RELIGION AND RITUAL IN
CHINESE SOCIETY

Contributors

Emily M. Ahern

John A. Brim

Donald R. DeGlopper

Stephan Feuchtwang

Maurice Freedman

C. Stevan Harrell

H. G. H. Nelson

Jack M. Potter

Michael Saso

Kristofer M. Schipper

Robert J. Smith

Marjorie Topley

Wang Shih-ch'ing

Wang Sung-hsing

Arthur P. Wolf

RELIGION AND RITUAL IN CHINESE SOCIETY

Edited by ARTHUR P. WOLF

Stanford University Press, Stanford, California   1974

STUDIES IN CHINESE SOCIETY

Stanford University Press, Stanford, California
© 1974 by the Board of Trustees of the Leland Stanford Junior University
Printed in the United States of America
ISBN 0-8047-0858-4   LC 73-89863

Preface

The essays in this book are the fruit of a conference held at the Asilomar Conference Grounds, Asilomar State Beach, Pacific Grove, California, October 11–15, 1971. The conference was the fifth of six conferences arranged by the Subcommittee on Research on Chinese Society of the Joint Committee on Contemporary China of the American Council of Learned Societies and the Social Science Research Council. Earlier conferences resulted in the publication of the four collections listed opposite. Two further volumes are in press: *The City in Late Imperial China*, edited by G. William Skinner, and *Women in Chinese Society*, edited by Margery Wolf and Roxane Witke. All six of these books contain materials relevant to the study of Chinese religion, and four of the six contain essays devoted to some aspect of religion or ritual. These essays are "Ritual Aspects of Chinese Kinship and Marriage" by Maurice Freedman and "Chinese Kinship and Mourning Dress" by Arthur P. Wolf, both in *Family and Kinship in Chinese Society*; "City Temples in Taipei Under Three Regimes" by Stephan Feuchtwang, in *The Chinese City Between Two Worlds*; "School-Temple and City God" by Stephan Feuchtwang and "Religious Organization in Traditional Tainan" by Kristofer M. Schipper, to appear in *The City in Late Imperial China*; and "The Power and Pollution of Chinese Women" by Emily M. Ahern, to appear in *Women in Chinese Society*. We have here eloquent evidence of the fact that religion and ritual are integral parts of Chinese society, as relevant to the study of kinship and the city as to the study of beliefs and values.

Seventeen papers were presented at the Asilomar conference. For various reasons, six of these papers—by John Brim, Myron L. Cohen, David K. Jordan, Michael Saso, Marjorie Topley, and myself—do not appear in this book; those by Professors Brim and Saso, Dr. Topley, and myself have been replaced by new papers. In addition, the conference was attended by S. J. Tambiah, Victor Turner, and Robert J. Smith as discussants, to which role they brought exceptional intelligence, wit, and good humor. We are particularly indebted to Professor Smith for contributing an Afterword to this book. We are also grateful to John Creighton Campbell of the Social Science Research Council, who served as staff for the conference, and to Muriel Bell, whose skillful editing has helped clarify our papers and has given them a measure of elegance they would not otherwise possess.

In his Preface to the first book in this series Maurice Freedman noted that "the company of sociologists and anthropologists working on China is small, and its joint competence to discuss China in the fullest sense of that noun is still further hampered by the inaccessibility of the People's Republic." In the five years since then our company has recruited many new members, and the People's Republic has become accessible for short visits if not for research. The effect of the first change is evident in the fact that seven of the contributors to this volume were still students when the first conference was held. The second change has not had such a profound impact; the papers in this book, like those in Professor Freedman's, are almost exclusively concerned with Hong Kong and Taiwan, and the result would probably be the same if another conference were held next year.

What is the point of lavishing so much attention on so small a part of a vast, complex society? It depends, I think, on what we seek to accomplish. Is our goal to generalize about China, or is it to explain the beliefs and practices of people who are Chinese? The first goal calls for surveys that cover the length and breadth of China, province by province, city by city, hsien by hsien. The second substitutes depth for breadth: it calls for meticulous, long-term studies of some segment or segments of China. Though we have followed the second strategy out of necessity, it seems to me a legitimate strategy, one whose legitimacy is amply confirmed by the impressive results represented in this book.

The question of how best to represent Chinese terms in an English-language publication is always a problem, exacerbated here by the fact that the people studied spoke Cantonese and Hokkien rather than Mandarin. Consider, for example, the complex question of how to transcribe an inscription taken from a temple in a Hokkien-speaking community. Some authorities would use a Mandarin orthography, on the grounds that written Chinese is conventionally transcribed following the Mandarin pronunciation. Others would argue that because the community was a Hokkien-speaking community, the inscription ought to be transcribed in a Hokkien orthography lest it be inferred that similar institutions and concepts occur in Mandarin-speaking communities, which might not in fact be the case. Of those favoring a Hokkien orthography, some would argue for rendering the characters in colloquial speech, others for using the more formal "character readings" on the grounds that the literate author of such an inscription would have composed it with the more formal readings in mind. Perforce I have allowed the authors of these essays to choose the orthography that best suits their views of Chinese society, insisting only that all Mandarin terms be transcribed in Wade-Giles. The reader who wants to know whether *yang, yeung,* and *iong* are written with the same character or different characters should consult the Character List.

By way of general advice to the reader, I should like to conclude with a perceptive passage from R. F. Johnston's *Lion and Dragon in Northern China,* one of the best books ever written about the Chinese. In reply to missionaries and others who regarded the Chinese as superstitious because they believed in such things as ghosts, Johnston wrote: "That the Chinese (like multitudes of Europeans) do believe in some outrageous and ridiculous things I am quite ready to admit, but it is necessary again to emphasise the undoubted fact that many Chinese (like multitudes of Europeans) seem to believe in a great deal more than they really do, and that what seems like active belief is often nothing more than a passive acquiescence in tradition." It should never be thought that people believe everything they tell the visiting anthropologist. Some do; others do not. Most believe some things and are skeptical about others. I recall asking one of my most sophisticated informants why he bothered making offerings to ghosts. He replied with a grin, "Suppose you were planning a trip through the mountains and had a choice of two roads. If someone told you there were bandits on one road, which would you take?"

A. P. W.

Contents

Contributors

EMILY M. AHERN
  Associate Professor of Anthropology, Johns Hopkins University

JOHN A. BRIM
  *Assistant Professor of Anthropology, Livingston College,
  Rutgers University*

DONALD R. DEGLOPPER
  *Assistant Professor of Anthropology and Asian Studies,
  Cornell University*

STEPHAN FEUCHTWANG
  Instructor in Sociology, The City University, London

MAURICE FREEDMAN
  *Professor of Chinese Studies and Fellow,
  All Souls College, Oxford*

C. STEVAN HARRELL
  *Assistant Professor of Chinese Studies and Adjunct Assistant Professor
  of Anthropology, University of Washington*

H. G. H. NELSON
  *Assistant Keeper for Chinese, Department of Oriental Manuscripts and
  Printed Books, The British Library*

JACK M. POTTER
  Professor of Anthropology, University of California, Berkeley

MICHAEL SASO
  Associate Professor of Religion, University of Hawaii

KRISTOFER M. SCHIPPER
  *Professor, Centre Documentaire d'Histoire des Religions,
  Ecole Pratique des Hautes Etudes, Paris*

ROBERT J. SMITH
  Goldwin Smith Professor of Anthropology, Cornell University

MARJORIE TOPLEY
  Associate Research Fellow, Centre of Asian Studies,
  University of Hong Kong

WANG SHIH-CH'ING
  Special Lecturer on Taiwanese History, Tan-chiang Wen-li Hsüeh-yüan

WANG SUNG-HSING
  Research Fellow, Institute of Enthnology, Academia Sinica

ARTHUR P. WOLF
  Associate Professor of Anthropology, Stanford University

RELIGION AND RITUAL IN
CHINESE SOCIETY

Introduction

ARTHUR P. WOLF

With the exception of Maurice Freedman's introductory essay and Robert Smith's Afterword, the papers included in this volume are all based on recent field research conducted either in Taiwan or in Hong Kong. Consequently, the reader cannot expect to find in these pages the full range of Chinese religious experience. The perspective offered is limited to the recent past and to one area of China. At the same time, he should not begin by assuming that these papers all deal with an essentially homogeneous culture. So great is the variation from Taiwan to Hong Kong and from community to community within these two culture areas, that regional and class differences and how to interpret them became one theme of the conference from which this volume derives. Viewing the conference as a discussant whose specialty is Japan, Smith noted that "each participant seemed to be dealing with all the others as though they were informants. Those who had conducted their research in Hong Kong expressed great interest—and sometimes polite incredulity—when informed of practices and beliefs found on Taiwan. Those who had worked in the northern part of that island interviewed those who knew the southern part, and often registered their surprise at what they learned. And there were others who found all these informants' accounts at such variance with orthodox practice and belief (as they understood them to be from documents and interviews with members of the vanished elite) as to be offensive and perhaps not Chinese."

The volume opens with an essay by Maurice Freedman, who appears to have anticipated the extent to which the conference would concern itself with the question of regional and class variation. Setting himself the difficult task of suggesting "some broad lines along which the sociological study of Chinese religion might develop," Freedman reviews the work of C. K. Yang, J. J. M. de Groot, and Marcel Granet, three men who take a global view of Chinese religion. He then emphatically aligns himself with those who would study that religion as a whole. We ought to begin, he argues, with the assumption that "a Chinese religion exists," and attempt "to trace ruling principles of ideas [and] ruling principles of form and organization." Pointing to the range of variation that runs from peasant farmers to the elite, Freedman suggests that the discontinuity we see is more apparent than real. In his view, elite religion and peasant religion "rest on a common base, representing two versions of one religion that we may see as idiomatic translations of each other." This line of argument leads to the bold hypothesis that "with the exception of prophecy and ecstasy, every religious phenomenon to be found among the common people of China was susceptible of transformation into belief and rites among the cultivated elite."

As an example of "transformation" Freedman offers his demonstration that the geomancer's conception of *feng-shui* can be restated in the language of ordinary religion. Another example appears in this volume in Marjorie Topley's fascinating analysis of Cantonese women's beliefs about pregnancy, childbirth, and postnatal adjustments. Topley reports that uneducated mothers commonly attribute certain classes of disease to encounters with persons, things, or spirits that are *kwaai*, "strange" or "queer." She then tells us that though Confucian-minded doctors are aware of these beliefs among their patients, they "do not talk about 'strangeness' because 'Confucius did not talk of strange things.' Where my informants spoke of queerness, these doctors spoke of 'polarization': some people or things were polarized in the direction of *yeung* (mandarin *yang*) or in the direction of *yam* (mandarin *yin*)." The willingness of traditional doctors to entertain the idea that "polarized conditions could be termed queer" looks like a perfect example for Freedman's hypothesis. But is it? Might it not be that some doctors use the notion of kwaai to explain as best they can ideas that are beyond the reach of their average patient? How do we distinguish full and accurate translations from mere metaphors?

The problem is raised in a more general form by Smith's comments on Freedman's paper. Freedman asks: "How precisely to consider Chinese religion as a whole?" His answer, in part, is that "one might predict from first principles that a society so differentiated by social status and power would develop a religious system that allowed differences in beliefs and rites to complement one another—or, to put the point more provocatively, that allowed religious similarity to be expressed as though it were religious difference." Smith counters by arguing that "it is equally likely that this society may instead have treated religious differences as though they were religious similarities." The sense in Freedman's view is that complex societies need to express differences in power and status. The sense in Smith's suggestion is that they also need to express social solidarity. But how are we to identify similarity expressed as difference and difference expressed as similarity? Some of Topley's doctors said that "polarized conditions could be termed queer." Did they mean that, or were they telling the foreign interviewer that all Chinese stand together? Others apparently denied the equation. Can we accept their answers, or should we conclude that the purpose was to distinguish themselves from their patients? I am confident that many readers will respond to Freedman's vigorous call for research that traces ideas across the vast and varied terrain of Chinese belief. They must take care, however, to distinguish statements that reveal belief from those that use belief to express social distance.

The question of variation—in this case, regional variation—is also the theme of Donald DeGlopper's account of religion in Lukang, a former seaport in central Taiwan. Early in the paper DeGlopper asks us to consider the contrast in ritual life between the towns of Erhlin and Lukang. "They are eighteen kilometers apart in western Chang-hua hsien in a region originally settled by people from the Three Counties (San Yi) of Ch'üan-chou. Both are market towns with the usual complement of shops and services. Erhlin, with a population of 11,000–12,000, has six temples, one for every 1,900 people, and a flourishing planchette divination (*pai-luan*) group.... Lukang, with 27,000–28,000 people, has 39 temples, one for every 690 people, and residents claimed never to have heard of pai-luan." How do we explain this degree of local diversity? DeGlopper outlines three approaches:

One is to stress the common pattern or core that is found in all places. Local diversity can then be dismissed as representing accidental permutations of a fundamental structure. Ritual is seen as floating on the surface of local society like an oil slick, having no determinate relation to the particular community that supports it, and thus giving the appearance of more local color than in fact exists. Alternatively, one may explain local cults and customs as traditions handed down from early settlers, who came from diverse places. Local religious variation is then meaningful, but only in relation to the past, and may be used as evidence for migration or diffusion. Or, one can attempt a functional interpretation and try to correlate religious variation with some other easily observed social factor. The hope is that one will discover that two apparently unrelated social facts covary.

DeGlopper focuses his paper by asking three questions: Why does Lukang have so many temples? Why is Lukang's ritual style so lacking in spirit, in what the Taiwanese call *lau-ziat*? And why, given their apparent lack of religious fervor, do the people of Lukang support so many temples and contribute large sums of money to build new ones? The answer DeGlopper offers suggests that the search for generalizations must begin with the histories of particular places. The secret of Lukang's many temples and its muted ritual style appears to be that a town which was once an important seaport and a center of Taiwanese culture is now an isolated market town serving one of Taiwan's least prosperous rural areas. The port has been filled in; the great guilds have vanished; the houses of rich merchants and imperial degree-holders are occupied by poor tenants; land reform has enriched the countryside at the expense of the town. The past is gone, but it is still valued. Were it not for their glorious past, "the men of Lukang" would be all too like the inhabitants of other small towns. The result is that Lukang cherishes its temples as tangible links with the past and eschews the competitive aspects of public ritual as a way of expressing solidarity vis-à-vis an unappreciative world.

Though the point is not made explicit, DeGlopper's argument rejects all three of the approaches he outlines at the outset. Lukang's peculiar ritual style is related to its past, but it is not simply a relic of the past. In fact, DeGlopper gives evidence that in the town's heyday, Lukang public ritual was competitive, noisy, and gaudy, very lau-ziat. The change is correlated with other social changes, but DeGlopper does not single out any particular variable as primary. Instead, he emphasizes the changed character of the town as a whole: its decline as a commercial and cultural center and the effect this has had on the residents' conception of themselves and their relationships with other communities. The spirit of the argument is that of Clifford Geertz (1972) on the Balinese cockfight rather than that of Meyer Fortes (1949) on Tallensi ancestor worship.

The potential inherent in DeGlopper's treatment of ritual as an expression of local culture will be apparent to anyone who compares his account of Lukang with Wang Shih-ch'ing's careful reconstruction of the religious history of Shu-lin. Though Shu-lin is now as large and important a center as Lukang, the two towns have strikingly different histories. Founded as a seaport and administrative center, Lukang originally was oriented to the China mainland and other cities on Taiwan. Its merchants and resident officials took little interest in the villages in the immediate vicinity. Shu-lin, by contrast, began its career as Feng-kuei-tien, Blacksmith's Shop, and grew up as a market town serving the needs of farmers and coal miners. The difference in the degree to which the two towns were oriented toward local rather than regional interests is clearly reflected in the residents' conception of the supernatural. Where people in Lukang like to think of their temples as the "roots" of other temples on Taiwan and ignore ritual relationships with the surrounding countryside, Shu-lin's residents conceive of their most important god, Pao Sheng Ta Ti, as the supernatural governor of Shu-lin town *and* the rural area it serves. Their god looks after the villagers that come to the town rather than over them to more distant places.

Wang's paper also contains valuable evidence relevant to the contention of G. William Skinner (1964) that the basic unit of Chinese society is the standard marketing community, not the village. Skinner's model suggests that the boundaries of the marketing community mark the horizons of the Chinese peasant's world. Given that Chinese peasants tend to conceive of their gods as bureaucrats (a view for which there is ample evidence in this volume), it follows that the most important god in any marketing community should be thought of as the supernatural governor of the territory bounded by that community. And if the standard marketing community is in fact the community of which villages and neighborhoods are the parts, it also follows that the gods representing these subunits should be seen as less important and ritually inferior to the god responsible for the community as a whole. Indeed, given the bureaucratic metaphor, they ought to be seen as his subordinates. And so it is, at least in Shu-lin. The emergence of the town as a distinct community was closely paralleled by the rise of one of several local gods to the status of supernatural governor. By the time the new town was consolidated around the railroad station, the T'u Ti Kung associated with the villages in its immediate vicinity were cast in the role of Pao Sheng Ta Ti's appointees. Today Pao Sheng Ta Ti is thought of as the immediate superior of all T'u Ti Kung in the area and is therefore called on to choose the sites of new temples and approve the relocation of old ones.

But there is another side to Wang's paper. We see that in addition to those gods who functioned as supernatural governors of the community and its constituent parts, there were others who served as patrons of the various ethnic groups that settled this part of the Taipei Basin. Some of the organizations represented by these deities were confined to the Shu-lin marketing area, but others united members of the community with fellow ethnics living in neighboring communities. Through participation in the Szu-ku Ma (an association devoted to worship of the god Kuan Yin Fu Tsu), Ting-chiao people residing in the southern half of the community were allied with fellow ethnics in market towns to the south and west, and by means of their membership in the Shih Pa Shou Kuan Yin Hui (also devoted to Kuan Yin Fu Tsu), Ting-chiao people residing near Shu-lin's northern border demonstrated solidarity with their fellows in several towns to the north. All these people were acknowledged members of the Shu-lin marketing community and loyal subjects of Pao Sheng Ta Ti, but their social horizons extended well beyond his realm.

The need to reconsider certain aspects of Skinner's model is even more apparent in John Brim's account of village alliance temples in Hong Kong. So far as their overt religious functions are concerned, these temples differ only in detail from Shu-lin's Chi-an Kung. The significant difference is that whereas the latter serves as the ritual center of a standard marketing community, the former have as their social base a cluster of villages that constitutes only a part of the catchment area of a single market town. Indeed, Brim tells us that in the past the alliances centered on these temples competed, sometimes violently, for control of the local market. Thus, where Wang's paper provides evidence of standard marketing communities cross-cut by religious associations, Brim's presents cases in which marketing communities were honeycombed by alliances organized around temples.

I will leave it to others to pursue the implications of these cases for models of local-level social organization. The point to note here is the suggestion that ritual does more than simply mark the boundaries of groups founded for other purposes. Brim argues that alliance temples solved what he terms the "latency problem," i.e., "the maintenance over time of the system's motivational and cultural patterns." Noting that "most of the activities undertaken by the village alliances were, by their very nature, highly intermittent," he argues that their temples helped maintain the alliances by promising supernatural rewards to those who engaged in private and collective worship. Wang's evidence goes further and suggests that in some cases an organization's religious role may have superseded its other functions. Though the intercommunity associations he describes originated in ethnic solidarity, they did not all wither and die when ethnicity lost its social significance. Instead, some of these organizations were redefined as territorial groups the primary purpose of which was to worship certain gods. The most striking case is that of the Shih Pa Shou Kuan Yin Hui, which not only survived its origins but expanded its scope to include communities scattered all across northern Taiwan. The role of religion in maintaining and transforming social forms created for other purposes obviously merits greater attention.

With Stephan Feuchtwang's paper we turn from religious organization to Chinese conceptions of the supernatural. This paper and the three that follow—my own, Wang Sung-hsing's, and C. Stevan Harrell's—

are all based on fieldwork in northern Taiwan and are all concerned with the beliefs of laymen: farmers, coal miners, fishermen, and shopkeepers. It is therefore encouraging to see that despite obvious differences in experience and interest, we arrive at remarkably similar conclusions. Where we differ it is on general questions that cannot be resolved on the basis of the study of religion in any one society. With regard to the essential facts and their meaning to our Chinese informants, we appear to be of one mind. Rather than treating the four papers separately, then, I will discuss them as a unit and attempt to summarize the conclusions drawn.

Feuchtwang sets the theme of the four papers early on when he notes that "the performance of ritual... implies three major categories of spiritual beings, which are arranged in pairs of cross-cutting oppositions. The three are ghosts (*kui*), gods (*cieng-sin*), and ancestors (*kong-ma* or *co-kong*)." Whether one begins with the architecture of homes and temples, the terminology used to refer to acts of worship, the form of offerings appropriate for the various classes of supernatural beings, or what people say about their behavior, the conclusion is always the same. Gods are contrasted with ghosts and ancestors; ghosts are contrasted with gods and ancestors; and ancestors are contrasted with gods and ghosts. For example, gods are offered uncooked (or whole) food, ghosts and ancestors are offered cooked food; ghosts are worshipped outside homes and temples, gods and ancestors are worshipped inside; ancestors are given an even number of incense sticks, ghosts and gods are given an odd number of sticks. Or, to take another set of oppositions: gods are offered gold money, ghosts and ancestors are offered silver money; ghosts are propitiated (*ce*), gods and ancestors are honored (*pai*); ancestors are worshipped "because one owes them something," gods and ghosts are worshipped "so they will help and not cause trouble." Taken together, the four papers offer impressive evidence that the Taiwanese recognize three classes of supernatural beings: gods, ghosts, and ancestors.

But the papers do more than this. They also show that the characteristics attributed to these three classes of supernatural beings are closely correlated with the attributes of three classes of human beings. Gods wear the robes of posted officials; they reside in temples guarded by divine generals; they punish people for crimes against society; they are easily insulted and can be bribed; they write reports, keep records, and are associated with discrete administrative districts. Obviously, gods are the supernatural counterparts of the imperial bureaucracy. Ghosts are worshipped outside of temples and at the back doors of homes; they are dangerous and sometimes malicious; they are offered masses of food and clothing that are thought of as handouts or payoffs; and they are explicitly compared to bandits, beggars, and gangsters. Clearly, ghosts are the supernatural equivalents of despised, dangerous strangers. And, of course, the ancestors are the senior members of one's own line of descent, the people to whom one is indebted for property, for social status, and for the gift of life. They have the right to be worshipped and are offered food in the form of a meal. As one of my informants put it, "They are your own people."

It would be ridiculous to conclude that the Chinese peasant's conception of spiritual beings is nothing more than a reflection of his perspective on society. Though the gods are not omnipotent, they possess powers far beyond those of human officials. And though the ghosts are often compared to bandits and beggars, they have monstrous qualities that set them apart from any human being. On the other hand, it is clear that the peasant's conception of the supernatural world was molded by his vision of society. All four of the papers we are discussing note that there are intermediate spirits, beings that are part god and part ghost or part ghost and part ancestor. They are exceptional in that they do not fit easily into any one of the three major categories of supernatural beings, but they also have their counterparts in society. Consider, for example, the residents of what are commonly spoken of as *san-mien pi*, "three-face walls." Some people offer them gold money, others offer them silver. They are supplicated as though they were gods, but their "temples" lack the architectural features that identify the residence of a real god. These demigods are often the spiritual remains of soldiers who died defending the community, or local gangsters with Robin Hood qualities. They occupy much the same position in the supernatural world as they did in this world.

What does this remarkable correlation imply for the study of Chinese religion? Since Feuchtwang, Wang, and Harrell each comment on this question in their concluding remarks, I will let them represent their own views. For me, it implies two things. In the first place, the study of Chinese religion must begin with the social and economic history of particular communities. Though concepts of the supernatural are products of people's relationship to their society, the supernatural world is never a simple projection of the contemporary world. The experience of each generation is passed on to the next through the medium of traditions that are only slowly modified by changing circumstances. Today people on Taiwan conceive of T'u Ti Kung and his temple as comparable to the local policeman and the police station, but Kristofer M. Schipper (1975) identifies the god's hat as "the *yüan-wai-mao* of wealthy country gentlemen with no official rank but of great influence." The example is trivial, but the point is not. To understand the beliefs held at any point in time, one must examine the history of the community as well as the contemporary situation.

Second, I think the evidence we have seen of the close correlation between the beliefs of laymen and their perspective on society argues that there has always been a vast gulf between the religion of the elite and that of the peasantry. I cannot imagine that wealthy merchants and powerful officials conceptualized their fears in the form of petty bandits and beggars. For them, kui must have had a very different meaning. It may be that such ideas as the opposition of yin and yang played a role in the religion of all social classes, but these must have been formulas that contained little or nothing of the visions that are at the heart of any religion. Consequently, where Freedman argues that we should begin with the assumption that "a Chinese religion exists," I would argue for exactly the opposite assumption. We should begin by reconstructing the beliefs of people who viewed the Chinese social landscape from different perspectives. Surely the imperial bureaucracy did not approach gods modeled on that bureaucracy with the same attitude as peasants who were understandably awed by the power of imperial officials. The fact that an idea was shared by people with such very different perspectives would suggest to me that it was relatively insignificant or that it was easily invested with very different meanings.

The next three papers take us from Taiwan to Hong Kong and thereby reintroduce the question of regional variation. The first of the three is Jack M. Potter's fascinating study of *mann seag phox,* "old ladies who speak to spirits." The paper, based on Potter's work in Ping Shan, a lineage village in the New Territories, contains rich material on many subjects, but it is his description of an annual group seance that most strikes one's attention. At the time of the Moon Cake Festival the entire village assembles at dusk in an open space near their ancestral temple to participate in a seance held free of charge by the village's three resident mediums. When one of the mediums falls into a trance and begins to chant, the gathering knows that she has contacted her familiar spirits, who are leading her upward and away toward the Heavenly Flower Gardens. The purpose of the journey is to inspect the flowers that represent the fortunes of individual villagers, but the villagers are less interested in this than in the ghosts the medium encounters along the way. These are the souls of deceased relatives and neighbors who take advantage of the opportunity to communicate with the living. They give advice, demand help, voice complaints, and occasionally scold their descendants.

One of the ghosts encountered at the session Potter attended was a villager's younger brother, angry and restless because "it was not time for me to die"; another was the soul of a child who accused her parents of having contributed to her death by not calling a doctor until it was too late.

There are many interesting aspects to this event, not the least of which is the fact that the entire community participates. Both A. J. A. Elliott (1955) and Maurice Freedman (1967) have noted that seances of this kind are usually held in the strictest secrecy and seclusion. "A skillful soul raiser is capable of laying bare the skeletons in a family's cupboard and bringing to light some of the personal animosities of which an outsider might well remain ignorant" (Elliott 1955: 136). One wants to know why people in Ping Shan are willing to risk communicating with the dead in a public setting. The more sophisticated among them must realize that the medium could take advantage of this opportunity to give village gossip dramatic exposure or even manufacture embarrassing messages from the dead. Potter tells us that the Tang lineage is "a hatchwork of competing families and sublineages." What an opportunity for an unscrupulous medium to score political points! The answer can only be a general understanding that the medium will avoid political issues and not bring up anything that could embarrass the leading citizens.

The judgment required by public seances and the sensitivity needed to conduct private sessions mean that mediums have to be highly skilled in the use of sociological knowledge. They have to know how to probe for information and how far to go in revealing what they learn. Margery Wolf suggests that this is the reason most soul raisers and mediums of the type Potter describes are women. "A Chinese woman trained from childhood to be sensitive to attitude change, to understand and make use of the kin and emotional relationships between people, and, in a sense, to 'live by her wits' clearly comes equipped with the basic essential skills of the soul raiser" (1974: 166). My own view is that if men lack these skills they are capable of learning them, and that they would do so if they thought it would be remunerative. My hypothesis is that women have an advantage because their male clients are not willing to reveal secrets to other males. In rural Taiwan a man who wants to borrow money from a neighbor and is afraid of being refused sends his wife to conduct preliminary negotiations with the neighbor's wife. Men carry the burden of representing their family's reputation in the community and are therefore unwilling to risk embarrassment in the presence of another man.

I have already introduced Marjorie Topley's paper in commenting on

Freedman's view of the relationship between elite and peasant religion. In addition to its relevance to the problems raised in that context, the paper is also relevant to the anthropologist's interest in anomalous things. This class of things is called *k'ei-kwaai*, "strange," or, in popular Cantonese speech, *m-saam, m-sz,* "not three, not four." Some things like brides and mourners are only temporarily k'ei-kwaai; others are, as Topley puts it, "permanently polarized." They include eels, which are both "fish" and "snakes," and a kind of spirit called *iu-kwaai*. Topley explains that iu-kwaai are considered strange because they are "something like a god, something like a demon." This adds weight to the view that Chinese popular religion recognizes three major categories of supernatural beings. It would not make sense to consider iu-kwaai anomalous if the class god and the class demon (ghost) were not fixed points of reference.

The paper also includes an intriguing discussion of the way kinship relationships are manipulated to deal with illnesses attributed to horoscope clashes and wrongs committed in a previous existence. In my view, however, the most important question is raised by Topley's description of the great variety of explanations available to Cantonese mothers. An illness on the part of either the mother or the child can be attributed to the mother's failure to observe certain dietary restrictions during her pregnancy. Or it can result from her failure to observe the restrictions that apply to the postnatal period. It can be a consequence of a horoscope incompatibility involving mother and child, father and child, or child and ancestors. It may suggest that the child will be difficult to raise because he has a kwaai fate. Or it can indicate that the newborn soul is someone "coming back" to settle accounts left unsettled in a previous incarnation. And though Topley does not discuss these possibilities, we can probably assume that a child's illness can also be interpreted as punishment inflicted by either the gods or the ancestors. How do people choose between these various ways of explaining an illness? Topley makes some suggestions and provides important evidence, but we need to know much more about this. We cannot claim to understand the beliefs associated with these various modes of explanation until we can specify the conditions under which one interpretation is preferred over another.

The third of the three Hong Kong papers is H. G. H. Nelson's study of ancestor worship and burial practices in a small, poor lineage in the New Territories. The paper sets out "to test the hypothesis that just as in nonliterate ancestor-worshipping societies, the structure of the localized Chinese lineage is determined by the political and economic relations of men on the ground; and that burial practices, and certain recurrent inefficiencies in the system of recording ancestral links, provide mechanisms whereby in a literate society the often inconvenient facts of biological descent can be bent to suit the changing needs of the living." Nelson then examines in meticulous detail the Lei lineage's written genealogies, oral tradition relating to the development of the lineage, the ancestral tablets found in halls and homes, lineage tombs, and land records. He discovers that though a gap in the lineage's genealogy is exploited to create the impression that its segments are roughly equal in size and status, the lineage's own records indicate that they are not in fact in balance. Hence, he concludes that "the lineage records are accurate; it is the interpretation put upon them that defines the political and economic balance of the lineage."

Though Nelson appears disappointed with this conclusion, I find it refreshing and encouraging. It confirms the hypothesis that changing circumstances affect people's view of their history, but it also says that Chinese genealogies can be used to reconstruct the past. Moreover, I am convinced that Nelson's conclusion applies to the records of most Chinese lineages. My first fieldwork on Taiwan was conducted in a community segmented along descent lines. The highest level of contrast was between what were referred to as the *wu-fang* branch and the *ch'i-fang* branch. People told me that the founders of these two segments of the lineage were brothers (sons of the same father) who had migrated to Taiwan together and jointly settled the community. Later I acquired a copy of the lineage genealogy and discovered, with the help of Wang Shih-ch'ing, that these "brothers" had as their closest common ancestor a great-great-grandfather. My guess is that lineage genealogies are not revised to conform to the group's perception of itself because they serve many purposes. They are more than group charters. People turn to them for information about their ancestors and use them as evidence in disputes over inheritance and claims made against the income from corporate property.

I would also like to draw the reader's attention to Nelson's description of the Lei lineage halls. Taken together with the results of Emily Ahern's work on Taiwan (Ahern 1973), this evidence suggests that we need to distinguish two types of lineage halls. What Nelson calls a *tz'u-t'ang* admits new tablets only when the hall is restored and then only for a price. The result is that tz'u-t'ang admit only the remote dead, and among the remote dead only those whose descendants can afford the price of admission. This is the type of hall assumed in Freedman's seminal analysis of Chinese lineage organization (Freedman 1958), but it now appears that there is a second type of hall. Nelson notes that in addition to the tz'u-t'ang that serves as ritual center for the entire Lei lineage, there are two other halls, belonging to two branches of the lineage. In the case of these *shen-t'ing*, "there is no rule, as there is for the tz'u-t'ang, that tablets can be installed only when the hall is restored—and then for a price." One result is that there are no tablets in the homes of members of these two branches of the lineage; the other is that ancestral tablets are not segregated along class lines.

Except for the fact that they serve branches rather than a lineage as a whole, the Lei's shen-t'ing are precise equivalents of the four lineage halls Ahern studied on Taiwan. The Taiwan halls also admit new tablets at any time and without charge, excluding only those lineage members who marry into their wife's family and thereby deprive the lineage of manpower and descendants (Ahern 1973: 123–24). Thus, we find both in Taiwan and in Hong Kong a type of lineage hall that differs significantly from the tz'u-t'ang. Where tz'u-t'ang select among the dead in such a way as to emphasize generational and class distinctions, shen-t'ing (they are called *kung-t'ing* on Taiwan) reduce the distance between the generations and ignore class distinctions altogether. In these and other respects they are much closer to domestic altars. Ahern says that both engagements and weddings are held in the hall rather than in the home, and even finds that "the domestic cult *par excellence*, the worship of the kitchen or stove god, also takes place in the hall" (1973: 94–95). Nelson is not so specific, but he does say "it was explained to me that shen-t'ing fulfilled the functions of domestic altars."

The reason for this difference appears to be simply that some lineages are smaller and more self-consciously solidary than others. The four lineages Ahern studied are all small, compact residential groups that suppress all signs of internal differentiation, and Nelson tells us that "the two shen-t'ing were located in parts of the village that differed from the rather more amorphous remainder in being occupied by clearly defined, self-conscious, closely related groups of kin." The significance for religious studies is that Freedman's important distinction between hall worship and domestic worship (Freedman 1958: 81–91) may need to be revised in one respect. The distinction contrasts the form of worship conducted in tz'u-t'ang with that performed before domestic altars in the home. The fact that there are intermediate types of altars suggests that there may also be intermediate forms of worship.

The four Taiwan lineages I have just mentioned are also the subject of Emily Ahern's paper for this volume, though she is here concerned with marriage rites and affinal ties rather than with ancestor worship. Judging from the lively debate an earlier version of the paper aroused

at the conference, it is destined to be the most controversial (and consequently the most productive) of the papers included here. The accepted view of affinal relations in China has been that marriage "leaves
the girl's family ritually and socially in a position of inferiority with
the boy's" (Freedman 1970: 185). Ahern turns this proposition on its
head, arguing that "in at least one pocket of Chinese society, the village
of Ch'i-nan [the community in which the four lineages are located], . . .
marriage creates a ranking in which wife-givers are distinctly superior
to wife-takers. From the time of betrothal the bride's family is defined
as ritually superior to the groom's, irrespective of the previous economic
and social position of the two families."

Much of the discussion at the conference related to Ahern's interpretation of her evidence. For example, how does one interpret the lavish
gifts wife-givers send wife-takers on the occasion of weddings and
birthdays? Ahern reads them as an expression of the wife-givers' need
to "validate their superior status by acting in a superior manner." In
comments he prepared as the discussant for Ahern's paper, Freedman
argued that the same evidence could be used to support the opposite
conclusion. "People who make lavish gifts can be interpreted as trying
to narrow the gap between themselves and their superiors." Or, to cite
one more example, what is one to make of the exaggerated deference
shown the bride by the groom and his family? Ahern says this is evidence
of the bride's high status; Freedman suggested that it might just as well
be taken as evidence of her low status. "Ceremonial deference cannot
simply be taken as evidence of the inferiority of the person or group
which offers it. The offering of exaggerated deference may be a sign of
the inferiority of the person to whom that deference is shown."

Though I agree entirely with Freedman's view that the ritual acts
Ahern cites could be interpreted differently, I still accept her argument
that people in Ch'i-nan regard wife-givers as superior to wife-takers.
For me, the crucial evidence is that they say wife-givers are superior and
defer to them in other than ritual contexts. Freedman rejected this conclusion for various reasons, but primarily because it flies in the face of
what is known of affinal relationships elsewhere in China. "If there is a
systematic superiority of wife-givers over wife-takers, then the families
of brides must be either equal or superior in status to the families of
grooms. And this, so far as I know, is the very opposite of what one finds
in China. Most of us assume that the Chinese formula to the effect
that like status marries like is a reality accompanied by a practice
which ensures that if there is a status difference it is always in favor of
the groom's family. The girl does not marry down; she marries up."

But though Freedman saw this point "as disposing of the assertion that there is a social superiority of wife-givers," he conceded that it "does not dispose effectively of the theory that wife-givers are ritually superior. It may be that one half of Ahern's argument is correct and the other half incorrect. Maybe the argument about the social superiority of wife-givers is incorrect, but it could be that the argument about their ritual superiority is correct and absolutely unassailable." Ahern, in sharp contrast, insists that the ritual superiority of wife-givers reflects their social superiority, and, though she admits she cannot prove the point, thinks that this in turn reflects a tendency for women to marry down, not up. The debate raises questions fundamental to our understanding of Chinese kinship and the relationship between kinship and ritual. Does the relative social status of bride-givers and bride-takers vary radically from one area of the country to another? Are there communities in which brides are so valued that the gift of a woman in marriage confers automatic superiority on wife-givers? What do ritual statements say about social reality? We can only hope that the issues raised by Ahern's paper are pursued.

The last two papers in the volume, those by Kristofer M. Schipper and Michael Saso, deserve special attention. Where anthropologists typically look at Chinese religion through the eyes of laymen, these papers shift our perspective to that of the Taoist priest. We move inside the temple and are given an opportunity to see what Chinese religion means to this class of ritual specialist. Both papers make extensive use of Taoist texts and other documents, but these are not the texts that form the basis of most studies of Taoism as an elite philosophy. Consequently, there is also a shift in perspective for those readers who begin with a view of Taoism derived from the work of historians and theologians. The shift in this case is from philosopher to priest, from theory to practice.

Schipper opens his paper by pointing out how difficult it is to define Taoism and particularly to identify the functions of the Taoist priest. In present-day Taiwan the Taoist priest or Tou-su "is not just a ritual Master." "He also acts as an exorcist and healer, expelling and pacifying demons," functions that he shares with the Huat-su, the magician. "The Tou-su even 'borrows' a vestimentary element from the Huat-su: a red turban or headscarf, which he winds around his own headdress." But though Tou-su and Huat-su perform some of the same rites and sometimes wear the same headdress, Schipper tells us that "there is one essential difference between them: a pure Huat-su ritual does not make use of written prayers, whereas the same ritual performed by a Tou-su does."

For example, to effect the transfer of large sums of paper money to the Treasury of Fate, the Huat-su "often has a medium take his place at the altar, and it is the spirit of the medium that makes the journey and effects the transfer of funds." The Tou-su writes a memorial, and "it is the burning of the memorial that effects the transfer."

The fact that the Taoist priest distinguishes himself from the rival Huat-su by the use of written prayers termed "memorials" strikes me as significant for two reasons. In the first place, the Taoist is clearly placing himself on the elite side of the elite-commoner dichotomy, literacy being the traditional dividing line between these two classes. Second, labeling his prayers memorials suggests that the Taoist priest thinks of himself as something more than a ritual specialist. In his own view, his relationship to the common man is comparable to that of an imperial official. Schipper develops the evidence for this point by examining in detail a memorial written for a *chiao* held in A-lien village in southern Taiwan in 1969. He notes that the memorial uses formulas characteristic of documents prepared by the imperial administration, and he draws attention to the inclusion in the memorial of a complete census of the village. Indeed, in his view, "the periodic chiao sacrifice is nothing less than the constitutional assembly of an autonomous state, during which the Chiefs renew their alliance and infeudation, and a collective covenant is made."

I therefore think we are justified in drawing a sharp distinction between the social perspective of the Taoist priest and that of the laymen whose beliefs are the subject of most of the papers in this volume. Though the Taoist priest was not an official, he was, at least in his own view, a member of the elite and in some sense an administrator. Consequently, we should not be surprised to discover that though the Taoist priest grants the peasant's gods a place in the scheme of things, he does not worship these gods as his own. This is made strikingly evident by the way in which a temple is rearranged in preparation for a chiao. The peasant's gods, what the Taoist terms *shen-ming*, bright spirits, "are removed from their places of honor along the north wall of the temple and put in the south by the entrance, from which place the people usually worship." The object is to make the sacred area of the temple ready for "the bringing of the Heavenly Worthies, the special object of Taoist ritual worship" (Saso 1972: 33).

Where Schipper's paper helps us define the relationship of the Taoist priest to the larger society, Saso's paper takes us inside the Taoist's world and affords us a glimpse of the priests' relations with one another. We learn something of the criteria they use in judging one another's performance, the ranks of the priesthood, the means by which the novices advance, and even the issues that divide priests into competing camps. For me at least, it is a revelation to discover that the magic of one school is viewed as "mortally opposed" to that of another, and that "the opposition extends not only to name-calling ('heterodox' vs. 'orthodox'), but to great physical battles for control of a temple or a city, and to magical jousts fought with conjurations, mudras, and spirits." And it is also interesting to see that even today Taoism has a private as well as a public face. Saso tells us that for many priests "the striving for *hsien*-hood or personal immortality by means of internal alchemy takes priority over and sometimes supersedes motives of personal profit"; there are, he says, Taoist masters who "practice internal alchemy in private without making their powers known to the public."

The most important conclusion to be drawn from Saso's paper follows from his contrast between "the methods used by a Red-head Shen-hsiao or Lu Shan Taoist in curing a child's illness and those used by a Black-head Cheng-i Taoist performing Five Thunder Magic." In describing the two rites from the priest's point of view, Saso shows us that even Taoists differ radically in their ideas about the supernatural. And though Saso does not tell us what these rites mean to the clients of the two rival sects, it is obvious from what he says about the priests that the meaning cannot be the same. The gods envisioned by the Cheng-i Taoist as he builds the Mandala of the Prior Heavens around him are "various esoteric spirits unknown to the ordinary faithful and appropriate to his own sect and rank at ordination." The layman is systematically excluded from the Taoist's world by strict rules of inheritance and professional jealousy. "The names of the spirits, the mudras and mantras for summoning them, and the meditation with which the Taoist brings them under his control" are "carefully guarded secrets" that are revealed only "to one son of a priest's family per generation." There cannot be such a thing as a Chinese religion, it seems to me, in part because priests were not preachers. Rather than attempting to educate the masses, they treated their knowledge as a professional secret. This allowed different sects, and within each sect different lines of descent, to develop their own ideas, and eventually created a vast gulf between the ideas of the priest and the beliefs of the peasant.

It is appropriate that this volume should conclude with an Afterword that compares China and Japan, since that is the way the first volume in this series concluded. And it is also appropriate that the Afterword is addressed to the question of variation, since this is the first question that students of religion in complex societies must face. And since it is through debate that our understanding of any subject grows, it is fortunate that Smith's views on the subject should contrast so sharply with Freedman's in the paper that opens this volume. Where Freedman would have us focus on those ideas and principles that all Chinese hold in common, Smith would have us focus on variation and treat it as "intrinsically important." Though he avoids committing himself on the question of Chinese religion, Smith makes it clear that he doubts the existence of a Japanese religion. After briefly summarizing the history of Buddhism, Shinto, and Confucianism in Japan, he tells us that "the contemporary effects of this history are not far to seek. What has resulted is a layering of coexistent practice and belief, a variability of both even within small communities, and the setting out of genuine contradictions that may be subscribed to even by a single person." By this he means to suggest that "the totality cannot be reconciled into a systemic whole." I believe this to be true of China, and I would not have it otherwise. Where belief systems are uniform, there is little to interest the anthropologist beyond the historical origin of the uniformity. Where belief systems vary, there is the endlessly fascinating question of why.

On the Sociological Study of Chinese Religion

MAURICE FREEDMAN

Quand vous gémissez sur la politique de Mao Tse-
toung à l'égard des religions, vous montrez simplement
que vous ignorez tout de l'histoire de la Chine.
          —Etiemble, *Connaissons-nous la Chine?*

The character of this paper is in part explained by the purpose for which
its earlier version was composed. As the reader of this volume will by
now know, it arises from a conference on Chinese religion and ritual,
one of a series of meetings on the sociology and anthropology of China.
In ignorance of what my fellow contributors to the conference would
say in their papers, I took it upon myself to play the programist and in
that role to suggest some broad lines along which the sociological study
of Chinese religion might develop. As matters turned out, some of my
sermonizing proved embarrassingly unnecessary, but in this revised version of my paper I have retained its original spirit,[1] in order to reinforce
what I consider to be, in the present state of the sociology of China, the
proper trend it has taken.

I began the exercise of thinking myself into my subject by rereading,
among other standard works, C. K. Yang's *Religion in Chinese Society*.
That book is, after all, the latest of the very few works of its kind: an
attempt to characterize Chinese religion as a whole and in relation to
the society within which it was thought and practiced.[2] I then went back
to the review of the book I had written in 1962, to discover that I was

---

[1] The present version reflects not only the discussions at the conference itself,
but also comments made when a shortened version of the paper was read at a
meeting of the University Association for the Sociology of Religion held at the
London School of Economics and Political Science on December 15, 1971.

[2] Yang's chief predecessors within sociology were Max Weber and Marcel Granet,
to whom I shall be referring presently. One might consider the candidature of
Edwin D. Harvey's *The Mind of Modern China* (1933), which was written by a
sociologist with a long experience of China. But there is not enough sociology in
Harvey's book, and although a case can be made for saying that he tried to see
Chinese religious ideas as a whole, he does not appear to have considered Chinese
society central to his inquiry. In method the book strikes me as a loosely aggregated

now less in sympathy with the review than with the book it criticized. It seemed to me that in 1962 I was perched on an anthropological high horse (irritated by Yang's simpleminded treatment of ancestor worship) and skeptical about the possibility of making an advance in the study of Chinese religion without, as I put it, "a change in method and an accession of new data. One could argue that the next step would be to formulate a series of clearly defined problems and then tackle them on the basis of a detailed scrutiny of the literature and painstaking field investigations of Chinese behaving and expressing their beliefs in re-ligious contexts." (Freedman, 1962: 534–35.) I do not now much care for the way in which the point is made, although I was not, I think, alto-gether wrong in making it. But I wish that in 1962 I had not passed so quickly over Yang's main achievement and the possibilities of our build-ing upon it; I mean his interpretation of Chinese religion taken as a whole. And that is the topic upon which this essay effectively opens—and upon which it ends.

A Chinese religion exists; or, at any rate, we ought to begin with that assumption: the religious ideas and practices of the Chinese are not a congeries of haphazardly assembled elements, all appearances and the greater part of the extensive literature to the contrary. Consider, for example, Doré's and Wieger's compilations, which, precious sources of data though they unquestionably are, reduce the reader to a state of stunned resignation before a mass of non-aggregative facts.[3] Behind the superficial variety there is order of some sort. That order might be ex-pressed by our saying that there is a Chinese religious system, both at the level of ideas (beliefs, representations, classifying principles, and so on) and at that of practice and organization (ritual, grouping, hierarchy, etc.). But it is easy to see that to use the word "system" systematically would be to run the constant risk of appearing to impute to Chinese religion a thoroughgoing unity and tightness that manifestly it does not have. The starting assumption made here is both more modest and more complex. It says that there is some order—of a kind that should allow us (if we take the trouble) to trace ruling principles of ideas across a vast field of apparently heterogeneous beliefs, and ruling prin-ciples of form and organization in an equally enormous terrain of varied action and association. Ideas and forms need not be uniform to be com-

---

assortment of facts from literary sources and rather unsystematically observed field data. (Full bibliographical data for all works cited in the text and in footnotes will be found on pp. 351–54.)

[3] The recent (1970) republication of Doré's *Manuel* demonstrates the continuing usefulness of the data scattered over his many volumes on Chinese "superstitions," but while it classifies and systematizes, it does not analyze.

mon; they may be reflections, perhaps misshapen reflections, or idiomatic translations of one another, as in their transmission back and forth between social strata, between sect and "church," between "church" and "church," between text and living language, between the cultivated and the popular. Their Chineseness lies in a basic stock upon which complex social and intellectual life works and elaborates variety. Chinese religion is not all of a piece, and in the end there may be much that we shall not be able to fit into any sort of order; but we should try to push out toward the limits so that we may know them.

One way in which to approach order—it is only a beginning—is to grasp the relations among the different parts of Chinese society. (I mean of course traditional Chinese society and its extensions into our own day and direct purview, especially in Taiwan and Hong Kong, from which areas of China my colleagues in this volume draw most of their data. I am not at all concerned here with modern changes as such.) We may start with two simple and connected propositions. First, Chinese religion entered into the unity of a vast polity. Second, it was an intrinsic part of a hierarchized society.

The narrowly political significance of Chinese religion can hardly have escaped the notice of early observers, but I can recall no study of it to compare with C. K. Yang's other than one first published in 1882 by Sir Arthur C. Lyall, the eminent Anglo-Indian scholar-bureaucrat (1835–1911). I think his work so striking that I am giving him an honorary place among the small band of social scientists to whom I am limiting myself. (An odd thing about Lyall's essay is that it is generally unknown to people who write about China; I myself came across it only by accident.) Lyall knew about Chinese religion what he picked up from a very few sources: Edkins, De Groot, Giles, and above all the English translations of the so-called *Peking Gazette*.[4] What his study (Lyall 1907) demonstrates in the first place (and disenchantingly) is that the advances in our understanding of a society are not necessarily made by people who know a great deal about it. Lyall began from an interest in Indian government and comparative religion that prompted

[4] This material is vivid. Here, for example, is a fine illustration of the religious foundations of bureaucratic practice, from the *Translation of the Peking Gazette for 1882* (Shanghai, 1883, p. 110): it was reported in August that in a postscript to a memorial from the Censor of Kwangsi, an official "advocates a return to the practice of 'slaying the water-dragon...' in the sixth moon as recommended in the Monthly Rules (of the Records of Rites). This custom, though never enforced by law, is recollected by the farmers and aged country-folk.... The animal will always be discovered after digging to a depth of five feet or so. Would it not be better to destroy the hidden evil instead of merely providing against the floods it causes...?"

questions about, as he puts it (1907: 107), "that empire which at one time had attained, as a government, the highest level yet reached by purely Asiatic civilisation." He had earlier said that, to pass from the "intolerant monotheism" of Islam, it might be "more interesting . . . to examine the relations of the civil government to religion in a country where creeds and rituals still preserve their primitive multiformity, where they all have, nevertheless, free play, and where the ruler finds it possible and advantageous to preside over all of them" (p. 106).

I reproduce the following passages from Lyall to illustrate the quality of his argument. It will be noticed that he took much of the religious variety at its face value but saw it as being brought to the service of political unity.

. . . China has attained this superiority over India, that she succeeded centuries ago in bringing her religious doctrines and worships [sic] into practical cooperation with her secular organisation. (P. 108.)

All this system harmonises with and favours the policy of associating religion with every department of the public service, and of identifying the laws of the Government with the decrees of Heaven. (P. 110.)

It becomes thus possible to form some trustworthy conception of the principles that underlie this vast organisation—unquestioned authority; lofty ostentation of public morality; the affectation of profound reverence for churches, rituals, and all things pertaining to divinity; deep respect for tradition and ancestral usage coupled with steady encouragement of classic learning; entire religious toleration conjoined with the peremptory assertion of civil supremacy; provincial home rule controlled, at least in form, by a despotic central executive; in short, the continuous experience of many ages applied to the management by a foreign dynasty of miscellaneous tribes and races, and an immense mixed population. (P. 118.)

It will be fairly obvious that Lyall's interest in China was that of somebody on the alert for solutions to the kind of problem faced by the British in India: how a foreign dynasty may succeed in reconciling religious toleration with effective rule. It follows that, from our point of view, Lyall may have seen the problem too narrowly (for in religious matters the Ch'ing rulers of China may not have differed substantially from their native predecessors); but I think it will be recognized that Lyall attained to an understanding of the politics of Chinese religion that was not to be matched until C. K. Yang wrote his first general study of Chinese religion (Yang 1957). The Englishman wrote as an outsider; Yang wrote as somebody brought up in China and sociologically formed in the United States. Somehow both encompassed a whole religio-political system, one of them by ignoring the details and proceeding unencumbered by specialist knowledge, the other by having that knowledge and transcending it. Nearly all other writers on Chinese religion either have lacked sociological insight or, if they have had it, have restricted its range to something less than the total system of religion-in-politics.[5]

Let us pass to the second proposition, that Chinese religion was part of the hierarchization of Chinese society. It is less obvious than the first proposition, and indeed more difficult to bring home, precisely because of the stratification that forms its subject. The great "discovery" by English-speaking social scientists in an earlier part of the century (say, from the thirties to the fifties) was that behind the Confucian smoke-screen there lay hidden a different way of life and a different set of values: roughly, the culture of the peasants. The second half of the century has seen the further "discovery" that the first was an illusion. That is to say, elite culture and peasant culture were not different things; they were versions of each other. To read much of what is still written about Chinese religion one might not realize that the second advance had been made. For example, C. P. FitzGerald tells us (1969: 389, 391):

In broad general terms it might be said that the people were both Buddhist and followers of the old polytheism which came to be known as Taoism: the scholars were Confucian. . . . Popular religion was thus confused and inchoate, lacking any accepted overall theology, or central organization. . . . Agnosticism, instead of being a rare and unpopular attitude only safely adopted by the rich and powerful, was the acknowledged and proclaimed view of the ruling class, the basis of higher education, indeed of all education. Popular religion was not under the guidance and inspiration of dedicated men of learning, but left to persons of little education and often of less probity.[6]

---

[5] Max Weber does not, in my opinion, quite escape inclusion among "all other writers." True, he tried to deal with the whole religious system, and put his finger on a number of crucial points—e.g. when he discusses the imperial promotion and demotion of gods (Weber 1951: 29–32), drawing, though less extensively than Lyall, upon the *Peking Gazette* (*ibid.*, pp. 260–61, notes 57, 60, 63); but, in his preoccupation with the nonemergence of capitalism in China, he fails to reach a satisfying synthesis. One might say that he threw away the advantage he enjoyed of writing totally from outside by a somewhat fussy attention to detail. And cf. Weber's remarks on China in *The Sociology of Religion* (1965), especially p. 95, where he gives "animism in China" as an example of religion among "the lower middle class, and particularly among the artisans." However, I am relieved of the necessity of evaluating the work by the forthcoming appearance of Sybille van der Sprenkel's "Confucianism and Taoism" in a symposium on Weber's work on religion. Cf. also C. K. Yang's Introduction to the 1964 reissue of Weber 1951; and Otto van der Sprenkel 1964.

[6] For a similar view by a Chinese scholar, see Hsiao 1960: 225: "Crude polytheism was thus a way of life with the masses."

But the newer view is firmly lodged in Yang's *Religion in Chinese Society*, and we may expect to find it more and more commonly expressed.[7]

Before dealing with Yang's book in some detail I think it may be instructive to go back in time and beyond the English-language social science tradition to consider the views taken of the interrelations between peasant and elite religion by the Dutchman J. J. M. de Groot (1854–1921) and the Frenchman Marcel Granet (1884–1940), in my opinion the two most important sociological-sinological contributors to the debate. I am not the first to give pride of place to these two writers or to see striking differences between them (cf. Eberhard 1971: 338 *et seq.*, 362 *et seq.*), but neither has yet been adequately studied, and I have thought it useful to sketch in here their significance as a complementary pair.[8] Both seek the source of the various forms of Chinese religion and discuss their transmission through the hierarchy of Chinese society, but De Groot, in his maturer work, begins from an elite-classical version from which all others are, so to say, debased aberrations (unless they are spiritualized sectarian movements), whereas Granet appears to build up the elite-classical version from its alleged peasant origins. De Groot was during several crucial years of his career a fieldworker—an official of the Netherlands Indies service sent to China to familiarize himself with Chinese life—who, as his studies developed, sought to anchor in the classical past what he saw of the present. Granet, the

[7] A more sophisticated version of the surviving and (as I think) mistaken view that popular and elite religions are divided by a gulf is to be found in Barbara E. Ward (1965: 131), where the author, pursuing her general thesis that areas of social conduct not governed by elite models show great variation, says: "Because formally the literati despised the popular cults we should perhaps expect the greatest variety of all to appear in this sphere. There is a good deal of evidence in support of this contention. In other words, there being no literati-derived model for religious behaviour outside the state and ancestral cults (which were uniform), the popular cults could develop to suit local fancy—and did." Is it really true that there was as great a variety in "popular cults" as is envisaged in this formulation? I think not. And it seems to me a mistake to imagine that there was not also variation between the elite and the common people in the sphere of the ancestor cult. But surface variation is in any case one thing, underlying similarity another.

[8] What follows on De Groot and Granet derives from a study in which I am now engaged. Since the first version of this paper was prepared I have carried out "field research" on the two men in Leiden and Paris, in connection with which I gratefully acknowledge the financial support of the Social Science Research Council (London). Given the complexity of the documentation, which I shall be discussing in later publications, I see no point in trying to justify my statements here with bibliographical references and citations of unpublished material. What appears here is the merest summary of one part of my researches as of August 1973. But in September 1973, after the present version of the paper was completed, I finally traced De Groot's manuscript journal, which will enable me to say more about, *inter alia*, his religious ideas, education, and reading.

student of China's ancient past through her classical literature, aimed in much of his work at getting behind that past to a humbler origin that the classical literature was taken as trying to conceal. Both sought to explain at least in part by origins, but they moved in opposite social directions: De Groot, beginning as a fieldworker, from the popular to the elite; Granet, starting from the Chinese classical texts, from the elite to the popular. Each was a sort of deflater, one diminishing the popular, the other the elite.

We know De Groot best for his unfinished monumental work in six volumes, *The Religious System of China* (1892–1910), which has as its subtitle *Its Ancient Forms, Evolution, History and Present Aspect. Manners, Customs and Social Institutions Connected Therewith.* Even if we were to take that work on its own, ignoring the rest of the author's considerable literary output (in English, Dutch, German, and French), we should obviously be dealing with a man who set himself the task of producing a comprehensive study. It is important to understand how and why he came to compose that great work—and since nearly all writers on Chinese religion pick at his books (as I have myself done in the past) without an idea of his intellectual background,[9] I want to discuss it very briefly here. After studying Chinese at Leiden, in preparation for a career as a Chinese interpreter in the Indies service, in 1877 he went off to spend a year in China, chiefly in Amoy. During that 'prentice year he collected the data for the study that we usually consult in its French translation, *Les Fêtes annuellement célébrées à Emoui (Amoy): Etude concernant la religion populaire des Chinois* (De Groot 1886). That fruitful year of field study (in which, with no formal social science background, he invented a field method for himself)[10] was in fact the shorter of two stays in China; the career that he began in 1878 in the Indies as a civil servant specializing in Chinese affairs (and to which we owe, among other works, his important study [De Groot 1885] of the "kongsis" of West Borneo) came prematurely to an end when, during sick leave in the Netherlands, he was granted a request to return to his investigations in China. His second sojourn lasted from June 1886 to April 1890, most of it again spent in the region of Amoy, the chief area of interest to the Dutch in connection with Chinese immigration to their eastern empire.

[9] Illustrated by C. K. Yang's astonishing description of De Groot as an "embittered Dutch missionary"; p. xxxix of his 1964 Introduction to Weber 1951.

[10] De Groot may have attended lectures on the ethnography of the Dutch East Indies while studying at Leiden, but his time there was devoted primarily to learning Chinese. At Delft, before he went to Leiden, he certainly received some instruction in the ethnography of the Indies.

In *Les Fêtes* De Groot in at least one respect shows himself a true pupil of his teacher at Leiden, the sinologue Gustave Schlegel, who was, in his ideas, an extension of the eighteenth century into the second half of the nineteenth. The picture painted of China in *Les Fêtes* is complimentary (more so in the original Dutch than in the French translation). China is an alternative civilization, having roots in common with Europe. It is to be compared with Europe, in some respects very favorably. The book expresses anti-Christian, especially anti-Catholic, sentiments, and emphasizes the religious tolerance prevailing in China. De Groot links the "three religions" with popular religion (the latter being the chief object of his study—he wanted to see how people behaved before committing himself to what was written in Chinese texts); and although he does not make a system of them, it seems to me that he was now ready to do so. But that system was to be achieved only after a break in his intellectual development and a complete transformation of his view of China. When exactly the change took place is difficult to pin down; but it must have occurred between 1886 and 1891, possibly as the joint result of his experience during his second stay in China and his switch to an academic career.

He returned to the Netherlands in 1890 to teach Chinese and Malay in Amsterdam, but he was soon called to occupy the chair at Leiden vacated by Wilken. He became Professor "in de Land- en Volkenkunde van Nederlandsch-Indië." He was now a professor of ethnography not because he was an ethnographer (although of course he had written descriptively on the Chinese in both China and the Indies and drawn upon comparative ethnography ever since he had begun to write on them); he became an ethnographer because he undertook to profess the subject. And his manner of presenting China after his appointment to Leiden reflected the anthropology of the day. Spencerian evolution of a sort is present in his earliest work, but there countered by an eighteenth-century respect for China; De Groot now adopted a far less inhibited European view. In 1904 he reluctantly allowed himself to be translated to the Chair of Chinese vacated by Schlegel. His more narrowly sinological career was, so to say, confirmed when he finally accepted an invitation to a chair of Chinese in Berlin, where he installed himself in 1912. (One may amuse oneself by speculating about the turn Chinese studies might have taken in the United States if De Groot had accepted an invitation he received from Columbia University in 1902.) He saw the war through in Germany, and died there in 1921, broken by the tragedy of the country with which he had come closely to identify himself.

Although in both China and the Indies De Groot concerned himself with practical affairs (and wrote on them), it is clear that religion above all commanded his attention; and of course his greatest work falls in that field. In the General Preface to the first of the six volumes of *The Religious System of China* he points out (p. vii) that Chinese religion had never up to then been studied as a whole and as it was lived: "Sinologists have never taken any serious pains to penetrate into the intimate Religious life of the nation." And he goes on to say (p. viii) that his aim in the work was precisely to depict "the Chinese Religion as it is really practised by the nation." But the social and religious matters he is to discuss, being "founded upon the past . . . rightly to understand them, a knowledge of Antiquity is necessary" (p. x). It is for that reason that a work of ethnography, based upon fieldwork (indeed, what must have been the first sustained and systematic fieldwork ever done in China) is—as it must seem to many readers—cluttered up with references to and quotations from the classical literature.[11]

De Groot's exposition has another aspect: he had always taken a vaguely evolutionary view of religion and culture, but the Chinese had now become for him a semicivilized people, and he thought himself obliged to try to relate his findings on the Chinese to those of comparative (or as we should now say, indiscriminate) ethnography. "Many rites and practices still flourish among the Chinese, which one would scarcely expect to find anywhere except among savages in a low state of culture" (De Groot I: xi). (The alternative Europe has disappeared.) Happily, for editorial reasons, De Groot cut out nearly all the comparative references, but as he says himself, we shall "soon become aware that those references have left a distinct mark upon this work, a mark chiefly manifested by the fact that the author has followed the beaten track of Science for the study of Religions and Sociology in general" (De Groot I: xi–xii). One might well wish that he had kept away from Science and been faithful to the humanism of his early work.

De Groot saw Chinese society from the top down. In the first place,

[11] For ease of reference, individual volumes of this work will be referred to as De Groot I, De Groot II, etc. Large as it is, *The Religious System of China* realizes only six of the twelve to fourteen volumes planned; and of the six "Books" foreseen we have less than two, "Disposal of the Dead" being complete, and "On the Soul and Ancestral Worship" unfinished. On the other hand, much of the matter intended for the missing four Books was published elsewhere. For example, the yearly round of festivals we have in the form of *Les Fêtes* (1886), while *Le Code du Mahâyâna en Chine* (1893) probably represents part of the missing fifth Book. But whatever the possibilities open to us for reconstructing the unrealized work as a whole, we must be saddened by the thought of the enormous amount of information irretrievably lost to us.

The customs described in the Book as observed by the Chinese of the present day are by no means conformed to by all classes of society. As has been remarked already by the ancient *Li-ki* . . . "the rites and ceremonies do not go down to the common people", whose means are small and manners rude. As a basis for our descriptions we have selected the well-to-do classes and families of fashionable standing, amongst whom, in China, we chiefly moved, and these may be said best to maintain the whole systems of the rites and ceremonies prescribed by the laws of custom. (De Groot I: 1–2.)[12]

Second, the customs seen and recorded for the well-to-do and the fashionable (slipping into De Groot's language one may have the pleasure of the snobbery without the responsibility for it), and mainly in one provincial corner of the Empire, are shown to be directly dependent upon the classical norms.

So determined is he to demonstrate this last connection that De Groot traps himself into contradicting his own field evidence when he comes to describe how tombs are arranged.

Down to this day, clan life and family life have undergone no change of any importance, the ancient method of burying the dead in family grave-yards or clan grave-grounds and of placing very near relations . . . in the same tomb, has probably remained in vogue uninterruptedly. (De Groot III: 831.)

The current editions of the Rituals for Family Life generally contain an appendix, stating how the tombs should be arranged in family grave-grounds. . . . The Rituals for Family Life being the chief vademecum of the people for their domestic rites and ceremonies, we may assume that family grave-grounds certainly in most cases are laid out in accordance with those instructions. (De Groot III: 832.)

Now, the arrangement prescribed in the Rituals involves a complicated pattern in which unmarried descendants of the apical ancestor are buried to the north of him, and his descendants with wives and children to the south; the latter group is so disposed that members of adjacent generations do not lie next to one another on the north-south axis (see diagram, De Groot III: 833). How did De Groot come to imagine that the graveyards of his day were usually so arranged unless he somehow persuaded himself that what was classical was right and

---

[12] One wonders of course how, having been sent to China to gain an understanding of the background (in its widest sense) of Chinese emigration overseas, De Groot justified his choice of the upper class as the one with which to associate and to investigate the most fully. From the ranks of the people he knew best, very few of the migrants to the Indies could have originated. The quotation from the *Li Chi* is a handy one for scholars wishing to stress the distinction between elite and people, or to show the difficulties experienced by the common people in conforming to elite ideals. For the latter, see Levy 1949: 99.

therefore followed? All the other evidence we have contradicts his generalization for "modern" China, and, more important, he contradicts it himself when later he turns to discuss the influence of geomancy (*feng-shui*) upon burial (De Groot III: 1017 *et seq.*). What he there says implies dispersed burial and flies in the face of his earlier account. The passage quoted above is a telling example of the triumph of theoretical scheme over observed fact. Or consider what he says about mourning, which, though it illustrates his sensitivity to changes over time, shows him hard at work to justify his historical method. In Volume II (pp. 474 *et seq.*) we are treated to a detailed account of ancient mourning practices. De Groot interrupts the flow of his exposition to remark (p. 533), "No doubt our readers will have had the question on their lips: Why weary us with these tedious mourning lists of the ancients? Why fill up so many pages with such uninteresting stuff?" It was to be expected that those questions were introduced in order to justify answers at length. They culminate in the

chief reason, outweighing by far all the others . . . : that the mourning codex of the *I li* . . . has through all the ages exercised a mighty influence upon Chinese society and its organization, because, with modifications and revisions of more or less importance, it has always been used by legislators in assigning to each individual a fixed place in the circle of his family. (De Groot II: 534.)[13]

We are soon plunged into an exposition of the mourning regulations laid down in the Ch'ing code, after which follows a section (pp. 585–602) dealing with the "modern mourning attire at Amoy," showing

that, in this respect, the inveterate conservatism of the Chinese race abnegates itself to no small degree. The nation's idiosyncrasy of closely imitating everything bequeathed to posterity by the holy ancients has indeed not been strong enough to prevent the people of the present day from indulging in considerable deviations from the mourning dress of olden times, which cannot properly be ascribed to a wrong understanding of the ancient works. (De Groot II: 586.)[14]

Then why the deviations? That question is not answered, for it is not posed. De Groot is saying throughout that the Chinese he knew followed

[13] De Groot's tracing of the kinship system of ancient China (De Groot II: 507–11) is a flat contradiction of the assertion quoted above, that "clan life and family life have undergone no change of any importance" (De Groot III: 831).

[14] As a matter of fact, one suspects that the mourning practices De Groot witnessed were still wider of the classical mark than he allowed. And it seems to me that a recent sinological writer has been misled by De Groot's exposition: Laurence G. Thompson says that in Volumes I and II of *The Religious System* "nearly every detail of late nineteenth-century practice is shown to conform to the scriptural injunctions" (Thompson 1969: 111).

in the steps of their ancient forerunners—and if they did not, then they were being irritatingly inconsistent.

It may be recalled that Lyall wrote of "entire religious toleration conjoined with the peremptory assertion of civil supremacy"; and the nature and extent of religious tolerance in China are a theme that recurs in many branches of the literature on that country. De Groot's view (that is, his later view) of this important matter is interesting in part because it is of a piece with his general attitude toward the Chinese in his later years. He had come to disdain the people he had studied so long and so intensively. And despite the sinological apparatus and learning he brought to his work, one detects in him some of the less instructed arrogance of the late-nineteenth-century Western European confronting an empire in collapse. There is little of the Christian missionary about De Groot in most of his writing,[15] but in one important context he springs to the defense of the missionaries. In *Sectarianism and Religious Persecution in China: A Page in the History of Religions* (De Groot 1903–4) one kind of indignation is made to do for both the imperial persecution of heterodox sects and the harassment of Christian missions. De Groot then argued that intolerance was built into China's system of political control, and in intemperate language expressed the hope that if ever Western politicians had again to consider whether, as during the Taiping Rebellion, they ought to "uphold the Confucian tyrant on his throne against his bloodily persecuted people rising in arms against him and his satraps," they would decide not to do so (1903–4: 565).[16] The Chinese society of this book is the nightmare version of the conservative, dull, and irrational China of *The Religious System*. In *Sectarianism* there are of course some heroes, the sectarians; but they are not enough to redeem China in De Groot's eyes. Evolutionary theory pushed De Groot toward an expectation of increasing civilization; that expectation was canceled by another theory embedded in his work: degeneration from antiquity. At times one detects yet a third contradictory theme: China never changes. The first theory De Groot clearly owed to European thought;

[15] He was brought up in a Catholic family but at the age of twenty left the Church. *Les Fêtes* shows us his religious views during his early manhood; his later work demonstrates his respect for the missionaries in China. Religion was obviously something he took seriously.

[16] The book is dedicated "To all missionaries of every Christian creed labouring in China." Cf. his Lamson Lectures, given at the Hartford Theological Seminary in Connecticut (De Groot 1910), in which he shows his contempt for Confucian materialism ("it is a religion of a lower order"; p. 131) and his assimilation of the Chinese sects to Christianity (pp. 222–23). The last words of the book (p. 223) are: "Is it too idle a suggestion that those humble sects are destined to be the precursors of Christianity in China?"

the second and third, perhaps partly to different phases of that thought and partly to the Chinese self-image. It is just possible, I suppose, that his occasional messianic hopes for the triumph of both unorthodox Chinese and Christian religions were a way out of the impasse created by his two leading and mutually contradictory ideas.[17]

In turning from De Groot to Granet we enter an entirely new intellectual world, where we find so completely different a China that we must wonder at the outset whether the two sinologists were studying the same country. With Granet we are of course in the realm of Durkheim (who along with Chavannes was Granet's teacher), of Mauss (Granet's close friend), and of the *Année Sociologique* in general. The China that Granet saw was remote, and it is not surprising that some of his readers regard him as an earlier Arthur Waley, never venturing to see for himself what China was like. In fact, after his sociological and sinological training in Paris (first at the Ecole Normale Supérieure and then at the Fondation Thiers), he went on a scholarship to Peking in 1911 and stayed there until 1913, having witnessed some of the events of the Revolution. And he passed a few months in China in 1919 on his way back to France from service with the Allied forces fighting the Bolsheviks in Siberia. But what he did in China was nothing approaching fieldwork, for his sociology was entirely Durkheimian, little touched by the Maussian version of it that moved up direct observation to a position of honor.

The China that engrossed his attention for nearly his whole career as student and teacher in Paris was the China that spanned the primitive and "feudal" and the beginnings of the imperial age. (At the end of his life, cut short by the events of 1940, he was doing research as far forward as the T'ang.) He was much preoccupied with the origins of imperial China, and with the peasant sources of high Chinese culture and social organization. Yet his sociological method was professedly antihistorical in one sense, and explanation merely by origin anathema.[18]

---

[17] The line from *Les Fêtes* to *The Religious System* is extended to De Groot's last great work on Chinese religion, *Universismus: Die Grundlage der Religion und Ethik, des Staatswesens und der Wissenschaften Chinas* (1918); we are now finally in the world of pure textual sinology, the field observations having vanished from sight; and China's single religion, "Universism," is cast in its final form.

[18] In his first book on religion Granet castigates De Groot for writing in the tradition that seeks to explain current religious practices by a purpose ascribed to them by the Chinese themselves or by reference to some fashionable theory such as Naturism or Animism. "The search after the beginnings of things is generally misleading: particularly is this the case in China, where native scholars devote their attention to discovering, not the actual beginnings of things, but only the date when the characters employed to denote these things were first used" (Granet 1932: 2–3).

Durkheimian method called for a rigorous dissection of a body of facts and an analysis of their connection. (What Granet meant by a fact is too complex a matter for discussion here.) In his first great book, *Fêtes et chansons anciennes de la Chine* (1919), he took "the most ancient facts of the religious history of China" (Granet 1932: 207) from the *Shih Ching* and, by an act of scholarly prestidigitation that still astonishes his readers, inferred a peasant way of life that he was later so to elaborate along with other forms of Chinese social order that it was to furnish models for students of society uninterested in China itself.[19]

So far as religion is concerned (I take the word in its broadest sense), the method was to be seen at work again chiefly in *La Religion des Chinois* (1922), *Danses et légendes de la Chine ancienne* (1926), and two general works, *La Civilisation chinoise: La Vie publique et la vie privée* (1929) and *La Pensée chinoise* (1934). But I want to pay particular attention here to the first of those works, which, although it belongs among his early writings, states positions that he was for the most part to maintain. It is, moreover, the only one of his books in which he attempts to cover the whole span of Chinese history and all aspects of Chinese religion. Its brevity and comprehensiveness are due to its being written in response to a publisher's request for a short general study of Chinese religion to fit into a series.

The structure of the book implies a large part of its argument. It opens with peasant religion, moves to "feudal" religion, and thence proceeds to official religion. We are now two-thirds of the way through. The remainder is taken up with "religious revivals" (Taoism and Buddhism) and concluding remarks on religion in contemporary China.

Peasant religion and "feudal" religion together precede imperial religion; of the first two, peasant religion is prior. True enough, Granet sometimes writes as though peasants and nobles, rural and town life, were an aboriginal complementary pair. But in fact, he looks upon peasant life and thought as the ultimate foundation of all Chinese culture. It was the source from which "feudal" and imperial religion sprang, and from which many sectarian movements were later to derive. And were we to question the peasant mass, the very stuff of the country, in order to describe religious life as it is now, we should perhaps discover that common peasant base all over again (Granet 1922, 2d ed.: xi). And for Granet, one might add, that peasant religion was essentially gentle, free of objectionable features of the religious forms to follow on from it (p. 107).

[19] Note the importance of Granet's work on Chinese kinship and marriage for Lévi-Strauss in chaps. 19–21 of *Les Structures élémentaires de la parenté* (1949).

Peasant life and religion are described and analyzed with the assurance characteristic of Granet's writing—except when he briefly turns to present-day China. The closer we get, under his guidance, to the modern and the more fully documented, the remoter and more indefinite it seems to be. The peasants led their distinctive way of life, marked by the aristocratic ritual formula: the Rites do not go down to the common people (p. 1).[20] They lived in villages on high ground and enclosed within quickset hedges, and the men for part of the year in huts in the fields. The seasonal rhythm of work was different for men and women, the men at their labors during the warmer season, the women during the colder weather. Each village consisted of a homogeneous group barely differentiated by descent—sex and generation were the two chief organizing principles. (Descent began by being matrilineal.) Exogamy tied these close-knit communities one to another. And from this there arose the elaborate and colorful institutions of ritual centers ("Lieux Saints") and peasant festivals, marking the seasonal and social changes of the year and the crucial significance of sexual and marital relations. We are now in the presence of the origin of the calendar, destined of course to remain a key element in Chinese religion, and of the fundamental concept of *yin-yang*. The agrarian base of this early society provides the ritualization of the Earth and the first form of the ancestors (pp. 2–26). We know at once that we are in the same world as Durkheim's Australia (although paradoxically Granet, working on a literate civilization, had worse documentation than Durkheim upon which to draw); and we may well gasp at the vividness and richness of the description, wondering after the first impact whether it relates to very much outside Granet's superb sociological imagination.[21] Fortunately, that is a problem I am not obliged to consider here.

In the chapter on "feudal" religion (pp. 31–79) we are given the corresponding account of social life and its correlates in the towns, the seat of noble life. Here Granet's eloquence is devoted to expounding the agnatic and primogenitory kinship system and the concomitant elaborations of the ancestor cult; the worship of Heaven, a dynastic and official cult superimposed on the agrarian and ancestor cults; and the

[20] Granet contrives to put some life into this tired formula. Cf. note 12 above.

[21] Most modern studies of ancient China are more restrained in their reconstructions, and Granet *as historian* seems to have been largely left behind. But we may note that one of his French successors takes some of his assertions about the ancient peasantry as though they were historically established facts: Jacques Gernet, *Ancient China from the Beginnings to the Empire* (1968), pp. 51 *et seq.* A parallel American study—Joseph R. Levenson and H. Franz Schurmann, *China: An Interpretive History, From the Beginnings to the Fall of Han* (1969)—does not even mention Granet.

worship of Earth, which built upon and expanded the agrarian cult of Earth.

In the section on "La religion officielle" Granet reaches the climax of the book, for the remaining chapter and the conclusion slide down to a less arresting finish. Now both the peasant and the noble forms of religion are seen to be worked up into beliefs and cults serving the needs of an imperial state and its functionaries, the literati. China has become a unified country whose dominant system of ideas reaches down into all levels of society. In Granet's eyes, it was not a religion that was at all points commendable, but at least religious life remained dominated by a practical spirit that for the most part preserved China from mystical adventures (p. 99). Confucianism had triumphed even when it had at times to reckon with Taoism (pp. 88–120).

But Taoism began from the same source as its greater rival and, along with its "foreign" companion, Buddhism, complemented the official religion. Just as Taoism had to be called to the aid of the official religion in order that the forces of Nature might continue to render their services to the Chinese people, so Buddhism established its prestige by pacifying the world of the dead (p. 150). We have arrived at a synthesis in which beneath the surface variety and literate sophistication there lie a few simple and basic religious ideas, a heritage from the peasant past (pp. 121–75).[22]

De Groot and Granet, each in his own manner, have pointed the way to an understanding of how in modern times the vast hierarchized society of China might be seen to display a single underlying religion taking many guises. One of these sinologues thought (in his maturer work) that a classical tradition would account for nearly everything; the other assumed that by penetrating the literary deceptions practiced and the distortions worked in the name of the same tradition, we could reach a source from which all Chinese religion ultimately stems. We may now return to C. K. Yang and his analysis of the total religious system of China.

Yang opens the chapter of his book called "Political Role of Chinese Religion in Historical Perspective" by pointing out that the relation between the Chinese state and religion is an unsettled question: "in China the political role of religion was somewhat obscured by the dominance of Confucian orthodoxy in the function and structure of the state,

---

[22] Of the many crucial passages, let me quote just one example (from p. 170): "The religious life of the Chinese people is inspired by a few simple and deep-lying beliefs, the heritage of an ancient peasant past; they provide a meaning in life for the humblest Chinese; among the more cultivated, religious feeling is manifested in an effort of inner cultivation pursued within the framework of national traditions."

for Confucianism had very prominent non-religious, secular features" (Yang 1961: 104). In fact, Yang says, religion in China has in recent times stood in every possible relation to the state—by suffusing and supporting it, by struggling against it (as in the case of the rebellions started by the sects), and by withdrawing into seclusion from it (as with the monasteries). To understand these three solutions, we need to survey the history of the relations between religion and state; and at the end of the survey Yang undertakes (pp. 105–26) we can see that by the modern period Buddhism and Taoism had adopted more or less passive roles, submitting to the state, but not submitting so far as to be incapable of acting on occasion as inspirers of rebellion.

The next chapter deals with the Mandate of Heaven, a topic which lends itself admirably to an analysis of the connections between the religious and the political, but which in Yang's hands turns into something more, for (on p. 134) he asks the key question: how did the common people come to believe in the idea of the Mandate of Heaven and to accept "the supremacy of imperial power partly on the ground that it was a predetermined course ordained by the gods? . . . The question is particularly pertinent in view of the relatively tenuous tie between the central imperial power and the intimate life of the common people." I think Yang slips into a phraseology uncongenial to his thought when he refers to "the magic-oriented common people" (p. 135), for his argument supposes a systematic coherence between elite ideas and those of what he calls the common people.

Observers have generally regarded these practices of divination and geomancy as a chaotic mass of ignorant superstitions. Actually they represented a well-coordinated system of religious concepts containing the belief in the power of Heaven and Earth to predetermine the course of all events, large and small, by controlling the time and space within which they occurred. . . . In this sense, the theology of Yin-yang and the Five Elements served as a link between the supernatural basis of the affairs of state and the intimate life of the people. (P. 136.)

Moreover, he goes on to argue:

The universal acceptance of the supreme power of Heaven over all gods and man provided the imperial power with an important religious basis for the political integration of a vast country. . . . Under this system the peasants in Chekiang or Kwangtung province might be intensely devoted to local gods and spirits stemming from a particular ethnic background, but these deities were a part of the hierarchy of supernatural powers subordinated to Heaven, the formal worship of which was monopolized by the central political power. (Pp. 136–37.)

The next chapter, "Ethicopolitical Cults," *inter alia* demonstrates the interlocking of official and popular cults (see especially p. 145), and brings out the untenability of a view such as Weber's, which makes official religion seem merely formal and conventional and so distanced from the religious fervor of the masses (pp. 178–79).

I jump to Chapter 10, "Religious Aspects of Confucianism . . . ," where we find a clear expression of a thesis I am holding up for approval:

Even taking into consideration the relative difference in the belief in magic and miracles, the Confucians did not constitute a group separate from the general current of religious life of traditional Chinese society. They shared with the rest of the population a basic system of religious belief in Heaven, fate, and other supernatural concepts. More important was the steady inter-flow of religious ideas between the Confucians and the general population. . . . The Confucians, therefore, cannot be regarded as a distinctively different group on religious grounds, but must be regarded as part of the general pattern of Chinese religious life with only relative differences due to their social and economic position. (Pp. 276–77.)[23]

Let us leave Yang at that point.

In what I have said so far I have tried to show that there is a sociological tradition, culminating for the moment in Yang's book, which takes Chinese religion to be one entity. When we survey the sociological work done on Chinese religion in the last thirty or forty years, Yang's book excepted, it is difficult to believe that there has been such a tradition to adhere to. I think we may in part trace the anomaly to two consequences of the fact that the adjective "sociological" in the last sentence in reality means "anthropological." Those consequences are, first, that some fragment of Chinese society and religion is studied, not Chinese society and religion as a whole;[24] second, that a special

[23] In chap. 8, "State Control of Religion," I think Yang errs on one point. He argues (pp. 192–93) that the persecution of religious heterodoxy by the Confucian state was due not to religious motives but to political ones. Certainly religious sects seemed often, perhaps usually, to be politically threatening, but there is more to it that that. Heterodoxy was also an affront to Confucian social principles, which in turn, of course, rested upon religious foundations. The best discussion I know of this point is in R. A. Stein, "Les Religions de la Chine" (1957), a truly remarkable synthesis. Stein writes (p. 54-5) that the *yin-ssu*, "immoral cults," implied a forbidden social promiscuity and a forbidden religious promiscuity—divinities incarnating and mixing with men.

[24] But I should really limit myself to anthropologists in the Anglo-American tradition. From other traditions of anthropological research, broader views might issue. Cf. the criticism by the eminent Russian S. M. Shirokogoroff of the choice of the "village" as a unit of study (Shirokogoroff 1942: 3). And note his remark at p. 6: "If one reads the works like that by *Hsiao-Tung Fei* or that by *D. H. Kulp* one may get quite a wrong impression of the ethnographical investigations in general."

peasant's-eye view of China is promoted that inverts but otherwise reproduces the distortion of the Confucian's-eye view in the course of the wholly admirable effort to move from bookishness to fieldwork (see Li 1938; Freedman 1963: 9–10). We find ourselves in the rather tired intellectual world of the Great and Little Traditions.[25] For the fieldworker is aware in a general way of the difference between the religious ideas and practices of the people he studies and those ascribed to the fully literate elite of the country—but in fact he does not know enough about the religious ideas and practices of that elite (for he does not study them)[26] to realize the extent to which elite and peasant religion rest upon a common base, representing two versions of one religion that we may see as idiomatic translations of each other. And so it comes about that fieldworkers in China are confident of having made a discovery in establishing that peasants do not belong to merely one of the Three Religions, but are heirs to a long syncretic tradition.[27]

Now, the question might be raised whether the fragmentary view of local religion obtained from anthropological studies is due solely to professional deformation. It may well be asked why it is that the Chinese anthropologists themselves, who presumably differ from their Western colleagues in knowing a great deal about the religion of the strata of Chinese society from which they come, seem to paint much the same distorted, or at any rate incomplete, picture as anyone else. I shall not presume to talk about scholars whose intellectual and social backgrounds I do not know well enough beyond observing that they may illustrate one aspect of that very polymorphism of Chinese elite religion to which I shall be referring presently: as literati they are licensed by their society to ignore or even to despise the religion of the common people by adopting one of the several positions open to them within their total religious field. That the religion of the masses was quaint, superstitious, or negligible was not an attitude suddenly produced by modern currents of thought. It is, of course, an old theme of elite Chinese culture—and one consistent with the fact of that culture's shared basis with peasant culture. But

[25] For some pertinent comments on the Redfieldian approach, see Tambiah 1970: 3–4, 367–77.

[26] And if he were to confine himself to the texts he might be seriously misled. One can too easily slip into the fallacy: text = elite, oral culture = peasantry. The matter is, of course, vastly more complex.

[27] For an early example see Kulp 1925: I, 308. More recently Norma Diamond has written in *K'un Shen, A Taiwan Village* (1969: 84–85): "The folk traditions and the literary traditions of China are inextricably combined in the total belief system. . . . The religious life of K'un Shen cannot be discussed in terms of a fixed and systematically elaborated doctrine; it can only be seen as a totality of eclectic practices and beliefs which to the villager's mind presents an integrated whole."

whatever the reason, Chinese intellectuals in this century have not shown
any marked interest in the religion of ordinary people.[28]

But how precisely to consider Chinese religion as a whole? It is reasonable to assume (I think) that a country of China's extent and political cohesion would demonstrate a large measure of agreement on
religious assumptions among all its people. And, more important, one
might predict from first principles that a society so differentiated by
social status and power would develop a religious system that allowed
differences in beliefs and rites to complement one another—or, to put
the point more provocatively, that allowed religious similarity to be
expressed as though it were religious difference. When an educated
Chinese, writing about Chinese religion as though from the outside,
says that a rational agnosticism characterizes the elite and an indiscriminate superstition the masses, he is in reality writing from the *inside*
and expressing the elite's view of the difference between the two great
layers of his society. An example that springs to mind is one provided
by Wing-tsit Chan, who, in his rightly celebrated *Religious Trends in
Modern China*, says: "I have always urged that instead of dividing the
religious life of the Chinese people into three compartments called
Confucianism, Buddhism, and Taoism, it is far more accurate to divide
it into two levels, the level of the masses and the level of the enlightened"
(Chan 1953: 141).[29] He proceeds (p. 143) to distinguish the two levels
above all by the differential vocabulary of religious service: *pai* and *chi*.
"The masses *pai*, that is worship in the formal, orthodox, strictly religious
sense, but the enlightened *chi*, that is, sacrifice or make offerings....
The idea of propitiation or expiation is never present."[30]

[28] Note the passage in Wing-tsit Chan, *Religious Trends in Modern China* (1953:
144), where he remarks upon the neglect by Chinese writers of the topic of the
"religion of the masses": "Not a single book on Chinese folk religion has been published in the last five decades.... For information about the religion of the Chinese
masses, we still have to rely on Maspero, Soothill, Hodous, Doré, Day, Shryock and
Latourette." Certainly Francis L. K. Hsu has added considerably to our store of
knowledge of popular Chinese religion in *Under the Ancestors' Shadow* and *Religion,
Science and Human Crises*, but he appears up to recently to have been an exception.

[29] But it must be noticed that Chan (p. 142) defines "enlightened" and "masses"
in an unconventional way, for "By the masses is meant the 85 per cent of the Chinese people who are devout but ignorant. By the enlightened is meant the intelli-
gentsia and the illiterate farmers, fishermen and similar humble folks who may often
use a smaller vocabulary but often express greater wisdom."

[30] Note how this sort of characterization in turn affects the view formed by Western scholars. See, for example, Huston Smith, "Transcendence in Traditional China":
"We must first distinguish between the views of the peasants and those of the intel-
ligentsia. Peasants believed the unseen world to be peopled by innumerable spirits,
both benign (*shen*) and malevolent (*kuei*), who could dwell in idols and natural
objects and be used or warded off by magic and sacrifice." (Smith 1970: 109.)

But the pragmatic-agnostic interpretation of elite religion is made possible by the very assumptions upon which that religion rests: there is an order in the universe presided over morally by *T'ien*, Heaven, whose workings may be analyzed by recourse to the ideas of yin-yang and the Five Elements. (See, for example, Topley 1967.) With all that simply taken for granted, it becomes possible to look upon the entities to which sacrifices must for official-political reasons be made as convenient fictions—if one chooses. But we, the outsiders, are not entitled to conclude that the pragmatic-agnostic interpretation was the common one among the elite. Apart from any other complicating factor, we would be hard put to distinguish between what a literatus believed qua official and what qua private citizen (cf. Welch 1970: 616; Stein 1957: 54–4). The polymorphism of Chinese religion allowed variation not only among the elite but also within the religious life of the individual literatus. With the exception of prophecy and ecstasy, every religious phenomenon to be found among the common people in China was susceptible of transformation into beliefs and rites among the cultivated elite. Heterodoxy might be a transformed version of orthodoxy, and vice versa. That is a point I made more narrowly a few years ago in the context of feng-shui. I said then that even though the geomancer and the priest are separated in function and the beliefs that surround their different roles, the "metaphysical" gulf between them

is no gulf at all, but rather a neat transformation. Most of the elements of *fêng-shui* can be restated in the language of ordinary religion. Just as in the Neo-Confucian philosophical writings the concretising words *shên* and *kuei* ... are used for positive and negative spiritual forces, being stripped of their anthropomorphic connotations ..., so in popular religion a reverse transformation is worked by which the disembodied forces of the geomancer are turned into personal entities. (Freedman 1969: 10.)

At first sight, the baroque elaboration of popular feng-shui may seem to contrast sharply with the austere religious imagination of the elite; but on closer inspection it becomes evident that both sets of beliefs are products of the same assumptions and manipulate versions of the same concepts. I am suggesting now that similar transformations will be found in many other spheres of Chinese religion.[31]

How could China fail to constitute a community of ideas when the political center made itself responsible for disseminating its beliefs by

---

[31] Cf. the brief discussion on the possible connections between gentry thought and the ideas associated with such things as traditional Chinese "boxing" in Wakeman 1966: 27–28. And see Muramatsu 1960 and Dunstheimer 1972 for some relevant data.

the spoken and written word, when literacy, however thinly spread (Mote 1972: 110), was an institutionalized part of rural life, when the elite were based as much in the countryside as in the towns,[32] and when social mobility ensured a steady interchange of style between the common run of men and the high-literate? Members of the elite might stand by a puritanical version of Chinese religion, and in that posture deplore the antics of the superstitious masses; but the elite as a group was bound to the masses indissolubly by its religious beliefs and practices. Within that union of belief and ritual action, rebellion might occur, sects crystallize out, unorthodoxy provoke; Taoism might elaborate local community organization and Buddhism sanctify a withdrawal from the world. But let us take it as a working hypothesis that all religious argument and ritual differentiation were conducted within a common language of basic conceptions, symbols, and ritual forms.

And this great community of religion was achieved without a church, unless we choose to call the state itself a church, in which case one of the two terms becomes superfluous. Mandarins performed rites and commanded (or, as sometimes happened, pretended to command) spirits in their official capacity;[33] they were not priests. There were priests, Taoist and Buddhist; they were, generally speaking, men of low standing.[34] Among religious specialists only the geomancer seems consistently to have attracted the respect attaching to civil virtue, for religious practitioner though he was, he was a version of the literatus (Freedman 1969: 9–10). Chinese religion was in a sense a civil religion —not austere and cunningly calculated to serve political interests, but based upon a view of the interpenetration of society and the universe, and upon a conception of authority that in the last analysis would not allow the religious to separate off from the secular. Caesar was Pope, Pope Caesar. And if the sectaries were sometimes tempted, by turning away from normally constituted society, to introduce a sharp difference

[32] The systematic interpenetration between town and country and the channels for the movement of ideas and practices back and forth between them are best seen in the work of G. William Skinner, in his articles "Marketing and Social Structure in Rural China, Part I" (1964: especially p. 40), and "Chinese Peasants and the Closed Community: An Open and Shut Case" (1971: especially pp. 272–74). See also Freedman 1974.

[33] Shryock (1931: 14) mentions the extension of the practice into the Republican period. See also Ch'en 1939: 239. On the implication of religion in administrative matters, see Balazs 1965: 63–64 (on Wang Hui-tsu); and Giles 1882: 163–68. And see Hsiao 1960: 22–35; and Bodde and Morris 1967: 271–78, 288–92.

[34] The generalization is not meant to exclude the possibility of special contexts in which Taoist and Buddhist priests were held in high esteem and accorded high status.

between the secular and the religious, they incurred a reaction from the state which, in killing and maiming them, should convince us, the outsiders, that the powerholding elite was not prepared to tolerate a bifurcation of authority. The Chinese state has on the whole been very successful—and to this day—in muting religious authority. That is one aspect of the religious unity of China.

Religion and Ritual in Lukang

DONALD R. DEGLOPPER

In almost every community on Taiwan, temples stand out from their drab surroundings in bursts of polychrome splendor. Processions, in which the images of deities ride in sedan chairs accompanied by bands and costumed troupes, are a common sight in both city and countryside. For most people religious festivals (*pai-pai*), with their attendant feasts and public entertainment, provide the major holidays. Popular religion flourishes despite the opposition of the central government, the routine labeling of ritual as "superstition" in all schools, and the supposedly secularizing and modernizing forces of urbanization and industrialization. Taiwanese devote a good deal of time and effort to the practice of their religion, and one is struck by the ubiquity of ritual, its vitality, and its sheer exuberance.

Equally striking and perhaps more difficult to understand is the extreme diversity and differentiation within what may loosely be called Taiwanese popular religion. Annual festivals that provide the year's greatest holiday in one place are scarcely noticed ten miles away; deities who are wildly popular in some places play only minor roles in others; and such practices as firewalking, competitive presentation of mammoth hogs, or divination with the planchette by organized groups are common in some communities and nearly unknown in others. Even so simple a matter as the date of Ch'ing Ming (105 days after the winter solstice) is a matter of some confusion in central Taiwan, with people distinguishing between "old" Ch'ing Ming on March 31 and "new" Ch'ing Ming on April 5.

There is, to be sure, a common ground of basic notions and practices, and it is not difficult to abstract a general pattern or system that can be called Taiwanese or Chinese religion. People all over the island worship

their ancestors and tidy up their graves at Ch'ing Ming; divining blocks
are interpreted in a standard way; all temples have incense pots; and
festivals everywhere are managed by ritual officers called *lo-cu* and
thau-ke. There are a number of common themes, but the degree of variation on these themes strikes me as surprising and hard to account for.
The forest of symbols may be homogeneous, but the kinds and numbers
of trees seem to differ markedly from place to place. Here I intend to
concentrate on the trees rather than the forest.

Some sorts of variations do not strike me as problematic. Much of the
apparent diversity one observes is a consequence of one's own imposition
of the blanket category "Taiwanese popular religion" onto a multitude
of practices, cults, and customs which have nothing in common save that
they are observed by Taiwanese. There is no more reason to expect various Taiwanese customs or beliefs to form a coherent, logically consistent, and uniform system than there is to expect the doctrine of the
Trinity, the tooth fairy, and Easter eggs to fit together in a consistent
"American popular religion." The religion of the Taiwanese, which after
all has no name, is not characterized by the elaboration of doctrine and
dogma one finds in Christianity or Islam, and the individual Taiwanese
has much more latitude than an Irishman or a Saudi Arabian in what he
chooses to believe or do. Modern Taiwanese society is complex and differentiated, and it is not surprising that semi-literate rice farmers and
educated owners of Taipei factories should go at their religion differently.

Such diversity, which stems from the undiscriminating nature of the
category "popular religion," from the relative indifference to doctrine
and the minimal role of the professional clergy in most Chinese religion,
from individual interpretations of symbols, and from the differentiation
of Taiwanese society, does not seem difficult to understand. But local
variation does. If one restricts one's attention to public ritual in Hokkien-
speaking communities, one finds striking differences between apparently
similar settlements. Most villages have temples and celebrate an annual
festival, but some, which differ in no obvious way from their neighbors,
do not. Some communities devote a great deal of attention to placating
hungry ghosts, and shrines for the bones of the unknown dead are common. Other settlements slight the hungry ghosts in favor of their own
ancestors, and most of the small shrines in the fields house the Earth God
(T'u Ti Kung). Examples could be multiplied, and each new bit of fieldwork provides another variant case.

Consider the contrast in ritual life between the towns of Erhlin and
Lukang. They are eighteen kilometers apart in western Chang-hua hsien

in a region originally settled by people from the Three Counties (San Yi) of Ch'üan-chou. Both are market towns with the usual complement of shops and services. Erhlin, with a population of 11,000–12,000, has six temples, one for every 1,900 people, and a flourishing planchette divination (*pai-luan*) group, which in 1968 was preparing to build its own temple. Lukang, with 27,000–28,000 people, has 39 temples, one for every 690 people, and residents claimed never to have heard of pai-luan. Processions and small-scale public rituals are much more common in Lukang.

The problem, to me, is why, on a fairly small island settled for the most part only in the last 250 years by people from the same small region of China, one should find such great local diversity in ritual, when most other aspects of culture—language, cuisine, architecture, categories of disease, etc.—are fairly uniform. Or, to put it another way, while such diversity might have been understandable a hundred years ago when the island's population was divided into scattered settlements that had little contact with one another, its existence today is puzzling. Much of the history of Taiwan, at least since the 1880's, can be summed up in terms of increasing integration, centralization, and standardization. Today communications, in the all-inclusive sense of the Chinese *chiao-t'ung*, are good, and no place on the plains could in any way be described as isolated. Primary education is well-nigh universal, as is military service for men. People go to cities to seek work or visit relatives, they read newspapers of island-wide circulation, they go to films, listen to the radio, and tend to have clear if somewhat inaccurate ideas about life in other parts of the island. Urban fashions and fads are quickly and enthusiastically adopted in the villages. Pilgrimages to distant shrines are popular, and most temples are involved in ritual visits with temples in other communities.

Yet ritual, public communal ritual, remains surprisingly unstandardized, and provides the most obvious way of distinguishing otherwise similar communities. Religion seems the most mutable, labile, and differentiated aspect of modern Taiwanese culture. Instead of "secularization," *Entzauberung*, or the sort of "modern" religious movement Clifford Geertz discusses in *Islam Observed*, each of which might seem likely on Taiwan, one finds a hundred flowers blooming, each in its own plot.

If one assumes that there is some relation between ritual and other aspects of people's lives, or between religion and social structure, then one faces the problem of accounting for patent differences in ritual and trying to find something that goes along with such differences. If one restricts one's attention to variation between communities, the problem can be approached in several ways.

One is to stress the common pattern or core that is found in all places. Local diversity can then be dismissed as representing accidental permutations of a fundamental structure. Ritual is seen as floating on the surface of local society like an oil slick, having no determinate relation to the particular community that supports it, and thus giving the appearance of more local color than in fact exists. Alternatively, one may explain local cults and customs as traditions handed down from early settlers, who came from diverse regions. Local religious variation is then meaningful, but only in relation to the past, and may be used as evidence for migration or diffusion. Or, one can attempt a functional interpretation and try to correlate religious variation with some other easily observed social factor. The hope is that one will discover that two apparently unrelated social facts covary.

The first approach, concentrating on system and general structure, dismisses the problem as trivial or unanswerable. The second atomizes the subject into a cluster of traits and ultimately pushes the question back one step, so that one ends up asking about local variations in Fukien 300 years ago. The last approach is attractive but runs into the difficulty already noted: there appear to be no obvious differences between communities to correlate with ritual variation. In this paper I begin with the assumption that local religious diversity is not necessarily trivial, and examine one case in detail, hoping to discover less obvious relationships that may provide some suggestions for a solution to the general problem. My case is public ritual in the city of Lukang.

As of October 1968 Lukang, which had a resident population of between 27,000 and 28,000 people, had 39 temples. It is my impression that Lukang has more temples than do most Taiwanese communities of equivalent size. By temple I mean a structure that houses an image, altar, and incense pot, and is freely accessible to the general public. In speaking of the 39 temples of Lukang, I am omitting the numerous small shrines to the unknown dead (Yu Ying Kung), buildings dedicated to ancestors rather than deities (two), Christian churches (four), incense-burner associations that keep their incense pot or image in private homes, and private shrines such as the domestic altars of *tang-ki* (spirit mediums) or the shrine of the now defunct Ch'üan-chou guild, found in the back room of a drugstore endowed with the guild property. Nor am I counting deities enshrined in rear or side courtyards of large temples.

Lukang, seen in comparative perspective, has a lot of temples. Why do its inhabitants need or want so many temples, when most of their compatriots get along with far fewer? This is one of the questions I explore; the other concerns what might be called the "style" of public ritual. It is my strong impression, based on my own observation of public ritual in other places and on the accounts of my fellow fieldworkers, that public ritual in Lukang, especially that connected with temples and processions, is characterized by a restricted range of activity and expression. Out of the many things other Taiwanese do, of which the people of Lukang are quite well aware, the natives of Lukang choose to do only a few. In very crude terms, most Lukang ritual could be described as conservative, stereotyped, plodding, and rather dull.

It is difficult to support this generalization without a tediously detailed ethnographic account of just what is done elsewhere that is not done in Lukang, and vice versa, and I will make do with a few apt illustrations or epiphanies.

One event that seems quintessentially Lukang is *am-hang*, a nocturnal procession of deities, mostly Ong Ia, for the purpose of expelling malign influences from an area. It is an occasional rite that can be performed at any time and for any area, but every spring there is an am-hang for the entire city of Lukang. After dark a procession of perhaps fifteen sedan chairs, led by those of T'u Ti Kung and the Ch'eng Huang, passes along every street and alley in the city. It takes all night to cover the route. The procession winds through the city in near silence and near total darkness, the only light coming from a few dim electric bulbs on the gods' chairs and from glowing incense sticks. Householders, usually in their night clothes, stand in their doorways with incense sticks and *pai* (bow slightly with the hands together, the gesture of respect and supplication to the gods) as the chairs pass. They receive charm papers, *hu*, from the men who accompany the procession.

Most religious processions in Taiwan are, by definition, *lau-ziat* (Mandarin *je-nao*)—that is, exciting, gay, crowded, offering maximum stimulation to all the senses. Religious festivals and processions are often referred to simply as "lau-ziat." Am-hang in Lukang is not lau-ziat; it is spooky. There are no bands, no floats, no costumed troupes of performers, none of the great puppets one sees in processions in northern Taiwan. The participants are mostly young men in their regular clothes, who take turns carrying the sedan chairs through the silent streets at a trot. There are no tang-ki, and chairbearers are not expected to go into trance. (One I observed who showed signs of possession was immediately replaced and left behind by the rest of his group.) All the deities are from temples in Lukang; there are none from any other place. No one watches the procession; indeed it is hard to see anything but lurching points of light. No feast is associated with the am-hang, and it is certainly not an event one invites guests to. There is an intense but somewhat hurried and furtive atmosphere about the whole event. As far as I know, this silent, distinctly eerie procession through the sleeping streets is the only ritual event that includes every household in the city of Lukang. Whatever else it is about, it is clearly concerned with territory and locality, and every household, rich or poor, is "served" equally and in an order determined only by its location. The procession, in an understated way, defines the limits of the city and deals with the inhabitants in terms of their most basic and common status, that of city resident. No one has very much to say about the procession, and people do not discuss it as they do Ma Tsu's birthday, the festival for the hungry ghosts in the seventh month, or the dedication of a new temple. "That's am-hang. It's an old Lukang custom."

A more usual sort of event is the birthday of the god in one of the 39 temples. All morning local housewives come to the temple with hampers of food to be offered the god. They set out the food, burn incense, and return home with the food, which will be served to guests of the family. In the afternoon the puppet show or opera begins, attended until midnight by a large crowd. The feast and puppet show are the essential parts of a festival, especially at a neighborhood temple. No professional clergy, *tao-shih* or Buddhist, play any role in the festival, and such lay figures as tang-ki or *fa-shih* (magicians) are seldom seen. In the afternoon the god may be carried about his neighborhood, escorted by a distinctly amateur band. Gods from other temples may be invited to the festival as guests, and then there is sure to be a procession. If the guests are from outside the city, the procession will pass down the main street to entertain and impress the general public.

It is on these occasions, when groups from outside Lukang come to the city, that the distinctions in ritual style between residents and outsiders become most apparent. Since Lukang with its ancient Ma Tsu temple is something of a center for pilgrimages, and since many of its natives have left to seek their fortunes in other places but return along with the gods they worship in those other places, processions and displays by groups representing temples outside the city are quite common. They bring spectacular displays by tang-ki, possessed chairbearers, smartly dressed drill teams, floats, dragon and lion dancers, drum majorettes, and bands of all sorts. It is all very exciting, and the people of Lukang enjoy watching the visitors' displays.

In October 1968 many deities from temples as far away as Taipei City and Kaohsiung came to Lukang as guests for the formal installation of

Su Fu Ta Wang Yeh (locally known as So Tua Ong or Tua Ong Ia) in his impressive new temple. Thousands of guests came, and the procession through the streets was so long it took two hours to pass a given spot. That evening, after most of the banquets in Lukang homes were over, the god was formally installed in his new temple. There are, in the Taoist repertoire, ceremonies for dedicating new temples, and there are specialists who can be hired to perform the ritual. They were not hired, though the managing committee of the new temple certainly could have afforded to do so. Instead, the man charged with raising funds for the temple, a businessman quite active in a local political faction, accompanied by his associates and a few hangers-on, burned through the paper seals on the closed doors of the temple with a handful of lighted incense sticks. A string of firecrackers was set off, and he repeated the procedure at the burner for spirit money. The temple doors were then opened, and people wandered in to admire the decor. The whole ceremony, which was the ostensible reason for the invitation of thousands of guests from all over Taiwan, took no more than two minutes. It attracted little attention from the immense crowd in front of the temple, which was watching two operas and a very skillful lion dance team from Puli, and patronizing the games of skill and chance and snack stalls ranged around the edges of the square. The focus of the celebration, which people in Lukang had been discussing and looking forward to for the previous two months, was on the procession, the entertainment, and the domestic banquets. The unsealing of the temple and installation of the deity were carried out in a hurried, rather offhand fashion by a small group of local merchants and political figures.

In the Lukang style of public ritual, the focus is on frequent, small-scale celebrations at neighborhood temples. Processions typically consist of a group of local lads carrying a sedan chair, followed by another group of local lads beating gongs and blowing trumpets. Possession and displays by tang-ki are rare. Ritual in temples, whether performed by tao-shih, Buddhist monks, or less professional folk practitioners like tang-ki or fa-shih, is rare, and when performed is usually done in a sketchy fashion. The ancillary aspect of processions and celebrations, represented by military drill teams, elaborate floats, costumed children, and all the other things that contribute to the excitement, the lau-ziat, of a festival, is hardly present. Most of the festivals at the smaller temples resemble one another, and after one has seen a few, one has in a very real sense seen them all. Festivals at the major temples are enlivened primarily by the visitors, who bring exciting things like tang-ki, lion teams, and dragons carried by teen-aged girls.

The people of Lukang enjoy mass displays of tang-ki, skillful military

drill teams, and ingeniously constructed floats when they come to town.
But they apparently feel no desire to do these things themselves, though
they could if they wanted to. They could hire professionals to put on
rituals in their temples, or train local people to act as fa-shih. But they
do not. One of the functions of the ancillary performers that accompany
the gods in processions is to impress other people, to make a good show,
and to distinguish the group represented by the god. Much of the elaboration and innovation one observes in the popular art form of the procession, especially in the major cities—things like bigger and more elaborate floats, troupes of performing girls—can be interpreted as contest
and emulation. But the people of Lukang seem to deliberately eschew
this. Rather than use their processions to say "our group is different from,
more impressive and therefore better than your group," they seem to be
saying, "our group is distinct from yours, but otherwise quite similar."
This, however, applies only to relations between groups within the city.
In Lukang the more flamboyant, individualizing aspects of public ritual
are played down, and stress is put on domestic feasting, a reciprocal arrangement, and on public entertainment such as puppet shows, which
can be enjoyed equally by everyone.

A different spirit prevails in relations with groups and temples from
outside the city, and at this point it is necessary to say a bit more about
the 39 temples of Lukang and their relations with one another and with
outside temples. All the temples of Lukang are, in the opinion of its
inhabitants, divided into two categories, pan-Lukang (*hap-kang-e*) and
neighborhood (*kak-thau-e*). The pan-Lukang temples, supported financially by all the citizens, are the largest and most elaborate, and are the
ones most actively involved in relations with outside groups. They are
the goals of pilgrimages by groups from Taipei City, Taichung, and
Kaohsiung, and every visitor to Lukang is dragged off to admire them.
They are managed by committees drawn from the local elite—wealthy
businessmen, retired provincial assemblymen, the mayor, and the like.
The ritual officers for their festivals are chosen from large contributors
to previous festivals or to building funds, and they are almost always
wealthy and prominent men.

The pan-Lukang temples are best exemplified by the Ma Tsu temple.
It is by far the largest and best known of the three temples dedicated to
Ma Tsu, and was founded sometime in the early eighteenth century, soon
after the first settlement at Lukang, by immigrants from Ch'üan-chou.
It is now claimed that its image was brought directly from the original
shrine of Ma Tsu, on Mei-chou Island off the Fukien coast, by Admiral
Shih Liang, who conquered Taiwan for the Ch'ing dynasty in 1684. He

is supposed to have left the image off at Lukang to serve as patron god
for his lineage-mates, the Shihs of Ya-k'ou hsiang, in Chin-chiang hsien
in Ch'üan-chou, who were already settled at Lukang. The land the present temple stands on is said to have been donated by the son of Shih
Liang's younger brother, who is commemorated with a statue in a side
room. There is no historical foundation for this story, but it supports the
claim that the Lukang Ma Tsu is the oldest such cult on the island, and
is the rightful "root" of nearly all the island's Ma Tsu temples. The
people of Lukang claim that their Ma Tsu temple is ritually superior to
all other Ma Tsu temples on Taiwan, including the vastly more popular
one at Peikang.

The temple has been rebuilt many times in the last 250 years, and
today takes in more than fifty *wan* a year (NT $500,000; U.S. $10,250)
in contributions alone, the money being used for decoration and building. Every household in the city contributes at least a few New Taiwan
dollars to the celebration of Ma Tsu's birthday, and some wealthy households contribute substantial sums. The managing committee of the temple, chosen, according to government regulations, by the "disciples"
(*hsin-t'u*) at the banquet held in the temple on the eve of Ma Tsu's birthday, is popularly thought to include the most powerful men in Lukang.
They are said to constitute the dominant local political faction, which
controls the town (*chen*) government, the Farmers' Association, and
most of the area's seats in the Chang-hua County Assembly. The managing committee, at least since 1958, has assiduously promoted the temple
as one of Taiwan's oldest and most important, and their success is evident in the scores of pilgrimage groups that come each year, and in the
newspaper publicity Lukang's Ma Tsu temple receives at the time of
Ma Tsu's birthday. The temple is decorated with eulogy boards presented by Admiral Shih Liang, the Ch'ien-lung emperor, the Kuang-hsü emperor, and the previous governor of Taiwan, and a photograph of the
visit of the American ambassador in the early 1960's is prominently displayed. Subsidiary images (divided bodies) from the temple circulate
through the rural areas surrounding Lukang,[1] though little attention is
paid to this within Lukang and members of the temple committee are
not interested in discussing it. They would much rather talk about the
pilgrimage groups who come from Taipei City, Kaohsiung, and even
Taitung, or explain why a delegation from the Peikang Ma Tsu temple
no longer comes to acknowledge its position as a "branch" of the Lukang
temple.

[1] Bernard Gallin, *Hsin Hsing, Taiwan: A Chinese Village in Change* (Berkeley,
Calif., 1966), pp. 251–52.

The Ma Tsu temple is the site of a *chiao* on the fifteenth of the seventh month, the festival of hungry ghosts. The temple committee operates an incense and spirit money stall, which brings in a small profit, and a member of the managing committee can usually be found behind the desk to the right of the altar, chatting or doing bookkeeping. Children play in the courtyard, and old men lounge on the front steps. There is usually someone in front of the main altar burning incense and dropping the divining blocks, seeking Ma Tsu's help for some domestic problem. The temple has scores of small images that are lent out to anyone who asks for one, as people do to seek Ma Tsu's intercession or to fulfill a vow. One frequently sees people riding down the main street in pedicabs, dressed in their best clothes and piously holding a two-foot-high image of Ma Tsu. Most young men who serve in the army take along a sachet of ash from the temple's incense pot, pressed on them by their anxious mothers. In 1958, after the Taiwan Straits crisis had subsided, the court-yard of the temple was full of pigs, presented to Ma Tsu by families keeping their vows to so thank the goddess if she preserved their conscripted sons from harm. Many people credit Ma Tsu with preserving Lukang from the American bombing that devastated the nearby cities of Chang-hua and Taichung in 1945. The booklet published by the managing committee lists several instances of her intervention in the past, saving the city from pirates, bandits, and armies of rebellious Chang-chou men. Nearly everyone in Lukang knows and can tell a version of the story of Ma Tsu, the poor fisherman's devout virgin daughter, and many can add a personal anecdote about the efficacy (*ling*) of the goddess. "My sister's husband's mother was very ill, and then she prayed to Ma Tsu. . . ." In short, more things and more kinds of things happen at the Ma Tsu temple than anywhere else, and it seems to satisfy most of the local people's ritual needs.

Five other large temples are considered pan-Lukang by everybody in the town, although their popularity, support, and activities are less extensive than those of the Ma Tsu temple. Fewer pilgrimage groups visit them; their annual festivals are celebrated less elaborately; their managing or festival committees, though drawn from all over the city, generally consist of less powerful or important men; and fewer people bring their private problems to them. They are the New Ma Tsu Temple, founded by a Manchu general in 1787 and in most respects a pale reflection of *the* Ma Tsu temple; the Lung-shan Ssu, a Buddhist temple dedicated to Kuan Yin; the Ti Ts'ang Wang Temple, dedicated to the god popularly regarded as the ruler of hell and custodian of hungry ghosts; the Ch'eng Huang Temple; and the Wen-wu Miao. This last, a "pseudo-official" temple, is dedicated to Confucius and Kuan Ti and was in the past the site of the local academy, the Shu-yüan. Occupied by soldiers in 1947 as living quarters, it is today in ruins. After years of petitions and pleas by Lukang's leaders, the soldiers finally vacated one of the three remaining buildings in the summer of 1968. Money was collected all over the city, and by autumn the ruined structure was being completely rebuilt. At that time the city had two other temples dedicated to Kuan Ti.

Three other temples may or may not belong to the pan-Lukang category; opinions on their status differed. The small T'u Ti Kung temple is a pan-Lukang temple in that it is the only T'u Ti Kung temple in the city, and its deity in his sedan chair leads every major procession. On the other hand it is a small, inactive temple, supported largely by the people living in the immediate vicinity, the neighborhood called Ship Head, who are the only ones to contribute to its annual festival. Two other large temples, one dedicated to a deity known as the Big General (Ta Chiang Yeh) and the new temple of Su Fu Ta Wang Yeh (whose inauguration festival in the autumn of 1968 was described earlier), are considered by their managing committees to be pan-Lukang, but their support, though wide, is far from universal. The remaining 30 temples are unequivocally neighborhood temples.

At first glance the neighborhood temples have nothing in common save their role as neighborhood temples. Some date back to the eighteenth century; others were founded in the 1960's. Some are newly rebuilt and resplendent with gilt and dragons; others are decrepit near-ruins. Their deities range from such mighty *shen* as Ma Tsu, Kuan Ti, or Shang Ti Kung to obscure Ong Ia who seem totally devoid of personality. One temple that has stood on Lukang's main street since 1737 is dedicated to San Shan Kuo Wang, a deity identified in publications on Taiwanese ritual as peculiar to Hakka from Ch'ao-chou. There have been no Hakka in Lukang within living memory, and there probably have been none since the eighteenth century; the people who live around and support the temple seem quite ignorant of their god's ethnicity. All the neighborhood temples, in spite of their distinct histories and deities, are regarded as functionally equivalent members of the same class. The personality or reputation (ling) of their gods is of little importance. Indeed, many people do not know the name of the god who resides in their neighborhood temple, and when I asked people which gods they worshipped I often got such replies as *"kak-thau-sin,"* the neighborhood shen, or "Ong Ia Kong," the Noble Lord. If someone wants a god's active help, he will usually go not to his local shen, but to the Ma Tsu temple or to a fortune teller, tang-ki, or Taoist private practitioner. Neighborhood temples are usually dusty and unfrequented, and many of them serve as workshops or living quarters. It seems more important that there be a temple which is a *neighborhood* temple, than it is that there be a particular deity in that temple.

Across the street from the house I lived in stood a small temple called the Shun Yi Kung, which housed two deities, Hsüan T'ien Shang Ti and Shun Yi Wang Yeh (Sun Gi Ong Ia). The latter looks like nothing more than the name of the temple (Accord with Righteousness) with the honorific title "Ong Ia" (kingly or noble lord) tacked on, and no one could tell me anything about this deity, who scarcely has an identity. The temple also houses a very poor family, whose meager domestic possessions and fowl share the space with the altar and images. The burner for paper money, missing several bricks, is in imminent danger of collapse. Save for its two annual feast days, no one ever enters the temple to burn incense or consult the divining blocks, and for 363 days of the year nothing happens at the Shun Yi Kung to indicate that it is a temple.

Its two annual feasts, the third day of the third month and the first of the sixth month, are celebrated with puppet shows and domestic banquets. The second of these, the first of the sixth month, is the more elaborate, and everyone in the neighborhood invites guests to a banquet. In the afternoon the band that has been playing in front of the temple accompanies the temple's incense pot on a brief tour of the neighborhood. In the evening people circulate from house to house, as hosts stand in their doorways and drag their neighbors in for a toast. In 1968 there was an opera on the first of the sixth, and a puppet show the following night. The opera was paid for by money collected from every house by old Mr. Huang, a respected former landlord. The usual donation is NT $20 (a skilled workman earns NT $60–70 a day). Some households give more, up to NT $50, and some give less, but everyone must give something. A family that refused to contribute would offend the god, and, perhaps more to the point, would be mocked and scorned by their neighbors. The puppet show was paid for by one family alone, that of a very powerful and influential local political figure who is on the managing committee of the Ma Tsu temple but plays no part in the Shun Yi Kung. The Shun Yi Kung has no managing committee, and its affairs, such as they are, are handled by "the old men of the neighborhood." Most of the chores, which consist of collecting money and hiring the opera troupe, seem to be in the hands of old Mr. Huang.

As the people of Lukang explain it, there are two categories of temple, pan-Lukang and neighborhood. The whole city participates in the first, only sections of it in the second. All temples are defined by reference to a territory; at present none is associated with a group defined by any other principle, though in the past occupational groups and those who came from certain places in Fukien had their own temples. Every household in the city participates in—that is, contributes money to—at least two temples, one neighborhood, one city-wide. "You give about NT $5 to the Ma Tsu temple, and perhaps $50 to your local temple." The major temples are known to have managing or festival committees composed of wealthy or powerful men from all over the city. Neighborhood temples have no committees, and one is told over and over that their affairs are handled informally by all the men of the district. "Around here, everyone knows everyone else, and when something has to be done they just get together and do it." Participation in the affairs of neighborhood temples is inclusive, and people say of the ritual offices, as lo-cu and thau-ke, that anyone may serve. On closer inspection things are sometimes more complicated, but it is important that nearly everyone in Lukang describes neighborhood temples in terms of a simple model which stresses community solidarity and participation by everyone, and which assumes that all neighborhood temples operate in the same way.

The temples of Lukang form a closed, self-sufficient system. Though the major temples claim other temples on Taiwan as their "branches," they recognize no "roots" on the island. Their founding temples are all back in Fukien, so that if one speaks of ritual hierarchies on Taiwan, from the townmen's point of view the Lukang temples are at the top. Ritual exchanges with temples outside the city are regarded either as the return of "branch" temples to their source, or as friendly visits between equals, "like inviting a guest to your house." Most of the ritual exchanges of the major temples are with temples located either in the major towns of Chang-hua and northern Yün-lin hsien, or in such major cities as Taipei, Taichung, Kaohsiung, and Chiayi. The villages around Lukang, although they have temples too, play no part in formal exchanges with the city's temples. The situation thus differs considerably from that around San-hsia in the Taipei Basin, for example, where during one entire month representatives of rural districts take turns visiting the temple of Ch'ing Shui Tsu Shih Kung.[2] Nor do the temples of Lukang exchange visits with those of such old Taiwanese cities and seaports as Tainan, Hsinchu, Peikang, and Tamsui.

Within the city there is no clear hierarchy of temples or of linked groups of temples, only the distinction between pan-Lukang and neighborhood temples. The neighborhood temples do not recognize other temples in the city or elsewhere as their "root" temples. The origins of

[2] Arthur P. Wolf, personal communication.

the neighborhood temples' cults are not a subject of great interest or discussion, and those stories that I did hear ascribed the foundation either to the direct act of the god himself (the god appeared in a dream, or the image came floating in from the open sea), or to some person who brought the image or some incense ash from Fukien in the distant past.

During the year and a half that I lived in Lukang, from May 1967 through October 1968, two entirely new temples were built, raising the total number from 37 to 39; Su Fu Ta Wang Yeh moved into his new temple; the Wen-wu Miao was resuscitated after twenty years of army occupation; and many old temples were extensively renovated. A considerable sum of money went into temple construction and renovation, as well as into the festivals that marked each event. The inhabitants of East Stone (Tung Shih) describe their neighborhood as coterminous with the *li* (ward) of the same name, and when their new temple was dedicated in the summer of 1968, the li had a registered population of 236 households and 1,708 people. East Stone is a relatively poor neighborhood on the edge of the city, inhabited by fishermen, oystermen, farmers, and unskilled factory workers. The new temple cost twenty wan (NT $200,000; U.S. $5,000). The average contribution per household would be NT $850, which is a month's wages for a textile worker, or ten days' wages for a skilled cabinetmaker. Renovating a small temple in Cart Field neighborhood cost NT $71,084 (U.S. $1,773). Not only does Lukang have a large number of temples; its inhabitants care enough about them to spend a sizable portion of their incomes renovating them and even founding new ones.

Why, in a small and not extraordinarily prosperous city, does one find such an inordinate number of temples, most of them small and apparently otiose, all enthusiastically supported by the inhabitants? Other towns of the region, of similar size and economic structure, make do with far fewer temples. I want to examine a series of explanations, none of them entirely convincing, for this problem.

At present the city of Lukang differs in no obvious way from the scores of other market towns or small cities that dot the plains of western Taiwan. A casual observer who stepped off the bus on the main street would find little to surprise or puzzle him. The people dress much as those elsewhere do, appearing neither especially poor nor especially prosperous; the same sorts of shops line the streets; the usual patriotic slogans and advertising posters decorate the walls; the temples look much like those in other settlements. By all available statistical indices the differences between Lukang and other towns are either marginal or readily explained by Lukang's place as a center of light industry and handicraft.

This is not to say that it is exactly like all other places, or that it is a "typical" market town or small city. No place is. Each of the market towns of central Taiwan has its own peculiarities, and if one looks hard enough or listens to the inhabitants, one can find something "unique" about each of them. But there is no simple or obvious way of distinguishing present-day Lukang from all other settlements in the region. It has more temples, and perhaps a distinctive style of public ritual, but no other unique feature with which to correlate the number of temples.

If we look at the past, however, the picture changes. Today Lukang is an undistinguished, placid, and rather out-of-the-way small city. But in the past it was the main seaport of central Taiwan, the node of an extensive economic network linking central Taiwan with the Chinese mainland, and the second largest city of the island, surpassed only by Tainan. It occupied this position for at least a century, from the 1760's to the 1860's, and as late as 1911 was the fourth largest city on the island. From the mid-eighteenth century on, wealthy merchants from Ch'üan-chou settled in Lukang and prospered, controlling the trade between central Taiwan and southern Fukien. They formed eight guilds, which dominated the economic, public, and ritual affairs of the city. The guilds built temples; owned farmland and urban real estate; collaborated with the imperial officials in regulating trade and collecting taxes; supported the Ch'üan-chou militia, the dominant military force in the area; and cooperated in the celebration of the two great annual festivals, Ma Tsu's birthday and the festival of hungry ghosts. The city was never an official administrative seat, but officials, including a subprefect who outranked the hsien magistrate, were stationed there to control and tax trade, and a large imperial garrison guarded the port. From the mid-eighteenth century through the 1880's, Lukang was a center of wealth, power, and learning, and all the major temples date from this period. Their foundation and renovation is recorded on stone tablets built into their walls as due to joint action by the guilds and officials. Until the land reform of 1953 the major temples at least were endowed with farmland, and five *chia* (one chia is 2.4 acres, 1.03 hectares) of rice land belonging to the Lung-shan Ssu and one chia from the Ch'eng Huang Temple were donated to the new junior middle school in 1948.

Trade at Lukang declined slowly in the latter half of the nineteenth century. The decline accelerated after the Japanese occupation of the island in 1895, and trade practically ceased when the railroad, which reached Chang-hua from Kaohsiung in 1905, was completed in 1908. In the first decade of the twentieth century businesses failed, the guilds dissolved, and thousands of people emigrated to Taipei and the other major cities. Emigration has continued to the present, and Lukang's population has remained nearly static since 1900 (growing from about 20,000 to 27,000 or 28,000), while that of Taiwan has increased from 2.6 million to 14 million.

Since the turn of the century Lukang has been an emigrant community. Thousands of people have left, but no outsiders have moved in. By the end of the nineteenth century there was a Lukang guild in Taipei City, and today there are formal Lukang associations in Taipei, Taichung, and Kaohsiung. The emigrants, or at least a significant number of them, retain their identity as Lukang men, as they demonstrate by remittances to their kin, contributions to Lukang's temples, and occasional return visits. Some businessmen who have done well in the metropolitan cities retire to Lukang. The stereotype of the emigrants is that they are very good at doing business and stick together, helping one another out. One man observed that Lukang men who moved to other parts of Taiwan were just like overseas Chinese in Southeast Asia. Many stories are told of poor young men who made a fortune in Taipei or Kaohsiung, and people like to identify prominent industrialists as Lukang men.

From the early years of this century to the period after World War II, Lukang's economy remained stagnant. The harbor, which had always suffered from silting, was finally filled in by the Japanese in the 1930's. The people who remained in the city supported themselves as landlords, rice millers, moneylenders, craftsmen, shopkeepers, or minor public functionaries. Many families depended on remittances from men working in the major cities. The city quickly slipped down the central-place hierarchy, serving as a market town for the arid and windswept coastal region, one of the most sparsely populated and poverty-stricken areas of central Taiwan. Few temples were renovated in this period, and no new temples were founded.

After the war Lukang's leadership, composed of old landlord families and upward-mobile, rather Snopes-like, merchants, raised a fair amount of money from residents and well-to-do emigrants and attempted to excavate a new harbor and thus revive the glorious past. The harbor project had no financial support from the government, and failed utterly. Money was raised in the same way to found a community middle school. The school was built, but the goal of the project was not achieved, for the school was and still is considered inferior to the middle schools of Taichung and Chang-hua City, which were supported by the provincial and hsien governments. The harbor and school projects demonstrated an impressive capacity to mobilize support from residents and wealthy emigrants, but the money raised in this fashion was never adequate to meet the goals. Since the early 1950's local politics has taken the more common form of attempts to secure funds from the hsien and provincial governments for projects in Lukang.

The land reform of 1953 destroyed the landlords as a class, and many of the old elite families left for Taipei City. But the 1950's saw the beginning of industrial growth in Lukang, in the form of small, locally owned factories that made everything from furniture to rope to hand tools. As Taiwan's economy expanded during the 1950's and 1960's, so did Lukang's light industry, which benefited from improved transport, depending on trucks rather than the railroad that bypassed the city, and from wages averaging 10 percent less than those in the major cities. The thousands of emigrant men in the major cities probably played some role in the expansion of industry in their home community, but I have no definite information on this. By 1967 Lukang, though not in relative terms as prosperous as in 1767 or 1867, was not an exceptionally depressed or poor community. Apart from the shops and craftsmen serving the now prosperous farmers, the city's economy was based on about five hundred small and very diversified factories. A wave of temple construction began in the late 1950's and has continued to the present.

All of the major temples and most of the smaller ones date from before 1895. It is easy to see the temples of Lukang as relics, survivals from the glorious past. Although the city has not been settled any longer than most of the rural areas of central Taiwan, its inhabitants were in the past much wealthier than the peasants. They had more money to spend founding temples and did so. Many other towns or minor cities of the area, like Erhlin or Yüan-lin, which today have populations as large as Lukang or larger, either did not exist or had only a few thousand inhabitants at the turn of the century. It does not seem surprising that today they have fewer temples per capita than Lukang. But the superficially obvious relation between the age of a settlement, its population, and the number of temples it supports depends on some assumptions about the way temples are founded and maintained, assumptions that are worth examining.

We can assume that a Taiwanese community of a certain critical size will automatically generate a temple. Or we can say that over time a community will produce temples at regular intervals, like an oyster producing pearls. Either Lukang reached the critical size earlier than other settlements, and so has more temples, or, simply by virtue of being there longer, it has had more time to produce temples.

If we accept the first assumption, then it follows that at some point an optimum number of temples is reached, and a steady state exists. Then settlements like Erhlin, which have grown very rapidly in a short time, are simply lagging behind Lukang, but may be expected to keep founding temples until they, too, reach the ideal ratio of one temple for every 700 people. Clearly there must be some limit to the number of temples a community can support. But two entirely new temples were built in Lukang in 1968. Perhaps the neighborhoods that built temples, one of which was clearly poorer than most, were simply catching up with the rest now that they, too, had the money to build a temple. If we assume that temples are produced every so many years, then the number of temples in a community would be a direct function of its age and previous population. It would follow that the other settlements would never catch up with Lukang, unless the time required to generate a new temple increases with the number that already exist.

Of course either hypothesis, or any less simpleminded one along similar lines, assumes that once founded a temple must endure. In other words, a straight and simple historical explanation for the number of temples must, it seems, assume that like souls, temples and shen may be freely created but never destroyed. This seems unlikely. If it were the case, cities that are both old and populous, like Canton or Sian, would be overrun with temples and cults. Although the ethnography of the dissolution of temples and cults is unclear, the force of the argument and inference from a few recorded cases suggest that cults and their shen can and sometimes do softly and suddenly vanish away. The point is that while some of the temples of Lukang have existed for nearly two hundred years, we have no reason to assume that all of the temples or cults that existed two hundred years ago are still around. This means that the survival of the ones that exist now is problematic, and that they cannot be regarded simply as relics.

The problem then becomes why so many old temples continue to be supported by the people of Lukang. I never asked this question of them, but I feel fairly certain that the reply would be: "Because we Lukang people are very conservative and traditional." One hears this sort of remark all the time, and both outsiders and natives agree that Lukang is a very conservative place, full of all sorts of peculiar old customs. One is sometimes told that there are many people in Lukang whose "thought" is very old-fashioned. But exactly what is being conserved or what the content of the tradition is, is never made very clear. Examples are hard to produce. While most people agree that there are some special old Lukang customs, they are hard pressed to list them, or to point to evidence of their existence in daily life. People often discuss how greatly life has changed since "the old days," and no one doubts that much has changed.

Indeed, with respect to those aspects of the style of public ritual and celebration discussed earlier, until fairly recent times they apparently resembled what is now done in places like Taichung and Taipei City. Old men recall immense, flamboyant processions with elaborate floats and troupes of musicians and performers. So intense was the spirit of emulation and rivalry then that processions often ended in brawls. Within living memory the entire seventh month was devoted to communal feasting and elaborate public celebrations at the city's major temples. Elderly people in Lukang reminisce about the fame of the town's children's marching bands, about competition between troupes of acrobats in the square before the Ti Ts'ang Wang Temple, and about tang-ki from Lukang temples challenging one another to climb sword ladders. "Things were very lau-ziat then." Things still are lau-ziat in other places, but in Lukang only when outsiders come.

These and many other distinctive "old customs," such as the annual rock fight between the major surname groups, held as late as the 1930's, have fallen into disuse, and no one seems eager to revive them. It is not clear why some practices have died while others persist. To say that the people of Lukang are in some general sense conservative or traditional begs the question. One must specify what is conserved and what is not, and then account for the distinction. That the people of the city claim to be exceptionally traditional and conservative is an important social fact, but it does not account for the preservation of old temples.

As I see it, sheer persistence is not self-explanatory. To say that people in Lukang support old temples because they are traditional in outlook leads into a circular argument: they're traditional because they do certain things, and they do them because they're traditional. Functional explanations provide a way out of the circle, and the survival of temples may be explained by specifying their social functions. In very general terms one could say of any Taiwanese temple that it serves to symbolize, support, or reinforce the solidarity of the people united in common worship. Ritual offices such as lo-cu and thau-ke give men honor and recognition as public-spirited citizens, concerned with the common welfare and the good opinion of their fellows. Rich and powerful men such as local political figures may gain prestige and some degree of public acceptance and legitimacy by contributing to temples and serving as ritual office holders. Festivals provide everyone with entertainment and a break from the daily round. Temple festivals are among the few occasions on which householders invite guests to a banquet. Banquets and reciprocal feasting are in turn important parts of Taiwanese social organization, with their own functions. Some people worship and support temples because they believe in the gods. All these explanations help us to understand why Taiwanese, in general, support temples. But such arguments seem inadequate to explain variation from place to place or the proliferation of neighborhood temples in Lukang.

Functional arguments would account for much of the support of Lukang's Ma Tsu temple, which in a fairly straightforward way symbolizes the solidarity of the entire city and lends legitimacy to its native political leaders. The construction of the new So Tua Ong Temple directly across the square from the Ma Tsu temple can be explained in terms of factional rivalry. A group of men who oppose the faction associated with the Ma Tsu temple are promoting So Tua Ong as a means of gaining prestige and recruiting support. Some of them had previously tried to build a political base by organizing a surname association for the Shihs, the city's most common surname. This failed, so they turned to So Tua Ong, a deity with a reputation for efficacy, and are trying to promote a small neighborhood temple to the status of a pan-Lukang temple.

The pattern of ritual exchange between Lukang and other settlements can be explained in terms of the past extent of the city's trading network, within which branch temples were founded, and the present distribution of emigrants, who found branches of Lukang temples and set up exchanges between the temples they support in the major cities and those of their old home. The emigrants settled in the growing major cities or in such frontier areas as Puli and the east coast, but not in cities such as Tamsui, Hsinchu, or Peikang, whose economic situation was more like that of Lukang itself. For the same reasons that Lukang people emigrated, scarcely anyone from the villages around the city has moved into it. They, too, head for Taichung or Taipei City. In this regard Lukang's population differs considerably from that of other minor cities of the region, such as Yüan-lin or Erhlin, where many inhabitants are recent migrants from nearby villages who maintain ties with their home villages and temples.

Lukang, which owed its past prosperity to its position as the node of a trading system linking central Taiwan with southern Fukien, never had very close ties with its immediate rural hinterland, an arid region inhabited by poor farmers, fishermen, and bandits. Marriage with villagers was very rare, most Lukang people marrying either within the city or with those of the same class in other market towns and cities of the region. When the port declined, the people of Lukang seem to have done everything possible to maintain the social distance between themselves and the rustics who surrounded them and on whom they were forced to rely for a livelihood. Lukang's brick and tile houses were the dwellings of the landlords, whose tenants lived in mud and thatch huts in their villages among the sweet potato fields. Growing rural prosperity in the last twenty years has done much to erase the gross distinction between town and country, and now the farmers have brick and tile houses, too. The quiet streets of Lukang with their ducks and water buffalo carts resemble village lanes much more than they do the taxi-choked boulevards of Taipei City. Today the people of Lukang, those who have not emigrated, have much more in common with the villagers than they did twenty or fifty years ago, and they resent it. Perhaps because they do resemble rural folk in at least outward ways, they go to great lengths to maintain the distinction between themselves and their former tenants. Shopkeepers make acid remarks about illiterate farmers who have two motorcycles and now want television, and many stories testify to the vulgarity, gullibility, and crudeness of the rustics whose "cultural level is still low, even if today they're rich." The people of Lukang look down on villagers and keep their distance, and the gods of Lukang prefer to deal with their counterparts in other cities, holding themselves aloof from the deities of neighboring settlements.[3]

Once one understands something of the demography, economy, and social history of Lukang, much of its ritual life becomes comprehensible. But it remains difficult to understand why people contribute money and support to such apparently otiose temples as the one across the street from my house. My initial assumption was that the city was divided into named neighborhoods, each with its own temple, much as the country-side is covered with compact villages, each with its temple. Ritual re-flected social structure, and there were neighborhood temples because there were neighborhoods. But it proved much more difficult to define neighborhoods than to define villages, which have sharp boundaries, often consisting of hedges of thorny bamboo. Neighborhoods have names, but some names like "the north end" or "*gu-thau*" are applied to large sections of the city. These are further subdivided, with "the north end," for example, consisting of Ship Head, East Stone, Back Hut, Oyster Hut, and Kuo Village. I lived in a part of the city generally known as Vegetable Garden. This subsumed Upper Vegetable Garden, Lower Vegetable Garden, and Cart Enclosure. A short alley is known to some people at least as Behind the Wall, possibly because ninety-odd years

[3] For documentation on the history of Lukang, see my Ph.D. dissertation, "City on the Sands: Social Structure in a Nineteenth-Century Chinese City" (Cornell University, 1973).

ago it was behind the back wall of the subprefect yamen. Vegetable
Garden, or some part of it, may also be referred to as Huang Neighborhood, because so many people surnamed Huang live there. The situation is further complicated by the administrative division of the city
into fifteen li or wards, with their own usually more classical names.
While the li have practically no political functions and are not recognized social units, still they have been there since the Japanese period,
and some people, especially relatively educated men or those connected
with local government, may use their names to refer to places or people.
It is very hard to ascertain just where the north end begins, and people
disagree about whether Ship Head is a part of the north end or not.
Neighborhood names do not form a neat segmentary system, and every
household, indeed every person, names the sections of the city from a
personal perspective. There is probably no one who knows all the names
for the various parts of the city. Names do not correspond with discrete
social units or groups, and if there are significant territorial units within
the city they are not defined by names.

I also tried to define neighborhood boundaries by looking at temple
areas. In Lukang any household that contributes to a festival gets in
return a charm paper, a hu, with the name of the temple on it. This is
pasted up outside, over the front door, serving to protect the household
and to declare that "we gave." Usually every house in the immediate
vicinity of a temple will display its hu. As one moves away from the
temple in any direction, one eventually comes to a house without that
hu, one with, three without, one with, and so on. Charms trail off, their
distribution being that of a scatter diagram. Houses may have more
than one hu over their door, and most display charms from several temples. Temple areas overlap. Occasionally one finds a hu from a small
temple on the other side of town. In such cases the distant temple may
be that of the wife's original neighborhood. Or it may be that a close
business associate of the household head is serving as lo-cu. Or it may
be that one of the women of the family has decided that the god of the
temple is especially efficacious. If the hu of all temples were represented by dots of different colors and the dots were all projected onto
a map of Lukang, the result would resemble a picture by Monet rather
than one by Mondrian.

Households may contribute to the annual festival of more than one
neighborhood temple, but they need not contribute the same amount
of money to each, or hold a banquet on the festival of each. Thus the
edges of temple areas are blurred, and participation slopes down on a
gradient of money contributed. Over time, furthermore, temple areas

are fluid. When a new temple is built in an old neighborhood, and in Lukang all neighborhoods are old neighborhoods, a new area is created. Some areas disappear. Before the Japanese period the main street was divided into five segments by street gates. Each segment took turns putting on the annual festival of the San Shan Kuo Wang Temple, halfway down the street. Today the temple is still there, but people living on the kilometer-and-a-half-long street no longer take turns putting on its annual festival or consider themselves residents of its area. Both Upper and Lower Vegetable Garden have a temple, that of Upper Vegetable Garden being the decrepit Shun Yi Kung. In 1968 the other temple was rebuilt and celebrated its festival in an elaborate fashion. Its thau-ke came to Upper Vegetable Garden soliciting more than token contributions. They argued that both halves of Vegetable Garden were really one neighborhood, and formed a li as well, and that their temple was therefore common to everyone and deserved support. The looseness of neighborhood nomenclature permits this sort of argument, and if the solicitors from Lower Vegetable Garden convince enough people, their newly rebuilt temple will have extended its area and the Shun Yi Kung will become yet more otiose. There is no reason to assume that a similar process has not been going on for the last two hundred years.

The more one looks at neighborhoods, the less they resemble villages. Their boundaries are unclear; people make no effort to draw sharp lines and define people beyond them as outsiders. There is no reason for them to do so. Neighborhoods in Lukang have never been corporate groups. They are composed of diverse populations who bear different surnames, who earn a living in different ways, and whose income ranges from high to very low. They have nothing in common except residence in an arbitrarily and rather vaguely defined area, and they do nothing in common except worship. Temples, rather than reflecting or reinforcing some other sort of structure, are the only structure there is. Rather than neighborhoods creating temples, it seems as though temples create neighborhoods.

If people build and support temples in order to create neighborhoods, one must ask why they should consider neighborhoods worth so much expense and trouble. Part of the answer derives from the part played by neighborhoods in nineteenth-century Lukang. Very briefly, the city's social structure then can be described in terms of overlapping groups that recruited members on three different principles—occupation, surname, and place of residence in the city. There were guilds, surname groups, and neighborhoods, each cutting across the others, and all expressing their solidarity and mutual relations in public ritual. Today the guilds are gone, the surname groups, which were never the classic southeastern Chinese corporate, segmented lineages, are of little importance, and only the neighborhoods survive, although neighborhoods today are of course not quite the same things as their counterparts of the previous century. Then, neighborhoods, like surname groups, occasionally fought each other, and frequently competed in street processions, which sometimes ended in brawls. The seventh month was given over to a rotating festival, with the whole city feasting on the first, seventh, fifteenth, and thirtieth of the month, and a different neighborhood putting on a festival and inviting guests from other parts of the city on every other day of the month. This practice is today forbidden by the police, who restrict the celebration of the hungry ghost festival to one day, the fifteenth day of the seventh month. Of course the present system of thirty-odd neighborhood temples, each with its own annual festival and invitation of guests to domestic banquets, may be seen as providing just as many feasts and opportunities for the creation and reinforcement of social relations as did the old seventh-month festivals.

Of the several ways of organizing groups of people once practiced in Lukang, only residence survives today. Temples that once united in common worship people of the same occupation, people who traced their descent to the same native place in Fukien, people with the same surname, and people who lived in the same area of Lukang, today unite only people who reside in the same area. But temple organization based on residence, either in the city as a whole for pan-Lukang temples, or in some section of it for neighborhood temples, represents considerably more than a survival from the past. It also represents an affirmation of identity, and a statement of the kind of community Lukang is today, or, rather, of the kind of community Lukang would like to think it is. My explanation for the particular style of ritual in Lukang and for the support of so many neighborhood temples rests on an argument about the ways residents think and talk about their society and their city. My assumption is that because of the city's history and present economic and social structure, its people publicly and collectively define themselves in certain terms, which are those of temples and ritual. These provide the only idiom of fellowship, community, and common identity available to the people of Lukang.

Much of Lukang's self-definition rests on a picture of the city's glorious past. The details of the city's history—what happened when and why— are only faintly understood by most of the present inhabitants. But they regard that history as important, and as having some meaning for them today. What the present natives of the city share, apart from mere propinquity, is a common past. But the past is gone. The guilds are gone, the harbor has been filled in, and even the shoreline has changed, the city now being three kilometers inland. The crumbling houses of rich merchants and imperial degree-holders are now inhabited by poor families who send their rent to the emigrant owner's office in Taipei City. The postwar attempt to bring back the good old days by excavating a new harbor and building a school to take the place of the Shu-yüan that had produced four *chin-shih* (holders of the highest degree in the imperial examination system) ended in bitter failure, and by now it is clear that what happens in Lukang depends largely on the decisions of bureaucrats in Taipei City. One of the things that makes Lukang different, its people say, is its past, and there are no obvious continuities, no links between then and now, except the temples. As the only link with the highly valued past, temples are tangible proofs of identity. The pilgrimage groups who come to the Ma Tsu temple from all over the island provide evidence that Lukang is indeed a special place of great importance, and no one ever mentions that the groups often continue on to the far more popular Ma Tsu temple in Peikang, which in Lukang is regarded as a mere branch of the Lukang temple.

Temples also provide an acceptable way to describe the present condition of the city and what we would call its social structure. The people of Lukang are very much aware of their identity as Lukang men, and stress the differences between their city and every other place. They describe it as very old, very traditional and old-fashioned, as a center of Taiwanese culture and learning, and as occupying a position halfway along the rural-urban continuum, marked neither by the rural idiocy and crudeness they ascribe to villages, nor by the depravity, chaos, and urban impersonality of Taipei City. The boundary between Lukang and the rest of the world is very clear. Internally, the picture is less clear. The city is described as a place where everyone knows everyone else, where people care about one another, and where there is a lot of *jen-ch'ing wei*, a term that might be glossed as human feeling, affability, or folksiness. People recognize no distinct groups between individual households and the city itself. In one mode of discourse they discuss, often as malicious gossip, the habits and affairs of particular townsmen who are usually known within the city by nicknames. In another, more public mode, they speak of "Lukang people" in very general terms, and talk of the city as a whole as if it were an undifferentiated continuum, a pure gemeinschaft. To an outside observer this presents the rather odd spectacle of an industrial city of 28,000 people, with extensive economic and personal ties with the rest of the island, whose inhabitants describe it as if it were a closed, corporate community.

Temples, whose membership embraces everyone who resides in the same area, whose ritual language so stresses community and solidarity, and whose festivals are opportunities for reciprocal feasting, thus provide a model for the internal organization of such an undifferentiated community. If one first asserts that the community exists, and is composed of the same stuff, as it were, one can then subdivide it into any number of equivalent units that exchange gifts and so bind themselves more closely together in mechanical solidarity. This is the model of Lukang's social structure that is provided by its temples and their festivals. Neighborhood temples, defined as equals, invite one another to their festivals. The pan-Lukang temples and their festivals provide opportunities to invite guests from outside the community, but, as several people pointed out to me, one can hardly invite a fellow townsman to a feast when he, too, is giving one. If everyone is a host, no one can be a guest. Temples that define people only in terms of common residence provide a way to assert the solidarity of the city, and neighborhood temples provide a way to divide the populace into equivalent categories, which can then interact with one another in well-defined and amiable ways.

Lukang of course is not a gemeinschaft, and its people have far less in common than they claim. Economically and politically it is firmly integrated into a rational modern state; the personal networks of its natives extend beyond its boundaries to every part of Taiwan, and beyond Taiwan to Japan, Brazil, and North America. Its ritual pretensions to self-sufficiency, while not unimportant, are only pretensions. While the population of the city has remained nearly static, the economy and the occupational structure have become more and more differentiated. The organization of work serves to separate men, who have less and less in common. A man who unites with the other members of his occupational category ends up with but a small number of fellows and remains isolated from most of the people he lives among. Furthermore, the economy has been growing rapidly, many new occupations have sprung up, and new shops and factories have been founded. Some of these fail, others prosper. The old class structure of landlords, merchants, and tenant farmers is gone, and for the past fifteen years or so the class structure has been fairly fluid and mobility fairly common. The educated, the ambitious, and the poor who can find no work there continue to leave Lukang, and every adult male in the city has made a deliberate choice to stay, a commitment to residence in the city. Although its people are better off and their lives are different, the city itself has not grown appreciably or changed in any striking way in the past twenty years. Very few new buildings have been constructed; the city still lacks a public water supply and sewers; most of the factories are small and housed in sheds along back alleys or on the edges of the city. There is little feeling that the city as a whole is progressing or going anywhere in particular. Local political figures are regarded more as distasteful scoundrels and factional figures than as leaders who can define the future of the city and the shape of its new social structure. The old Lukang is changed and gone, and the present society resists definition or description. Ritual, with its model of mechanical solidarity, does not describe the present situation very well, but it does at least provide a model and an idiom for talking and thinking about some sorts of social relations.

If this is the case, the muted and unelaborated style of public ritual is understandable. Its purpose is to assert a very dubious unity, and not to call attention to distinctions. When no other way of uniting people presents itself, one can always fall back on residence and territory, even if the residents have little in common and the territories do nothing but get together a few days a year for temple festivals. Neighborhood temples permit a semblance of unity within an area. "Anybody can be lo-cu. We don't have any committee to run the temple. Around here everyone knows everyone else, and when something has to be done, why the men of the neighborhood just get together and do it." Temple festivals provide a standardized and restricted mode of sociability and a comfortable way of interacting with the other inhabitants of the city. If, as I have assumed, the people of Lukang do want some way of asserting a common identity, and some way of publicly describing the society they feel committed to, then they can do this by concentrating on their city's past rather than its present and future, and by identifying themselves in terms of residence rather than occupation, class, or political opinions. And that is why they support 39 temples.

Religious Organization in the History of a Taiwanese Town

WANG SHIH-CH'ING

Apart from groups concerned primarily with ancestor worship, religious organization in rural Taiwan commonly takes one of two closely related forms.[1] On the one hand, there are groups based on territorially defined communities, all of whose residents in some way support the worship of a god whom they consider their protector and supernatural governor; on the other, there are what are known as *shen-ming-hui*, self-selected communities in which membership is not defined solely on a territorial basis but on the basis of kinship affiliation, ethnic identity, or devotion to a particular god.

The Settlement of Shu-lin

The aim of this essay is to trace the development of these religious groups in one small Taiwanese town, noting the criteria employed to define membership and the way these criteria change as the town grows, commercializes, and finally becomes an industrial suburb. My thesis is simply that the religious organization of a Chinese town is best understood as an aspect of its social history. The organization of temple cults and shen-ming-hui is but one concrete expression of the various criteria that distinguish groups of people at one level and unite them as members of larger communities at another.

To illustrate this theme I have chosen a town located on the southwestern side of the Taipei Basin, approximately ten miles west of Taipei City. The town and the rural area associated with it include most but not all of Shu-lin *chen*. During the early Ch'ing the area was part of a much

---

[1] This essay emphasizes the sociological implications of the development of religious institutions in Shu-lin. For a more detailed history of these institutions, see Wang 1972.

larger administrative district known as Hai-shan *chuang*; locally it was known as Feng-kuei-tien, alternatively as Shu-lin. The latter name gained preeminence during the Japanese occupation, and Shu-lin is now both the official and the popular name for the town and the surrounding rural area, as well as the name of the chen.

Settlement of the Shu-lin area followed a course typical of northern Taiwan: the government made large grants of land to prominent men, who recruited poor farmers and laborers from the China mainland to settle and develop their estates. In return for their work developing the land, and perhaps also because the grantees could not prevent it, these settlers usually acquired permanent rights to the land they settled, including the right to sell their rights. Many settlers took up large tracts of land and eventually became landlords themselves. The result was a two- and sometimes three-tiered system of land rights. The original grantee, the *ta-tsu* holder, received rent from the settler, the *hsiao-tsu* holder, who in turn collected rent from the farmer who cultivated the land.

Although the original land grants were very large, few of the grantees prospered. The original grant that included what is now Shu-lin was made in 1713 to four men, Cheng Chen, Wang Mo, Lai K'o, and Chu K'un-hou. In 1724 Wang and Chu sold their shares to Teng Hsüan, who, unable to pay his taxes, soon sold the share that included Shu-lin to Hu Chao. Hu Chao developed irrigation facilities and brought some of the property under cultivation, but failed to make his fortune. In 1751 Hu and his sons sold half their estate to Chang Pi-jung, Wu Lo, and Ma Chao-wen, for 3,500 taels of silver; in 1752 the Hu family sold more land to Chang and Wu for 1,500 taels of silver; and then, after Hu Chao's death in 1754, the Hu family mortgaged and finally sold the remainder of their estate to Chang, Wu, and Ma.

Chang, Wu, and Ma created what was known as the Chang-wu-wen Corporation and appear to have succeeded where their predecessors had failed. After buying up all of Teng Hsüan's estate that had been sold to Hu Chao, the Corporation purchased another large parcel of Teng Hsüan's property from his son, who was forced to sell to pay for his father's funeral. The Corporation was divided in 1757, when Ma sold his shares to one Lung Erh, and was finally dissolved in 1760, when Wu withdrew his share and established an independent corporation known as the Wu-chi-sheng. The Chang family then divided their estate into two separate corporations, naming one after Chang Pi-jung and the other after his relative Chang Fang-ta. The former, which included Shu-lin, appears to have been exceptionally successful. In the next two decades Chang Pi-jung's descendants extended the area of their ta-tsu rights, bought up many of the settlers' hsiao-tsu rights, purchased water rights over much of the area, established five granaries, and successfully negotiated for control over much of the land owned by the aborigines. By 1783, when the Corporation's rules were inscribed on a stone tablet, the Changs controlled almost all of what was then known as Hai-shan chuang. The only other landlords of any importance in the Shu-lin area were Liu K'un-shan and a Lai family from Chang-chou.

With the exception of some Hakka families surnamed P'eng who set-tled what is still known as P'eng-ts'o, the settlers recruited by Hu Chao and Chang Pi-jung all came from either Chang-chou or Ch'üan-chou *fu* in southern Fukien. The result was a population that had a language and many customs in common, but at the same time was ethnically diverse. Depending on the precise location of their native place, people spoke different dialects of Hokkien and exhibited distinctive customs at wed-dings and funerals. It is therefore worth noting that the early settlers did not cluster together along ethnic lines, but were interspersed in ethnically mixed settlements. For example, the settlers of P'eng-ts'o, lo-cated on the southern side of the present town of Shu-lin, included (in addition to the Hakka P'engs) Liaos, Changs, Wangs, Hungs, and Lins from Ch'üan-chou, Chous and Ch'ens from Nan-an (Ch'üan-chou), and a Lai family from P'ing-ho (Chang-chou); the settlers of T'an-ti, on the north side of the present town, included Wangs from Nan-an (Ch'üan-chou), Wangs and Chungs from T'ung-an (Ch'üan-chou), Lais from P'ing-ho and Nan-ching (Chang-chou), and Lius and Lins from Lung-ch'i (Chang-chou).

The most important ethnic distinction was between Hakka and Hok-kien, and among the Hokkien, between people from Ch'üan-chou and those from Chang-chou. But the fact that a family came from, say, P'ing-ho rather than Nan-ching also made a difference. Among the Ch'üan-chou settlers people from Nan-an, Chin-chiang, and Hui-an were grouped together as Ting-chiao or San-i people and as such contrasted with settlers from T'ung-an and An-ch'i, while among people of Chang-chou origins a distinction was made between those from P'ing-ho and those from Nan-ching. The largest ethnic group was the Ting-chiao group, followed by Chang-chou settlers from P'ing-ho and Nan-ching, and Ch'üan-chou settlers from T'ung-an and An-ch'i. The An-ch'i group, though only a small percentage of the total population, were important in local affairs because of their close ties with the An-ch'i settlers who dominated the San-hsia area immediately south of Shu-lin.

Because the location of communities with respect to one another plays

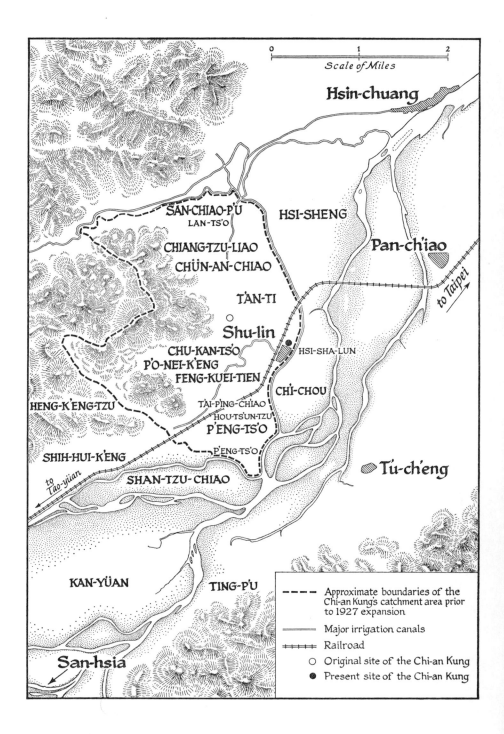

Scale of Miles

Hsin-chuang

SAN-CHIAO-P'U
LAN-TS'O

HSI-SHENG

Pan-ch'iao

to Taipei

CHIANG-TZU-LIAO
CHÜN-AN-CHIAO

T'AN-TI

Shu-lin

HSI-SHA-LUN

CHU-KAN-TS'O
P'O-NEI-K'ENG
FENG-KUEI-TIEN

CHI-CHOU

HENG-K'ENG-TZU

T'AI-P'ING-CHIAO
HOU-TS'UN-TZU
P'ENG-TS'O

SHIH-HUI-K'ENG

P'ENG-TS'O

Tu-ch'eng

to Tao-yüan

SHAN-TZU-CHIAO

KAN-YÜAN

TING-P'U

San-hsia

- - - - Approximate boundaries of the
Chi-an Kung's catchment area prior
to 1927 expansion

————— Major irrigation canals

+++++ Railroad

○ Original site of the Chi-an Kung

● Present site of the Chi-an Kung

an important role in local history, the reader should have some idea of the territory under discussion and the way it is divided. As the accompanying map indicates, the area consists of a long strip of low, fertile land, bordered on the west by the Tamsui River and on the east by the Kuei-lun Mountains. During most of the period that concerns us, the inhabitants divided this area into eight communities. The names used during the Ch'ing and most of the Japanese period were, from north to south, San-chiao-p'u, Chiang-tzu-liao, Chün-an-chiao, T'an-ti, Chu-kan-ts'o, Feng-kuei-tien, P'eng-ts'o, and, in the mountains to the west, P'o-nei-k'eng. Until the railroad was extended to Shu-lin in 1901, T'an-ti was the ritual and commercial center of the area; after that, the present town of Shu-lin developed around the railroad station located in Feng-kuei-tien. The reader should also note that San-chiao-p'u contains a hamlet known as Lan-ts'o, "The Lans' House"; and that P'eng-ts'o is divided into three named areas: T'ai-p'ing-ch'iao, Hou-ts'un-tzu, and P'eng-ts'o.

The Gods of Shu-lin

Though northern Taiwan contained much rich agricultural land and a plentiful water supply, it was hardly a comfortable environment for the early settlers. At first they had to contend with raids from the native peoples they displaced; later they suffered even more from the exactions of the Chinese bandits who replaced the aborigines in their mountain strongholds. Worse yet, unfamiliar diseases took a heavy toll. The impression northern Taiwan made on its Chinese settlers is dramatically depicted in the 1717 edition of the *Chu-lo hsien chih* (History of Chu-lo Hsien). The northern half of the island is described as a place with "too many negative natural elements. The mountain mists and ocean fogs are heavy. People are dazed even when they are wide awake, suffering from diseases that cannot be cured because they are carried on the wind." (1968: 284.)

For protection against these dangers, the immigrants brought with them from the mainland the more famous gods of their native places. We cannot say who all these gods were or where they came from because we have to assume that many of the wooden images or sachets of incense ashes were destroyed or lost when the family that had brought the god to the island died out. But just as some of the settlers survived to establish a Chinese colony on the island, so did some of their gods, whose histories cast light on the processes by which the society itself was constituted. In Shu-lin the four most important gods brought from the mainland were Ch'ing Shui Tsu Shih Kung, Pao Sheng Ta Ti, Hsing Fu Wang Yeh, and T'ien Shang Sheng Ma, better known as Ma Tsu.

Ma Tsu was brought to Shu-lin from Nan-ching (Chang-chou) by the Chien family, which settled Chu-kan-ts'o and the low-lying part of P'o-nei-k'eng. The original Chien settlement, Chu-kan-ts'o-ch'eng-chai, "Walled Chu-kan-ts'o," was destroyed in the 1860's during a fight between Chang-chou and Ch'üan-chou people, but the Chiens themselves survived and became the dominant group in Chu-kan-ts'o and most of P'o-nei-k'eng. Ma Tsu was established as the patron deity and public symbol of the Chien lineage. The lineage itself set up a religious association known as the T'ien Shang Sheng Mu Hui, or, more simply, the Chien Ma Tsu Hui. As long as people can remember, members of the Chien lineage have taken turns serving as *lu-chu*—master of the incense burner—for the Ma Tsu Hui.[2] The lu-chu makes daily offerings to Ma Tsu and organizes the annual festival held on the second day of the third lunar month. Membership in the Ma Tsu Hui and attendance at the annual feast are limited to members of the Chien lineage.

Ch'ing Shui Tsu Shih Kung was "invited" to Shu-lin by the four branches (*fang*) of the Lan lineage, who settled what is still known as Lan-ts'o. The relationship between the Lan lineage and Ch'ing Shui Tsu Shih Kung is essentially the same as that between the Chien lineage and Ma Tsu. Every year on the sixth day of the first lunar month, lineage members kill an animal as an offering to Ch'ing Shui Tsu Shih Kung and participate in a *kuo-huo*, a "fire-walking," "to make the god lively and efficacious." The lu-chu responsible for organizing these activities is always a Lan, and attendance at the feast held the same day is limited to lineage members. The rule is that each of four branches of the lineage must contribute 80 *shih* of rice to pay for the feast, with any deficit being borne by the family whose head is serving as lu-chu.[3]

The Wang Yeh Kung Hui, organized by members of the Lin lineage in P'eng-ts'o for the worship of Hsing Fu Wang Yeh, resembles in most details the Chiens' Ma Tsu Hui and the Lans' Ch'ing Shui Tsu Shih Kung Hui. Again, it is a religious association, a *shen-ming-hui*, whose membership coincides with that of a localized lineage. The only one of the four gods from the mainland that did not remain the exclusive property of a localized lineage was Pao Sheng Ta Ti. Brought to Shu-lin by the Lai family who settled most of T'an-ti, Pao Sheng Ta Ti was first worshipped in a small thatched hut at the foot of the mountains. Later, the Lai lineage set up the Ta Tao Kung Hui to organize worship for the god, paying the costs out of the rent collected from land owned by the

[2] The lu-chu is responsible for care of the burner and the organization of worship. Usually chosen by divination, he holds office for one year.

[3] One *shih* equals 100 catties or approximately 133 lbs.

Lai Sacrificing Association. At this point one might have expected Pao Sheng Ta Ti to remain the Lais' private patron, but instead the god became supernatural governor of all Shu-lin, the property and concern of all its population irrespective of kinship affiliation or ethnic identity.

The emergence of Pao Sheng Ta Ti as Shu-lin's supernatural magistrate is not easily explained. One story has it that he became famous because children who played with his incense burner immediately fell ill with a stomachache that could be cured only by their asking the god's forgiveness. More sociologically persuasive is the story that the powerful landlord Chang Pi-jung fell ill and, having heard of Pao Sheng Ta Ti's powers, asked one of his foremen to worship the god on his behalf. Chang immediately recovered and, to thank the god, contributed a large sum of money to build him the temple known as the Chi-an Kung or Ta Tao Kung Miao. There is also the possibility that T'an-ti's location near the wharf over which all imports and exports had to pass gave Pao Sheng Ta Ti the advantage of a location conducive to widespread renown. Still another possibility is that Pao Sheng Ta Ti served to "mediate" ethnic contradictions that gave rise to many conflicts and much distrust. The Lais who brought Pao Sheng Ta Ti to Shu-lin were Chang-chou people from Nan-ching and P'ing-ho, but tradition has it that Pao Sheng Ta Ti was a famous official in T'ung-an and therefore a respected deity among a large proportion of the Ch'üan-chou population.

Whatever the reason, or reasons, for Pao Sheng Ta Ti's rise to power, it is clear that the landlord Chang Pi-jung in fact played an important role, for he contributed the money with which the original Chi-an Kung was built in 1788. The temple was rebuilt in 1812, a fact noted in the 1871 edition of the *Tan-shui t'ing chih* (History of Tamsui Subprefecture; 1968 ed., 6: 148), and again in 1836. Temple records list the contributors to the 1836 reconstruction as the Pei-tsung Chung-ying Tu-min-fu, 12 silver dollars; Chang Pi-jung, 40 silver dollars; Lai Yung-ho, 24 silver dollars; Chang K'e-mei, 20 silver dollars; and Chien Pi-ming, 20 silver dollars. The last reconstruction, before the Japanese occupation of Taiwan precipitated more fundamental changes, was in 1893, when the existing temple was repaired and an opera stage built next door. At that time eight *fen* of paddy field and two fen of forest land that belonged to T'an-ti's Fu-te Kung were transferred to the ownership of the Chi-an Kung.[4] The rent from these properties provided the temple with an annual income of 418 shih of rice.

Since the founding of the Chi-an Kung, Pao Sheng Ta Ti's birthday

---

[4] A fen is one-tenth of a *chia*, which is equivalent to 0.9699 hectares or 2.3968 acres.

has been marked by an opera performed for the god's entertainment and a parade that takes the god on a general "inspection tour." At first the lu-chu was chosen by lot from among all the heads of household in Shu-lin, and he gathered all the young men in the community to take turns carrying the god's sedan chair. This procedure continued until some-time in the 1880's, when a new form of organization was initiated, pri-marily because the growth of Shu-lin's population had made the old procedure too cumbersome. The entire area was divided into four ku— T'an-ti and Chün-an-chiao, Chiang-tzu-liao and San-chiao-p'u, Feng-kuei-tien and Chu-kan-ts'o, and P'o-nei-k'eng and P'eng-ts'o—which from then on took turns providing the lu-chu and the god's chair-carriers.[5] This new organization reflected the emergence of these eight districts as distinct social entities, which together constituted the larger community centered on the Chi-an Kung.

The next major event in the history of the Chi-an Kung reflects another kind of change. Almost as soon as the Japanese had crushed the last native resistance, the colonial government chose a new route and began modernizing Liu Ming-ch'uan's experimental railroad. The new route took the line from Keelung to Taipei City, and from there to Pan-ch'iao, Shu-lin, and Ying-ke, and eventually on to Kaohsiung at the southern end of the island. The tracks reached Feng-kuei-tien in 1901, and a station was built there the following year. As the name Blacksmith's Shop sug-gests, Feng-kuei-tien had long been a small commercial center, but be-fore the railroad arrived, the wharf in T'an-ti had made that district the crossroads of the area. The railroad replaced the old river boats, and soon the center of gravity had shifted south to Feng-kuei-tien. Within a few years numerous shops had opened in the immediate vicinity of the new station and the school and administrative offices set up by the Japanese. Although I would be reluctant to argue that religious or-ganization always follows the lead of social organization, clearly this is sometimes the case. In 1922 two prominent members of the Chi-an Kung, Huang Ch'ün-ch'ing and Wang Tu-lung, feeling that the old temple was decayed beyond repair, suggested building a new temple and asked the god to choose a site. Pao Sheng Ta Ti chose a location a few hundred yards south of the new train station. In the next five years Huang and Wang raised a total of 43,455 silver dollars, and on the twenty-fourth day of the tenth lunar month, 1927, the new temple was completed. A *chiao* was performed for the benefit of souls in purgatory

[5] As the example given indicates, the term ku refers to a share or turn in a rotation.

on the twenty-third day of the eleventh month,[6] and with that Feng-kuei-tien, now better known as Shu-lin, had become the religious as well as the commercial center of what once had been Chang Pi-jung's estate.

In the years since 1922 the area regarded as falling under Pao Sheng Ta Ti's jurisdiction has been expanded twice. In 1927, when the new Chi-an Kung was completed, a fifth ku was added to the original four, incorporating Shan-tzu-chiao, Heng-k'eng-tzu, and Shih-hui-k'eng as part of the Chi-an Kung's catchment area. Thirty years later, in 1957, the five-ku system was reorganized to accord with the administrative districts established by the Nationalist government, and Hsi-sha-lun, part of Pan-ch'iao chen, was added to the third ku. The result is that at present the area supporting the Chi-an Kung temple includes most of Shu-lin chen and a small part of Pan-ch'iao chen. With the important exception of Ch'i-chou, which is a part of Pan-ch'iao chen but on the same side of the river as Shu-lin and only a five-minute walk from the new Chi-an Kung, the area under Pao Sheng Ta Ti's jurisdiction is approximately the same as that served by the Shu-lin station and the shops clustered around it.

The inclusion of the Shan-tzu-chiao area and Hsi-sha-lun in the Chi-an Kung organization and the continued independence of Ch'i-chou underline the role of commercial and ethnic ties in the community's formation. Obviously, Shan-tzu-chiao and Hsi-sha-lun were drawn into the Chi-an Kung organization by their participation in the markets that grew up around the new station, and, in the case of Hsi-sha-lun, despite inclusion in an administrative district with offices in another town. But though most of Ch'i-chou is closer to the station than either Shan-tzu-chiao or Hsi-sha-lun and is an integral part of the marketing area centered on the town, it has never participated in any way in the Chi-an Kung organization. Individual residents of Ch'i-chou seek Pao Sheng Ta Ti's help in time of need because he is known as an efficacious deity, but the community does not contribute money to his temple and has no role in its formal organization. The reason, clearly, is that the great majority of Ch'i-chou's inhabitants are descendants of settlers from An-ch'i and therefore have close ties with the An-ch'i majority in San-hsia. We will see later that the only external organization in which Ch'i-chou does participate is the one centered on the great Ch'ing Shui Tsu Shih Kung temple in San-hsia.

[6] A chiao is an esoteric ritual performed by Taoist priests to consecrate a temple or renew its religious charter. An excellent account is available in Saso 1972; see also the paper by Kristofer Schipper in this volume.

The Emergence of Communities

Just as the growth of the Chi-an Kung was made possible by the development of Shu-lin as an integrated community, so the creation of
other religious organizations in local hamlets and neighborhoods reflects
their emergence as communities. From the time of its earliest settlement,
the history of Shu-lin has been one of amalgamation, of people of diverse
origins uniting to create organizations that overcome their differences.
The earliest local example was the establishment of the Fu-te Kung in
T'an-ti in 1765. The residents of T'an-ti built a small temple for the
tutelary deity T'u Ti Kung at a place still known as T'u-ti-kung-p'u, and
contributed money to buy eight fen of paddy land that was given over to
the support of the temple and annual worship of the god. This joint
effort, along with the general view of T'u Ti Kung as the supernatural
governor of a territorially defined community, indicates that by 1765 the
residents of T'an-ti considered themselves a community and were able
to act as a community despite their diverse origins and ethnic strife.

About the same time as the construction of the Fu-te Kung, the farmers of T'an-ti established a *ch'ih-fu-hui*. The ostensible purpose of such
an association is to meet once or twice a year, share a feast, and worship
T'u Ti Kung, but the fact of its creation also says a great deal about the
community that organizes it. These organizations provide the institu-
tional means of organizing work parties to repair irrigation ditches and
roads; they also provide a forum for negotiating disputes over boundaries and water rights. The existence of a ch'ih-fu-hui says that the members recognize joint interests and can cooperate to advance them even
though they may belong to groups that are at odds on other issues.

By 1800 most of the villages in the Shu-lin area had established T'u
Ti Kung temples and an associated ch'ih-fu-hui, many with incense
taken from the Fu-te Kung in T'an-ti. The ch'ih-fu-hui set up in San-
chiao-p'u is of particular interest because the membership included
several ethnic groups and both landlords and small farmers. The association was established with sixteen shares, the holders of which were, in
annual rotation, responsible for organizing four feasts. Two shares were
held by Li Shen-fa, an important landlord, two by a Chung family from
T'ung-an, and one each by a Cheng family from Nan-an, a Ch'en family
from Ting-chiao, a Chiang family from P'ing-ho, a Li family from somewhere in Chang-chou, a Chien family also from Chang-chou, the Chien
lineage's Sacrificing Association, and six families, with the surnames
Ch'en, Li, Chiang, Tseng, Wu, and Chang, whose origins I have not been
able to trace. The only residents of San-chiao-p'u who did not partici-

pate in the ch'ih-fu-hui were the members of the Lan lineage in Lan-ts'o, who set up their own T'u Ti Kung temple and acted as an independent social unit.

The history of the Ch'ung-hsing Kung T'u Ti Kung temple in P'eng-ts'o is also interesting as an example of the relation between ethnic ties and the creation of community temples. The Ch'ung-hsing Kung was built by representatives of two ethnic groups to symbolize a truce that ended years of conflict. Of the eight named districts into which the Shu-lin area was partitioned during the Ch'ing period, P'eng-ts'o had the deepest ethnic divisions, its settlers including Hakka from Kwangtung as well as Hokkien from both Chang-chou and Ch'üan-chou. Perhaps because of this diversity and the conflicts it engendered, P'eng-ts'o was the last area to establish a T'u Ti Kung temple, despite its early settle-ment and its importance as the site of the Chang Kung-kuan, a rent-col-lection station set up by the Chang-wu-wen Corporation. The area's Chang-chou and Ch'üan-chou residents fought each other in 1853 and again in 1859, and then, neither side having gained an advantage, de-clared a truce in 1861, at which time they blamed their troubles on their Hakka neighbors and drove them out of the area. To affirm the truce, and perhaps also to celebrate their victory over the Hakka, a Liao family from Ch'üan-chou and a Lai family from Chang-chou suggested build-ing a T'u Ti Kung temple. They jointly purchased one chia of paddy land, donating its earnings to the Ch'ung-hsing Kung as an endowment. We see in this example both the divisive effects of ethnic differences and the way their resolution was expressed through the creation of local-level temples.

Although ethnicity has played a more important role in Shu-lin's his-tory than kinship, it would be a mistake to ignore the effects of lineage organization. The Lan lineage in San-chiao-p'u is the only lineage in the area that has its own T'u Ti Kung temple and does not participate in the organization created by the larger community, but it is not the only lineage to maintain independent links with the supernatural. We have already noted the Chien lineage's Ma Tsu Hui, the Lin lineage's Wang Yeh Kung Hui, and the Lai lineage's Ta Tao Kung Hui. Still another example is provided by the Chung lineage in San-chiao-p'u. Although the Chungs hold a share in the local ch'ih-fu-hui and help support the community T'u Ti Kung, they also have their own T'u Ti Kung temple and an independent organization. The dozen or so households that be-long to the lineage take turns burning incense every morning and eve-ning for the benefit of the lineage's god, and seven times a year, on the second day of the first and second lunar months, the fifteenth of the eighth month, the fifteenth of the twelfth month, the first day of the new year, and the anniversaries of the dates on which construction of the temple was started and completed, every household prepares a more elaborate offering.

The concern of most lineages to maintain an independent identity is most striking in the case of the Lai lineage in T'an-ti. Although members of the lineage supported the creation of the Chi-an Kung and are listed as contributing to the rebuilding of the temple in 1836, the lineage did not abandon its private rites for Pao Sheng Ta Ti when the god became supernatural governor of all Shu-lin. Instead, the Lais changed the date of their private festival from the fifteenth to the sixteenth day of the third lunar month, holding their private rites after participating in the community festival the previous day. The Lais appear to be proud of the high status achieved by their protector, but at the same time jealous of the symbol that represents their position as an independent social entity.

Segmentation

Amalgamation of the various ethnic groups that settled Shu-lin and the growth of local communities were accompanied in later years by a process of segmentation. As the population of Shu-lin grew, new communities appeared within established communities. The history of P'eng-ts'o offers a relatively simple example. As mentioned earlier, the residents of P'eng-ts'o think of the community as divided into three hamlets known as Hou-ts'un-tzu, T'ai-p'ing-ch'iao, and P'eng-ts'o. All three hamlets joined in founding the Ch'ung-hsing Kung in 1861 and all three participate in its annual festival to this day, but in the meantime two new temples have been established, one in Hou-ts'un-tzu and another in T'ai-p'ing-ch'iao, giving ritual recognition to the fact that they are distinct segments of the P'eng-ts'o community. The oldest of the two is the Ts'un-te Kung in Hou-ts'un-tzu, founded in 1925 at the suggestion of Chang Feng-shun, a descendant of Chang P'ei-shih, who was a relative and important ally of the landlord Chang Pi-jung. Without knowing the circumstances of Chang's suggestion, we can assume that its acceptance had something to do with the fact that eight of the fourteen households who joined the new organization were surnamed Chang.

The temple in T'ai-p'ing-ch'iao was built by a man named Hung Shui-lung, who later gave the establishment to the community. The story I have is that Hung's son was so ill he could not walk, and that after consulting both Chinese and Western doctors, Hung became desperate and sought the advice of the god Shang Ti Kung. The god told Hung he would have to build a temple and worship T'u Ti Kung and Ma Tsu or his son would never recover. Hung tried to bargain and offered to build the temple *if* his son recovered, but the god insisted that the boy would not recover *until* the temple was built. Hung then spent NT $10,000, and the temple was completed in December 1959. Hung's neighbors hired a Taoist priest to perform the temple's inaugural ceremonies and now regard the god enshrined there as a local tutelary. The god's considerable popularity is attributed to the recovery of Hung's son early the following year.

The recent history of T'an-ti affords a more elaborate example of segmentation. Despite the quarrel occasioned by the transfer of the old Fu-te Kung's property to the Chi-an Kung, this temple remained the sole T'u Ti Kung in T'an-ti until 1965. The district's *li-chang* and their representative to the chen assembly then decided that an open-pit mine near the temple had destroyed its geomancy and suggested building a new temple elsewhere. The community agreed and within a few months raised NT $15,000 to construct what is known as the T'an-te Kung. At the same time the organization that had supported the old Fu-te Kung was restructured in recognition of the district's greatly increased population. The new organization followed the example of the Chi-an Kung and divided T'an-ti into five ku, which now rotate the responsibility for choosing a lu-chu and raising funds for the temple's annual festival.

Although the image enshrined in the old Fu-te Kung was moved to the new T'an-te Kung, the old temple was not abandoned. Instead, a few families living in its immediate vicinity obtained a new T'u Ti Kung and placed him in the old building, which they now treat as a neighborhood temple.

A third T'u Ti Kung was established in T'an-ti a few months later after a dispute over the direction in which the T'an-te Kung should face. As is now the custom in most of the Shu-lin area, Pao Sheng Ta Ti was asked to choose the site of the new temple, the local god to decide its orientation. The god indicated that he wanted the temple to face south, but a man named Lai Huo-lien argued that it should face west instead. When the building committee rejected Lai's suggestion, he joined with seven of his neighbors and raised NT $4,000 to build a temple called the Te-an Kung. Like the small group of families that purchased a new image for the old Fu-te Kung and continue to make offerings despite the threatening coal mine, Lai and his neighbors participate in the community-wide T'an-te Kung organization while supporting regular worship at their neighborhood temple.

Three years later, in 1968, a fourth T'u Ti Kung temple was established in T'an-ti, this one in a neighborhood populated by a number of families from the mainland and some two hundred Hakka households living in the dormitories of the Railroad Bureau. The story is that shortly before the local elections in 1968, a local T'u Ti Kung, who had long been housed in a small stone temple, appeared in a dream of a female shaman (Hokkien: *sian-si:-ma*), and asked her "to please build a temple for me before the election." The woman quickly raised NT $20,000, and a new temple was constructed a few months later. The neighborhood then set up a lu-chu system and began holding a regular festival in honor of their god on the second day of the second lunar month. Until 1970, when this area of T'an-ti became a separate administrative district equivalent to T'an-ti, the followers of the new temple contributed to the support of the T'an-te Kung and participated in its annual festival; but with administrative independence, the neighborhood severed relations with the T'an-te Kung and became a separate religious community.

The history of Feng-kuei-tien, the site of Shu-lin town, illustrates segmentation of another kind. The first T'u Ti Kung temple was established in Feng-kuei-tien in 1766 by Chang P'ei-shih, a relative of Chang Pi-jung. The occasion was the completion of the Chang-ts'o Ch'uan, the Chang Family's Canal, the source of water for most of the area's irrigated fields. So far as I know, the temple functioned like any other T'u Ti Kung through most of the Ch'ing period, its diocese being Feng-kuei-tien, an area that included many farmers as well as the shopkeepers who gave the district its name. The first major change occurred in 1903, by which time Feng-kuei-tien was well on its way to becoming the commercial and administrative center of all Shu-lin. Two businessmen, Huang Hsien-shui and Ch'en Chin-shih, suggested building a new temple "to thank the god for our prosperity," and Chang Feng-shun, a descendant of Chang P'ei-shih, contributed 51 *p'ing* of land and raised 430 silver dollars.[7] The new, expanded temple, named the Shu-te Kung, then became the ritual center of the town that was growing up around the railroad station. Its catchment area included, in addition to Feng-kuei-tien, most of Chu-kan-ts'o, part of T'an-ti, a part of Ch'i-chou known as Fan-tzu-p'u, and Hsi-sha-lun.

The Shu-te Kung was rebuilt and enlarged again in 1951, at a cost of NT $22,500, the initiative coming from the administrative head of Shu-lin chen, the *chen-chang*, and the li-chang of the three districts into which the town was now partitioned. Huang Te-shih, a native of the

[7] One p'ing equals 35.6 square feet. The measure is used in describing the size of buildings and building sites.

town and professor at National Taiwan University, was invited to compose a couplet to be inscribed on the temple door, and—whether intentionally or not, I do not know—in his lines underscored the change in the institution's character. He wrote: "Go to the temple and burn incense, address the people as grandfather and uncle; go out and do business, respect the elders and men of excellent virtue." Because of their wealth and the influence it gave them, the businessmen with shops along Shu-lin's main street had long controlled the Shu-te Kung. Now their position was given public recognition; the Shu-te Kung became a businessman's temple. Other people could worship in the temple and participate in its annual festivals, but only businessmen could serve as lu-chu or join the ch'ih-fu-hui. It does not require much sociological imagination to see this change as reflecting the gradual decline of the landlords and the rise of a new business class. The 195 registered members of the ch'ih-fu-hui include the wealthiest men in Shu-lin and the great majority of its elected officials.

The relationship of the Shu-te Kung to other temples and the status of its god vis-à-vis other gods also mirror the importance of the town. The temple that Chang P'ei-shih founded was for many years only one of a number of T'u Ti Kung temples, its god nothing more than the tutelary deity of one of the eight districts governed by Pao Sheng Ta Ti. At present the god enshrined in the Shu-te Kung is acknowledged "head" of all the T'u Ti Kung in the Shu-lin area, a sort of hegumen of this class of gods. The resident of the Shu-te Kung is often invited as a "guest" when other T'u Ti Kung associations stage an opera or a puppet show for the entertainment of their local deity, an honor otherwise reserved for deities of higher status, such as Pao Sheng Ta Ti, Ch'ing Shui Tsu Shih Kung, and Ma Tsu. Moreover, the Shu-te Kung is the site of an annual *p'u-tu*, a ritual event that is seldom performed in a T'u Ti Kung temple but is a customary annual activity of major temples like the Chi-an Kung.[8] The resident of the Shu-te Kung is in fact a little Ch'eng Huang. On the one hand, he is the chief god of the town, and on the other, the chief of the tutelary deities responsible for the adjacent rural districts.

The Shu-te Kung is not the only religious organization in Shu-lin to recruit followers on the basis of some principle other than ethnicity, residence, or kinship. In 1872 a man named Chien Lien, dissatisfied with the state of society and feeling that Confucian reform was the only

[8] The primary purpose of the p'u-tu, from the layman's point of view, is to feed and thereby pacify the hungry ghosts released from the underworld during the seventh lunar month. Cf. Schipper's description, pp. 321–22 below.

solution, raised a hundred dollars and built the Hsi-tzu T'ing, Love-the-Written-Word Arbor, next to the old Fu-te Kung in T'an-ti. This example encouraged Wang Tso-lin, a private tutor, to organize the Wen-ping She, also known as the Tzu-chih T'ing Hui, the Association of the Arbor for Inscribed Paper. The eighteen members of the Wen-ping She raised a sum of money, the interest from which was used to finance an annual sacrifice in honor of Ch'ang Chih, the reputed inventor of Chinese writing. Until Wang Tso-lin died in 1935 the Wen-ping She met once a year in front of the Hsi-tzu T'ing to worship Ch'ang Chih and discuss Confucian principles.

The Wen-ping She was essentially an association of Shu-lin's literati and aspiring scholars. An organization more narrowly defined by occupation is the Ta Tao Kung Hui, founded by Chien Wu-shih. Membership in this association is limited to coolies who work in the Shu-lin railroad station, the majority of whom are Chien's sworn brothers. These men have taken as their patron deity Pao Sheng Ta Ti, and they founded their organization with incense taken from the Chi-an Kung. Obviously, despite their low status, they identify with the community and want their organization to be regarded as one of its constituent parts.

Ethnic Organizations

Because Shu-lin's population was divided into several competing ethnic groups, the appearance of territorially defined units can be seen as a process of amalgamation. But this does not mean that ethnicity did not affect religious organization, or that its only effect was to retard the growth of organizations based on residence. The emergence of the Chi-an Kung as a community symbol and the founding of a number of local T'u Ti Kung temples were paralleled by the creation of shen-ming-hui that were the exclusive property of particular ethnic groups. These organizations cut across the communities defined by the T'u Ti Kung temples, and in three instances allied segments of the Shu-lin population with fellow ethnics elsewhere.

Three of the most important ethnic-based shen-ming-hui are confined to Shu-lin. These are the San Chieh Kung Hui in Chiang-tzu-liao and San-chiao-p'u, another San Chieh Kung Hui in T'an-ti, P'eng-ts'o, and Hsia-shan-tzu-chiao, and the K'ai Chang Sheng Wang Hui, more commonly known as the Ch'en Sheng Wang Hui. The first of these three organizations was founded during the Ch'ien-lung period (1735–96) by the landlord Liu K'un-shan, who endowed the association with 1.9 fen of paddy land, the rent going to pay for two annual festivals. Until shortly after the Japanese occupation, membership in the association was limited to people of Chang-chou origins living in Chiang-tzu-liao and San-chiao-p'u. The Chang-chou residents of these two communities alternated the responsibility for choosing a lu-chu, who was entrusted with organizing a festival on the fifteenth day of the first lunar month and again on the fifteenth day of the eighth month. Worship was conducted in the home of the lu-chu, who held the god's incense burner during his tenure in office and then passed it on to his successor in the other district.

The second San Chieh Kung Hui, founded in the Chia-chin period (1796–1820), was similarly organized. Again membership was limited to people of Chang-chou origins living in geographically defined communities, in this case T'an-ti, P'eng-ts'o, and a village at the foot of the mountains known as Hsia-shan-tzu-chiao. These three communities rotated the responsibility for choosing a lu-chu who would organize a festival, usually held sometime between the second and the fifteenth day of the eighth lunar month. We need only note the peculiar belief in T'an-ti that the family of the lu-chu will suffer a death during his year in office, the not very surprising result being that people there are reluctant to serve as lu-chu for the San Chieh Kung Hui. This probably is also the reason why the lu-chu in this community usually stores the god's incense burner in either the Fu-te Kung or the Chi-an Kung rather than in his own house.

The primary difference between the two San Chieh Kung Hui and the Ch'en Sheng Wang Hui is that whereas the former recruit members on the basis of residence and ethnicity, the latter recruits on the basis of surname and ethnicity. In theory, the Ch'en Sheng Wang Hui includes everyone in the Shu-lin area who is of Chang-chou origins and bears the surname Ch'en. The religious rationale for these recruitment principles is the belief that K'ai Chang Sheng Wang is the deified spirit of Ch'en Yüan-kuang, the official credited with opening Chang-chou to Chinese settlement. He is therefore both a patron deity of people from Chang-chou and an "ancestor" of people surnamed Ch'en.

The role ethnic ties have played in shaping religious organization in Shu-lin is even more strikingly evident in the case of three other ethnic shen-ming-hui, which cut across marketing areas and unite people whose only shared characteristic is their ancestors' native place. One of these is the Szu-ku Ma, an association devoted to the worship of the god Kuan Yin Fu Tsu. The membership of the Szu-ku Ma includes all the Ting-chiao people living in T'u-ch'eng, Ting-p'u, Kan-yüan, and Feng-kuei-tien. T'u-ch'eng and Ting-p'u are south of Shu-lin, across the Tamsui River in the Pan-ch'iao marketing area; Kan-yüan is a part of Shu-lin chen but is closer to San-hsia and is part of its marketing area; and in this context the name Feng-kuei-tien refers to the southern half of Shu-lin's marketing area and includes Shan-tzu-chiao, P'eng-ts'o, P'o-nei-k'eng, and Ch'i-chou, as well as the part of Shu-lin that was once known locally as Feng-kuei-tien. The Szu-ku Ma thus extends over an area that is as large as Shu-lin itself and that cuts across the marketing areas of the three most important towns on the southwestern side of the Taipei Basin.

The Shih Pa Shou Kuan Yin Hui is also a Ting-chiao organization and is also devoted to the god Kuan Yin Fu Tsu. Whereas the Szu-ku Ma takes in the southern half of the Shu-lin marketing area and extends southward, the Shih Pa Shou Kuan Yin Hui includes only the northern tip of the Shu-lin marketing area and extends over a vast territory to the north and west. Organizationally, the association is doubly segmented: it is divided into three sections, each of which is subdivided into several ku. The first section is P'ing-ting with six ku; the second, Shan-chiao with three ku; and the third, Kuei-shan with twelve ku. The overall organization is sustained by the belief that the gods worshipped by the three sections are duplicate images of the same deity, while the ku that make up each section relate to one another by rotating the responsibility for an annual festival in honor of their section's image. Integration of the larger community is indicated by the staggering of the three sections' annual festivals in the fashion of periodic markets so that members of one section may attend the other two's festivals. The P'ing-ting section holds its annual festival on the nineteenth day of the ninth lunar month, the Shan-chiao section on the fifteenth day of the ninth month, and the Kuei-shan section on the ninth day of the third month.

Ting-chiao people living in Shu-lin's San-chiao-p'u participate in this organization as members of the P'o-chiao ku of the Shan-chiao section. This ku receives the god on the fourteenth of the ninth month from the Hsi-sheng ku to the south and passes it on one year later to the Hsia-shan-chiao ku to the north. To mark the handing over of the god's image and censor to the next ku, Ting-chiao residents of the area that has been keeping the god hold a festival known as Kuan Yin Kuo-t'ou, "Transferring Kuan Yin." The community receiving the god sends its lu-chu and a band of young men to bring the god home in a sedan chair, and then on the following day, the fifteenth of the ninth lunar month, all the Ting-chiao residents of the ku kill pigs and assemble them in front of the god in the form of a sacrifice. So strong has the organization been in recent years that over a thousand pigs are annually killed and assembled for presentation to the god.

To assess the last association to be considered here, that of Shu-lin's An-ch'i minority, we must first understand the organization of the Ch'ang-fu Yen temple in San-hsia, an establishment devoted to the worship of Ch'ing Shui Tsu Shih Kung. The responsibility for the annual festival at the Ch'ang-fu Yen is rotated among seven ku that together embrace almost everyone living in San-hsia's marketing area. In this case, the rotation is by surname rather than by place, except for a village known as Chung-chuang, which participates as a community. The first ku is for people surnamed Liu; the second for people of miscellaneous surnames; the third and fourth for people surnamed Ch'en and Lin; the fifth for Chung-chuang; and the sixth and seventh for people surnamed Li and Wang. An-ch'i people who live outside San-hsia's marketing area also worship the god enshrined in the Ch'ang-fu Yen, but invite the god to their own districts rather than attend the San-hsia festival. One of these districts is Ch'i-chou, which is itself divided into four ku. The others are scattered across the western half of the Taipei Basin as far north as Shan-chiao and as far east as San-chung-p'u.

One of the largest groups of An-ch'i people in Shu-lin, the Lans of Lan-ts'o, do not participate in the worship of San-hsia's Ch'ing Shui Tsu Shih Kung, probably because they have their own image of the god and their own organization. But until twenty or thirty years ago, most of Shu-lin's An-ch'i residents did participate. The Wangs in Chün-an-chiao and the Hungs in P'eng-ts'o belonged to the seven-ku system that supports the annual festival at the Ch'ang-fu Yen. The Wangs killed pigs and attended the San-hsia festival in concert with the seventh ku, while the Hungs participated as one of the second ku's miscellaneous surnames. The Hsiehs in Feng-kuei-tien took the other option and joined the four-ku system that supports the annual Ch'ing Shui Tsu Shih Kung festival in Ch'i-chou. Many of them attended the San-hsia festival as guests and observers, but they killed pigs and worshipped as though they were residents of an area of Ch'i-chou known as Fan-tzu-p'u.

Community Precedence

The six organizations I have just described were founded in the late eighteenth and early nineteenth centuries and continued as ethnic provinces throughout the Japanese occupation, but today only one of them, the Szu-ku Ma, retains its original form. The K'ai Chang Sheng Wang Hui, once the exclusive domain of people surnamed Ch'en from Chang-chou, now accepts anyone surnamed Ch'en, regardless of origin. The two San Chieh Kung Hui continue to hold an annual festival in honor of their patron deity, but they are now community organizations that expect Chang-chou and Ch'üan-chou families to participate on an equal basis. Of the three An-ch'i groups in Shu-lin who participated in the worship of San-hsia's Ch'ing Shui Tsu Shih Kung, only the Hungs remain loyal to their An-ch'i origins. The Wangs and the Hsiehs have both joined the Shih Pa Shou Kuan Yin Hui. The community, clearly, has come to take precedence over both ethnic and kinship affiliations. The Lan lineage's Ch'ing Shui Tsu Shih Kung Hui remains restricted to members of that lineage, but both the Lins' T'ien Shang Sheng Mu Hui and the Chiens' Wang Yeh Kung Hui now admit their neighbors as members. In 1970 only ten of the seventeen families belonging to the Wang Yeh Kung Hui were also members of the Chien lineage.

This does not mean that native religious institutions in Taiwan have been overwhelmed by the many changes that have swept the island in the past forty years. Though transformed by these changes, they have retained their vitality. The recent history of the Shih Pa Shou Kuan Yin Hui provides a striking case in point. While losing its original ethnic identity, the organization has greatly expanded its scope. Just prior to World War II the Shan-chiao section expanded to include Hsin-chuang as a fourth ku, and shortly after the war jumped across the Taipei Basin to include San-chung-p'u and then across the island to include Tung-kua-shan in I-lan hsien. At the same time Chün-an-chiao, Chiang-tzu-liao, T'an-ti, and Shu-lin were all added to the Hsi-sheng ku. The result is an organization that now spans the northern half of the island and counts as members more than 100,000 people.

Now that we have seen something of the various groups that together constitute the units of religious organization in Shu-lin, we must briefly consider their relation to one another. The most important point to be made is that almost all these groups are ritually linked to Pao Sheng Ta Ti and the Chi-an Kung. These links say that the other gods in Shu-lin are to Pao Sheng Ta Ti as the groups they represent are to the larger Shu-lin community. The intensity of these links varies with the degree to which the members of a given religious organization are integrated into the community governed by Pao Sheng Ta Ti. The gods of socially or spatially distant groups are less closely tied to Shu-lin's supernatural governor than the gods of groups fully integrated into the community.

Consider first the various shen-ming-hui we have discussed. With the exception of the Wen-ping She, separated from the Chi-an Kung and the community by ideological commitments, all these organizations maintained some ritual tie with Pao Sheng Ta Ti. At one extreme we find the Ta Tao Kung Hui, founded with incense from the Chi-an Kung, and organizations like the K'ai Chang Sheng Wang Hui, which houses its god in the Chi-an Kung and holds its annual festival there; at the other, organizations like the P'o-chiao ku of the Shih Pa Shou Kuan Yin Hui, which invites Pao Sheng Ta Ti as a guest to its annual festival but does not otherwise keep up any formal tie with the Chi-an Kung. The typical case is that of the Lin lineage's Wang Yeh Kung Hui. The Lins always invite Pao Sheng Ta Ti as a guest when they stage an opera or a puppet show to entertain their own god, and on the occasion of Pao Sheng Ta Ti's annual inspection tour always carry their god in the procession as though he were a part of Pao Sheng Ta Ti's entourage. The relationship between the two gods is much like that between a posted magistrate and the educated elite in the area under his jurisdiction.

The relationships between Pao Sheng Ta Ti and the numerous T'u Ti Kung that govern segments of the Shu-lin community is even more explicitly bureaucratic. Although the popular religion of most Taiwanese holds that T'u Ti Kung's immediate superior in the supernatural bureaucracy is the Ch'eng Huang, practice in Shu-lin makes Pao Sheng Ta Ti the deity to which the local T'u Ti Kung are responsible. The temples of major segments of the community in or near the town invite Pao Sheng Ta Ti as the guest of honor to their annual festival, ask the god to choose a site if the temple needs to be relocated, and also consult the god if a fire in the T'u Ti Kung's incense burner indicates that something is amiss. That these ritual links represent the structure of the Shu-lin community is clearly shown by the fact that their intensity varies with the size and location of the village or neighborhood served by the T'u Ti Kung temple. The temples of small villages and those some distance from the town invite Pao Sheng Ta Ti to their festival and usually ask him to decide the site and orientation of a new building, but they do not seek his advice in the case of a fire in the incense burner. The temples of insignificant hamlets and of villages located on the periphery of Shu-lin either ignore Pao Sheng Ta Ti or limit their relationship to inviting him to their annual festival. The case of the Fu-te Kung in San-chiao-p'u is particularly interesting because it illustrates the precision with which ritual events can be used to express social distance. San-chiao-p'u's location on the northern edge of the Shu-lin area and its close ties with communities to the north are neatly expressed by the practice of inviting Pao Sheng Ta Ti as a guest but seating him below two gods from other communities.

This brief exposition does not do justice to the full complexity of religious organization in Shu-lin, particularly the changes that have occurred in the past few years. Rapid population growth has been accom-

panied by the appearance of new shen-ming-hui, the expansion of existing hui, and the establishment of many new T'u Ti Kung temples (there
are now more than 35 of them in the area). Although it would be a
mistake to write off these new organizations as simply more of the same,
the form they have taken is at least consistent with the general direction
in which Shu-lin's religious institutions have been moving. In broad
terms, we can think of the history of these institutions as involving two
phases. During the first phase, extending from the time of settlement
through the late Ch'ing, the growth of a self-conscious community with
clearly defined segments gave rise to the Chi-an Kung as a ritual center
and the appearance of T'u Ti Kung temples as the symbolic foci of
villages and neighborhoods. This process involved amalgamation of
people belonging to competing ethnic groups, but not a rapid deterio-
ration of ethnic ties. It was not until after the Japanese occupation that
ethnicity began to lose its social significance. During this second phase,
initiated shortly after the turn of the century, place of residence became
the primary criterion for defining membership in religious organizations.
Shen-ming-hui organized by lineage or with reference to ethnicity either
disappeared or were transformed into community organizations. It now
seems likely that organizations long confined by exclusive criteria will
rapidly expand as the communities they represent expand their own
horizons.

Village Alliance Temples in Hong Kong

JOHN A. BRIM

Although much of traditional Chinese religious life was focused on temples, comprehensive studies of Chinese temple organization are rare. Moreover, most studies of Chinese temples treat them in isolation from their social milieu, emphasizing such topics as iconography while slighting details of temple organization and of its relation to other elements of the social structure. This paper will discuss a type of temple of great importance in the area of China that became the New Territories of Hong Kong and probably in other parts of China as well—the village alliance temple. It will describe the organization of village alliance temples and attempt to elucidate the relationship between these temples and their social milieu.[1]

Village alliance temples serve and are owned and controlled by organizations of allied villages.[2] Although other types of temple are found in the New Territories—some serving individual villages and others special interest groups such as lineages and voluntary associations—village alliance temples had special importance in the religious life of the New Territories because of their size, the wide range of religious services they provided, and the vital role they traditionally played in supravillage social structure. Before discussing village alliance temples, let me briefly

[1] This article is based on fieldwork in the New Territories, primarily in Yuen Long district, carried out in 1967–68 and the summer of 1970, and on research in the archives. I would like to thank S. K. Fung, H. H. Lo, and K. K. Wong, all of the Hong Kong Government, for their valuable assistance, and James Hayes, Hong Kong City District Commissioner, for supplying the copy of the official map of New Territories subdistricts that served as a basis for the map on p. 96.

[2] So far as I know, New Territories residents have no special term for village alliance temples as a generic type. They refer to them by their specific names, often prefixed by the name of the village alliance to which they belong—e.g., "Tun Men K'ou-chiao Miao," the K'ou-chiao temple of Tun Mun (Village Alliance).

outline the nature of the village alliance organizations with which they were associated.

Village Alliances

Village alliances, commonly referred to as *yüeh* or *hsiang* by the people of the New Territories, have long been a feature of the area's social organization. Village alliances are referred to in temple inscriptions dating from the mid-eighteenth and nineteenth centuries, and there is no reason to suppose that their existence does not antedate these references. Pale reflections of these alliances persist to this day.[3] Typically including from five to twenty villages, alliances traditionally had important parapolitical and paramilitary as well as ritual functions.

The village alliances of the New Territories can be divided into two major types, the distinguishing feature being the degree to which an alliance is dominated by a single lineage. The lineage-dominated village alliance is composed primarily of villages populated almost entirely by members of one higher-order lineage. These villages might be dispersed throughout the alliance's territory or virtually contiguous. Not infrequently a lineage-dominated village alliance included several satellite villages, whose inhabitants were not members of the dominant lineage. Describing such satellite villages, a well-informed British observer, Stewart Lockhart, wrote: "Small villages and hamlets often place themselves under the protection of large and influential clans, to which they refer all their complaints, and from which they expect assistance in case of attack, robbery, and lawsuits. In some instances the smaller villages pay their land tax to the Government through the influential clans." (Lockhart 1900: 20.)

The second major type of village alliance was composed primarily of villages that did not share membership in one dominant lineage. Generally the member villages of such an alliance were not contiguous, but were scattered throughout the alliance's territory.

After the British takeover of the New Territories in 1899, the colonial government incorporated the major village alliances into the administrative structure it established, conferring semiofficial status on recog-

---

[3] Within a few years of the British takeover in 1899, agencies of the British Colonial Government superseded the village alliance organizations in many important areas—especially defense and the settlement of cases at law. Subsequently these organizations declined greatly in importance. After World War II, the Hong Kong Government attempted to revive the village alliance organizations by establishing "Rural Committees" that more or less paralleled the old village alliances. The powers of these bodies, however, are very limited compared with those of the traditional village alliance organizations.

nized alliance leaders (Lockhart 1900: 251). The village alliances thus recognized are shown in the accompanying map, which reproduces an early official map. When this outline map is compared to a detailed map of the area, it can be seen that, as Lockhart (1900: 251) observed, the member villages of an alliance often occupy a common drainage system, which suggests that one important determinant of alliance membership may have been participation in a common irrigation system. In an area as heavily dependent on irrigation as the New Territories, it is clearly advantageous for villages sharing an irrigation source to band together in parapolitical organization, if only to facilitate the settlement of irrigation disputes and to coordinate water use.

Besides providing a mechanism for the resolution of irrigation disputes, the village alliance organizations were active in the adjudication of other types of disputes arising within their boundaries. In some cases, the legal machinery of a village alliance became relatively elaborate. At least one village alliance in the New Territories is known to have maintained a formal legal code. A tablet kept in the alliance temple of the Tung Chung village alliance on Lantao Island, dated 1893, specified the fines to be paid for various common offenses and procedures to be followed in trying accused persons before the village alliance council (Hayes 1962: 84). A village alliance might deal internally even with very serious crimes, which by Chinese law were the province of the district magistrate. During the brief military resistance to the British takeover in 1899, for example, a Ha Tsuen man thought to be a British collaborator was put to death by the leaders of his village alliance (Dispatches 1900: 47). After surveying the area to be leased by Great Britain as the New Territories, Lockhart reported in 1898 that the majority of legal cases never went beyond the village alliance council, though appeal to higher authorities was theoretically possible (Report 1898: 192–93).

A village alliance also had a strong paramilitary aspect, with its member villages on occasion fighting together against outsiders. The major village alliances maintained formally constituted militia units (*t'uan-lien*).[4] The New Territories area, like much of China's southeastern seaboard, was plagued by pirates and bandits who periodically raided the villages. The gazetteer of Hsin-an hsien, to which the New Territories belonged prior to 1898, records numerous instances of fighting between village alliance forces and pirate or bandit groups (Wang et al. 1891, ch. 13). As late as the years immediately following World War II, banditry continued to plague the New Territories (Barrow 1950: 7).

[4] On the t'uan-lien, see Wakeman 1966. See also Groves 1969 for a discussion of militia organization in the New Territories.

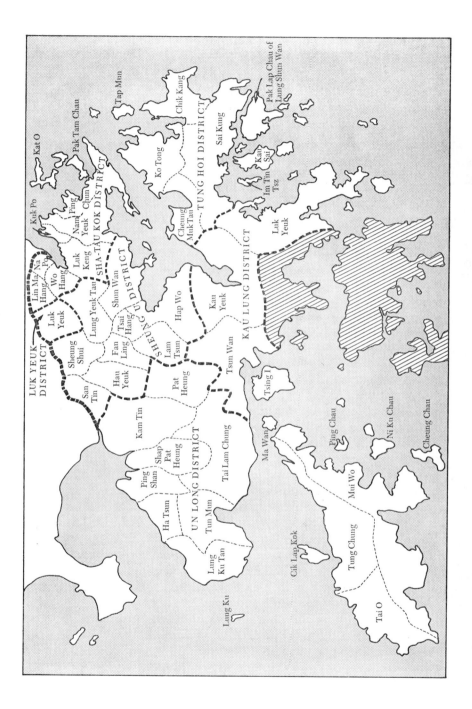

In traditional times village alliances in the New Territories fought engagements not only with pirate and bandit forces, but also with other village alliances. One important cause of such conflicts was disputes over land rent—between, for example, an alliance composed largely of major landlords and an alliance mainly of tenants. For example, according to a tablet dated 1777 in the Shap Pat Heung village alliance temple, a dispute arose between landowners in the Kam Tin village alliance, a wealthy stronghold of the powerful Teng lineage, and their tenants in the Shap Pat Heung village alliance, composed of several mixed-surname villages, over the size of the grain measure to be used in collecting rent. The Shap Pat Heung tenants withheld their rent for two years; according to the tablet the people of Kam Tin retaliated by invading Shap Pat Heung and seizing livestock and crops, killing at least one Shap Pat Heung man in the process. Subsequently, the size of the grain measure was fixed by the provincial authorities, which presumably resolved this particular dispute. Another such conflict, this one between Kam Tin and the Pat Heung alliance, which also took place during the eighteenth century, is documented by a tablet in the Chau-wong Temple at Kam Tin Pak Pin.

Clashes between village alliances were not isolated incidents. Three major outbreaks of armed warfare between village alliances, each resulting in loss of life, are documented for the New Territories' Yuen Long district alone during the last half of the nineteenth century (Hayes 1962: 88; Baker 1968: 183). In addition to disputes over rent, struggles over water rights and control of markets could also precipitate combat between alliances.[5] Control of markets was important because markets generated substantial income in the form of "scale charges" and other types of commissions.[6]

In the New Territories the village alliance took on still another function in at least two instances, and possibly in many others. Both the Ha Tsuen and Tun Mun village alliances undertook to provide their members with insurance against the theft of crops and livestock. In return for money paid over to the alliance, certain men were delegated to collect insurance fees from the member villages' inhabitants, based on the amount of land farmed by each household and the number of animals it owned. At the same time, the men in the consortium were responsible for reimbursing victims of theft. They attempted to minimize

[5] For a relatively recent example, see Tratman's (1922: J2) account of the response of the Kam Tin village alliance to an attempt by a leader of the Ping Shan alliance to launch a land reclamation project that would have disrupted Kam Tin's irrigation system.

[6] On alliance rivalries over control of markets, see Sung 1935 and Brim 1970: 9f.

losses by patrolling the fields of the alliance villages at night when the crops were nearly ready for harvesting.

Relations between village alliances were not inevitably hostile. It was not unusual for two or more village alliance organizations to combine forces against common enemies. The Ha Tsuen and Shap Pat Heung alliances, for example, were longstanding military allies. In recognition of this relationship, the Ha Tsuen alliance to this day sends a delegation to the god's birthday celebration at the Shap Pat Heung alliance temple. Moreover, virtually all the village alliances in the New Territories joined forces to oppose the British in 1899.[7]

In sum, then, village alliances provided an organizational framework within which villages could cooperate to rout common enemies, to settle disputes, to coordinate water use, and to provide crop insurance. Another important activity of village alliance organizations was, of course, the operation of village alliance temples.

Village Alliance Temples

Village alliance temples are built in locations thought to have superior *feng-shui* (or geomantic influence). The geomantic aura of the temple is believed to benefit the entire territory of the alliance. Consequently many alliance temples are situated in open country, within the alliance boundaries but at some distance from any member village. A typical alliance temple consists of a large main hall, where the major temple gods are enshrined, and a number of side halls used for secondary shrines, meeting rooms, kitchen facilities, caretaker's quarters, and the like. Each temple is dedicated to one or two principal gods, although a number of secondary divinities are also enshrined. One of the most popular principal alliance temple gods in the New Territories is T'ien Hou, the Goddess of Heaven. Other popular alliance temple gods are Pei Ti, Kuan Yin, Ch'e Kung, and Yang Hou Wang. Among the secondary divinities commonly found in alliance temples are Chin Hua Fu Jen, who can ensure smooth childbirth and the birth of sons; Kuan Ti; Hung Sheng, the flood god; and the virtually ubiquitous Earth God. A number of alliance temples also have a side hall in which the spirit tablets of men who died fighting for the alliance are enshrined.

The village alliance temples, in contrast to the smaller village temples,

---

[7] There existed a level of organization above that of the village alliance—the *tung*—which was responsible for coordinating the military forces of the various village alliance organizations to meet a major outside threat and which was activated in 1899. See Groves 1969 for a discussion of the tung organization in the New Territories.

offer a wide range of ritual services. These include various kinds of divination; rituals in which children are "adopted" by a god in order to assure them of the god's protection; ritual transactions for procuring divine assistance in connection with childbirth, business ventures, long journeys, serious illness, and so forth. This variety of ritual services is made possible by the temple's full-time religious specialist, the *miao-chu*, who assists worshippers with rituals.

Routine, day-to-day activity at an alliance temple consists mainly of small-scale transactions of the sort just described between the gods and individual worshippers. Major temple activities occur at intervals throughout the year. Each temple has several small images of its principal god or gods called "traveling images" (*hsing-hsiang*). A member village that experiences a crisis such as an epidemic may have one of the traveling images brought in so that the god's beneficent influence will focus upon the stricken village. Traveling images of the temple gods may also be taken to a member village for an important village ceremony such as the *tien-teng* ceremony, at which infant boys gain formal membership in their lineage or village.

The gods in the alliance temples are regarded as more efficacious than those in the small village temples (although the same gods may be enshrined in both village and alliance temples).[8] As a result the alliance temples are heavily patronized by individual worshippers on the occasion of "make blessing" (*tso-fu*), an annual religious event, usually held early in the second lunar month, during which the worshipper requests the gods' favor in the coming year, and during "repay the spirits" (*huan-shen*), a religious observance at the close of the year held to repay the gods for their beneficence throughout the year.

Another important class of rituals is performed not simply on behalf of individual worshippers or villages within the alliance, but on behalf of the alliance as a collectivity. The miao-chu performs a daily ritual on behalf of the alliance and sees to it that the spirit lamps before the temple gods are kept burning. The major collective ritual event in New Territories alliance temples, however, is the birthday celebration for

---

[8] Many villages in the New Territories have their own small temples, which are important in local ritual (Brim 1970: 41–87) but typically lack professional attendants and hence also lack such specialized services as divining. Most villagers consider the gods in their alliance temple, represented as effigies, to be far more powerful than their village temple counterparts, usually represented only by tablets.

Arthur Wolf has suggested to me that some village temples may be subordinate branches of the village alliance temple. Unfortunately I have no evidence bearing on this hypothesis, which has important implications for the ideological underpinnings of village alliance systems.

the temple's principal deity. This is an occasion for elaborate offerings
to the god from representatives of the allied villages and mass worship
by the inhabitants. In addition, the god's birthday observance traditionally incorporates operas, puppet shows, and other forms of entertainment for the gods and the masses of assembled worshippers, making
the god's birthday celebration one of the religious and social high points
of the year. Many alliance temples feature, as part of these festivities,
a "rocket-snatching" (ch'iang-p'ao) contest, during which teams of
young men from alliance villages vie with one another to capture lucky
rockets fired off by officers of the temple. These rockets are considered
relics of the principal temple deity, and are thought to bring good fortune to villages that win them. They must be returned to the temple
with a thank-offering to the god on his or her next birthday.[9]

Some of the excitement of a typical god's birthday celebration is conveyed by the following description of T'ien Hou birthday celebrations
at the Shap Pat Heung alliance's T'ien Hou temple near Yuen Long
market, written by a resident of the alliance:

Every year on the eve of T'ien Hou's birthday, the managers from the
villages whose turn it is to take charge must abstain from meat and go together
to the temple to spend the night. Just past midnight on the morning of the 23d
[of the third lunar month], all the managers must burn incense to T'ien Hou
and offer her birthday greetings to show their respect. Every year, from the
22d to the 23d of the third lunar month, there is a continuous stream of
devout men and women going to the T'ien Hou temple to worship, filling the
temple to overflowing.

On the morning of the 23d, the rocket associations proceed to return their
rocket [captured during the preceding year's competition]. These are received
by the managers. At two in the afternoon the firing of the rockets begins.
There is an explosion and the rocket shoots up into the sky. The crowds of
rocket seekers rush toward the spot where the rocket fell, competing with one
another to be the first to snatch it up. If the person seizing it does not break
away from the crowd quickly, they will surround and pile on him. It is extremely dangerous. You can imagine, under these circumstances, how much
concern there was over the possibility of an accident. As a result, misunderstandings between individuals or between villages started easily, and there
were frequent fights. No matter how severe the injuries sustained, no one has
ever been killed. This is due to T'ien Hou's protection. (Lin 1964.)[10]

---

[9] Gods' birthday celebrations have ceased at some New Territories alliance
temples.

[10] The writer goes on to note that owing to tremendous population growth in the
area after World War II, fighting over possession of the rockets became a serious
problem. Consequently it was decided in 1949 to have participants draw lots for
the rockets to reduce the chance of violent clashes. This system is still in effect.

Another important collective ritual held in many alliances is the *ta-chiao*, a ceremony performed periodically with the primary intent of succoring hungry ghosts (ghosts of persons who have died unnaturally) and freeing the alliance of their malign influence. Although the ta-chiao need not be held at the alliance temple, the alliance temple gods are essential participants and their traveling images are conveyed to the site of the ritual, when it is not the alliance temple, in order to enlist their powers.

Ta-chiao ceremonies are typically carried out at ten-year intervals and last several days. All members of the alliance are expected to abstain from meat before and during the rites. At the site of the ta-chiao, a number of large sheds are constructed of rice-straw mats to house the ritual equipment, the gods, and the human participants. Various rites are held in these enclosures and, to extend their benefits throughout the alliance's territory, a procession of ta-chiao participants, accompanied by lion-and-dragon dance teams, goes from village to village performing rituals. The ta-chiao culminates in the burning of great quantities of paper clothing and money to meet the needs of the hungry ghosts, the celebration of a mass to succor their souls, and the burning of a memorial to the Jade Emperor containing the names of the alliance residents to apprise Heaven of their contribution to the ritual. After all the rites are completed, operas are performed for several days to entertain both human and divine participants.[11]

The operation of village alliance temples is supervised by the alliance's governing body. Traditionally, this seems generally to have been a *t'ang* organization to which the various allied villages named members.[12] This governing body is responsible for appointing a miao-chu to preside over temple ritual, for maintaining the temple, and for managing its endowment. The routine maintenance expenses of an alliance temple and the salaries of the miao-chu and his assistants are generally paid out of income from the endowment—generally land or shops donated by members of the alliance—and fees collected from worshippers. Extraordinary expenses such as those incurred in reconstruction of a temple are defrayed by assessment of the member villages and by additional contribu-

[11] A description of a recent ta-chiao held by the Ha Tsuen village alliance may be found in Teng 1965.

[12] T'ang organizations, found in great numbers in the New Territories, run the gamut from purely business organizations, to lineage organizations holding land in common, to quasi-political organizations such as those that constituted managerial bodies for village alliances. (For further information on New Territories t'ang, see Hayes 1963, 1964.) The postwar Rural Committees seem in most, but not all, cases to have replaced the traditional t'ang organizations as the governing bodies of the alliance temples.

tions from persons or corporate groups residing in or having some special relationship to the alliance.

Traditionally, an alliance temple often served not only for religious gatherings, but as a meeting place for the leaders of the alliance. There were few other buildings in traditional times large enough to accommodate a good-sized meeting.

The Village Alliance Temple and Its Social Milieu

Contrary to the usual implications of the literature on Chinese religion, village temple alliance organizations in the New Territories are *not* loose assemblages of the devout existing in relative isolation from other aspects of the social structure. Instead, they are deeply rooted in local-level social structure.

One possible explanation for the intimate linkage between these major temples and the village alliance organizations is that such temples, along with their associated rituals, may have helped solve the alliance system's "latency problem," i.e. "the maintenance over time of the system's motivational and cultural patterns" (Blau and Scott 1962: 38, paraphrasing Parsons et al. 1953). Most of the important activities undertaken by the village alliances were, by their very nature, highly intermittent. In times of relative security, many years might pass before a military show of force was required. There might also be long hiatuses between alliance efforts to defend or coordinate water use. The intermittent character of such activities must have aggravated the latency problem, which exists in all social systems.

If it is true, as much evidence suggests, that in general as the intervals between the benefits a social system provides for its members increase, the cohesion of the system tends to decrease, a village alliance system would be in danger of disintegrating during inactive periods.[13] Within such a system there exist a number of lower-level social systems—those built around lineage segments, lineages, and villages being among the most important—which harbor a high potential for conflict. If the cohesion of the overarching village alliance system dropped below a certain critical level, it is easy to imagine conflict between lower-level systems —which must have occurred in a muted way at the best of times—reaching dangerously divisive proportions.

Collective ritual can be viewed as one response to the latency problem. The existence of a village alliance temple with its associated ritual im-

[13] This assumes, of course, a general relationship between the degree to which a person sees a system as rewarding and his commitment to that system—an assumption supported by experiment and observation (e.g., Lott and Lott 1965).

plies, at least to the devout, that the residents of an alliance are continually being provided with supernatural benefits—through individual worship at the temple, through the frequent performance of ritual on their behalf by the temple's miao-chu, through the annual god's birthday activities, and through the temple's geomantic influence. The benefits that flow from a village alliance temple thus greatly increase the frequency of perceived rewards from the village alliance system, and should therefore contribute to system maintenance.

It might be expected that the system maintenance role of the alliance temple would be considerably reduced in the case of lineage-dominated alliances, most of whose residents share participation in another ritual system—the one centering on ancestral worship. The latter system, with its ideology of benefit from collective worship of ancestral spirits and the geomantic influence of common ancestral graves and ancestral halls, should also provide a steady flow of perceived rewards and thus contribute to system maintenance in much the same fashion as a village alliance temple. Although I have not gathered systematic data on this question, my impression is that, as a rule, alliance temples are more elaborate and more heavily patronized in non-lineage-dominated village alliances.

A question of some importance is why lineage-dominated village alliances do generally have alliance temples when ancestral worship seems to offer an alternative system-maintenance mechanism. One possible answer has to do with the fact that in most cases at least a few outsiders reside within a lineage-dominated alliance. Indeed, if one views women who marry into a lineage as non-members, as New Territories people apparently do, the proportion of non-lineage members resident in a lineage-dominated alliance is necessarily high. It may be that in these circumstances the highly particularistic ancestral cult, which restricts its benefits to lineage members, is insufficient to maintain alliance cohesion at an adequate level and must be supplemented by a more universal cult, such as that surrounding a village alliance temple.

In conclusion, village alliance temples have been an important focus of religious life in the New Territories. Traditionally, they were closely tied to an important unit of local-level social structure, the village alliance organization. The key to the intimate linkage between a village alliance temple and the alliance organization, I have argued, is the capacity of the temple and its associated ritual to alleviate the latency problem—a problem to which village alliance organizations, like all organizations with highly intermittent schedules of activity, were particularly vulnerable.

Domestic and Communal Worship in Taiwan

STEPHAN FEUCHTWANG

The place in which I most closely observed the ritual practices that I shall describe is a small town (of 1,140 persons in 1965, the year before I arrived), linked in a system of marketing, administration, and education as well as a system of festivals and feast visits with Taipei City, the commercial, industrial, and political capital of Taiwan.[1] It is situated at the confluence of two mountain streams that flow into the river basin in which Taipei City is built. At the point where the streams meet they have cut rocky gullies, leaving high above them a narrow flat area, and at the downstream angle of their confluence a broad triangle. On these areas the town's two- and three-story brick and concrete houses, shops, coal mine office, government office, school, and temple have been built. In the higher valleys of lesser streams and farther up the valleys of the main streams, the slopes are more gentle and have been terraced for paddy, orange groves, and tea gardens. The steeper slopes are cultivated for timber and sweet potato, and are bored here and there by small coal mines, the largest of which employs not more than a hundred men and women.

The town, which I shall call Mountainstreet, was settled by Chinese in the first decade of the nineteenth century. It became a market town in the next few decades, during which the temple was founded (in 1839, according to the Republican edition of the local history of Taipei hsien). The Mountainstreet temple was a branch of a temple in one of the more central market towns toward what is now Taipei City, and that temple was itself an offshoot of a temple in An-ch'i hsien, Ch'üan-chou prefecture, Fukien province, on the China mainland. The ritual

[1] Fieldwork was made possible by a fellowship from the Carnegie and Nuffield Foundations, through the London-Cornell Project in London.

affiliation to a root temple in An-ch'i is still maintained in the largest annual festival of Mountainstreet, in which a figure of the god from the temple of which Mountainstreet's is a branch visits and is carried in procession through Mountainstreet town and a festival area that includes several of the hamlets in its hinterland. The affiliation reflects the actual historical spread of settlement eastward across the Taipei Basin and into the mountains on its rim, and marks what is still a concentration in this area of descendants of immigrants from An-ch'i.

In festivals Mountainstreet people define themselves as a community. But Mountainstreet is not isolated economically, politically, or in religious practice. The first settlers must have been peasant farmers who produced camphor, dyestuffs, and timber for sale, and the history of the area has been one of increasing dependency on urban and overseas markets, especially after the introduction of tea as a major crop in 1869. Under the Japanese colonial administration truck transport stimulated the development of coal mines and the timber industry, and a government office and a primary school were built in the town. Small farmers still make up the bulk of the population of Mountainstreet and its hinterland, but no farm family is self-sufficient. At least one member of every family works as a clerk, a coal miner, or a trader.

The household is the smallest territorial unit of society for government registration. Households are also ritually defined. The mark of a fully established household—not just as a separate unit of property and budgeting, but also as a unit of membership of a community—is its domestic altar. Through their incense burners, domestic altars renew their ties to the local temple in Mountainstreet three times a year. The occasions for this are the three procession festivals, in which the temple's incense burner is carried past every household in the festival territory and incense sticks are exchanged between household representatives and the Master of the Incense Burner. The households are joined in a festival community through the selection, by divination, of one head of household as representative of each ward, and of one ward representative as Master of the Incense Burner.

I shall describe the religious system reproduced in the annual round of Mountainstreet's domestic and communal ritual, and will seek to extract the selective definition of society that the system implies. The definition itself and how it is constructed are my concern, and not either its function or its adequacy.

I should note at the outset that the performance of ritual in Mountainstreet homes implies three major categories of spiritual beings, which are arranged in pairs of cross-cutting opposition. The three are ghosts (*kui*), gods (*cieng-sin*), and ancestors (*kong-ma* or *co-kong*). One propitiates (*ce*) kui, but honors (*hok-sai, kieng-hong,* or *pai*) gods. The relation of the worshipper to the gods, but not to any other spiritual beings, is often referred to as that of disciple (*te-cu*). Kui and ancestors are together distinguished from the gods in having silver rather than gold spirit money burnt for them. Ancestors are distinguished from the other categories of spiritual beings in having an even number of incense sticks burnt to them; the other two categories are always offered an odd number of sticks.

Nearly all households, some more fully and regularly than others, perform a series of acts of domestic worship on the first and fifteenth days of every lunar month. Taking the fullest range of spiritual beings addressed on these occasions, it may be noted first of all that they are distributed spatially. Some are worshipped at the main doorway of the house, or the window of the main room when it is on the first floor, with the offerings and incense sticks being placed on the threshold and the worshipper facing outward. Others are worshipped at the domestic altar, which is at an inside, usually the back, wall of the main room (*thia:*), or guest room (*kheq-thia:*), as it is also called. In such cases the offerings and incense are placed on the altar table, and the worshipper faces it, with his or her back to the outside.

The domestic altar is most commonly called *thia:-thau,* "head of the main or guest room." When, for a formal and festive meal, guests are entertained in the main room and there is a hierarchical order of seating, the guest of honor is seated at the top of the table, nearest the domestic altar, and his host sits at the other end of the table, facing him. The order of honor goes down toward the host, with seats to the left of the place of honor taking precedence at the same level over seats to its right. The domestic altar is similarly divided, with at least two incense burners, one stage left and one stage right. Stage left are the various representations of gods known collectively as *put-kong,* or as *put-co* to those who give pride of place on their altars to the savior gods reckoned to be Buddhist. Stage right are the ancestors of the household head, or heads of two or more households sharing the altar. Ancestors are known collectively as *kong-ma.* The object representing them on the altar itself is an inscribed wooden tablet or slip of paper, never an image, although paintings and photographs of the more recent dead are often hung on nearby walls. The object that represents a god, by contrast, may be an image—a picture or a statue.

Now a household is part of a local community, which has as its own ritual focus a temple. Nearly every market town has a temple. As the guest room and the put-kong on its altar are to the household, so the temple and the gods installed in it are to the local community. Whatever the selection of gods in the temple, to the households it serves they are a fixture of the locality. The twice-monthly domestic worship is in recognition of the local temple or shrine and of the fixed gods. They may differ from the household's particular put-kong, but the gods' incense burner on the household altar is treated as a division of the local temple's main incense burner. The more punctilious will take a little ash from the temple's burner into the domestic burner when setting up a new domestic altar.

Everyone in Mountainstreet knows the name of at least one of the local temple's gods, but in any case there is a category (*sin-bieng* or cieng-sin) which includes household put-kong, the local temple's gods, and gods of smaller local shrines, and which is used by many people to refer to the gods they cannot identify but nevertheless address at the domestic altar twice a month. Depending on the number of lines commemorated, there may be more than one ancestral incense burner, but in no case is there more than one incense burner for the gods worshipped domestically. In the temple itself, on the other hand, there are incense burners specific to each enshrined god.

The local community is territorially defined. Its temple was built and its festivals are regularly financed by means of contributions collected from every household within certain territorial boundaries, with the amount of tax and the boundaries varying according to the festival. These territories are subdivided into the territories of smaller shrines, for the wards and streets of the town and the villages and hamlets of its market area. In most cases the only god represented in them is the territorial guardian, known as T'u Ti Kung. T'u Ti Kung is also always addressed, and separately named, at the domestic altar in the twice-monthly worship.

Facing outward, the worshipper invites the cieng-sin, including T'u Ti Kung, in to his altar, and sees them off again after making offerings to them. By turning outward before and after worshipping inward, the householder addresses himself to a deity that is at the center, is inside with reference to the community although outside the household itself, which is of a lower order of inclusion than the community of which it is part. When in festivals the local temple god is taken in procession past every door in the territory, each household makes offerings to it facing outward, but if possible exchanges its own incense sticks for sticks held with the temple's burner, which are then put inside, in the domestic burner.

Offerings to cieng-sin are made at the domestic altar. But other offerings in the twice-monthly ritual are presented at the threshold, facing outward, to spiritual beings never addressed through the domestic altar. Some are for the officers and troops of the local temple's gods. In northern Taiwan this offering is called *kho-kun*, "rewarding the troops." In southern Taiwan the same rite is called *siong-pieng*, "recompensing the soldiers," the same term as that used for the distribution of bonuses to the soldiers of Taiwan's living army. The local temple gods' troops guard the community against kui. Many people told me that it was particularly necessary to make twice-monthly offerings to the spirit troops in Mountainstreet because the community had not held a *ciou* (*chiao*). A ciou is a community ceremony of periodic retreat, but its profound and extremely complex symbolism is not available to the common people. Many parts of the ceremony are the professional secrets of the Taoist priests who guide the community's representatives through it. Mass participation is confined to the ceremonies that take place outside the temple, of which the most spectacular is the feeding of the kui. In this ceremony the priests come out of the temple and face out from its shut main door. The mass of the community brings embellished offerings from home to the space in front of the temple, pointing them outward, toward the kui. The people themselves, however, face the priests.

A version of this ceremony, always including the feeding of the kui, occurs at the annual temple procession festivals, and also especially, in central places larger than Mountainstreet, in the seventh lunar month. In Mountainstreet the seventh-month ceremony is still rated an important festival (*tua pai-pai*), although it is no longer celebrated communally in a temple ceremony accompanied by theatrical performances; rather, it persists as a festival of domestic ceremony, held on the first, fifteenth, and last days of the seventh month. But most Mountainstreet people have been invited to places where either ciou or the seventh-month temple ceremony is held, and so know of or have had the experience of facing the community's offerings to kui and seeing women, children, and some men, usually the sick, old, and poor, scramble for the small cakes and coins scattered by the priests in this ceremony, collecting them almost as if they were themselves kui.

At the beginning of a ciou the Taoist priests set up an altar within the temple, which establishes a yet more general order of interiority than that represented by the local temple itself. An expression of this greater generality is the representation of the community inside the temple. Only its selected representatives are allowed into the temple, and even they may not enter the central space where only the Taoists tread. The Taoists address themselves to spiritual beings in an order of inclusion in which the local temples' gods, taken in their totality, are only one element. It is to this greater order of inclusion that the domestic worship in the first, seventh, and tenth lunar months also refers. Thus, in the seventh month, on the first and fifteenth days, both spirit soldiers and kui are propitiated at the door facing outward. And on the first and fifteenth days of the first and tenth months, offerings to spirit soldiers are part of a series which includes, notably, the worship of the god or gods of heaven (Thi: Kong) facing outward at the main door. (Very few Mountainstreet households burn incense to heaven on the first and fifteenth days of other months.) Although the incense sticks to both the gods of heaven and the soldiers of the local gods are placed in the same holder or crack in the wall by the doorpost outside, the manner in which the offerings are presented makes a clear distinction between them. The offerings to the gods of heaven are set out on a raised table, whereas the offerings to the spirit soldiers are set out on a low bench. This is a spatial distinction like the inside/outside and left/right distinctions. The inside/outside distinction is often made between offerings to spirit soldiers and those to kui by placing the bench for spirit soldiers within the threshold and the presentation to kui beyond it, out of doors. The upper/lower distinction is also often used in separating these two categories of spiritual beings—spirit soldiers' offerings being placed on a bench, kui offerings on the ground. The two are distinguished in any case by the placement of incense: in the case of spirit soldiers it is placed in the holder at the door or alongside the food on the bench, whereas for kui it is stuck into the food presented to them, just as chopsticks are stuck into the food offered the spirit of a person at his or her mortuary rituals.

In conjunction with the spatial codes there is another means of making distinctions in the presentation of offerings. Offerings to the gods of heaven must not have been presented previously to any other deity, whereas the offerings to the spirit soldiers may consist of food that has already been presented to the gods of heaven and the other gods. This means of distinction introduces an entirely different kind of order altogether than the spatial codes taken on their own: a sequential order of access to offerings of food. It makes a pattern of movement from the outside to the inside, then from stage left to stage right, and back outside again: first gods of heaven, then local and domestic gods, then T'u Ti Kung; next there usually follow first ancestors, then spirit soldiers, and finally kui.

This order of privilege constitutes a syntagmatic, hierarchical, order. It brings continuity into the order of the pantheon and of the relations of its celebrants to the categories of spiritual beings, which the spatial order, taken on its own, does not. The spatial order is discontinuous and paradigmatic, an order of contrasts, and a similarly paradigmatic order occurs in the preparation of food offerings. They are ordered in two respects. One is according to their readiness for consumption: whether or not cooked, whether or not cut up, whether or not served with chopsticks. The other is according to their purity: whether or not vegetarian, whether or not sweet (= pure), whether or not great care is taken to keep them clean. Thus certain cieng-sin associated with Buddhism or with asceticism, Buddhist or no, are offered sweets and fruit, while their soldiers receive meat. But in addition, as with any gift, the exchange value of the offering introduces an ordinal, not a contrasting, order. The gods of heaven are offered the cleanest, purest (often vegetarian), and most valued food on the raised table, while meat and other, less valuable foods are placed behind it on a lower table for their retinue of lesser gods. Where expensive meat is offered to the gods, gods' soldiers and kui are offered only rice and vegetables and smaller amounts of less expensive meat, or such meat substitutes as egg and soy-cake. Whereas cieng-sin in general, including T'u Ti Kung, are offered uncut food without chopsticks, and the gods of heaven uncooked food, gods' soldiers and ancestors are offered cooked and cut-up food with chopsticks. Offerings to kui lack chopsticks and, an inversion of the top extreme, consist of uncooked but cheap food. Here we see that the exchange values of food offerings, like privilege in access to them, have the function of establishing continuity.

We have already seen that the internal/external code constitutes an order of inclusion, of domestic gods to local gods, and of these to the more universal gods of heaven. Thus, we find in the domestic and communal rituals of Mountainstreet three orders: a paradigmatic order of spatial contrasts, a syntagmatic order of sequence and expense, and an order of inclusion. The first distinguishes the spiritual beings into several classes; the second establishes order and continuity between the classes; while the third arranges the classes as parts of ever more inclusive categories.

Calendrical Contrast and Continuity

To begin to see how the three kinds of order work together, I turn now to the calendar of fixed days of annual worship and to an analysis of three such days in particular. This triad of domestic festivals can be expounded as referring, in sequence, to Heaven, Earth, and Man; to Heaven, Earth, and Water; to Heaven, Man, and Earth; or to Heaven, Water, and Earth.[2] Their formal written names, as found in common almanacs, are the upper, middle, and lower principles or points of origin (*shang yüan, chung yüan,* and *hsia yüan*). But they are known to most people in Mountainstreet only by their lunar dates: the fifteenth of the first lunar month, fifteenth of the seventh, and fifteenth of the tenth. The first and second refer in practice, as must already be clear, respectively to heaven and to purgatory. Both are primarily domestic in Mountainstreet. But the third coincides with Mountainstreet's largest temple festival. It is, indeed, paired with the first month's worship in its subject. Both are addressed to all three cosmological divisions taken at once, as a set either of brothers or of officers appointed by the god of heaven or simply as the gods of heaven (Sam Kai Kong, or Sam Kuan Tai Te, or Thi: Kong).

The three days are, then, in Mountainstreet paired off as follows: the two heavenly days, one of them more domestic and the other more communal, against the day of purgatory. All three are, in the orientation of domestic ritual, outward-facing, but the communal day, oriented toward the local temple and its visiting figure from the root temple in the central place of the next higher level, is only relatively outward-facing, as I have shown earlier. The other two refer to a more inclusive order, the one outward and up, the other outward and down.

A more extended analysis of these two domestic days of worship, the fifteenth of the first month and fifteenth of the seventh, and their ritual seasons gives us an idea of the structural components of domestic ritual's most general order. The deities celebrated at shang yüan, the fifteenth of the first, are for many people in Mountainstreet indistinguishable from the deities celebrated on New Year's Day and on the ninth day of the first month. All are known by the general term Thi: Kong. In any case shang yüan is both the first of the triad of annual festivals and one of the last festivals of the New Year's season. Shang yüan is linked to chung yüan by virtue of their shared association with seasons

---

[2] In a 1940 handbook I bought in Taiwan (*Tao-i i-wen chiao-ta* [Answers to questions about the right way], prefaced by Kuo T'ing-tung), a paragraph (p. 16) on the three kinds of *p'u-tu* festival explains them as: (1) the Upper, crossing the rivers of stars and dippers, the heavenly breaths (*ch'i*), and all those who have achieved immortality (*hsien*); (2) the Middle, crossing the world of men, plants, and all living things; (3) the Lower, crossing the Department of Earth, the dark and somber kuei and souls (*hun*). In a Taoist handbook—*Tao-chiao yüan-liu*—kindly summarized for me by Michael Saso, the order is (1) Heaven, (2) Earth, (3) Man. In a common Taiwanese almanac in my possession, the order is (1) Heaven, (2) Earth, (3) Water.

that emphasize ancestor worship. Indeed, it was remarked to me on New Year's Day that it and the seventh month were the year's two most important occasions for the worship of ancestors. In both seasons the predominant motif is, then, one of contrast between inward-facing worship of ancestors and the outward-facing offerings. In both cases gods mediate inside with outside: the emphasis in the one case is on the mediation of household with heaven, in the other on the mediation of household with purgatory. But the two cases differ in the character of the mediation and of the social unity that it confirms.

The difference is manifest in the diachronic organization of each season. The outer limits of the New Year's season fluctuate, but its center is fixed. The outermost possible limits are two T'u Ti Kung celebrations, the last day of the old year and the first of the new year, i.e., the sixteenth day of the twelfth month and the second day of the second month. The innermost possible dates for the New Year's season are the days of seeing off and welcoming back the household gods, i.e., the twenty-fourth day of the twelfth month and the fourth day of the first. Between the two brackets in the first month, apart from the already mentioned days for worshipping the gods of heaven, fall a number of days of worship whose exact date varies according to the worshipper's occupation and what the almanac indicates is the correct day for reopening business.[3] The seventh-month festival season, in contrast, has its outer limits fixed unvaryingly on the first and last days of the month. In the New Year's season before shang yüan, craft and commerce have particular times of celebration as if they were still following a guild system. But the celebrations are performed by and on behalf of each separate firm or household. In the seventh month around chung yüan, as at New Year's, guilds—and particularly merchant guilds, before they disappeared during the Japanese occupation of Taiwan—sponsored *p'u-tu*, the feeding of kui, on days that varied according to their patron deity. P'u-tu are celebrations on behalf of a locality, and the guilds were making a civic contribution to their section of town or city in sponsoring these festivals. In Taipei City in imperial times, each street or ward held a p'u-tu on a different day (Kataoka 1924: 61–62). In Mountainstreet, each settlement in the area used to hold a p'u-tu on a different day of the seventh month, in a series of rival processions, feasts, and cross-invitations.

[3] In the days following New Year's, the patron deities of various occupations are celebrated by their practitioners in their several places of work, especially on the tenth day of the first month, the day of Kuan Ti, patron of businessmen in general. In Mountainstreet, for instance, the Taoist ritual practitioner, the pig gelder, the herbalists, and the smiths all had their separate gods to worship on different days.

It must not be forgotten, of course, that ancestors are honored in the seventh month as well as at New Year's, but again it is done in a different way in the seventh month, accommodating social units larger than the household and with more of a neighborhood definition. In Mountainstreet and the nearby settlements, families and small local lineages worship their ancestors on different days within the seventh month, again allowing for cross-invitation of guests, whereas at New Year's all households worship their ancestors individually and at the same time.

The seventh month is the opening and closing of the doors of purgatory, the release of kui, which mingle with the ancestors of the locality during the month until they are shut outside it again on the last day. While the doors are open each territory and local lineage in turn feasts members of other territories and local lineages, along with their own kui and ancestors.

Instead of the doors of cemeteries, graves, and shrines of the unknown dead being in theory if not in fact opened and closed, in New Year's ritual it is the household that closes and opens again. The time of complete closure is the fixed point of the New Year, the moment of transition from old to new. That turning point is marked by a household feast at which all members are seated at the table together in the guest room. The household should be complete, and, whether or not in fact a new charcoal stove is lit under the table, its completion is called ui-lo, "around the stove." Immediately before the feast, offerings are made to the household ancestors and foundation spirit (Te Ki Co). Thus the household is ritually defined. The ancestors are worshipped in the main room at the domestic altar, the foundation spirit at the threshold to the kitchen or in the kitchen itself. In other parts of China the Stove God (Tsao Chün) is or was singled out for worship at the send-off of the household gods, a practice emphasizing that the unit is a household and not a larger descent group. In Mountainstreet the same emphasis is achieved by the name ui-lo for the New Year's feast and by the worship of Te Ki Co immediately before it.

Te Ki Co is an ambivalent category of spirit, worshipped inside but not at the domestic altar, and with silver money not with gold; he has been interpreted to me variously as the household's own T'u Ti Kung and as kui, and most consistently likened to the landlord of the house, his propitiation at New Year's being seen as rent. The social unit at New Year's Day is, then, the smallest descent group and territorial unit that can ritually be isolated: the household, its particular ancestors, and its particular kui or territorial guardian.

The household gods have, according to the accompanying myth, been sent off to report to heaven. There has been an estrangement between heaven and earth, a break. Earth is threatened with extinction. Many variations on this myth are told in Mountainstreet. Common to all of them is the theme that the disaster does not occur; they vary in their explanation of the threat of disaster, and in whether its non-occurrence is accounted for. All versions are an explanation of the congratulations exchanged as greetings on the first days of the New Year: people exchange congratulations on finding each other alive. New clothes and shoes are worn. The incense on the domestic altar has been renewed, this being the only time when it may be changed. New Year's Day is everyone's simultaneous birthday. The gods are welcomed back and heaven is worshipped. This New Year sequence is a reestablishment of order. In reestablishing its relation with heaven, the household's own hierarchical order is asserted. Only the male head of the household may address heaven. His wife may worship the ancestors. Children of the household, and, on another day, employees of a firm, are given bonuses by parents and bosses. The hierarchical order of worshipped beings is apparent at New Year's as at no other time because at this time all the spirits and deities of domestic worship are addressed in turn and the rule of privileged access to food must be applied. On the one hand, in the worship of ancestors, the continuity of the household as a patrilineal descent group is re-created. On the other hand, its continuity on earth as base unit of a cosmic empire is guaranteed in the worship of heaven and the return of the gods.

The asymmetry and continuity of New Year's order contrasts strongly with the symmetry and discontinuity of the order of territorial units and the separation of outsiders (kui) from insiders (ancestors) that is established by the end of the seventh month. The gods that mediate inside and outside are not, in the seventh month, the internal gods of the domestic shrine, but gods that face outward, erected outside temple doors. They are the controllers of kui, in Mountainstreet variously called Pho To Kong (gods of the p'u-tu) and Lau Tua Kong and likened to jailers. They are in an ambivalent category, like Te Ki Co, worshipped outside and facing outward, but with gold. They are separators of the living and their ancestors from kui.

A second kind of god worshipped in the seventh month is a charitable savior who redeems kui from purgatory for rebirth or paradise. This kind of god is worshipped inside at the domestic altar; it stands for the continuity of a particular person between life and death, but not between the groups of the living society and the mass of kui. Its chief example in Mountainstreet, sitting on a lotus pedestal at the top

of the standard altar-print stuck on the wall at the stage left side of domestic altars, is the bodhisattva (*pho-sat*) Kuan Yin. She is both savior
of individual souls and protector of individual births, and it is to her
that many women in Mountainstreet address themselves at New Year's,
seeking fertility for themselves and good health for their infants.

To sum up the analysis of New Year and seven-month ritual, in
New Year ritual the unit is the household and its ancestors, and it is in
a subordinate position to the main deity worshipped, who is the supreme
deity or group of deities. Between the supreme deity and the small base
unit are on the one hand the mass of gods, and on the other an individual savior god and a household god. In seventh-month ritual the
unit is a neighborhood and its constituents are the ancestors. This territorial unit is in complementary opposition with other such units and
with masses of kui. Between them, between the territorial group and
the mass of kui, are single guardian gods and individual savior gods.
At New Year's a continuity is reestablished that involves a hierarchical
relation, whereas in the seventh month a discontinuity is reestablished
that involves a symmetrical relation of opposition.

Re-creation of a Metaphor

Gods, gods' soldiers, ancestors, and kui are all thought of as former
human beings. They inhabit heaven (*Thi:*) and purgatory (*te-gak*, literally "earth-prisons"), separated and mediated by the world of man.
The world of man is often referred to as the living or yang world (*iong-
kan*), and contrasted with the world of the dead and of kui, which is
then called the yin world, *im-kan*. The living world mediates the two
parts of the other world as a social structure into which the various
offices of the other world fit and make their power felt, and through
which there is communication by ritual.

The beings of the other world once conceived can be considered by
the people of Mountainstreet metonymically as extensions of life and
metaphorically as symbols of life. The beings of the other world are not
in a direct relationship to the living world. Death is the point of discontinuity in the relationship; it renders them inaccessible to all the
senses of the living. They are accessible only through a ritual code, which
selects and transforms living concrete actions into a negation of the living
concrete world, creating a world which is *as if* living and concrete, a
world in which the beings "eat" the food that is offered them before it
is eaten concretely by the living. Rituals and beings from the other
world, both of them selections from the living and their behavior, are
thus *symbols* of the living concrete world. The separation and selection

from it of these symbols, however arbitrary they be and however anach-
ronistic they may have become, make possible the contemplation of the
concrete world. But what is metaphor or ideal or image is also made
into metonym and an existence directly related to experiential being.
Pragmatic results in the living world after "communication" with its
negation complete the realization of the metaphor. The living look upon
the living world as an extension of the work of the beings of the other
world, as well as looking upon the other world as one into which living
subjects enter on death.

The extension of the human being after death is extension of a parent after death as an ancestor, or of any self after death either in paradise, in permanent purgatory, or through purgatory to rebirth. Ancestor
worship and the lineal succession to it ensure a generational extension
of the existence of the now dead through the now living. The worship
of ancestors is the use of the biological fact of birth selectively for social classification and for claims on certain kinds of social relationships.
One is born into a socially established selective relationship with one's
parents. By the same selective principle and parentage, one is born into
a relationship to certain of the dead and through a parent and these
selected dead to certain others of the living. A break in the extensions
from life into death and death into life produces one definition of kui,
as orphan souls (*ko-hun*), those who have no descendants to worship
them as ancestors. Ancestors may become orphan souls if their descendants neglect them, whether because of separation from their home
and its ancestral altar or out of indifference or carelessness. Indeed, as
I was told not only by ritual specialists but also by two non-specialist
inhabitants of Mountainstreet, upon death all souls (*lieng-hun*) are kui,
or *kui-sin.* It is only in being remembered, ritually, that they become
spirits or gods (sin or sin-bieng). *Hou hia:-ti,* "the good brothers," the
most common euphemism for kui, have been expounded to me as *bou
sun e kui,* "kui without descendants."

Forgotten/remembered is a code by which the mass of undifferentiated dead is broken up. As a social object the mass of undifferentiated
dead is the undifferentiated history of the society of living persons. By
means of the forgotten/remembered code, the dead past and the live
present with its social forms become metaphors, one for the other. But
death is also a moment of discontinuity between the individual creature
and society's ongoing history. There is no equivalent point in that history itself, except perhaps a revolution resulting in such a profound
transformation that a society's present form could be seen as discontinuous with its previous form. As a biological reality men and women

are subject to the one kind of duration, and as a social reality to the other. The ritual code of remembering by worship establishes a relation of continuity between social time and its biological equivalent. By means of metonym, a relation of part to whole, continuity is established between the two kinds of time and between past and present, individual and group. By metonym the biological death of individual men and women is conceived of as the link between past person and present social group or between present person and present social group, and it also serves to link a number of present social groups related to a particular dead person. But the dead are also conceived metaphorically as a society of souls and spirits equivalent to the living social world. And as such, by rituals other than ancestor worship, this equivalence is realized in a relation of continuity between the social world and social history and their supernatural counterparts; for the inhabitants of the supernatural world are also present and influential in the events of natural time and the places of territorial space.

Funerals and deathday celebrations of ancestors pick out particular dead persons for the social definition and differentiation of living groups —household, branch, lineage, surname association. But funerals also establish a relation of continuity with a dead person as a soul in the world of souls and spirits. That relation is set up by a continuity between equivalents in the two worlds. The other, supernatural world is re-created diachronically in a lunar ceremonial calendar and synchronically in geomantic space, making possible at the same time calendrical and geomantic mediations between elements of the social world and the world beyond death. Standard forms of social communication between social persons in a historical past are used in ritual to mediate between living and dead worlds.

The ceremonies for the dead will show how ritual accomplishes this dual task of re-creating both continuity and discontinuity. Mortuary rituals in Taiwan are twofold. On the one hand are the ceremonies in which the dead person is mourned by the social segment of which he or she was part, led by its representatives and allies. On the other hand are the ceremonies in which the living take care of the dead as a particular person in the world beyond death through the mediation and under the guidance of specialists in ritual. I refer, of course, to Taoist and Buddhist priests. The kinship-segment aspect of the mortuary rituals leads eventually to deathday and to chosen spring and autumn days of ancestor worship. The world-beyond-death aspect, or eschatological ritual, leads into fixed calendrical ritual such as that of the seventh month.

In mortuary rituals and the subsequent ancestral worship, the dead are divided according to a single principle: whether or not they are worshipped. They are, in other words, selected. While the dead are still known it is possible ritually to revive them as ancestors. A diviner may attribute a sickness or some other misfortune to the neglect of an ancestral spirit; the troublesome spirit is always one alive within a generation or two, usually one within living memory. These diviners, who mediate between the worlds of the living and the dead, are, like the priests, a class of initiates with a special skill or gift. So far as I know, they are always either spirit mediums possessed by gods able to describe the state of the soul in purgatory, or else shamans, usually women who travel in spirit to the other world, and known in Mountainstreet as *khan-bong-hun*, "drawer-up of dead souls." Known but unworshipped, the dead are kui. Known and worshipped, they are ancestors. As records and memories fade, they become less known and less defined, masses of kui and masses of cursory ancestors whose deathdays go unobserved and who are worshipped only on the occasions in the ritual calendar when ancestors are statutorily worshipped as a category, collectively and not by name.

Jordan (1972: 134–40) has given an explanation based on social structure for the retrieval of spirits from oblivion: "to be troubled by a family ghost I must first *have* a family ghost. . . . If I know there is such a one among my family dead and I suspect that it is the cause of my problems, I am likely to go to a medium whose god is known to be capable of handling family ghosts." He concludes, I think correctly, that it is only the structurally anomalous kin who are remembered in this way. Certainly, I know of no claim that a direct and indubitable agnatic ancestor had at one point been forgotten and then subsequently installed for the first time on the domestic altar. A dead person may be said to cause misfortune or disruption to draw attention to some unfilial act, but in such cases she or he is acting as an ancestor not wanting to become a kui, and not as a kui wanting to become an ancestor.

The periods of selection and progressive phasing out of memory are marked off by the sequence of ceremonies: death, burial, calendrical days of mourning, merit-making, domestic deathday worship, second burial, and establishment as ancestor in lineage hall, ancestral home, or hall of a surname association. These ceremonies constitute a weeding out, a process of exclusion. The process involves an escalation of social exclusiveness—the greater the ceremonial, the greater the role of wealth and the desire for status in determining who is worshipped as an ancestor. Those weeded out, without wealth or status, are in limbo, orphan souls.

Mortuary ritual is a process of definition, a simultaneous extension and separation, the isolation of the mourning group from other groups, affines, and neighbors, and of the deceased from the living. A few elements in the minimal, least expensive, form of mortuary ritual for an adult in Mountainstreet should make the process clear. It begins with the making or buying of a table and a lamp at death; it ends with their being cast out after burial. The table carries the provisions of food for the deceased, and the incense for communication with him or her. The lamp, which is never allowed to go out, is placed on the table in the position that permits the spirit of the deceased to view his or her old home. Table and lamp are placed by the corpse, which is laid out in the main room. The domestic altar shelf is shrouded. As the ritual was explained to me, the deceased's soul, in wandering about after death, realizes it is dead when, while drinking or washing in special water, it notices its hands are beginning to rot.[4] It then returns home in sorrow. A bamboo and paper stand, sometimes inscribed *wang hsiang t'ai*, "platform for viewing home," must be erected on the table around the lamp and the mourning household must begin to wail by the time the sorrowing soul returns if the soul is to have a sympathetic welcome and not be left an orphan. Wailing is response, communication. On the other hand the dead one is firmly kept apart in a variety of symbolic statements. The incense container on the table, like the table itself, has been created specifically for this funeral, for this soul and no other. Into it, or into the coffin with the corpse, is placed a boiled egg or a stone. The message conveyed by the egg, as repeated to me, is "When this egg hatches you may join your descendants"; and by the stone, "When this stone powders (or melts) you can return to your family."

Some time after burial, some ash from the incense container is transferred to the ancestral incense burner on the main room altar. The deceased is henceforth worshipped on special days, but along with the household's other ancestors. The shroud is removed from the altar, but not before the table and all that stood on it, lamp and special incense container, are discarded and burned. This is an act of separating the dead from the living: "we no longer share the same things." Between the installation and destruction of the table, the passage to ancestral status is marked by a series of ambivalent statements of the kind already mentioned, statements that separate mourners from the dead one and also isolate those in contact with the dead one from the rest of the living in layers that reflect the degree of closeness to the deceased. In affixing

[4] The water is variously described as "soul water" to which T'u Ti Kung leads the soul, as water provided by the soul's own household, and as the water of the Frozen Water Pit (*lieng-cui khi*).

the degrees of mourning required, classes of affines are distinguished
from the lineal descendants of the dead one, and, in grades of nar-
rower distinction, collaterals from immediate descendants and daughters and granddaughters from sons and grandsons. Each degree is reflected in the duration of the prohibition against participation in the
rituals of the living, such as making New Year's cake or representing
the community at its temple festival. The outermost circle, the immediate neighbors of mourners and all those who have helped with funeral
preparations, are given firecrackers, charms, and other ritual means by
which to dissociate themselves immediately from the dead "so that
we may worship gods again." Households along the routes of burial
adopt the same means. The main doors of Mountainstreet's temple are
always closed when a burial procession passes, just as the altar shelf
of the mourners' own home is masked before the spirit of the corpse
is cast out. The gravesite is guarded by a special category of territorial
guardian called Hou T'u on the graveside inscription, distinguished in
ritual and myth from the T'u Ti Kung that guards hamlet, street, or
ward territory. In the common classification of rituals, those of mourning are, along with the exorcism of ill luck such as sickness, contrasted
with the rituals of birth and marriage, of chiao and celebrations of local
gods. The former are called *song-su* or *hiong-su*, "affairs of mourning or
misfortune," the latter are *hi-su* or *kiat-su*, "affairs of happiness or good
fortune."

Thus in mortuary ritual a continuity between living groups and a
particular dead person, a metonymic relation, is first asserted and then
broken, and two worlds and kinds of event ritually defined. The dead
are cast into another world, as kui and as sin, and ritual itself is divided
into (1) communication with the individual soul of a dead person or a
person in danger of death, and (2) communication with the beings of
the other world as equivalents of the living.

The ritual concept of *lieng* is a key to the ambivalence between continuity and discontinuity. I referred earlier to the distinction between
the representation of gods by an image and of ancestors by a tablet.
A consecrated image can be thought to have immanent power to respond, i.e., lieng or *lieng-kam*. A tablet, even when consecrated after
burial of the deceased, cannot. It is true that the soul (*hun*) is referred
to as lieng in the binome lieng-hun also meaning soul, but this refers to
soul as the extension of an individual person after death, not as a being
incorporated into a social group as ancestor. Lieng is identified not so
much with the gods or kui, past selves, as with the things or events by
which they are known, and it is both affirmed and denied in the most

current explanations given in Mountainstreet, which hold lieng to be a function of the reputation people have given the gods of their choice.[5]

One other ritual concept is a key to this ambivalence. The power of a place as such, without implication of another immanent presence, is called *hong-cui* (= *feng-shui*), its geomantic properties. Every grave and every house has properties that can be divined either by pure geomancy or with additional reference to an active principle that is subject to propitiation. The configurations of the earth, of the whole universe, are, according to Chinese metaphysics and geomancy, configurations of activity called *ch'i*, which are formed by the interflowing of the two powers yin and yang and the five forces (*wu hsing*). Depending on the relative strength of their yin and yang properties, the configurations of ch'i are referred to in almanacs and other manuals of geomancy as either *kui* (= *kuei*) or *sin* (= *shen*). Kui in this usage are metaphysical forces with a high yin component. In popular usage yin is associated with malevolence as well as death, yang with beneficence as well as life. So kui are to be avoided like death, and sin to be sought after for the cultivation of life-giving force. Points of the compass and times of day, month, year, and sixty-year cycle can be matched with a person's horoscope, and in almanacs general malevolent or beneficent properties of particular times are calculated.

The gradations between ancestors, gods, fixed active principles, and the properties of a place on earth or in the universe are many and fine. They are partly represented in the structure of domestic worship as relative interiority. The same relation may also be broadly understood as relative mobility: the earth relative to the human groups that move across it; the universe relative to the gods and kui that move within it. A household with its domestic altar of gods and ancestors moves in relation to the relatively fixed points of the temples of its ancestral home and subsequent places of residence and of the graves of the ancestors and the ancestral home or hall itself. The domestic altar thus represents a selection made in the course of migration, as families accumulate, discard, and retain ritual alignments. But the local temple, to which the domestic altar is related as mobile to a fixed point, is itself mobile in relation to two other yet more fixed points. The incense of the temple's

---

[5] As examples of the range of opinion about lieng in Mountainstreet, here are three people's answers to the question "Which god is most lieng?" "Most lieng-kam [responsive] is the god most people say is lieng-kam. They are all the same. It depends on one's own personal experience." "How lieng-kam a god is depends on people saying how lieng he is." "The most lieng are hou-hia:-ti ["the good brothers," i.e. kui], because they are scattered and uncontrolled sin [spirits] not bound by principle and will do anything if you feed them."

burner may derive from a division of an older temple's burner, and so on back to the temple at which the cult of its main deity originated. Each branch incense burner and image is a branch manifestation of that deity, but each of them is also related to the fixed properties of the place it inhabits and to the relatively immobile tutelary deities of place as such, typified as T'u Ti Kung. T'u Ti Kung are not the multiple manifestations of a single cult, as are, for instance, the myriad representations of Kuan Ti, patron of the military and mercantile occupations, and the thousands of temples to him throughout Taiwan and, formerly, the rest of China. The various kinds of T'u Ti Kung are a multiplicity of gods of fixed locations, without a cult center. Their relation to their locations may be conceived of as a posting, and T'u Ti Kung the title of a low office. On the other hand kui, the souls of those who have died a violent death and so retain unspent yang force, are also said to be fixed to a place, the place of their death. The relation of human spirit to property or place is even closer in the conception of Te Ki Co, god of the house foundations, and Hou T'u, god of the gravesite. And the relation is inverted, the human replaced as the monstrous, in the conceptions of Pe Ho, white tiger, and Lieng, dragon, which are the names of cosmological non-human principles of a place itself, and similarly inverted in the general conception of kui as the yin properties of a place, which may be pacified (an) and propitiated (ce) on the advice of diviners.

Thus mortuary and calendrical ritual is simultaneously intelligible as the reproduction of a metaphor of supersocial and supernatural beings and the metonym of an active universe combining person and place. Metonymically, each altar and each place is both a micro-universe, an active subject in itself, and understandable as a part of a greater whole—domestic altar unit to temple altar unit, T'u Ti Kung territory to temple god territory, geomantic site to cosmological configuration of time or place.

The Structure of the Religious Metaphor

In religious thought the relation of the gods to the natural world they inhabit and control is equated with political and judicial life. Heaven and earth in this sense are known as *hu*, "courts," or "prefectures." The sun, moon, five planets, and five dippers are the positions (not necessarily identified with observable heavenly bodies) of the hu of heaven. They have earthly counterparts, such as the five sacred mountains. Knowledge of their names is left to the experts, diviners and priests, who act as lawyers and bureaucrats issuing petitions and passes and advising and guiding the client through the sacred protocol and squeeze.

The structure of the religious world is described in terms of the present form of government. Mountainstreet people tell one that T'u Ti Kung is like the chief of the local police substation. And indeed, as guardians of peace and security with the most limited territorial definition, T'u Ti Kung do represent the "jurisdiction" of the local temple and the wider territory of the city god (Ch'eng Huang Yeh).[6] This jural hierarchy figures prominently in stories and in popular theater and puppet shows, with police and detective underlings controlling kui, and gods of higher bureaucratic rank controlling the lifespans of men and women and their fates after death. Kui are likened, by present-day Mountainstreet people, to rootless wanderers and the secret brotherhoods of protection gangs and bandits that used to abound in local-level politics.

Kui and T'u Ti Kung between them mark social territorial boundaries that have ancestors and local kin or compatriot groups and their gods as centers. T'u Ti Kung mark these boundaries from the inside, kui from the outside. We have already seen this to be so in domestic ritual, but it also works with respect to the local community as a whole. Just as the local T'u Ti Kung is supposed to protect one on journeys abroad, and just as it is a matter of common courtesy to burn incense in the temple of the god of any place to which one travels, so kui are supposed particularly to haunt paths, streams, and bridges. Kui connote the dangers of the road, of bandits and strangers, and of accidents beyond the reach of familiar people that put one in danger of becoming a kui oneself. Kui mark the edge of the home community. One euphemism for kui is *gua-sin*, "outsider spirit."

A few hundred yards from Mountainstreet the road that links it to the more central places in its marketing system passes through a tunnel. The tunnel marks the edge of Mountainstreet's local marketing area and of that area as a community centered on Mountainstreet town and its temple. "Within the tunnel," *tong-lai*, as the area is widely known, people use Mountainstreet's shops, send their children to its primary school, and share its temple's festivals. The people "beyond the tunnel," *tong-gua*, go elsewhere for these things. A great many stories of the haunting of the tunnel are told. One of the kui supposed to haunt it is a former gangster of the kind I have mentioned who came from the nearest market town "beyond the tunnel." He had a secret liaison with

---

[6] I was often told, "When you go out, you depend on [or, "you are the guest of"] T'u Ti Kung" or variants of this (*Chut mng, ciaq Tho Te Kong*). The function of the local temple god as territorial guardian is dealt with more fully in Feuchtwang 1974.

a married woman of Mountainstreet and paid her a visit the night of the
lantern festival (*shang yüan*), despite warnings from a diviner that he
was doomed if he went out that day, and from the Japanese police that
someone in Mountainstreet was after his life. As he made his way back
home in the middle of the night, three people hired by the cuckolded
husband killed him at the entrance to the tunnel.

Another haunting of the tunnel resulted in what amounts to a fatal
ritual accident. In a ritual no longer performed in Mountainstreet the
Taoist priest exorcised "outsider spirits" with a straw figure that was
then discarded, in this case at the tunnel. On one occasion the straw
figure was found there by a boy, who, it was said, kicked it and uri-
nated on it, and as a consequence died urinating blood soon after returning home.

At the outermost boundary of culture and society, kui are the equivalent of foreigners and aborigines, and Mountainstreet's local temple
god, Ang Kong, is said to have defended that boundary. Short of the
border with non-Chinese are lesser borders marking sub-cultural breaks
between regions, which were defended in their turn in the names of
their gods. Communal battles occasionally became serious enough to
warrant the dispatching of central government troops to suppress them,
always with the help of loyalist volunteers from one of the contending
sides, the other side then being treated as bandits. The dead of both
volunteers and bandits had collective shrines built for their bones, either
because individually they were unidentifiable and could not be returned to their ancestral homes, because they were too young to have
descendants, or because they had died violently and before their allotted
span was up—all these eventualities leading to trapped, uncontrolled
souls, i.e. to kui. But the loyalists were honored kui, their shrines frequently adorned by an official inscription, and there are even cases of
such shrines becoming new ritual foci for the compatriots of the slain
combatants, the spirits being, to them, beneficent rather than malevolent, honored rather than propitiated. By dint of special ritual care,
possibly instituted with the building for the dead of a temple to a savior
or guardian god, these potentially malevolent souls were saved.

The assistants of these savior gods, and some controllers of kui, are
themselves known to be redeemed kui.[7] They are described and de-

---

[7] Shrines for these ambivalent righteous kui go by several names. In Mountainstreet their shrines were called either Iu-ieng Kiong (*Iu-ieng* meaning "responsive")
or Tua-bong Kiong (big grave or mass grave shrines), which were more responsive;
there was also a special type of shrine for so-called Saintly Women (Sia: Ma) who
died childless. One such shrine in Mountainstreet was considered particularly efficacious. In Hsin-chuang district, Taipei hsien, a Iu-ieng Kiong (Yu-ying Kung

picted as having monstrous attributes, whereas gods higher in the heavenly order are fully human with dignified trappings and iconography modeled after imperial mandarins. In pictures of purgatory, such as those hung by priests at mortuary ceremonies for guiding the soul through purgatory, the souls in purgatory are also shown with fully human, though tormented, attributes, while their tormentors, the assistants of the mandarin-like judges of the purgatorial courts, have cleft heads or some other emblem of monstrosity. These monsters of humanity on the border between kui and gods, like the monsters of nature on the border between place and spirit, are the products in mythical knowledge of the transformation or solution of a relation of contrast or equivalence into one of continuity, the transition from kui into god, and from the natural into the supernatural.

Local warfare was brought to an end when a strong central government was established in Taipei City. But local rivalries are still expressed in religious festivals. Neighboring localities celebrate the same god but on different days try to outdo one another in the munificence of their feasts and the magnificence of their processions. Every small town or market area has at least one band, or a troupe of traditional military gymnasts or lion dancers, that competes with neighboring troupes for invitations to participate in distant festivals. Within its area it automatically accompanies the local god in procession. After the procession, the different contingents compete for invitations to individual households, a competition that often ends in scuffles.

The bands and troupes are frequently formed of just such brotherhoods as those people likened to kui, yet they accompany and perform for the local god in the first place and for the good luck of households in the second. As one lion dancer told me, they are acting out their offer

---

in Mandarin) for the bones of the dead after battles between descendants of immigrants from Ch'üan-chou and immigrants from Chang-chou in Fukien province had an adjacent savior god temple that won wide repute. The savior god was Ti Ts'ang Wang, king of the underworld and usually, as is likely in this case since the temple was called Tz'u-pei Ssu (temple of charity), presented as a bodhisattva, i.e., a being who has achieved buddhahood but renounces or postpones it to save the world. A similar shrine for the bones of dead combatants in another part of Taipei hsien was called Ta Chung Yeh, which is a common title given to kui guardians; and in Taipei City, in fact, a Ta Chung Yeh temple stands side by side with a Ti Ts'ang Wang temple. Also in Taipei City, the famous Hsia-hai Ch'eng-huang Temple, whose main god is of the type often labeled by Mountainstreet people as a judge and as a guardian of kui, has next to it a side shrine to the 38 T'ung-an martyrs, who died rescuing the figure of the god from a fire. Their savior god, in the same side shrine, is the bodhisattva Kuan Yin. For the records of all the above shrines and other cases in point (except the Mountainstreet and two Taipei City shrines, which can be observed now), see Li 1962: 72; Liu 1963: 72–77; and Ino 1928: 1, 41–42.

to be in military service to the god in the manner of the times when the god was alive. In other words, they act as mortal equivalents of spirit soldiers, not of kui. Indeed, to my knowledge kui are never propitiated as a group, only singly or as an undifferentiated mass. Nor have I seen them depicted in bands or any other formation of their own. The mortal equivalents of kui are beggars at the seventh-month festival and other occasions involving charitable distributions to the masses of kui (i.e. at any p'u-tu), when beggars are entitled to claim the food offered.[8]

Conclusion

I conclude with the proposal that gods are a metaphor for the system of authority, the state. The metaphor is one of gods as rulers and judges and the mass of kui as beggars and supplicants being judged and saved by the gods. Yet kui are also broken extensions of the living into this domain. And though gods are neither kui nor ancestors, they and ancestors are placed in the same category (sin) and worshipped as insiders, in contrast with kui, worshipped as outsiders. Where god is to a locality like the imperial bureaucrat, a stranger with authority, and ancestor a native of the locality, kui is unwelcome stranger and outcast native. Gods and kui are to ancestors as metaphor is to metonym. Yet so are kui and ancestors to gods as metonym is to metaphor. The mythical and magical resolutions of these incompatibilities traverse a borderland of ambiguity, a transition of which the imagery is monstrous. Where kui become gods they are fearsome and inhuman. On the other dimension of the metaphor, kui who haunt the living are identified as having monstrous features.[9] Both are distinguished, in various ways but by everyone in some way, as different in kind from the kui in purgatory.

Kui in purgatory as separated subjects are contrastingly paired with remembered ancestors and, as already mentioned, are depicted as more nearly complete humans. Where gods have reportedly manifested themselves and taken part in the world of the living, they are described as fearsome. The most common stories tell of their intervening as a terrifying vision of a general with his troops, who petrify or scare away the enemy. The higher in the hierarchy of gods, the further removed both from kui and from human affairs, the less military and violent and the

---

[8] Liu Ming-ch'uan, the famous Ch'ing dynasty modernizing governor of Taiwan, had to issue a regulation to temper this custom because beggars had been trampled to death in the rush for food. Beggars' rights are still respected at p'u-tu, as I saw for myself at a fairly large chiao. Beggars also seem to have rights to food at funerals, or at least to beg along the route of the burial procession.

[9] For instance, one apparition in Mountainstreet is described as so tall that "his penis rests on top of the tunnel."

more benign and human is a god's image. It is the reverse with offerings
to the god and favors asked. The less practical and the more mediated
or symbolic they are, the more likely are they to be addressed to a god
high in the hierarchy.

Within the metaphor of gods and kui itself, the kui in purgatory as an
unstructured mass are contrastingly paired with the gods' structure, a
structure that is, moreover, a hierarchy and the organ of domination
over the kui. Monster kui, the demon servants of savior gods and of the
gods who are judges in purgatory, are at the point of this contrast itself.
Ritual contrives a continuity not only thus within the metaphor, but also
between it and present society, where the point of transition is marked
by fierce, militaristic gods and their troops of gods' soldiers. These points
of ambivalence are in the religion of commoners filled with a multipli-
cation of kinds of kui, of grades of kui, and of gods' officials and officers,
which vary according to local culture. They are a negotiation of the
relations of rule themselves as reflected in the religious metaphor, and
they are a negotiation skewed upward. In fact the local-level organizations of commoners, such as feast rotations and festival communities,
which often use the gods of the religious metaphor as points of reference,
are themselves absent from the metaphor.

The social past invoked as a religious metaphor for the present is that
of imperial China. Yet in imperial China a great number of institutions
of self-government, from guilds to street and village associations, were
formalized as institutions around an incense burner to a tutelary or local
deity, the members sitting as equals at periodic feasts. The least functionally and locally specific of them were the most ritually formalized,
namely the sworn brotherhoods of kui fame. In present-day Mountainstreet, feast associations, with or without patron deities, abound. The
bands that are the organizations of those who are likened to kui have
no place in the organization of kui themselves in the religious metaphor.
In the metaphor are only bands of gods' soldiers. Action by kui is individual, amoral, anarchic, and massive. The incense burner and commen-
sal association is one of equals, but only before a god as ruler. Its meta-
phoric equivalent is the troop of gods' soldiers. An association of equals
has no metaphor equivalent. Brotherhoods of gods, where gods are
groups in sets, are always much fewer in number than the membership
of popular sworn brotherhoods. The commensality not of feast but of
offerings, that is of men with gods and of men with kui, is not that of
equals but of host to honored guest and patron or to outcasts and beggars. The metaphor is one of rulers as a ruling system of gods and of
ruled as an outcast mass of kui.

The rhythm of the ritual calendar and of every religious ceremony is a movement between the interiorizing of a central authority and the externalizing of a mass of subjects. In the externalizing movement a community is defined, and in the interiorizing movement its units are identified as internal subjects. The totality in which they, the internal subjects of the defined communities, and defined communities vis-à-vis one another, are all related, is identified in the central authority—the innermost point of the community ritual in the temple and the highest external point of the interiorizing New Year ritual. Consequently, when individuals or households combine by means of joint ritual and feast, they know their interdependence as a totality of subject units deferring to a central subject upon which they depend. They depend on it individually for being saved from joining, and communally from being attacked by, the externalized mass of subjects. In this way the very organization of the ruled classes of present society achieves order by an image of authority that is a metaphor for a past imperial state, but a metaphor in which the equivalent of the ruled classes have no order.

Gods, Ghosts, and Ancestors

ARTHUR P. WOLF

In the rural areas along the southwestern edge of the Taipei Basin, conservative families burn three sticks of incense every morning and every
evening.[1] One of these is placed in a niche outside the back door for the
benefit of wandering ghosts; one is dedicated to the Stove God, whose
image resides above the large brick structure on which all meals are prepared; and the third is placed in a burner before the tablets of the family's
immediate ancestors. The purpose of this essay is to examine the significance of these three acts of worship. I will argue that this significance is
largely determined by the worshippers' conception of their social world.
The reader should therefore note at the outset the limited scope of this
exploration. My informants have been farmers, coal miners, and laborers,
as well as a few shopkeepers and petty businessmen. Thirty years ago
the homes of many of these people were constructed of mud bricks and
roofed with straw thatch. Thus my social perspective is that of a poor
and politically impotent segment of the society. It is also that of the layman rather than of the religious specialist. Were we to look at the same
acts of worship from the perspective of government officials, wealthy
landlords, or the Taoist priest, we would find they had very different
meanings. The most important point to be made about Chinese religion
is that it mirrors the social landscape of its adherents. There are as many
meanings as there are vantage points.

[1] The first draft of this paper was written in 1965, for a seminar conducted at
Cornell University by Maurice Freedman. The paper has since been revised several
times to take account of new information and the comments of friends and colleagues.
I am particularly indebted to Maurice Freedman, Margery Wolf, Robert J. Smith,
Emily M. Ahern, and C. Stevan Harrell, all of whom have commented on earlier
drafts. I am also indebted to Freedman, Ahern, and Harrell for permission to report
data drawn from personal correspondence and unpublished field notes.

The geographic scope of my study is most appropriately defined with reference to the Ch'ing Shui Tsu Shih Kung temple in San-hsia. In 1895, when Taiwan was ceded to Japan, this god was regarded as the supernatural governor of much of the Taipei Basin. The area of his jurisdiction extended from the outskirts of Shu-lin in the north to just beyond Ying-ke and Chung-chuang in the south, embracing the entire valley that is bounded on one side by the Kuei-lun Hills and on the other by the lower reaches of the central mountain range. In cultural terms the boundaries of Tsu Shih Kung's domain were coterminous with the limits of an area dominated by the descendants of eighteenth-century immigrants from An-ch'i. To the west T'ao-yuan and Ta-ch'i were controlled by Chang-chou people, while to the east Tsu Shih Kung's subjects faced Ting-chiao and T'ung-an people at Shu-lin and Chang-chou people in the direction of Pan-ch'iao and T'u-ch'eng. Until the Japanese administration brought an end to years of internecine strife, An-ch'i people worshipped An-ch'i gods and married An-ch'i women. Although Hsia-ch'i-chou, the site of my first fieldwork, is only fifteen minutes' walk from villages controlled by Chang-chou people, it was not until 1918 that the first Chang-chou woman married into the community.

This is not to say that Tsu Shih Kung's domain existed as an isolated, self-sufficient kingdom. At the turn of the century at least half a dozen families in Hsia-ch'i-chou made their living as boatmen, and San-hsia's position as the area's leading commercial center depended on its role as a riverport. The area sent camphor, tea, coal, and wood down the river to Wan-hua and Tamsui, and received in return cotton, paper, and tobacco from Amoy, sugar and sweetmeats from Hong Kong, and occasionally flour and kerosene from the United States. Recognition of the area's position as part of the Chinese empire is clearly reflected in the natives' conception of their supernatural governor. The most enthusiastic of Tsu Shih Kung's subjects would never have claimed that he was an autonomous ruler. It was universally understood that his authority was delegated by a higher power, responsible for a much larger community. Tsu Shih Kung is but the local representative of a vast supernatural bureaucracy, headed by a deity whose every characteristic marks him as the spiritual equivalent of the human emperor.

I have probably given the reader the impression that my subject is a community that disappeared shortly after the turn of the century. There is a sense in which this is true. The bandits who used to parade through the streets of San-hsia shouting, "You trust the mandarins; we'll trust the mountains," have long since been dispersed (MacKay 1895: 159–60). The river that once carried the burden of all commerce was supplanted by the railroad seventy years ago. By the time I began my research in the area in 1957 many residents were commuting to jobs in Taipei City, and by 1970 the area's leading employers included Sony and Motorola. Everything has changed, and yet nothing has changed. Even new houses have ancestral altars and a Stove God as well as a television set, and I have seen a fire-walking performed on a baseball diamond. The reader will have to exercise some historical imagination to understand the conditions that gave rise to the beliefs I discuss, but he must not forget that these beliefs endure and will influence the future.

II

The Stove God, Tsao Chün, is not a god of the culinary arts, nor is his location above the stove a matter of convenience or coincidence. In northern Taiwan the large brick cooking stove on which most meals are prepared stands as a substantial symbol of the family as a corporate body. Possession of a stove identifies a family as an independent entity. The new independent segments of a recently divided household often share many of the facilities of a single house, including, occasionally, the kitchen, but independent families never share a stove, not even when the heads are brothers. When brothers divide their father's household the eldest inherits the old stove, while his younger brothers transfer hot coals from the old stove to their new ones, thereby inviting the Stove God to join them. For this reason, family division is commonly spoken of as *pun-cau*, "dividing the stove." In the view of most of my informants, the soul of a family, its corporate fate, is somehow localized in their stove. When a shaman informed one family that there were "ants and other things" in their stove, they demolished the structure and threw the bricks into the river. A neighbor explained, "There was nothing else they could do. A family will never have peace if they don't have a good stove."

The association of Stove God and stove is thus an association of god and family. The character of the relationship is essentially bureaucratic. The family is the smallest corporate unit in the society, and the Stove God is the lowest-ranking member of a supernatural bureaucracy. In the Yangtze delta village of Kaihsienkung, Stove Gods were viewed as the spiritual remains of foreign soldiers forcibly billeted in the houses of the region to act as spies and informers (Fei 1939: 99–102). In San-hsia the god is usually described as "a kind of policeman." The metaphors chosen to describe the god vary from one area of China to another, possibly as a result of political experience, but the god is everywhere looked upon as representing a supernatural bureaucracy. The glutinous rice cakes offered him at the New Year are explained as a means of forestalling an unfavorable report on the family. According to one of my informants in Hsia-ch'i-chou, "You have to give the god something so that he won't say things about your family and cause you a lot of trouble."

The prototype of the many gods in the Chinese pantheon is, in my view, Fu Te Cheng Shen, commonly known as T'u Ti Kung. This "earth god" is often introduced as the Chinese god of agriculture, but this is only partially accurate. "T'u-ti" is better translated as "site" or "locality" than as "earth" or "soil." T'u Ti Kung is a tutelary deity, the governor of a place, concerned with agriculture, to be sure, but no more so than any official responsible for the welfare of a rural community. T'u Ti Kung are just as common in the towns and cities of Taiwan as in the villages. Older residents of Tainan City claim that in former times every neighborhood had its own T'u Ti Kung, and evidence gathered by Kristofer Schipper appears to bear them out. A Taoist manuscript dated 1876 lists all of the city's divine agents from whom one must request forgiveness in time of disaster. Among the 138 cults mentioned in the list, 45 are devoted to T'u Ti Kung (Schipper 1975).

T'u Ti Kung is seen as having two functions, one of which is to police the kui (kuei), the "ghosts," the supernatural equivalent of bandits, beggars, and other dangerous strangers.[2] The association between T'u Ti Kung and the earth is in part a consequence of this role. The kui are creatures of the soil, spiritual residues of the most material part of man, often represented in experience by bones uncovered in digging a foundation or plowing a field. It is T'u Ti Kung's task to protect the living from the depredations of these unhappy, wandering spirits. Although the god thus serves the best interests of the human community, he is not that community's agent. His other role is to spy on the affairs of his human charges, keep records of their activities, and report regularly to his superiors. Commenting on H. A. Giles's view that T'u Ti Kung are worshipped "for anything that can be got out of them," Clarence Day (Day 1940: 65) notes, "Not only that, but all local events and proceedings must be duly reported to them: births, marriages, misfortunes, deaths." Most people in the San-hsia area report vital events to their neighborhood T'u Ti Kung as well as to the local police station, and in many villages people customarily ask the god's permission to build a new house or demolish an old one.

In imperial China every local official was responsible for a discrete ad-

[2] Place names and the names of familiar gods are romanized with their Mandarin pronunciation. Otherwise, all terms are given in Hokkien. Where Hokkien terms have a familiar Mandarin equivalent, I sometimes give the Mandarin in parentheses following the Hokkien.

ministrative district, and this was as true of the supernatural bureaucracy as it was of their human counterparts. Until only recently the jurisdiction of many T'u Ti Kung in the San-hsia area was defined by means of a circulating plaque, a piece of wood about twenty inches long and eight inches wide, inscribed on one side with the name of the god and on the other with the name of the community.[3] This token of the god's authority was passed from family to family, day by day, moving through the community along an irregular but exhaustive route. The family holding the plaque on any given day was responsible for making an offering of incense, fruit, and tea at the T'u Ti Kung temple. This it did in the morning after receiving the plaque and again in the evening before passing it on to a neighbor. In this way every family participated in honoring the local T'u Ti Kung and in so doing identified itself as part of the community.

This practice implies a conditional relationship between the god and his subjects. The family that moves from one community to another should see themselves as leaving the authority of one T'u Ti Kung and entering that of another. And so it is. R. F. Johnston's description of Weihaiwei at the turn of the century is entirely applicable to the San-hsia area in the 1960's. After describing a procession of mourners "wending their way along the village street in the direction of the shrine of T'u Ti to report the death of a relative or fellow villager," Johnston continues: "It is noteworthy . . . that no village in Weihaiwei, or elsewhere as far as I am aware, possesses more than one T'u Ti, though there may be two or more 'surnames' or clans represented in the village; moreover, when a man migrates from one village to another he changes his T'u Ti, although his connection with his old village in respect of ancestral worship remains unimpaired" (Johnston 1910: 372–73).

Johnston's point is that T'u Ti Kung serve localities, not kinship groups. This is right and explains why farmers in San-hsia who own land in more than one locality worship more than one T'u Ti Kung. However, Johnston makes an avoidable error when he observes that no village ever has more than one T'u Ti Kung. The library of the School of Oriental and African Studies contains Johnston's copy of Arthur Smith's *Village Life in China*. The book is inscribed "R. F. Johnston, Government House, July 6th, 1901," a year or two after Johnston's arrival in Weihaiwei and nine years before he published his *Lion and Dragon in Northern China*. Had Johnston consulted Smith on the T'u Ti Kung, as he did on many other sub-

---

[3] Sung Lung-sheng, recently returned from field research, tells me that one of the T'u Ti Kung plaques in the San-hsia area also lists the names of the heads of all households that receive the plaque. Thus the plaque makes explicit the relationship between the god, the community, and the residents who worship the god.

jects, he would have found this passage: "If the village is a large one, divided into several sections transacting their public business independently of one another, there may be several temples to the same divinity. It is a common saying, illustrative of Chinese notions on this topic, that the local god at one end of the village has nothing to do with the affairs of the other end of the village." (Smith 1899: 138.)

Smith, too, errs in implying that T'u Ti Kung temples are always thought of as independent of one another. In fact, many T'u Ti Kung are the delegated representatives of other T'u Ti Kung. This is sometimes made explicit in the ritual process by which a new temple is established or an old one refurbished. During my most recent trip to Taiwan, in 1970, the people of Chung-p'u on the west side of San-hsia decided to rebuild the residence of their local deity. On the day the old temple was to be demolished, the head of the village bent six long strips of bamboo into circles and tied them together with red string to form a large hoop. Before the god was invited out of the temple for the duration of the repairs, this bamboo hoop was lowered over the roof and thus made to encircle the entire building. I was told that the hoop represented the boundaries of the district governed by the god. The purpose of encircling the temple was to keep the god from deserting the community while his home was under repair. "This is the god of this place. We do not want him to leave and take up residence somewhere else."

This step of the ritual identified the god with the district for which he is responsible. The next made it clear that he is not conceived of as a sovereign ruler, but as the local representative of a higher authority. Once it had been ascertained by divination that the god agreed to leave the temple, the village head took a spoonful of ashes from the incense burner and wrapped it up in red paper. This packet was then conveyed to the town of San-hsia, where it was deposited in the incense burner of what is known as the Big T'u Ti Kung temple. The village head explained that this was done because "our temple in Chung-p'u is only a substation of the big temple in town." He also told me that upon completion of the new temple, he would get ashes from the temple in town and deposit these in the new burner in Chung-p'u. "This is like asking the god in the big temple to send someone to live in our temple and protect us."

The view that the T'u Ti Kung temples in villages and neighborhoods are substations of larger temples is not an unusual one. There are fourteen other temples in San-hsia and its immediate environs that are commonly regarded as branches of the Big T'u Ti Kung temple on the main street. Until the changing character of the town led to a reorganization in 1947, these relationships were given explicit recognition on

T'u Ti Kung's birthday. The puppet shows provided for the entertainment of each of the fourteen neighborhood gods were always organized and paid for by the individual neighborhoods. The responsibility for the far more expensive opera performed to entertain the Big T'u Ti Kung was rotated among the fourteen neighborhoods on an annual basis. Even today the special status of the Big T'u Ti Kung receives occasional acknowledgment. When families invite gods to their home for some special occasion, they usually include the Big T'u Ti Kung as well as their neighborhood T'u Ti Kung. "It's the same as inviting both the mayor and the head of your village."

In considering the implications of this equation of god and bureaucrat, it is important to remember that one side of the equation is objective, the other subjective. A T'u Ti Kung and the administration he serves do not partake of the same reality as the human bureaucracy. People with different perspectives can interpret the supernatural hierarchy in different ways. An interesting case in point is provided by the T'u Ti Kung temples in Ch'i-nan, across the river from San-hsia. The community comprises four hamlets, each of which is dominated by a single lineage and its ancestral hall. At one time all four hamlets were united under the jurisdiction of one T'u Ti Kung. One T'u Ti Kung plaque circulated from family to family and then from hamlet to hamlet, and the four hamlets rotated the responsibility for the show presented to the god on his birthday. Then, sometime in the late 1950's, the hamlet dominated by the Ong lineage decided to build its own T'u Ti Kung temple. Residents of the Ong hamlet continued to take their turn in sponsoring the show for "old T'u Ti Kung's" birthday, but stopped accepting the plaque from the old temple and began instead to make daily offerings at the "Ong temple."

According to a member of the Ong lineage who now lives in the town of San-hsia, this decision was prompted by the Ongs' fear that the old T'u Ti Kung was neglecting them. "All our pigs and chickens suddenly died, and so someone called a geomancer who told us that it was because the old temple faced away from the Ong settlement. The god couldn't see us." Emily Ahern has since discovered that there were other reasons for the Ongs' dissatisfaction, but I will leave that story to her.[4] The important point for my purpose is that the present situation in Ch'i-nan is reflected in differing accounts of the Ong temple's origins. My Ong

---

[4] A detailed account of the four Ch'i-nan lineages and the problems that led to the construction of the Ong temple is now available in Ahern's *The Cult of the Dead in a Chinese Village* (1973: 64–66). Readers who want another perspective on the topics discussed in this paper are urged to read Ahern's book and Wang Shih-ch'ing's paper in this volume. All three studies are based on fieldwork in San-hsia *chen* and its neighbor, Shu-lin chen.

informant claims that the incense used to found the temple came from the Big T'u Ti Kung temple on the main street of San-hsia. A senior member of the Lou lineage in Ch'i-nan insists that the incense came from the old T'u Ti Kung temple in Ch'i-nan. The disagreement reflects the social perspectives of the two informants. The Ong lineage would like to put their settlement on an equal footing with the rest of Ch'i-nan. The other three lineages put the Ongs down by insisting that their temple is only a branch of the Ch'i-nan temple.

I emphasize the influence different social perspectives have on what is said about T'u Ti Kung temples in order to underline my primary thesis. People would not argue about the age of temples or the source of their incense if they did not see this as a question of the relative rank of the gods in question and hence the relative status of the communities they govern. Conflicts are expressed in these terms because everyone thinks of the gods in terms of a bureaucratic hierarchy. John Shryock reports that the followers of a certain Tung Yo in Anking advanced his claims for godhood by claiming for him the governorship of the entire province. Skeptics countered by arguing that the god's activities were confined to the East Gate suburb. Even Buddhists and Taoists expressed their perennial opposition in the same idiom. A Taoist monk told Shryock that the Ch'eng Huang responsible for Anking prefecture was a Taoist deity, while the god responsible for the hsien, who differed from the prefecture god in no way except for the smaller size of the district he governed, was Buddhist (Shryock 1931: 87–88).

The view of the gods as bureaucrats is so pervasive that evidence to the contrary is itself explained away in bureaucratic terms. The picture of the pantheon with which many families decorate their ancestral altar has the Stove God in the lower left-hand corner and T'u Ti Kung in the lower right-hand corner. The reason for this has to do with the ritual specialist's view that the left side is the *iong* (*yang*) side and the right side the *im* (*yin*) side.[5] One of T'u Ti Kung's tasks is to escort the souls of the dead to the underworld, the im world, so he appropriately appears on the im side of the picture, the right side. But since etiquette makes the left superior to the right in seating guests, this positioning of the gods conflicts with the laymen's view of their relative status. T'u Ti Kung should be at the left and the Stove God at the right because Tu' Ti Kung

[5] I am following the Chinese convention of taking the ancestors' perspective in designating right and left. If one asks a native how he seats guests at a home banquet, he will almost always turn his back to his ancestral altar and say, "The guest of honor sits this way (with his back to the altar, facing the door), while the second guest sits at the left and the third at the right." Thus, right is stage right; left, stage left.

governs a community while the Stove God is responsible only for a single family. I first noticed the contradiction while attending a feast in San-hsia, and immediately raised the problem with my fellow guests. One of the older men present explained that the T'u Ti Kung and the Stove God are not comparable. "T'u Ti Kung is like a policeman who wears a uniform. He can only report to lower gods like the Ch'eng Huang. The Stove God is more like a plainclothesman. He reports directly to T'ien Kung [the supernatural emperor]." I asked: "But how is it that a little god like the Stove God can report directly to T'ien Kung?" Another old man answered: "The Stove God is not a small person like T'u Ti Kung. He is T'ien Kung's younger brother." The apparent departure from bureaucratic principles is thus explained away as nepotism.

Popular mythology in northern Taiwan as in other areas of China has it that T'u Ti Kung's immediate superior in the supernatural bureaucracy is Ch'eng Huang, the so-called City God, a deity posted to govern the spirits residing in each of the major administrative districts of the empire. When a small T'u Ti Kung temple in a mountain village near San-hsia was enlarged in 1967, the village head obtained incense from the Ch'eng Huang temple in Taipei City as well as the Big T'u Ti Kung temple in San-hsia. He felt this was necessary "because the Taipei Ch'eng Huang is overseer of all the T'u Ti Kung in Taipei hsien. There is no point in building a new temple if you do not ask the Ch'eng Huang to send someone to live in it." The residents of Hsia-ch'i-chou also obtained incense from the Taipei Ch'eng Huang when they built a new temple to replace the one destroyed by a typhoon in 1962. They were afraid that if they did not inform the Ch'eng Huang, he might post a new T'u Ti Kung without recalling the old one. Two gods in one temple might quarrel and thereby bring the village further misfortune.

As his relationship with T'u Ti Kung implies, Ch'eng Huang is also conceived of as a scholar-official. The god's image is always dressed in official robes and usually appears on a curtained dais flanked on either side by secretaries and fearsome lictors; his temples are laid out on precisely the same lines as a government yamen, even to the details of red walls in the courtyards and flagstaffs at the entrance. In most cities the god appeared in public three times a year to *ke-kieng* (*kuo-ching*), "tour the boundaries," or, as other informants put it, "to inspect the frontiers." Preceded by heralds carrying his gold boards of authority and his banners, the god passed through the streets in a covered sedan chair, accompanied by hundreds of young men dressed as servants, soldiers, secretaries, and lictors. By all accounts, the procession was awe-inspiring. Shryock says the tour in Anking commenced about nine in the morning and did not return to the temple until after midnight, the god visiting every street whose inhabitants had made known their desire to welcome him in the proper manner:

The parade took more than an hour to pass my point of observation. There were hundreds of ghosts like the wildest nightmare visions, their faces painted and lined with every colour under heaven, their robes bright with embroidered silks, beads, and tinsel glittering in their high head gear and banners streaming from their shoulders like wings. Soldiers with gags in their mouths, lictors bearing staffs of office, secretaries, giants and dwarfs passed two by two down the narrow, crowded street, until finally, to a continuous roar of firecrackers exploding under the feet of the marching men, and a deafening clash of cymbals and drums, came the god in the sedan chair of an official, curtains drawn for fear pictures might be taken. I caught a glimpse of his dark, impassive face, and he was gone. (Shryock 1931: 105.)

A somewhat subtler indication of the god's assimilation to the imperial bureaucracy is his loss of individual identity. Although some tales of the god's origins give him a specific identity, most people now treat Ch'eng Huang as a position rather than a person. For example, deceased notables are commonly assigned the status of Ch'eng Huang. Ch'ü T'ung-tsu identifies the Ch'eng Huang of Lou hsien in Kiangsu as a former magistrate, Li Fu-hsing, who died there in 1669 (Ch'ü 1962: 311), and, according to Florence Ayscough, the god governing Shanghai is a former member of the Hanlin Academy, Ch'in Yü-poi, who was assigned to his present position by the founder of the Ming dynasty (Ayscough 1924: 140–41). This is a particularly interesting case because it led commentators on the Shanghai gazetteer to recognize that the term Ch'eng Huang is nothing more than a bureaucratic label. Ayscough quotes one commentator as asking, "How is it that we know nothing of a former P'usa [bodhisattva]? Did the seat of Spiritual Magistrate wait for Ch'in Yü-poi?" Another commentator she cites comes to the conclusion that officials in the im world are moved around just like those in the iong world (1924: 141).

Ritual specialists and people who take more than a casual interest in temple affairs commonly distinguish two types of deities. On the one hand, there are the su (shih), the "officials," the most notable of whom are the T'u Ti Kung and the Ch'eng Huang; on the other, there are the hu (fu), the "sages" or "wise men," a category represented in the San-hsia area by such gods as Tsu Shih Kung, Pao Sheng Ta Ti, Shang Ti Kung, and Ma Tsu. The former are explicitly compared with the imperial bureaucracy and are often treated as administrative positions that can be occupied by different people. The latter are usually thought of as particular deified persons with saintly qualities, the emphasis being on the deity's moral character and good works rather than on his bureaucratic functions.

Most laymen, though aware of this distinction, do not trouble much about it. From the point of view of farmers, coal miners, coolies, and the keepers of small shops, all gods are bureaucrats. Whereas the managers of San-hsia's Ch'ang-fu Yen, the residence of Tsu Shih Kung, insist that the god is hu, "a wise man like your Lincoln," the great majority of the population think of the god as their supernatural governor. Local legend says that many years ago a god named Ang Kong saved San-hsia by warning its inhabitants of an impending raid by head-hunting aborigines. To thank the god for this timely warning, San-hsia now sends a delegation every year to invite Ang Kong to attend a festival in his honor. The god is brought from his home temple in Hsin-tien on a sedan chair, and is met at the San-hsia border by Tsu Shih Kung, riding in another chair. Asked why Tsu Shih Kung goes to meet Ang Kong at the San-hsia border, people explain that it is because "Tsu Shih Kung is the god in charge of this place and so must meet Ang Kong and show him the road." The custom is precisely parallel to that by which a hsien magistrate greeted a visiting colleague and escorted him to the yamen.

Elsewhere in this volume Wang Shih-ch'ing's account of the history of the Ch'i-an Kung temple in Shu-lin provides another example. Although the god enshrined in the temple, Pao Sheng Ta Ti, is classified as hu by ritual specialists, the populace treat him as the town's chief bureaucrat, comparable in many ways to the Ch'eng Huang found in administrative centers. He makes an annual inspection tour and is looked upon as the official responsible for the many T'u Ti Kung temples in the area. When a village or neighborhood decides to build a new temple or enlarge an old one, they usually invite Pao Sheng Ta Ti to choose the temple's site and orientation. There is even a legend to the effect that Pao Sheng Ta Ti was once an official in Ch'üan-chou *fu* and that he was deified in recognition of meritorious service.

The same habit of thought molds the views of people whose gods are not responsible for communities as large as San-hsia and Shu-lin. The small village in which I initiated my research in Taiwan is one of five hamlets that together constitute a rural community known as Ch'i-chou. The local gods are two T'u Ti Kung, one for each half of the community, and Shang Ti Kung, who is considered the supernatural governor of Ch'i-chou. The five hamlets rotate the responsibility for Shang Ti Kung's annual inspection tour on the occasion of his birthday. Preceded by the village band and the clatter-bang of firecrackers, the god visits the four landmarks that define the boundaries of Ch'i-chou, stopping along the way to exchange incense with the head of every family that resides in the community. The whole affair is a country version of the grand tours undertaken by the Ch'eng Huang of important towns. The only difference is in the number of people involved and the magnificence of the god's equipage, a matter of magnitude rather than meaning.

Shang Ti Kung's bureaucratic character is most evident in his relationship to the local T'u Ti Kung. Although the T'u Ti Kung are always invited to witness a play or puppet show performed for Shang Ti Kung, people are careful to place Shang Ti Kung in the center of the viewing platform with the two T'u Ti Kung at his right. Shang Ti Kung is thought of as a proud, somewhat arrogant official, who would take offense were he denied the seat of honor. A person can use the same foodstuffs to make offerings to the two gods, but he must present the offering to Shang Ti Kung before he presents it to T'u Ti Kung. A series of misfortunes that befell one family was widely blamed on a careless daughter-in-law, who thanked T'u Ti Kung before she thanked Shang Ti Kung. I was told that on one occasion Shang Ti Kung refused to leave his temple for his annual inspection tour because only two men were assigned to carry his chair. A god of his status would not deign to sally forth in a sedan chair carried by fewer than four men.

The relative status of the two gods is also apparent at the fire-walking that is held every year "to cleanse the gods and make them efficacious." Riding in sedan chairs carried by young men chosen by lot, the various images of the two gods are carried two or three times across a bed of hot coals. Every year some of the men carrying the chairs occupied by Shang Ti Kung are possessed by the god and carry on as though he were in complete command of their senses. The chairs charge the crowd and one another, sometimes meeting in violent collisions, causing bloody if not very serious injuries. This display of energy is looked upon by the villagers as evidence of Shang Ti Kung's great vitality. It therefore says something about their conception of T'u Ti Kung that the men carrying his chairs are never possessed, despite their exposure to the excitement of the occasion and the example of Shang Ti Kung's bearers. I think it is simply that people consider T'u Ti Kung "a little god," who lacks the strength and authority to take command of a person's body.

The greatest power the peasant can imagine does not escape the impress of the imperial bureaucracy on his thought. Yü Huang Ta Ti, Pearly Emperor and Supreme Ruler, the mightiest god in the peasant's pantheon, is but a reflection of the human emperor. Although there are temples for Yü Huang Ta Ti in some parts of Taiwan, there are none in San-hsia or Shu-lin. People say this is because "Yü Huang Ta Ti is a long way away and cannot be spoken to directly." All communication with the god must be by way of another god, who must himself be one of the higher-ranking deities. Lowly deities like the T'u Ti Kung cannot approach Yü Huang Ta Ti any more than a district magistrate could approach the emperor. As the Rev. Justus Doolittle puts it on the basis of his observations in Foochow, "In strict theory, the great gods, the divinities of high rank, may worship him, while the gods of lower rank may not properly worship him, in accordance with the established practice that only mandarins of high rank may wait upon the emperor in person and pay their respects, while officers of lower grade may not approach into the emperor's presence" (Doolittle 1865: II, 257).

In traditional China not all officials were assigned to territorial posts. Some served as general inspectors, traveling from one area to another and reporting their observations to the central government. The same practice is followed by the supernatural government. In her brief account of religion in a fishing village in southern Taiwan, Norma Diamond describes "two wandering inspector gods" who visit the village periodically. Their visits are announced through a shaman, who cries the news through the village streets. During their stay in the village the gods are housed in the village temple, where each household worships them in the morning and again in the evening. Diamond notes that there is some disagreement about what the gods do while they are present, but the opinions expressed by her informants suggest that most people think of them as carrying out bureaucratic functions:

One informant was of the opinion that the god came only to bring protection, to prevent illness, and to help people earn more money, and that he did this of his own volition during a pleasure trip. Another felt that he was specifically sent by the Jade Emperor to investigate men's activities, parallel to the secret police being sent by the government. A third informant explained that while the god himself was benevolent in his intentions, the troops that followed him were a mixed breed, some of whom would bring misfortune and harm. And some felt that illness or misfortune would strike evildoers shortly after the god reported back to his superiors. (Diamond 1969: 94.)

It is not only bureaucratic organization that is replicated in the world of the supernatural; the gods also display many of the most human characteristics of their worldly counterparts, including their fallibility. A temple history translated by Shryock (1931: 113–14) tells the story of a Ch'eng Huang who allowed an innocent boy to be identified as a thief. The boy, knowing he was innocent, wrote a report condemning the god and burnt it. The report was picked up by one of the wandering inspector gods mentioned by Diamond and brought to the attention of the Jade Emperor, who "immediately issued a decree banishing the City-God 1,115 *li* from his city for three years." Thus castigated, the penitent Ch'eng Huang testified on the boy's behalf and thereby managed to get his sentence reduced to 15 *li*. "So the City-God has a temple in San K'ou Cheng, because that place was just 15 *li* from the city. Anyone who does not believe this may go to San K'ou Cheng and see the temple."

In this case a culpable deity is punished by his superior in the supernatural bureaucracy. In other instances irresponsible gods are punished by human officials. The bureaucracy of the other world is not thought of as superior to the human bureaucracy with authority over it. Rather the two are parallel systems, in which the higher-ranking members of one bureaucracy have authority over the lower-ranking members of the other. When drought strikes part of a province, the governor does not appeal to the local gods to bring rain. Instead, he orders them to see to their duty, treating them with as little ceremony as he would treat one of his county magistrates. Gods who failed in their duties could be tried and condemned to a public beating. Shryock writes: "A year or so ago, at Nanling Hsien during a drought, a god was publicly tried by the magistrate for neglect of duty, condemned, left in the hot sun to see how he liked it himself, and finally, after enduring every kind of insult, was broken in pieces" (1931: 97).

Like their human counterparts in the imperial bureaucracy, the gods are far more powerful than ordinary men. They can quell rebellions, check epidemics, apprehend criminals, dispatch ghosts, cure illnesses, control the weather, and otherwise intervene in natural and social processes for the benefit of their subjects. One of the T'u Ti Kung in Ch'ichou is credited with the important capacity to control the market price of pork. Yet the gods are far from omnipotent. Like the capacities of powerful human bureaucrats, those of their supernatural counterparts have limits. One day while I was attending a shamanistic session an elderly woman appeared and asked the god to save her seriously ailing husband. The shaman, speaking with the authority of the god, told her that although her husband's fate was due, his death could be postponed one year. My assistant happened to be present when the woman returned a little over a year later. Again her husband was seriously ill, and again she appealed to the god. This time the shaman refused to hear her appeal, bluntly informing her that nothing could be done. "Your husband's time is up. He will die no matter what I do. If I were to tell you that he will live, he would still die, and then what kind of a god would people think I am?" Although this answer may have been the shaman's way of saving himself from an almost certain loss of credibility, the idea that the god was powerless was accepted without surprise by everyone present.

The resemblance between the gods and their human counterparts extends even into the realm of their personal lives. The temples of the gods often include living quarters for their families as well as the hall in which they conduct their public business. Behind the main hall of the Ch'eng Huang temple in Shanghai is a room for the god's father and mother and an apartment occupied by his wife and four daughters (Ayscough 1924: 147). Even the lowly T'u Ti Kung is usually provided with a wife, and some take it upon themselves to add a concubine. On inquiring why a T'u Ti Kung in Weihaiwei was accompanied by two female images, R. F. Johnston was informed that "the lady on his left (the place of honour) was his wife and the lady on his right his concubine. . . . Two explanations were offered as to why this particular T'u Ti Kung had been allowed to increase his household in this manner: one was that he had won the lady by gambling for her, the other was that the T'u Ti Kung had appeared to one of the villagers in a dream and begged him to provide him with a concubine as he had grown tired of his wife." (1910: 374.)

In sum, what we see in looking at the Chinese supernatural through the eyes of the peasant is a detailed image of Chinese officialdom. This image allows us to assess the significance of the imperial bureaucracy from a new perspective. Historians and political scientists often emphasize the failure of most Chinese governments to effectively extend their authority to the local level. Certainly many governments had difficulty collecting taxes, and some allowed this function and others to fall into the hands of opportunistic local leaders. Judged in terms of its administrative arrangements, the Chinese imperial government looks impotent. Assessed in terms of its long-range impact on the people, it appears to have been one of the most potent governments ever known, for it created a religion in its own image. Its firm grip on the popular imagination may be one reason the imperial government survived so long despite its many failings. Perhaps this is also the reason China's revolutionaries have so often organized their movements in terms of the concepts and symbols of such foreign faiths as Buddhism and Christianity. The native gods were so much a part of the establishment that they could not be turned against it.

III

When we turn to the other two acts of worship, we must shift our perspective. All people worship the same gods just as they live under the same government, but people do not all stand in the same relationship to the two other classes of supernatural, ghosts and ancestors. Whether a particular spirit is viewed as a ghost or as an ancestor depends on the point of view of a particular person. One man's ancestor is another man's ghost. A young man in Hsia-ch'i-chou was returning home late one night and saw "a white thing floating across the fields" near the village. He told me he had seen a ghost. When I appeared skeptical he assured me that in this instance there were solid grounds for identifying the object as a ghost. It had been moving in the direction of Lim Bi-kok's house, and the next day was Lim Bi-kok's mother's deathday. Surely, then, the object must have been Lim Bi-kok's mother on her way home to receive her deathday offerings. "The ancestor, though dead, is a person with rights and duties" (Freedman 1967: 99); the ghost, also dead, is a person with neither rights nor duties. The one is usually a kinsman; the other is always a stranger.

In a world in which every person married and produced at least one male child, it could easily be argued that the rites of ancestor worship are a function of descent. In such a world every male child would take his descent from his father, and every woman would, on marriage, become a member of her husband's line of descent. Under these conditions men would worship their parents, their paternal grandparents, and their remote lineal agnatic ascendants; women would worship their father's ascendants before marriage and their husband's ascendants after marriage. From the point of view of any living person, the dead would fall into two mutually exclusive classes. On the one hand, there would be those dead represented by the tablets on one's family altar, all of whom would be lineal agnatic ascendants and their wives, people who would have the right to receive regular deathday offerings; on the other, there would be those dead enshrined on altars in other people's homes, the deceased members of descent lines other than one's own, outsiders to whom no obligation was owed.

With the important recent exception of Emily Ahern's *The Cult of the Dead in a Chinese Village*, this is the world assumed by most analyses of Chinese ancestor worship.[6] It does not exist. Many people die as children or before marriage, and many of those who survive to marry fail to produce male descendants. When we examine what happens to these people we discover that descent is only one of a wide range of relation-

---

[6] And I must now note a second exception, having just received a draft of a paper by Wang Sung-hsing entitled "Ancestors Proper and Peripheral." The essence of Wang's argument is that Chinese on Taiwan classify ancestors into two categories: those who are patrilineal forebears and those who are not.

ships that create an obligation to care for the dead. Instead of two mutually exclusive categories made up of agnatic ascendants and everyone else, we find a finely graded continuum that extends from those people to whom one is obligated by descent to those toward whom one owes no obligation at all. At one end of this continuum are ancestors whose tablets are placed in the position of honor at the left of the altar; at the other, we find the despised ghosts whose offerings are set outside the back door. Between the two are people who contributed to one's line but were not members of the line, and people who died as dependents of the line and have no one else to care for them. The tablets of the latter are placed on the right of the altar and are treated as ancestors; the tablets of the former are placed in a corner of the kitchen or in a hallway and are almost ghosts.

The one class of dead neglected as a matter of course are those who die as infants or small children. In Taiwan as elsewhere in China, an infant's death is assumed to prove that the child was really an evil spirit or "someone from a previous life coming back to dun you for a debt." As Mary Bryson puts it in her account of life in Wuchang in the 1890's, "The very fact of a baby's death convinces the parents that the little one was not a precious gift to be treasured, but possessed by some evil spirit, and only a source of anxiety and misfortune from the first, and the sooner they forget about it the better" (Bryson 1900: 22). Mrs. J. G. Cormack claims that in Peking a child whose death seemed imminent was "stripped and placed on the floor just inside the outer door of the room. The parents leave it there and watch what takes place. If the child survives this treatment, it is recognized as a true child of their own flesh and blood; but if it dies, then it never was their child, but an evil spirit seeking to gain entrance to their family in order to bring trouble on them." (Cormack 1935: 243–44.) She also notes that small children are never buried in the family graveyard "as that would mean adoption, and to adopt an evil spirit into the family would be the height of folly" (1935: 244). On the Shantung Peninsula children were buried without a coffin, just covered with sufficient dirt to hide the body from sight. The result was that at night the bodies were dug up and eaten by dogs. According to Robert Coltman (Coltman 1891: 77), the parents intended it thus, "For they say, 'An evil spirit inhabited the child's body, otherwise it would not have died so young. If the dogs eat it, the bad spirit enters the dog and cannot again enter another child who may be born to the same parents.'"

The idea that children who die young are really strangers is a consequence of the Chinese view that ancestor worship is an act of obeisance that can appropriately be performed only by a junior for a senior. If a man dies as a young adult, he will be worshipped by his own children, but never by his parents. On the contrary, his father will usually beat the coffin to punish his son for being so unfilial as to die before his parents. Consequently, if a person dies as a child, there is no one who can appropriately provide for his soul. His parents must either deny that the child was their own offspring, or live with the disquieting thought that a member of their family is now a hungry, homeless ghost. The only way the person who dies as a small child can achieve security as an ancestor is to "return" a generation or two after his death. If a shaman or fortune teller suggests that some misfortune is due to the anger of a neglected forebear, the family may then "discover" an ascendant who died as a child, and in this case the solution is to erect a tablet and initiate regular propitiatory offerings. The person who died as a child is now grandfather's older brother, and can therefore be accorded a place on the family altar and worshipped as an ancestor.

Although the Chinese kinship system demands that younger children defer to their older siblings, an older child can appropriately worship a younger brother or sister. People say that "the child who dies first is the eldest" and ignore the reversal of roles. This means that the great majority of people who die after early childhood but before marriage can be provided for, despite the fact that they have no descendants of their own. But it does not mean that they are all enshrined as ancestors on a proper altar. The fate of the person who dies before marriage depends on whether that person is a son or a daughter. Because a son who survives the first years of life is automatically recognized as a member of his father's line, he is entitled to a place on his father's ancestral altar. A daughter can never be accorded this privilege because women acquire membership in lines only through marriage. From her father's point of view, a daughter is an outsider. She can achieve the right to a place on his altar only by marrying a man who agrees to reside uxorilocally. Were a family to place the tablet of an unmarried daughter on their altar, they would risk the possibility of ancestral punishment. As one elderly informant put it, "The ancestors would surely be angry if you put an ugly thing like that on the altar."

The souls of unmarried girls can be disposed of in any one of several ways. At most of the funerals I have observed in San-hsia the soul is represented not by a tablet but by a small red sachet of incense ashes. After the funeral this is placed in a little basket to which is attached a section of bamboo that serves as an incense burner. In Ch'i-nan, where lineage organization creates a stronger sense of agnatic solidarity than elsewhere in San-hsia, many people insist that this basket and its contents cannot remain on lineage property.[7] In most villages in the area the basket can be hung anywhere in the house except in the *kong-thia:* (*kung-t'ing*), the hall where guests are received and the honored dead are worshipped. The preference is for "someplace where it won't be seen"—a dark passageway, behind a door, the corner of a storeroom. Asked why the souls of daughters are discriminated against in this way, some people say it is because these things are ugly and hateful. Others explain that it is because "women are meant to marry out and don't belong to their father's family." Ahern's informants told her (Ahern 1973: 127) that the soul of an unmarried girl could not be seated on lineage property because "she does not belong to us. From birth on, girls are meant to belong to other people. They are supposed to die in other people's houses."

The view that the souls of unmarried women should not come to rest in their natal home is not unique to San-hsia or to Taiwan. In his colorful description of ancestor worship in Shun-te hsien in Kwangtung, P. Alfred Fabre notes that a woman of marriageable age is not allowed to die in her father's house. Instead, she must breathe her last in a tent set up outside the house. And, Fabre adds (1935: 114), the same applies "a fortiori to the old unmarried aunt." In San-hsia the sachet of ashes that serves as the seat of an unmarried woman's soul often remains indefinitely in some dark corner of the house, but it appears that in Shun-te the soul was either removed by means of a ghost marriage (to be discussed shortly) or sent off to the care of a Buddhist monastery. At least Fabre does not mention the possibility of the soul's remaining in the care of its natal family. He only notes (1935: 114) that while awaiting removal the soul is not placed on the family altar, but is temporarily shut off in an area near the back door to the parents' house.

In his paper for this volume, Jack M. Potter reports that in the New Territories of Hong Kong people are afraid to put the tablets of unmarried daughters in the house "because they might haunt the family." One solution is to pay a spirit medium to care for the soul in her *pay-dhaan* (Cantonese), the shrine in which she communicates with the dead. In San-hsia families that want to rid themselves of an unmarried daughter usually deposit the ashes that represent her in what is known as a *ko-niu-biou*, a "maiden's temple," an example of which can be seen in Lung-p'u

---

[7] By "lineage property" people in Ch'i-nan mean both corporate land held by the lineage and land owned by families who are members of the lineage. I suspect that this usage reflects the fact that lineage members once enjoyed preemptive rights with respect to one another's landed property.

on the west side of town. This particular temple was built as a community project and now houses the souls of 32 unmarried girls. These
girls receive occasional offerings from their natal families but derive
most of their support from prostitutes, who take their collective soul as a
kind of patron deity. These women go to the ko-niu-biou with requests
they would not dare take to a representative of the supernatural bureaucracy.[8]

Elderly people in San-hsia say that in "the old days" a girl's parents
could rid themselves of the responsibility for her soul by trapping a
husband for her. The girl's name and horoscope were written on a piece
of red paper, which was concealed in a purse or some other attractive
bait and placed beside the road. The girl's brothers then hid nearby and
waited until some unsuspecting passerby discovered the purse. The fact
that he picked up the girl's horoscope was taken as evidence that he was
fated to marry her, and so he usually did, in return for a small amount
of money offered as a dowry. It did not matter if the man who discovered
the purse was married. Indeed, I think married men were preferred
because they would have children who would be obligated to worship
the soul as a mother. Local custom made the soul the man's first wife,
and thereby gave her the right to be worshipped by all her husband's
children.

People in San-hsia no longer attempt to trap men to marry the souls
of their deceased daughters, but a more elaborate form of ghost marriage
still occurs. I heard of three such marriages in the San-hsia area in less
than a year, and was invited to attend one of them as a guest. The groom
was a young married man with two children who had recently suffered
second-degree burns at a fire-walking in which he had participated despite his father's warning that he was polluted as a result of attending
a funeral the day before. This experience convinced the young man that
his father might also be right in insisting that his son had a "two-wife
fate," which is to say that his first wife would die. Because a ghostly
wife becomes her husband's first wife whether the marriage is his first
or second marriage, the obvious way of forestalling the untimely death
of the young man's living wife was for him to marry a woman already
dead. He therefore agreed to let his father arrange a ghost marriage.
The go-between was his father's sister, whose neighbor had a daughter
who had died fifteen years previously. I did not have a chance to interview the bride's family, but was told that they had been trying to arrange
a marriage for their daughter for some time.

[8] A woman who feels indebted to the maidens in the ko-niu-biou will usually
leave a pair of children's shoes at the temple as an offering. People say they offer
children's shoes because women in the im world still have bound feet.

The first step in the marriage procedure was to prepare a contract, which identified the groom and stipulated that his two living children would become the bride's children. This document was then submitted to the bride for her approval. "Had she refused, that would have been an end of the matter," but she agreed. The two families then exchanged a series of gifts, the groom's side sending to the bride's wedding cakes and NT $120 as a bride-price, receiving in return a dowry consisting of a gold ring, a gold necklace, several pairs of shoes, and six dresses, all fitted for the use of the groom's living wife. On the morning of the wedding day the dead bride's family held a feast for her benefit, "feeding her the same as if she were alive." The bride's brother and the go-between then placed the girl's tablet in a taxicab and conveyed it to the groom's home, where his friends and relatives had gathered for a second feast. On leaving their own home the bride's brother invited her to get into the cab, and on arriving at the groom's home informed her of their arrival and invited her to descend. The bride was always treated as though she was alive and participating in the proceedings. During the wedding feast her tablet sat on a chair next to the groom, and after the feast it was put in his bedroom. Local belief has it that a ghostly bride has sexual relations with her husband on their wedding night, and that as a result the man is always exhausted the next day. One of the guests told me that a man who sleeps with a soul "doesn't ejaculate just once or twice, but many times so that he cannot work the next day. A soul is im and so it is very *li-hai* [severe]." I asked if the soul ever returned a second time but was assured that this was impossible. "The next day the tablet is put on the ancestral altar and becomes a *sin* [*shen*, deity]. It cannot return to sleep with the man after that." It appears that once a soul is installed as an ancestor, it loses many of its human appetites.[9]

Although much of the talk at a ghost marriage is about the sexual prowess of female souls, the purpose of these weddings is not to provide dead girls with sexual partners, but to give them children who will be obliged to worship them. The point is made strikingly by the case of a woman I will call Ong A-mui. One day on her way home from the school where she taught, A-mui was struck down by a young man on a motorcycle and suffered such a severe concussion that she died a few hours later. She was forty years old, unmarried, and a member of a household that included her elderly mother and two married brothers. I inquired

---

[9] It appears that the form of ghost marriages varies considerably. In south-central Taiwan, David K. Jordan found that the groom was usually the bride's sister's husband (Jordan 1972: 152–53); in San-hsia most ghost marriages join unrelated families and thereby create new affinal ties. I was told that the groom in the marriage I describe was urged to visit his wife's parents frequently and treat them "like a father and mother."

into the case because I was interested to learn how much compensation her family would demand and how they would press their claim. Much to my surprise I discovered that rather than demanding compensation, her family was offering the young man all Ong A-mui's savings if he would agree to become her son. A neighbor explained that A-mui's mother feared that her sons would divide their sister's savings and neglect her soul. She had therefore spent a night in Mu-cha's famous Hsien Kung temple in the hope that the god would appear in a dream and tell her what to do. The god told her that the young man was an orphan, and said that the accident was a sign that he was fated to become her daughter's son. Because the young man agreed, there was no need for Ong A-mui to marry.

It is important to understand that daughters are not excluded from their father's altar because they are young and female. They are excluded because they are outsiders without a place in the descent line. Before World War II the great majority of all families in the San-hsia area gave away their own female children and adopted in their place "little daughters-in-law" (*sim-pua*) as wives for their sons. Although sim-pua did not enter into a conjugal relationship until they had reached puberty, they were considered married at the time they joined their future husband's family. Consequently, they were members of their husband's line and entitled to all the rights of a married woman. Whether she died as an infant or as a young adult, a sim-pua had a right to a seat on her foster father's altar. The girl's intended husband was responsible for her soul and could not marry without obtaining her permission, which required a promise that one of his sons would worship the girl as his mother. My older informants say that this promise had to be submitted to the deceased in the form of a written contract signed by the girl's foster father, her intended husband, and the woman he wanted to marry. "You had to promise that she would get one of the children or her soul would come back and cause trouble."

Although people often say that "you have to do something for the soul of a daughter or she will come back and cause trouble," it is my impression that serious misfortunes are more likely to be attributed to wives of the line than daughters of the line. Because married women have more rights than unmarried women, there is more likely to be understandable grounds for indignation on the part of a deceased wife. One of the most common sources of trouble is the failure of a second wife to respect the rights of her predecessor. In addition to the right to a place on her husband's altar, a married woman also has the right to expect her replacement to treat her "like an older sister." The second wife should pay a formal visit to the first wife's home immediately after her marriage and thereafter observe all of the duties of a daughter with respect to her predecessor's parents. She should also prepare special foods for the first wife on her deathday and say, "I hope older sister will protect me and help take care of the children." One of my most reliable informants told me that his father's sister had died shortly after marriage and that her husband's second wife had not visited their family. "Her children were sick all the time until she did this, but then everything was all right. The first wife was happy."

It is also important to recognize that the rights women attain through marriage depend on their continued association with their husband's line. If a woman's husband dies and his parents arrange a second marriage with a man who agrees to reside uxorilocally, she retains all her rights vis-à-vis her first husband's line. But if she divorces her husband or marries out of his family as a widow, she forfeits all claims on members of her first husband's line, including the right to expect her sons to worship her after death. It is said that Confucius worshipped his mother despite the fact she had divorced his father, but his grandson Tsu-ssu told his disciples that he could not expect his own children to worship their divorced mother. "My grandfather was a man of complete virtue. I cannot aspire to his level. For me, so long as the deceased was my wife, she was my son's mother. When she ceased to be my wife, she ceased also to be his mother." (Giles 1915: 116–17.)

Although married women who remain identified with their husband's line have a right to a place on his altar, this right does not extend to members of their natal family. If a woman should bring her parents' tablets with her at marriage or be forced by a brother's death to assume responsibility for them later in life, these guests in her husband's home are relegated to an altar in a back room of the house or at best a subsidiary altar located at the right of her husband's altar in the kong-thia:. They are granted a place on her husband's altar only if the wife's responsibility entitles her to inherit a share of her father's estate. Property makes unwelcome visitors honored guests. In such a case the husband must treat his wife's parents with respect, and must assign one of his children to act as their heir and descendant.

In addition to the tablets of unmarried daughters and those introduced by women who married into the family, one occasionally finds in a back room the tablets of dead who are cared for "because they died here and had no one else to provide for them." A good example can be seen in a kitchen in the Song compound whose residents worship the dead of five descent lines. The eldest member of the compound is a woman named Song Suat, whose father and husband both married uxorilocally. Their tablets are located on the main altar in the kong-thia:, alongside the tablets of the original Lim line of Song Suat's grand-father. The remaining two sets of tablets belong to a Ti: line and a Tiu: line and are located on a small shelf in the kitchen of Song Suat's second son. Song Suat insists that these tablets cannot be allowed on the family altar in the kong-thia: "because these are people who just came back here to die." Her story is that one of her mother's sisters married a man named Ti: and bore one child, a daughter. When her parents died the daughter married a man named Tiu: who died a few years later, leaving his wife with one child, an adopted daughter, and the responsibility for both the Ti: and the Tiu: tablets. At this point Song Suat adopted the adopted daughter to raise as a wife for her second son, and the girl and her mother came to live with Song Suat's family. The death of the adopted daughter, and shortly thereafter the death of her mother, left Song Suat's family with two sets of tablets belonging to unrelated lines. They felt they could not abandon them "because they had no children of their own," and so they put the tablets on a shelf in the kitchen, where they are now cared for by Song Suat's son.

We have so far identified two classes of dead. First, there are those dead who are not worshipped because no one has an obligation to care for their souls. They include strangers and children whose deaths are taken as evidence that they are in fact strangers. Second, somewhat closer to the core of the family, is the class of dead best described as dependents of the line. This class includes unmarried daughters, rela-tives of women who married into the family, and dead who are cared for because someone feels sorry for them. These dead are not worshipped on their individual deathdays, and their tablets cannot be placed on the family altar in the kong-thia:. The best they can hope for is a shelf in some corner of the house and occasional offerings on such calendar holi-days as the lunar New Year.

Until recently most homes in the San-hsia area were built in a style that allowed the house to expand into a large U-shaped compound as the family itself was expanded by the marriages of the founder's sons and grandsons. Approaching one of these homes by way of the open end of the U, one faces heavy double-leaf doors that lead into the kong-thia:, and beyond these doors, facing them from the opposite wall, a high, dark wooden table—the ancestral altar. The altar is more than just a table for tablets and an incense burner; it is the seat of the head of the family's line and is generally regarded as the exclusive property of the line. The tablets of other lines may be placed on the altar, but only with the permission of the dead who own the altar. Some people say their ancestors would punish anyone who placed a guest tablet on the altar without first obtaining the ancestors' permission, and everyone agrees that if other tablets are added, they must be placed in the inferior position to the right of the owners' tablets. People also feel that the tablets of different lines must be separated from one another. Altars with guest lines always contain an incense burner for each line, and on many of these altars the lines are separated from one another by a small wooden partition. Some people say that the purpose of these partitions is to save the owners the embarrassment of eating in the presence of guests; others insist that if the dead of different lines are not kept apart, they will quarrel and bring disaster on their descendants.

We can therefore add two further classes of dead to the two already identified. The first occupies the position of honor on the altar located in the kong-thia: and consists of deceased members of the family head's descent line, typically his lineal agnatic ascendants and their wives. The second occupies the inferior position at the right of the altar and consists of a heterogeneous class of dead whose one common characteristic is that their line somehow contributed to the welfare of the host line. Lou Hok-lai's father-in-law qualifies because he gave Lou a share of his estate. Probably because he was too poor to afford a bride price, Lou married a woman whose father was looking for a son-in-law who would help him support his family until his own sons were old enough to cope. Although men who marry in this way sometimes demand a small piece of land as well as waiver of the usual bride-price, this was not part of the agreement Lou reached with his wife's father. It therefore came as a pleasant surprise when his father-in-law gave him a small piece of property "to thank me for helping him raise his children." The result was that when his father-in-law died, Lou made a tablet for him and placed it on his altar next to that of his own parents. He told me that he does not have to worship his father-in-law, "because he has sons of his own," but added that he felt that he ought to "because he was very good to me and gave me a share of his property."

Since inheritance of landed property ordinarily follows descent, it is unusual to find people obligated to worship the dead of other lines as a consequence of inheritance. The only other case I have encountered in San-hsia is that of Tan Thian-lai, whose altar contains the tablets of four lines. In addition to his own parents and grandparents in the Tan line, Tan Thian-lai worships three people surnamed Hong, a man named Ng, and three people who bear the surname Yu:. By his own account, Tan Thian-lai's obligation to these people derives from his inheriting

property from Yu:, who had inherited it from Ng, who had in turn inherited it from Hong. Tan told me that the land in question once belonged to a man named Hong Hue-lieng, whose only child was an
adopted daughter. To perpetuate his line and provide for his old age
Hong married his daughter to a man named Ng Jong-kuei, who agreed
to reside uxorilocally and assign some of his children to the Hong line.
Unfortunately, Ng Jong-kuei and his wife died childless, at which point
the Hong estate and the responsibility for the Hong and Ng dead passed
to a man named Yu: Chieng-cua, "the manager of the Hong land." When
Yu: Chieng-cua also died without descendants, his wife "called in" as
her second husband Tan Thian-lai's father, who brought with him the
tablets of his own forebears. The result was that Tan Thian-lai inherited
what had once been the Hong estate and an ancestral altar that contained the dead of four lines. He told me that he has to worship the Hong,
Ng, and Yu: dead as well as his father and his Tan ancestors "because
all of the land we have used to belong to them."

A more common reason for worshipping the dead of another line is
that one's father belongs to it. Although the Chinese ideal is for all a
man's children to take their descent from him, in practice a large percentage of all children take their descent from someone other than
their father, most commonly their mother's father. When a family has
no sons who survive to marry, they ordinarily must arrange an uxorilocal
marriage for a daughter or an adopted daughter. Occasionally a man
can be found who is willing to resign his place in his own line and allow
all his future children to take their descent from his father-in-law. But
most men who marry uxorilocally insist on retaining their own surname
and the right to name some of their sons to their own line. One arrangement is to name the first-born son to his maternal grandfather's line and
all other children to their father's line; a common alternative is to
alternate the children's descent without regard to their sex.

Those children of uxorilocal marriages who take their descent from
their father must worship their mother as well as their father and his
forebears, but this obligation does not necessarily produce a mixed ancestral altar. They can simply ignore the fact of the uxorilocal marriage
and worship their mother as their father's wife. For example, if a man
surnamed Lim marries into an Ong family, those children who take their
descent from him usually worship their mother as Lim Ma, Ancestress
Lim, ignoring the fact that their brothers worship the same woman as
Ong Ma. But this solution to the problem of uxorilocal marriages is not
available to those children who take their descent from their mother's
father. They are obligated by descent to worship him and his forebears,
from whom they inherit their property. But they are also obligated to

worship their father. "You have to worship your mother's father because he gave you his property, but you also have to worship your father because he raised you. How could you not worship your father?" Since it is inconceivable that a man should be treated as his wife's husband rather than as a representative of a line, these obligations always produce mixed altars.

When a man marries into his wife's family he contributes labor and children to their line, while they provide him and his children with a home and the use of land. The result is a strong sense of mutual obligation that often endures for several generations. If the marriage produces enough children to carry on both lines, these obligations are not expressed in ancestor worship beyond the first generation. But if one of the two lines should lack descendants, the other is required to care for their dead. The inevitable result is that many ancestral altars contain tablets devoted to the remote dead of guests' lines as well as tablets representing the worshippers' parents and the senior members of their own descent line.

Ong Hok-lai's altar is unusual only in that it contains the tablets of two guest lines. Ong's maternal grandmother was an only child whose husband, a man named Lim, married uxorilocally, bringing with him his parents' tablets. Had this couple produced enough children to represent both lines, the responsibility for the Ong and Lim dead would have been divided when Ong Hok-lai's parents died. But his parents were even less fortunate than his grandparents. Their only child was an adopted daughter, who was assigned to the Ong line. Because she was an only child, she had to worship her father and his parents as well as her mother and her ancestors in the Ong line; and, for the same reason, she also married uxorilocally, to a man surnamed Tan, who brought with him his foster parents' tablets. Consequently, by the time Ong Hok-lai was born the family altar contained representatives of three lines. At the left, in the position of honor, were the tablets of the original Ong line; at their right, the Lim tablets brought by Ong Hok-lai's maternal grandfather; and, at the right of the altar in the lowest position, the Tan tablets introduced by his father. Ong Hok-lai's parents proved more fertile than his grandparents and his great-grandparents, bearing six sons and three daughters. Ong Hok-lai was the eldest son and was assigned to the Ong line; his second and fourth brothers were given to the Lim line; and his third and fifth brothers, to the Tan line. Unfortunately for the dead, Ong Hok-lai was the only filial son in the lot. His brothers all tired of the hard life of upland farmers and moved away to the city, deserting the tablets on the family altar. By descent, Ong Hok-lai is obligated only to his mother and her ascendants in the Ong line, but in fact he worships all the dead represented on the altar. These include, in addition to his deceased wife, his mother, his maternal grandmother, this woman's parents, grandparents, and great-grandparents; a man Ong identifies as his mother's mother's grandfather's younger brother's son; Ong's father and his foster parents; and Ong's maternal grandfather and his parents: a total of sixteen people. When I asked Ong Hok-lai how he could remember the deathdays of sixteen ancestors, he showed me a notebook that lists the names of the dead in one column and their death dates in another.

Ong Hok-lai's case is also interesting as an example of a tendency to divide the dead into classes representing degrees of obligation. The Ong tablets at the left of the altar are divided from the Lim and Tan tablets by a partition, but the Lim and Tan tablets are not separated from one another. Thus, whereas the altar contains tablets belonging to three descent lines, these are presented as divisible into two classes: those dead to whom Ong Hok-lai is obligated by descent and those to whom he is obligated as a consequence of uxorilocal marriages. The difference between these dead and those to whom Ong owes little or no obligation is shown by the location of a set of tablets introduced into the house by Ong's second wife. These have been relegated to a little shelf in the corner of a storeroom behind the kitchen. Ong Hok-lai insists that they could not be placed on the family altar or even in the kong-thia:. "These people didn't marry into the family. They aren't really members of the family."

Although Ong Hok-lai's arrangement of his ancestral tablets is a common one, it is by no means universal. The degree to which the various classes of dead are separated varies with the size and corporate solidarity of the group that owns the altar. One seldom finds partitions on domestic altars that serve a single household. These appear only later, when the house has grown into a compound occupied by several agnatically related families who worship their common ancestors at what I call a communal altar. If further growth does not destroy the residents' solidarity, they may even bar the tablets of other lines on the altar in the kong-thia:. The tablets of guest lines are then relegated to subsidiary altars in the private quarters of those people who are responsible for their care.[10] The extreme case in San-hsia is Ch'i-nan, where communal altars have been replaced by true lineage halls. Although the altars in

[10] In the course of our work in the San-hsia area, C. Stevan Harrell and I have examined 33 altars whose owners worship guest lines in the same house. Twenty-two of these were domestic altars belonging to a single family; eleven were communal altars serving two or more families living in one house. In eleven of the 33 cases the tablets of the guest lines were divided from those of the host line either by a partition on the altar or by removal of the tablets of the guests' lines to subsidiary altars. The difference between domestic altars and communal altars is evident in the

these halls admit the recent dead as well as the remote dead and serve as domestic altars for weddings and funerals, they are rigidly exclusive, admitting only lineage members who have given all their sons to the lineage (Ahern 1973: 121–25). The result is a situation in which the dead of lines that belong to the lineage are worshipped in halls at the center of the community; the souls of in-marrying men are worshipped only at private altars in the homes around the hall; and the souls of un-married daughters are entirely excluded from the community. The order is the one found throughout the San-hsia area, the difference being that in Ch'i-nan more rigorous distinctions are drawn between the three classes of dead.

My thesis is not that people in San-hsia classify the dead into three or four mutually exclusive categories, but rather that they recognize a con-tinuum of obligation and arrange ancestral tablets in a way that expresses their relative degree of obligation to particular people. After her husband died Lim Chun-ki lived for a number of years with a man named Tan Tsui-ong, who helped her raise her four sons. When Tan died Lim felt obliged to worship him "because he helped me raise my children," but she did not want to place his tablet on her family altar, probably because she and Tan had never married. On the other hand, she felt that she could not relegate his tablet to a back room "like someone who didn't matter." Her solution was to locate Tan's tablet on a small shelf next to the family altar in the kong-thia:. The important point is that however they arrange their tablets, people in San-hsia recognize a continuum of obligation that runs from those dead to whom the living are obligated by descent to those to whom they are hardly obligated at all. The dead at one end of the continuum are true ancestors; the dead at the other end are almost ghosts.

IV

In China ancestor worship is by nature an act of obeisance. Many people make regular offerings to dead who are not members of their line, sometimes even to quite distant relatives. But no one would con-sider worshipping a child or grandchild. Although people are under-standably reluctant to contemplate the possibility, all agree that parents will abandon the soul of an adolescent son rather than worship him them-selves. "Parents can never worship their own children. Children are supposed to worship their parents."

The offerings made to the gods also express obeisance, but the mo-

---

fact that hosts and guests are separated by one or the other of these devices in eight (72.7 percent) of the communal altars as compared with only three (13.6 percent) of the domestic altars.

tives are entirely different. A person worships his ancestors because he is obligated to do so as an heir or descendant; he worships the gods in the hope of gaining their sympathy and good will. Since a man is no more obligated to worship a god than he is to make gifts to an official, there is no thought that a god might punish a person for neglecting him. But neglect of worship is the most common reason given for misfortunes attributed to the agency of the ancestors. A man who used to live in Hsia-ch'i-chou married and moved out of the village, leaving his sister and her husband to care for his parents' tablets. A few years later his wife fell ill, and then one of his children. Frightened by these events and a doctor's inability to cure the illnesses, he consulted a shaman and was told that they were caused by his father, who wanted his son to care for his tablet. The shaman explained the essential difference between the gods and the ancestors in these terms: "A man is free to believe in the gods or not believe in the gods, but he has to believe in the ancestors. If he doesn't, they will come back and cause him trouble."

People ordinarily worship the god under whose jurisdiction they live because worship is often a community activity and because it is prudent to maintain good relations with such powerful figures, but it is clear that the average man does not feel morally obligated to make offerings to any god. If a particular deity is uninterested in his subjects or lacks the authority to be of any use to them, they turn to another god who is more sympathetic and more powerful. According to stories now told in Hsia-ch'i-chou, there was a period in the late 1930's and early 1940's when Shang Ti Kung was less efficacious than he is at present. During this period the god and his temple were neglected. The roof of the temple leaked; the garden in the courtyard filled up with weeds; and the god himself sat unconsulted and unhonored on a dirty altar. It was not until Shang Ti Kung was credited with predicting the political troubles of the late 1940's that his temple was repaired and interest in the god revived. What I think is the essential attitude toward the supernatural bureaucracy is revealed in the advice an old woman claims to have given Shang Ti Kung during the period of his decline. In her words, "I went to the temple every day, and every day I said to the god, 'You are a god with great ability, so why do you sit here and say nothing? You ought to show what you can do and let people here know what kind of a god you are. It is because you don't show what you can do that people all go elsewhere to worship. If you would do something to make your ability known, the people would all come here to worship.'"

When people encounter misfortunes it is usually to the gods that they appeal for help, but occasionally the aid of the ancestors may also be solicited. Because the ancestors are not so powerful as the gods, one cannot expect as much of them. They may even choose to ignore requests made of them, and if they do their descendants have little ground for complaint. A person's ancestors are his parents and grandparents, and parents and grandparents have no obligation to heed every request of a child or grandchild. But even though the relationship favors the ancestors as seniors, there is still an assumption of reciprocity. The ancestors may ignore many of their descendants' requests without endangering the relationship, but they cannot consistently ignore urgent and repeated supplications. If they do, their descendants may forswear their obligations. This is an extreme step, comparable to a man's abandoning his aged father, but it is not unheard of. Conversion to Christianity is often attributed to the failures of the convert's ancestors, and one man I know destroyed his ancestors' tablets in a rage at what he took to be their indifference. When Lim Bun-iek's wife became seriously ill, Lim appealed to his ancestors to help her recover. Unfortunately, and much to Lim's distress, she died. Two years later Lim's mother became ill; again he appealed to the ancestors for aid, and again without success. His mother also died. For a man with a temper as violent as Lim Bun-iek's this was more strain than his bonds with his ancestors could bear. He seized the ancestral tablets, chopped them into small pieces, burnt the pieces, and then threw the ashes into the river, telling his neighbors that he was henceforth a Christian. When I asked him why he no longer worshipped his ancestors, he replied, "What use are your ancestors? You spend money making offerings to them all the time, and then when you need their help they don't do anything for you."

In making the point that a son does not have an absolute obligation to worship his father, Ahern notes (1973: 155) that if a man has more than one son and fails to leave one of them property, the man who is disinherited need not worship his father. "Most of the people I asked about this replied, 'Why would that son want to worship his father if he didn't get any property?'" But some of Ahern's informants added that although "a son was justified in not making offerings to his father under these conditions, he still risked his father's anger; an angry deceased father could easily bring sickness or misfortune on him. No matter how strained a son's relations with his father, he may be held accountable to his father anyway simply for the gift of life." Although the obligation a son owes his father is not absolute, then, this evidence suggests that it is very nearly so. That a man could be disinherited and still be held accountable for "the gift of life" argues that the burden of obligation favors parents and gives them the right to demand unquestioning loyalty.

Although revolutionaries in China have destroyed images of the tutelary deities as symbols of the establishment, most Chinese would not blame a god for failing to answer a petition. Because the gods are not conceived of as having obligations to their subjects, there would be no cause for indignation. When a man appeals to an ancestor he appeals to a kinship relationship involving a certain degree of mutual dependence, but when he appeals to a god he negotiates for his good will just as he would in attempting to secure a favor from a magistrate or a policeman. He makes a small sacrifice and promises a larger one if the god will grant his petition. If divination reveals that the god is not inclined to grant the petition, he then promises a more substantial gift, repeating the process until the god finally agrees. The god is always treated with all the courtesy owed someone of such high status, but the larger gift is not produced until after the desired outcome has been obtained. Having promised a pig's head if a child's illness is cured or the price of pork raised, a person does not actually sacrifice the pig's head until the child has recovered or he has sold his pigs at a profit. As is always the case in negotiations with officials and petty bureaucrats, small gifts and respect are offered in promise of larger gifts to come, but the larger gifts are not delivered until the results are safely in hand.

Although neither the gods nor the ancestors are conceived of as essentially malevolent, both are considered capable of inflicting misfortunes on the living. These misfortunes are always interpreted as punishment, but very different motives explain the penalties attributed to the gods and those attributed to the ancestors. Like their counterparts in the human bureaucracy, the gods are thought of as proud and exceedingly jealous of their prerogatives. Any derogation of their high status is likely to bring a quick and angry response. A few years ago a man in Hsia-ch'i-chou fell at a fire-walking and was so badly burned that he later died of his wounds. Some of his neighbors now say that the god was punishing him for having failed to observe three days of sexual abstinence prior to the event. "The god was angry because that man came there dirty." Another man in the same village suffers from severe palsy, which people say is a consequence of his having made fun of a god he saw at a procession when he was a child. That this view of the gods was widespread in traditional China is suggested by Mrs. William L. Pruen's comments on the death of one of her neighbor's children in Chengtu: "At another home in this compound a little fellow, about eleven years of age, was suddenly taken dangerously ill. The poor boy was very worried because he had in some way insulted an idol shrine and thought he was being punished for his fault. He died the next day." (Pruen 1906: 101–2.)

The gods are sensitive to insult and may punish a man for personal reasons, but they are also officials who promote the general welfare. They are said to reward those who lead virtuous lives and to punish anyone who violates the moral code. An elderly man in Kan-yüan told me that a typhoon had washed away his neighbor's field and not his own "because the gods were punishing that man for always stealing other people's water. He was a bandit who took whatever he wanted." Several people in Ch'i-pei, on the other side of San-hsia town, claim that one of their neighbors used a potion to make her husband impotent (because she was a sim-pua and didn't like her husband), and that as a result the gods punished her with a protracted illness. Any particularly striking death is likely to be interpreted as supernaturally administered punishment. One day Hsia-ch'i-chou was struck by an unusually violent electrical storm. As one villager described it to me six years later, "There was lightning everywhere. The rice stalks in the kitchen looked like they were about to burn." Ong Hok-hin, returning from his fields, stopped to rest in front of the village store. "After watching the storm for a while, he said, 'I wonder who the lightning will kill today.' Then he got up and walked toward home. He was killed just as he was entering his house." Although Ong Hok-hin was generally thought of as a man of good character, the manner of his death was taken as evidence of some unsuspected crime. "He always seemed to be a good man, but he must have done something very bad that no one knew about or the gods wouldn't have punished him that way." A more sophisticated informant made the same point about a relative who had been killed by a truck, adding that "this is the reason people say it is better to die of an illness than to die a violent death."

Most people in San-hsia say that the gods only punish people "who are really bad," but the belief that the gods do administer punishment leads a few people to assume that they can be induced to avenge private wrongs. When Li A-hong's uxorilocally married son-in-law persuaded his wife to move out of her mother's home, Li A-hong was furious and "asked the gods to let him be crushed to death in a mining accident." "A year later when I heard that his shoulder had been broken in an accident, I was very happy. But then he recovered, and so I told the god that if he would let that man be killed, I would burn a hundred sticks of incense in an open field." When her son-in-law was killed in a second accident in the mines, Li A-hong was delighted. "My neighbors came and told me that that man had been crushed beyond recognition in the mines, and I was so happy that I laughed and laughed and laughed."

Just how punitive the ancestors are is the subject of sharp disagreement. On the basis of his extended experience as the British magistrate of Weihaiwei, R. F. Johnston concluded (1910: 286–87) that "ancestral spirits are regarded as beneficent beings who never causelessly use their mysterious powers to injure the living; but if their descendants lead evil lives, or neglect the family sacrifices, or treat the sacred rules of filial piety with contempt, then the spirits will in all probability exercise the parental prerogatives of punishment. . . . The father does not, by the mere accident of death, divest himself of his patriarchal rights of administering justice and inflicting punishment on his sons and grandsons." Essentially the same view is expressed by J. T. Addison (Addison 1925) and by Maurice Freedman, who summarizes his view of "the characteristic behaviour imputed to Chinese ancestors" as follows (Freedman 1967: 92–93): "While they will certainly punish their descendants if they suffer neglect or are offended by an act of omission which affects them directly (chiefly, the failure to secure for them a firm line of descent), they are essentially benign and considerate of their issue. Before taking action against their descendants they need to be provoked; capricious behaviour is certainly alien to their benevolent and protective nature."

In his study of West Town in Yünnan and in his generalizations about China as a whole, Francis L. K. Hsu argues (Hsu 1963: 45) not only that the ancestors are benevolent, but that they do not punish at all. "It can be stated unequivocally that ancestral spirits, in every part of China, are believed to be only a source of benevolence, never a source of punishment to their descendants. This is shown by the fact that when the Chinese is suffering some misfortune, such as sickness or fire or flood or the lack of male progeny, he will suspect that the fault lies with any of a variety of deities or ghosts, but never with the spirits of an ancestor." Emily Ahern, on the other hand, challenges the view that the ancestors are "essentially benign" and offers impressive evidence of their occasional capriciousness and malevolent intent. Her informants told her that the ancestors sometimes inflict misfortunes just because they are "mean" or have "a bad heart," and that even when a person makes regular offerings to his ancestors, he cannot be certain that they won't come back and cause trouble (Ahern 1973: 199–200).

In the version of this paper written in 1965, after my first field trip, I characterized beliefs about ancestral punishment in much the same terms as Johnston and Freedman. Since then I have returned to the field twice, and on each occasion have come away convinced that the ancestors are more punitive than I had previously thought. Ahern notes that many people in Ch'i-nan refused to tell her their version of a story that reflects hostility between the dead and their surviving descendants (1973: 207). This seems to me only one manifestation of a conflict between an ideal that says the ancestors are always benevolent and a fear that they are in fact punitive. Asked if they believe that their ancestors would punish them for neglect, people usually insist that they would not. But when they suffer a series of misfortunes, most people give serious consideration to the possibility that the ancestors are responsible.

I cannot cite here all the evidence that led me to this conclusion, but the following excerpts from my field notes should suffice to make the point that ancestors are not always benign and considerate:

1. The wife of a doctor in the town of San-hsia married out of her natal family despite being an only child. When her children suffered a series of illnesses, this was widely interpreted as punishment inflicted by her neglected ancestors. Apparently she and her husband accepted this interpretation, for they named one of their children to her father's line and now worship her forebears as well as her husband's.

2. Tan Kim-hok told me that if one of three brothers dies without children, the survivors have to give him one of their sons in adoption. "If they didn't, the man who died would come back and cause trouble." He explained that this is why he and his sons worship his younger brother even though he died after the family was divided.

3. I asked Li Chieng-cua if a man's sons have to have their father's permission to divide the family. He insists that they do, and that the ancestors would punish anyone who talked about dividing the family when their father was unwilling.

4. A man whose registered name is Ong Kok-hua told me that his real name is Ong Ng Kok-hua. He was given the second surname as a child, when it was discovered that an illness was caused by "an early ancestor" named Ng who wanted him to be his son. He also told me that two of his four children died because he did not give them the Ng surname, and made a point of noting that the two who survived had been given the surname Ng.

5. The wife of a farmer for whom Tan So-lan picked tea mistreated her sim-pua so badly that the girl committed suicide. To get revenge the girl's parents pulled an edge of her clothing out of the coffin before it was buried. "That girl came back all the time to scare her [foster] mother. When the mother's son married, the daughter-in-law was very aggressive and fought with her mother-in-law. Their quarrels made the son feel so bad that he ran away to the mainland and became a bandit. All this was because that woman treated her sim-pua so badly."

6. Hong Hai-a told me that the ancestors will punish anyone who dis-

turbs their tablets. He says nothing will happen if a cat or dog disturbs a tablet because the ancestors understand that animals do not know any better.[11]

7. One of Ui A-chan's neighbors told me that when Ui's grandmother died, the family arranged a *kong-tik* (a "merit" ceremony) for all their ancestors. Unfortunately, they wrote the wrong name for one ancestor, writing A-hok, the name he was always called by, though his real name was Thiam-hok. When they discovered the mistake they asked a shaman to intervene, but he said it was too late. By that time someone else had received all the money they had burned for Thiam-hok. The neighbor claims that Ui A-chan's family is so poor because of this unwitting slight to their ancestor.

8. Ong Lai-ho used to live next to a family who made their living as wood cutters. Because it was inconvenient for them to worship their ancestors on their individual deathdays, they decided to worship them all together on the ninth day of the ninth lunar month. "After that the husband and wife were sick all the time. The husband even lost one of his eyes."

9. Ong Lai-ho also told me that one of her neighbors inherited his brother's land and built a house on it, but did not bother to worship his brother. "His family was very troublesome until he went to see a god and found out the reason. After he began to worship his brother, the trouble stopped."

10. Lou Mui-mue told me that when her husband was about ten years old, his parents went to ask a god why he was so often sick. The god said it was because his mother's first husband wanted the boy to worship him. After his death this man's wife had married out of his family and left his tablet in charge of an adopted daughter. This girl worshipped her foster father and took his tablet with her when she married, but he was dissatisfied because his tablet was placed on a subsidiary altar in a back room. He wanted his wife's son to worship him and place his tablet on the main altar.

11. Ong Cin-tik's daughter says that an American missionary persuaded her mother's brother's son to throw away his ancestral tablets and become a Christian. "He died a few months later, and his father the following year. It's not a good thing to become a Christian and neglect the ancestors."

---

[11] Hong Hai-a's attitude is not unusual. Ahern (1973: 201) quotes one of her informants as follows: "Several years ago a Ui man accidentally bumped and moved the incense pot for the ancestors in the hall. As a result, another man in the lineage died shortly thereafter. When they opened the box to insert the man's tablet, two more people died."

12. I asked Lou Kim-lan if the gods would punish a mother-in-law who mistreated her daughter-in-law. She agreed that the gods would punish a woman who mistreated her daughter-in-law, adding that the ancestors would punish a daughter-in-law who mistreated her mother-in-law.

13. When his younger brother died, Li Ai-cu's neighbor drove his sister-in-law out of the house and claimed all the family's property for himself. Li Ai-cu says that as a result the man still cannot use the rooms that were once occupied by his brother's family. "Anyone who tries to live in those rooms sees that man who died and gets scared."

14. A former head of the Lou lineage in Ch'i-nan told me that Lous never marry their neighbors the Uis. "The Uis tried to steal our land and we told our ancestors we would never marry anyone named Ui." He also told me that when a Lou family broke this pledge and gave a daughter to a Ui family as a sim-pua, the girl died before she was old enough to marry her foster brother. He attributes the girl's death to the anger of his lineage ancestors.[12]

15. After fathering one son Lim Iu-chan was killed by aborigines, and his wife called in as her second husband a man named Ti: Cin-cai, who fathered three sons. When Ti: died the family prepared a gravestone that indicated he had four sons, counting Lim Iu-chan's son along with Ti:'s three. When several members of the family fell ill shortly thereafter, everyone agreed that this was because Lim did not want his son counted as one of Ti:'s sons. Neighbors say the sick members of the family did not recover until the gravestone was changed.

These cases and those mentioned earlier should not be taken as evidence that everyone in San-hsia fears their ancestors or attributes most misfortunes to their agency. Even when confronted with examples provided by their neighbors, many people insist that the ancestors do not ordinarily punish their descendants. At the same time, the fact that many people do not attribute misfortunes to their ancestors does not necessarily mean they consider them benign. When I asked Tan A-bok if she thought the ancestors would punish their descendants for neglecting them, she replied, "Oh, no, that wouldn't happen. Wouldn't everyone be rich if their ancestors were so powerful?" I think that Hsu is right in saying that Chinese never attribute such major disasters as epidemics to their ancestors, but I feel he is wrong in taking this as evidence that the ancestors are essentially benevolent (1963: 45–46). In my view the ancestors are

---

[12] Similar instances involving the same two lineages are mentioned by Ahern as evidence that people attribute serious illness and even death to their ancestors (1973: 201).

not propitiated as possible causes of major catastrophes because people do not think them powerful enough to affect the living in such a dramatic fashion. Freedman has argued that ancestors are not feared in China as in some West African societies because the living are not conscious of having displaced their ascendants from coveted positions of power (1966: 143–54; 1967: 90–102). A simpler explanation might be that Chinese ancestors are not feared because they are not conceived of as powerful beings. The African societies Freedman discusses are stateless societies in which the senior men of the lineage dominate the social landscape. In traditional China the authority of senior kinsmen was overshadowed by the far greater power of the imperial bureaucracy. People did not attribute great events to the spiritual remains of kinsmen because kinsmen were not capable of controlling the course of events. Great events were more appropriately attributed to gods, gods who were modeled on the imperial bureaucracy.

The essential difference between the gods and the ancestors is not that the former are punitive while the latter are essentially benevolent. It is, rather, that while the gods are powerful and represent public morality, the ancestors are relatively weak and concerned only with their own welfare and that of their descendants. The gods often punish people for crimes against society at large, the ancestors never. Quintessentially members of kinship groups, they remain identified with their best interests. When I asked people if they thought their ancestors would punish them for stealing from a stranger, they seemed genuinely surprised by the question. "Why should they want to punish you for a thing like that?" one of my more outspoken informants replied. "Aren't your ancestors your own parents and grandparents?"

This difference between the gods and the ancestors is evident in the way the two are supplicated. When a man asks the help of a god he must accompany his petition with an offering to gain the god's attention and assure his good will. Without an offering, there is no reason to expect the god to hear and respond to his plea. But when a person appeals to his ancestors, he need not make an offering then and there. Insofar as senior kinsmen are obliged to heed the requests of their juniors, they are under a general obligation to do so, just as juniors are under a general obligation to provide comfort and support for their seniors. Where relations with the gods must be continually renewed with offerings and shows of respect, any favor being dependent on an exhaustible good will, a man's relations with his ancestors are general and permanent, involving an assumption of a common welfare and mutual dependence. One is a kinship relationship; the other a political relationship.

V

Although the gods and the ancestors differ in many important respects, they also have a great deal in common. The extreme contrast, from the Chinese point of view, is between the gods and the ancestors on the one hand, and ghosts on the other. The gods and the ancestors are granted the respect due social superiors; ghosts are despised, "like beggars." Where the gods and the ancestors can be appealed to for protection and help, ghosts offer men nothing but misfortune of every kind. The terms used to refer to the two forms of the supernatural denote the sharpest spiritual and moral opposition. The gods and the ancestors are sin, "gods" or "deities"; the generic name for ghosts is kui, "demons" or "devils." In Chinese metaphysics the positive, immaterial, and celestial aspect of the human soul is termed sin; the negative, material, and terrestrial side of the soul is called kui. Philosophers associate sin with growth, production, and life, and hence with light and warmth; kui is identified with decline, destruction, and death, and, by extension, with darkness and cold.[13]

The catalogue of human misery attributed to ghosts is a lengthy one. Accidents, barrenness, death, and all varieties of illness are laid to their agency, as are crop failures, business losses, bad luck in gambling, and the wasteful and disruptive habits of individual men and women. One woman in Ch'i-chou blames ghosts for her husband's frequent visits to wine houses and prostitutes, and another sees their malevolent influence at work in her son's lack of enterprise and her daughter-in-law's stubborn independence. Any contact with ghosts, however brief, is likely to result in misfortune. One night Tan Chun-mui was returning home late from the market town and saw "something black" ahead of her on the path. Frightened by the apparition, she stopped, thinking it might be wise to return to town and spend the night with friends. While she hesitated, "the black thing flipped over into the field and was gone." Tan Chun-mui was so shaken she had to crawl all the way home to the village, and she and her friends now say the encounter resulted in an illness "lasting for months and months."

Some ghosts are purposely harmful, "like a man who is mad at you," whereas others are only passively dangerous, "like a hot stove." In the view of most of my informants the character of a ghost depends upon his

---

[13] In his paper in this volume C. Stevan Harrell discusses cases in which ghosts acquire a reputation for great power and come to be regarded as gods. The important point with respect to my thesis is that powerful spirits become gods and are then clothed in bureaucratic trappings. It is as though the peasant cannot imagine great power that is not essentially bureaucratic.

social and economic circumstances. Most dead people have descendants obligated to make offerings for their benefit, and their souls are therefore supplied with all the means of a comfortable existence in the next world. The spiritual remains of these people are content and bear no malice toward the living. The malicious ghosts are those discontented souls who are forced by their circumstances to prey on the living. They include the neglected dead—those who have no descendants because they died childless or as children, and those who died away from home and were forgotten—and also those hateful souls who receive no sacrifices because they remain at the scene of death seeking revenge—murder victims, suicides, and the unjustly executed. Some are angry because they are hungry and homeless, and some are hungry and homeless because they are angry. The weaker of these unhappy beings gather outside temples to beg for a living like the derelicts of this world, while the more powerful among them roam the countryside like so many bandits.

Although people in San-hsia differ on how one should deal with these malevolent creatures, they agree that dealing with a ghost is like dealing with *lo-mua:*, the gangs of young toughs who use threats of violence as a means of extortion. According to Ong Thian-co, "You have to make offerings to ghosts. They are just like the lo-mua:. If you don't give them something so that they will go away, you will never have any peace." Ong Zi-ko also views an offering to a ghost as comparable to paying off a lo-mua:, but he takes a more defiant attitude toward the use of such offerings. In his view it is a mistake to make an offering to a ghost "because the more you offer them the more often they come. They are like the lo-mua:. If you give a lo-mua: something when he comes to your house, he'll come back every day." As poor men with little means of defending themselves, Ong Thian-co and Ong Zi-ko fear both the ghosts and the lo-mua:. Their affluent and politically powerful neighbor, Li Bun-tua, fears neither. One day at a funeral Li told me that his relatives would not have to burn spirit money to keep the ghosts from harassing his soul on its journey to the underworld. "The next world is just like this one. If you are a strong man like me, big and fat, no one will bother you, but if you are old and weak, the ghosts will bully you just as the lo-mua: bully the old and weak in this world."

When pressed to explain their conception of ghosts, most of my informants compared them to bullies or beggars. Why do you have to make offerings to ghosts? "So that they will go away and leave you alone. They are like beggars and won't leave you alone if you don't give them something." Why is it that people usually call ghosts "the good brothers"? "Because they would be angry if you called them ghosts. Calling a ghost kui is like calling a beggar 'beggar.' " Ghosts ordinarily appear to the living as evil, formless objects, seen lying next to an irrigation channel or lurking in a dense bamboo grove. The one exception in Hsia-ch'i-chou was a creature who was said to walk through the village every night "beating two bamboo sticks just like a beggar." The dozen or so villagers who claimed to have seen this particular spirit agreed that it was the spiritual remains of a former beggar. "He used to come here all the time before he died. That was a long time ago now, but he still comes every night. He didn't have any children, so there is no one to make offerings."

The association of the destitute of this world with those of the next is also clear in the Reverend Doolittle's description of funeral customs in Foochow in the 1860's: "When burials connected with wealthy families take place on the hills, or the regular sacrifices to the dead are about to be performed in the spring at their graves, beggars often interfere for the purpose of getting food or money. . . . Oftentimes a considerable sum of money is distributed on such occasions among the beggars before they will allow burial or the sacrifice to proceed without interruptions, and with the desirable solemnity and silence." (1865: II, 262.) Just as the mourner must bribe the beggars to keep them from interfering, he must also pay their supernatural counterparts to save the deceased from similar annoyances. After the coffin has been lowered into the grave, "an offering is also made to the distressed and destitute spirits in the infernal regions, such as the spirits of lepers and beggars. . . . According to the general supposition, they, on receiving what the friends of the dead are disposed to bestow upon them, allow the sacrifice to the dead to go on without interruption." (Doolittle 1865: I, 206.) Each year when people return to the grave to make offerings to the deceased, they must also offer something to the ghosts. This, Doolittle says, is "in order to prevent departed friends from being molested by the importunity of beggars and lepers in the unseen world" (1865: II, 49).

In the Chinese view a beggar's request for alms is not really begging. It is a threat. Beggars are believed capable of laying terrible curses on anyone who ignores their entreaties. The man who sends a beggar away empty-handed risks the possibility of illness or damage to property. Beggars are thus like bandits and ghosts in that they are feared, and bandits and ghosts are like beggars in that they are socially despised. The social identities of the three are so similar that bandits and beggars are sometimes treated like ghosts. It was once the practice in northern Taiwan for every village and town to make a massive offering to the ghosts during the seventh lunar month. A high bamboo structure was erected in some central place, a market or a village square, and then hung with firecrackers and a wealth of food: chickens and ducks, both dead and alive, slices of pork and pigs' heads, fish of every kind, rice cakes, bananas, pineapples, melons, etc. This great feast was first offered up to all the wandering spirits who had answered the summons of the gongs, and then, after the ghosts had had time to satisfy themselves, the entire collection was turned over to the destitute humans who had gathered for the occasion. The Rev. George MacKay witnessed one of these festivals in Taipei City in the 1880's:

It was a gruesome sight. When night came on and the time for summoning the spirits approached, the cones were illuminated by dozens of lighted candles. Then the priests took up their position on a raised platform, and by clapping their hands and sounding a large brass gong they called the spirits of all the departed to come and feast on the food provided. "Out of the night and the other world" the dead were given time to come and gorge themselves on the "spiritual" part of the feast, the essence, that was suited to their ethereal requirements. Meanwhile, a very unspiritual mob—thousands and thousands of hungry beggars, tramps, blacklegs, desperados of all sorts, from the country towns, the city slums, or venturing under cover of the night from their hiding-places among the hills—surged and swelled in every part of the open space, impatiently waiting their turn at the feast. When the spirits had consumed the "spiritual" part, the "carnal" was the property of the mob, and the mob quite approved of this division. . . . At length the spirits were satisfied, and the gong was sounded once more. That was the signal for the mob. . . . In one wild scramble, groaning and yelling all the while, trampling on those who had lost their footing or were smothered by the falling cones, fighting and tearing one another like mad dogs, they all made for the coveted food. (MacKay 1895: 130–31.)

All ghosts are like bandits and beggars, but not all ghosts are the spiritual remains of bandits or beggars. The reader will remember the case of the young man who saw "a white thing" moving across the paddy. His argument for labeling this apparition a "ghost" was his belief that it was the soul of another man's mother. This woman had not been a beggar during her lifetime, and she was not destitute in the next world. She was on her way to her son's house to receive deathday offerings made in her honor. I suggest that the category "ghosts" includes the souls of all people who die as members of some other group. They are not all malicious because the great majority are cared for by their living descendants, but they are all potentially dangerous because they are all strangers or outsiders. The malicious among them are malicious for the same reason some strangers are malicious. They are souls who have been insulted or injured in this life or the next, or souls who can support themselves only by begging or banditry. The crucial point is that the category "ghosts" is always a relative one. Your ancestors are my ghosts, and my ancestors are your ghosts, just as your relatives are strangers to me, and my relatives strangers to you.

This is not a point one can prove by asking people if the ghosts they see are their neighbors' ancestors, or, worse yet, by asking them if their own ancestors are ghosts to their neighbors. The two categories are polar opposites, like day and night, good and bad, and iong and im. Hence it is impossible for people to seriously consider the idea that what is an ancestor from one point of view is a ghost from another. The few informants on whom I tried such questions replied, "How could your ancestors be ghosts? Your ancestors are your own people and help you. Ghosts make you sick and cause trouble." Only the rare informant can look at his own society from a vantage point other than his own. Tan Cin-chiong was such a man because of his education and his academic interest in Chinese folklore. In his view kui is the generic term for all spirits or souls of the dead. "Sin is just a polite name for kui. Your ancestors are sin to you, but they are kui to other people. It just sounds better to call them sin."

Most people realize that their ancestors are other people's ghosts only when unusual circumstances make them look at their own dead from another point of view. One of my best examples was recorded by Ch'en Cheng-hsiung, who worked as my field assistant for a few months in 1967. A woman named Peq A-mui was telling Ch'en that her mother had once quarreled over water with one of her husband's cousins. "That man went to see a famous *hu-a-sian* and got something and put it in my mother's tea. Ten days later a red stripe appeared on my mother's neck and she died. Exactly one year later his neighbors heard that man scream, saying that someone was squeezing his testicles. When the neighbors ran to see what was happening, they saw my mother coming out of the house." Ch'en then alertly asked his informant if her mother was a ghost to that man. She seemed surprised by the question, but agreed that her own mother was a ghost from the other man's point of view. "If he wanted to make an offering to my mother, he would have to do it outside the house rather than in the house."

Maurice Freedman has kindly allowed me to report another striking case in point, which he collected in Hong Kong. Talking to a man who had grown up in Kwangtung province, Freedman asked him about the difference between *shan* and *kwai* (the Cantonese equivalents of sin and kui). "He was horrified at the suggestion that the ancestors were other than shan; kwai are evil, ancestors never are, they help. But when I got him on to the festival of the hungry ghosts in the seventh lunar month, it occurred to him that other people's ancestors could be kwai and therefore harmful." A few weeks later Freedman asked the same informant to explain the use of the term kwai in the context of female mediums who are hired to call up customers' ancestors. One term of these mediums in Cantonese is *man kwai p'o*, "old women who talk to ghosts." "My informant patiently explained that everybody else's dead are kwai to you: the word kwai in such expressions as *man kwai p'o* . . . refers to the fact that the customer's ancestors are not the medium's ancestors. Your own ancestors cannot possibly be kwai to you; kwai means (implies) stranger."

The essential point that ghosts are the supernatural equivalent of feared strangers need not rest on contemporary evidence alone. Thanks to the careful work of Shen Chien-shih, we have a detailed account of the evolution of the character *kuei* (the Mandarin equivalent of kui and kwai). Drawing on both paleographic and documentary evidence, Shen (1936–37: 19) reconstructs the character's history as follows:

1. *Kuei*, like *yü*, was originally the name given to some strange anthropoid or simian creature.
2. From the name of an animal, *kuei* was extended to denote a people or race of alien origin.
3. From the abstract idea of an animal, *kuei* was extended to express the abstract ideas of "fear," "strangeness," "large size," "cunning," etc.
4. *Kuei*, the name of a corporeal creature, was "transferred" to represent the imagined appearance of a spiritual being, i.e., the ghost of the dead.

One could argue that the meaning of the character kuei has not changed at all. The term still refers to strange creatures who are regarded as aliens and are feared. The only difference is that whereas kuei once referred to real beings, it now refers to their supernatural counterparts. As the horizons of the Chinese world expanded, aliens became fellow citizens, making it impolite and impolitic to refer to them as kuei. But from the point of view of the average villager, people who are nothing more than fellow citizens are still strangers, and still to be feared. Consequently, their souls become kuei.

Until the Japanese occupied Taiwan and established an effective police system, the average village was a small community surrounded by a largely hostile social environment. The mutual animosity of the various racial and ethnic groups occupying the Taipei Basin made it a cauldron of internecine strife. The Chinese settlers fought the aborigines; Hokkien-speaking Chinese fought their Hakka neighbors; while among the Hokkien, people from Chang-chou and Ch'üan-chou competed bitterly for land and control of ports. In the hills surrounding the Basin, law and order gave way entirely to the rule of bandit chiefs and fugitives from the mainland. Under these conditions much of a peasant's contact with strangers was with bandits, beggars, bullies, and equally rapacious ya-men hirelings. When a man left his village it was usually to visit relatives in a neighboring community, and the only outsiders welcomed in the village were those recommended by ties of kinship. The world beyond the bamboo walls that encircled each community was dangerous be-cause it was inhabited by strangers, and strangers were feared because they were represented in experience by bandits and beggars. The ghosts are the product of this experience. They are dangerous because they are strangers, and strangers are dangerous because experience has proved them dangerous.

The conception of the supernatural found in San-hsia is thus a detailed reflection of the social landscape of traditional China as viewed from a small village. Prominent in this landscape were first the mandarins, rep-resenting the emperor and the empire; second, the family and the lin-eage; and third, the more heterogeneous category of the stranger and the outsider, the bandit and the beggar. The mandarins became the gods; the senior members of the line and the lineage, the ancestors; while the stranger was preserved in the form of the dangerous and despised ghosts. At a more general level the ancestors and the gods, taken together as sin, stand for productive social relationships, while their spiritual opposites, the kui, represent those social forces that are dangerous and potentially destructive.

As an example of the Chinese peasant's "singular and unscriptural sentiments" concerning the soul, the Reverend Doolittle observes (1865: II, 401–2) that people in Foochow believe "each person has *three dis-tinct* souls while living. These souls separate at the death of the adult to whom they belong. One resides in the ancestral tablet erected to his memory, if the head of a family; another lurks in the coffin or the grave, and the third departs to the infernal regions to undergo its merited pun-ishment." The soul enshrined in the ancestral tablet clearly represents the dead in his role as kinsman, while the soul subjected to judgment in the underworld is just as obviously the dead in his role as citizen of the empire. Although the Chinese peasant's conception of the underworld was inspired by the Buddhist imagination, it has long since become a multi-layered yamen staffed with supernatural bureaucrats. The great amounts of spirit money transmitted to the Bank in Hell at the end of a funeral are only partly intended for subsistence expenses. Everyone knows that most of it will be expended to bribe officials who might otherwise subject the deceased to his merited punishment and perhaps some unmerited punishment as well.

This leaves for identification the soul that goes into the coffin and the grave. In Freedman's view the rites performed at the grave are the reverse of those performed before the ancestral tablets in homes and lineage halls. Where the soul represented by an ancestral tablet is involved in a moral relationship with its descendants, the soul associated with the bones in the grave is the source of an amoral power that can be manipulated by impersonal means. The former is iong; the latter, im (1966: 140–42; 1967: 86–88). I am inclined to extend this interpretation, and to argue that the soul in the grave represents the social role of the stranger. Division of the social world into strangers, bureaucrats, and kinsmen means that every man plays the role of stranger as well as the role of kinsman and citizen. At death the kinsman takes his place on the ancestral altar, where he continues to perform many of his rights and duties as an ascendant; the citizen is conducted to the underworld by a representative of the supernatural bureaucracy and is there judged and punished; while the stranger goes into the grave and becomes the source of an amoral and impersonal power.

VI

In China, as in most societies, eating and the exchange of food are socially significant acts. The family is commonly defined as "those people who eat together," and it is often in terms of food that a family expresses its relations with other people. While most families give a bowl of rice or sweet potatoes to a beggar who stops outside their door, they never invite the beggar into the house to eat. He squats outside the back door and leaves his bowl on the threshold when he is finished. The only people invited to eat a meal as guests are the family's relatives, friends, and other persons of approximately equal social status. A family will invite a schoolteacher, a policeman, or a petty bureaucrat to dinner, but they would never invite a senior official such as a hsien magistrate or one of his principal secretaries. When I naively invited the heads of several of Hsia-ch'i-chou's more prominent families to dinner with the magistrate's secretary and another senior official, my guests from the village all found reasons to absent themselves. Eating together implies intimacy and a certain degree of social equality, and it is therefore impossible for a farmer or a coal miner to eat a meal with a ranking official. If a farm family wishes to curry the favor of an official, they often use food as a means of establishing a relationship, but it is presented through a go-between as a gift rather than in the form of an invitation to dinner.

The offerings of food made to the various forms of supernatural express the same social distinctions. As kinsmen and people with whom one is on intimate terms, the ancestors are offered food in very much the same form as a family's guests. The table in front of the altar is set with chopsticks, rice bowls, soup spoons, and a selection of common spices and condiments: salt, soy sauce, vinegar, and perhaps a hot sauce. The food is presented in the form of fully prepared dishes, hot from the stove, and always includes cooked rice. The offerings to the ancestors are meals, in both form and intent. By means of these offerings the living support and succor their kinsmen in the next world just as they supported them during their last years in this world. The intimate nature of the relationship is reflected in the efforts many families make to respect the personal tastes of individual ancestors. When an ancestor is known to have been particularly fond of certain dishes, these are commonly included in the offerings made on the anniversary of his deathday. One woman told me that she always makes rice cakes to offer to her father-in-law and something made from flour for her mother-in-law "because my father used to like rice cakes very much and my mother loved things made of flour."

The offerings prepared for a god's birthday also include the elements of a meal, but this meal is intended for the god's soldiers and attendants rather than the god himself. Despite their considerable power, a magistrate's personal attendants and other members of his staff had very little status in traditional China. During most of the last dynasty they were officially designated *chien-jen*, "mean people," and excluded from competition in the civil service examinations. It was therefore conceivable for a farmer to invite these people or their supernatural counterparts to a meal, but it would have been presumptuous for him to issue an invitation to either a magistrate or a god. The offerings for the gods usually consist of what is known as *sieng-le*, i.e., three or five kinds of meat—for example, a duck, a large slice of pork, and a fish, or, alternatively, a chicken, a duck, squid, a slice of pork, and liver or kidney. Except on the occasion of special offerings to the supernatural emperor, T'ien Kung, these foods are cooked, but they are never seasoned or sliced as for a meal. The only items on the table aside from the offerings themselves are three cups of wine and perhaps a bowl of fruit. There are no eating utensils, no spices or relishes, and, most significantly, no rice. The ancestors are dependent on their living descendants and must be sustained. The gods, on the other hand, are in no way dependent on their subjects, and their high status makes it inappropriate for them to eat in the home of a farmer or coolie. The offerings to the gods are essentially gifts, presented in the same spirit as a gift of food to a magistrate. As one of my informants in Hsia-ch'i-chou explained, "The gods don't really eat the things you give them. These are just to show them that you respect them so they will help you and protect you."

The form and manner of offerings to the gods also reflect their relative status in the supernatural bureaucracy. When people worship T'ien Kung, the offerings for the god and those for his soldiers and attendants are placed on separate tables. The table with the meal for the soldiers and attendants stands on the floor, but the table with the offering for T'ien Kung must be raised by being placed on four stools. T'ien Kung's status is infinitely higher than that of any of the subordinate officials in his empire. If a rooster is included among the offerings made to such deities as Shang Ti Kung or Tsu Shih Kung, the tail feathers must be plucked. Only T'ien Kung can command a rooster with both a "head" and a "tail."

The ranks of the various gods are also expressed in ritual protocol. While they are not ordinarily observed in practice, there are rules on the number of prostrations to which each of the gods is entitled. If the deity is the lowly Stove God, at the very bottom of the hierarchy, a petitioner need only prostrate himself twice. The much higher ranking Shang Ti Kung, comparable to a hsien magistrate, is accorded one hundred prostrations, while, ideally at least, a person who approaches the supernatural emperor, T'ien Kung, should prostrate himself a thousand times.

The content of offerings made to ghosts varies more than that of offerings made to the gods or the ancestors. Although everyone agrees that the spirits inhabiting the little Yu Ying Kung temples are ghosts, it is customary to offer them sieng-le just as one would a god.[14] The shopkeepers in the San-hsia market also offer whole ducks and chickens and large pieces of cooked meat to the ghosts during the annual festival for hungry ghosts. In many villages, however, the offerings made on this same occasion consist of fully prepared dishes of food laid out in the form of a meal. Aside from the fact that offerings to ghosts often consist of masses of food "because there are so many of them," their only characteristic feature is a wash basin and towel. People say that the gods and the ancestors "don't need these things because they have homes of their own." Many families also set next to the wash basin a pack of cigarettes and occasionally a bottle of beer. As one man explained, this is because

[14] The name Yu Ying Kung refers to an inscription found over the doors of most of these temples: yu ch'iu pi ying, "a request gets a response." A common alternative name is Pai Hsing Kung: the honorific kung plus the most common Chinese term for "the people." This suggests that from the point of view of any particular person, the people are ghosts as well as strangers.

ghosts are like lo-mua:—"They all smoke and drink." Another man said that "you have to treat the ghosts as you would treat a policeman who stopped at your house." I am confident that his point was not that the ghosts represent law and order, but rather that like the police, ghosts are demanding and dangerous. In the peasant's view the modern police-man, the traditional yamen runner, the bandit, the beggar, and the ghost all belong to the same category. "You have to give them something so they will go away and not cause trouble."

Although ghosts are sometimes offered sieng-le like the gods and some-times meals like the ancestors, the location of offerings to them shows that they form a distinct class of supernatural. Whereas offerings for the gods and the ancestors are always presented in the house (facing out-ward in the case of the gods and inward in the case of the ancestors), offerings for ghosts are always presented outside the house. If the object of the offering is a single spirit who has been identified as the cause of an illness or some other misfortune, the offering is usually placed on the ground outside the back door, "the same as for a beggar." The great mass of ghosts placated during the seventh lunar month usually receive their offerings on tables set in front of the house. But no matter who the spirit is or what the occasion for the offering, ghosts are never served in the house. They are despised and disreputable strangers, not guests. "It would be dangerous to invite them into the house." The bowls used to offer food to a ghost are turned upside down and left in the yard for three days to protect the family from pollution. Anything that has come in contact with ghosts is contaminated and dangerous.

The offerings made to the various forms of supernatural usually in-clude several types of "spirit money" (*gun-cua*), as well as food and incense. The different categories of spirit money reflect the division of the supernatural world into spirits modeled on senior kinsmen, on strang-ers, and on the imperial bureaucracy. Confused by the various kinds of spirit money I had seen for sale in San-hsia, I once asked an elderly man with some reputation as a geomancer to explain their use. He kindly prepared for me a chart that divided the supernatural into categories, and listed for each category the appropriate monies for their worship. Because this was the first time we had met and I had not yet discussed with him my own view of the Chinese supernatural, I am confident that his chart lists native categories and not artificial ones prompted by my questions. All I have added, for the convenience of the reader, is the numbers.

1. For Yü Huang Ta Ti, colloquially known as T'ien Kung: *thi:-kim, gou-ci:, siu-kim, hok-kim,* and *kua-kim.*

2. For Ch'ing Shui Tsu Shih Kung and T'ien Shang Sheng Ma, colloquially known as Tsu Shih Kung and Ma Tsu: siu-kim, hok-kim, and kua-kim.

3. For Fu Te Cheng Sheng, colloquially known as T'u Ti Kung: hok-kim and kua-kim.

4. For worshipping the souls of dead people (i.e. the ancestors): *tua-gun, siu-gun,* and *kho-ci:.*

5. For begging peace of the *gua-sin* (i.e., ghosts): kua-kim, hok-kim, siu-gun, *kieng-i, kim-ci:, ka-be, tai-lang, ngo-kui, peq-ho, thi:-kau,* and *pun-mia-ci:.*

On completing the chart my informant placed parentheses around the hok-kim and kua-kim listed under T'ien Kung. "These," he explained, "are not for T'ien Kung himself, but for his followers—his secretaries and his soldiers." Thus, the gods are divided into three ranked classes, as one would expect given the fact that they are conceived of as bureaucrats. At the bottom of the hierarchy is T'u Ti Kung, whose offerings are the same as those made to T'ien Kung's soldiers and secretaries. Above T'u Ti Kung are Tsu Shih Kung and Ma Tsu (and my informant agreed that one could add to this class such gods as Shang Ti Kung and Pao Sheng Ta Ti). Their offerings include the hok-kim and kua-kim offered T'u Ti Kung, but also one of the three types of money offered T'ien Kung. Finally, at the top of the bureaucracy but still part of it, is T'ien Kung. He, like such middle-ranked gods as Tsu Shih Kung and Ma Tsu, receives siu-kim, plus two types of money that are reserved for his exclusive use.

My informant also explained that kho-ci: is offered only to the recent dead, the typical offering for ancestors whose tablets are established on an altar being tua-gun and siu-gun. We therefore find that where the gods are usually offered *kim,* gold, the ancestors are usually offered *gun,* silver. The use of gold money for the gods and silver for the ancestors divides these supernatural into two classes and at the same time suggests that the gods are superior to the ancestors. We need make only the obvious assumption that Chinese think of gold as superior to silver. The one problem is that both T'ien Kung and the recent dead are offered a form of *ci:,* "copper cash," or more generally "money" and "wealth." Since ghosts also receive two forms of ci:, kim-ci: and pun-mia-ci:, it appears that ci: alone is not a diacritical mark. What is crucial in this case is the form of ci:, which is different for each of the three classes of supernatural.

The fact that hok-kim and kua-kim are listed as offerings for ghosts as well as for T'u Ti Kung and T'ien Kung's retainers appears to conflict with the assertion that money offerings separate the supernatural into three categories. But in fact this is not the case. When questioned on this point my informant explained that offerings to ghosts always include an offering to T'u Ti Kung, "because he is the god responsible for policing ghosts." The hok-kim and kua-kim are intended for T'u Ti Kung, not for ghosts. Thus, there is only one type of money that is used for more than one class of spirit, i.e. siu-gun, listed as an offering both for the established ancestors and for ghosts.[15] This offers some support for Stephan Feuchtwang's contention elsewhere in this volume that the fundamental opposition is between the ancestors and ghosts on the one hand and the gods on the other. But it is nonetheless clear that by the most obvious criteria, the supernatural are sorted into three classes. While ghosts are sometimes offered siu-gun, "little silver," they are never offered tua-gun, "big silver." And while the ancestors and ghosts share one form of money, they are distinguished by the use of nine or ten others. Perhaps the most important point to note is that the ancestors are never offered kieng-i, "contributed clothing," the one form of spirit money that is almost always included in offerings to ghosts. Although it is considered a form of gun-cua, kieng-i is not actually imitation money. It consists instead of rectangular sheets of paper, each of which is printed with pictures of such common apparel as pants, shirts, and shoes. This suggests that where the gods get gold and the ancestors silver, the ghosts get a handout—like beggars.

Both the use and the interpretation of gun-cua vary considerably. One man who made his living recovering children's lost souls told me that the "money" offered to the gods is not money at all, but is more "like the petitions people send to the government." He scoffed at the idea that the gods would be interested in money. On the other hand, Ahern's informants in Ch'i-nan gave her monetary equivalents for many of the various types of gun-cua offered to the gods, for example, NT $100 for the siu-kim burned for Tsu Shih Kung, Ma Tsu, and T'ien Kung. She also discovered that on special occasions, the monies normally reserved for the higher spirits can be offered the lower spirits. Such ritual escalation occurs, for example, when people in Ch'i-nan kill pigs for Ch'ing Shui Tsu Shih Kung. On this occasion the ancestors are offered kua-kim; T'u Ti Kung receives siu-kim in addition to hok-kim and kua-kim; Tsu Shih Kung gets siu-kim, gou-ci:, and thi:-kim; while T'ien Kung is honored with the usual offerings plus a special form of money known as *ciok-pik-siu-kim*. But Ahern's evidence indicates that whatever the occasion, the

---

[15] Michael Saso tells me that in Hsin-chu the souls of unmarried daughters are offered siu-gun, little silver, but never tua-gun, big silver. This appears to support my argument that the souls of unmarried daughters are almost ghosts.

monies offered always divide the gods into ranked classes and distinguish them both from the ancestors and from ghosts.[16] The idea that there are gods, ghosts, and ancestors is expressed differently in different contexts, but it appears that whenever peasants think about the supernatural, they think in terms of these three classes.

[16] Personal correspondence.

Taiwanese Architecture and the Supernatural

WANG SUNG-HSING

The domestic architecture of Taiwan's Chinese population reflects their beliefs about the supernatural as well as the need for shelter against both cold, damp winters and hot, humid summers. These beliefs influence the choice of a building site, the orientation of the house with respect to prominent features of the landscape, and the number of rooms and the uses to which they are put. They even affect the way people treat the men hired to build the house: because carpenters and brick masons are thought capable of altering a structure in subtle ways that can bring the inhabitants either good fortune or enduring misfortune, they are treated like guests rather than laborers.

The typical home in rural Taiwan is a large U-shaped compound, constructed, as nearly as possible, to conform to an ideal of perfect symmetry. A home of this type is usually built in stages, the growth of the building reflecting the growth of the family. The original structure is a long, rectangular building partitioned internally into three, five, or seven rooms. It is expanded by the addition of wings, first to the left side and then to the right, and, occasionally, by the addition of rows of rooms outside the original U.[1] To preserve symmetry, the roofs of these additions are all kept to the same height, always lower than the roof of the original building, and an effort is usually made to partition the house into an odd number of rooms.[2] Odd is "good" because it creates symmetry; even is "bad" because it results in asymmetry.

[1] In speaking of the right and left sides of the house I follow Chinese usage, taking the perspective of a man standing with his back to the front of the house rather than that of a man facing the house.

[2] For further details on house construction, see Kajiwara Michiyoshi 1941; and Dillingham and Dillingham 1971.

Entering a completed compound by way of the open end of the U, one faces a heavy, double-leaf door that leads into a large room, the ceiling of which is often blackened by smoke from incense. This is the ritual and social center of the house, the *cheng-t'ing*. It is here that the family receives guests, and it is here that they worship their ancestors and the gods enshrined on their domestic altar. Images of the gods and the ancestral tablets are located on a high table facing the door and the open end of the U, the gods at stage left in the position of honor, the ancestors on their right. On the wall behind the altar one usually finds a colorful picture of the Buddhist deity Kuan Yin, and in front of the altar a table where offerings are placed and guests are served at banquets. Every cheng-t'ing also contains an incense burner devoted to Yü Huang Ta Ti, the supernatural emperor, commonly referred to as T'ien Kung. This is hung from the ceiling a few feet inside the door that opens onto the courtyard between the wings of the house.

The rooms on either side of the cheng-t'ing are classified as *fang* or *chien*, depending on whether they are occupied by a married couple or an unmarried son or daughter. The first room to the left of the cheng-t'ing is the *ta-fang*, "the big fang." This serves as the parents' bedroom until their eldest son marries, at which point he and his wife take over the ta-fang and his parents move into the *erh-fang*, the "second fang," located directly to the right of the cheng-t'ing. In a small house partitioned into five rooms the kitchen is usually located in the room at the left end of the house, to allow easy access by the housewife who sleeps in the ta-fang. The room at the opposite end of the house is known as the *wu-chien-wei*, "the tail of the five rooms," and commonly serves as a bedroom for unmarried children, as a guestroom, or for storage.

If more than one son survives to marry, these men will eventually divide their father's household. The cheng-t'ing and the ancestral altar remain common property, but the other rooms become the exclusive property of one or the other of the households created by the division. As a rule, the ta-fang and original kitchen are assigned to the eldest son, the erh-fang and the wu-chien-wei to the second son. If there are more than two sons and the house has been expanded by the addition of wings, the wing at the left goes to the third son and the wing at the right to the fourth son. The allocation of space in the house reflects, on the one hand, the social principle that older brothers take precedence over younger brothers, and, on the other, the architectural principle that the cheng-t'ing is the center of the house.

Figure 1 shows the allocation of space in a large compound in Shen-

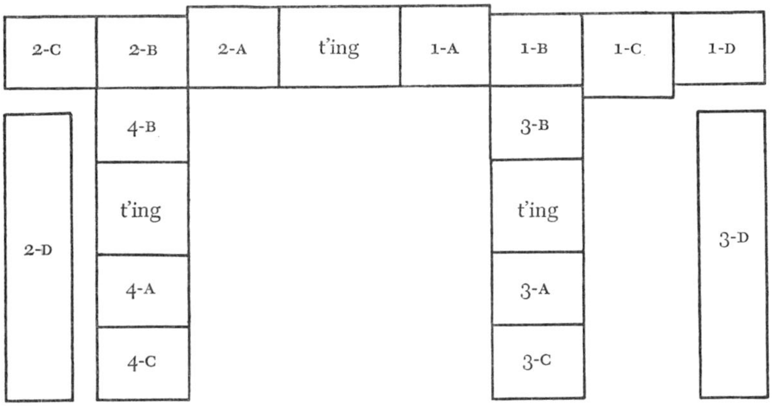

2-C	2-B	2-A	t'ing	1-A	1-B	1-C	1-D

	4-B		3-B
2-D	t'ing		t'ing
	4-A		3-A
	4-C		3-C

3-D

FIG. 1

kang *hsiang*, Chang-hua *hsien*, in central Taiwan.[3] The residents of this house included four married brothers, the eldest of whom had two married sons. Room 1-A is the senior bedroom or ta-fang, and was once occupied by the eldest brother and his wife. When their eldest son married they passed this room to him and his wife, and they now sleep in 1-B with their third, unmarried son. The second son and his wife occupy room 1-D. These people constitute an undivided domestic group and share the stove and kitchen located in room 1-C.

The second brother and his family occupy the right side of the main part of the house. The parents sleep in room 2-A, their children in room 2-B; room 2-C serves as their kitchen. The left wing of the house is owned by the third brother and his family, and the right wing by the fourth brother and his family. In the left wing of the house room 3-A is the parents' bedroom, room 3-B the children's bedroom, and room 3-C the kitchen. In the right wing, 4-A is the parents' bedroom; 4-B is used for storage; and room 4-C is a kitchen.

The outer left wing is less important and is occupied by a married sister and her uxorilocally married husband; the outer right wing, 2-D, was built by the second brother and serves as a storeroom and cattle shed.

This type of U-shaped dwelling is the most common style of house among farmers who live in such rich agricultural areas as the Taipei Basin and the Chang-hua Plain. In small towns and fishing villages another type of house predominates. Figure 2 presents the floor plan of

[3] This example was collected by Li Yih-yuan and Ch'en Chung-min, who have kindly allowed me to use their unpublished material.

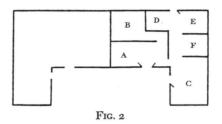

FIG. 2

a house in a small fishing village on Kuei-shan Island, off Taiwan's east coast (Wang 1967: 20). In this case room A is the cheng-t'ing and contains the family's domestic altar. Room B is considered the ta-fang and was once occupied by the owner of the house and his wife, but was passed to the owner's eldest son and his wife when the son married. The elderly owner of the house and his wife now sleep in rooms D and E. Room C is the kitchen. In addition to the family stove, it contains a subsidiary ancestral altar with a tablet the owner's wife brought with her when she married into the family. Room F is a storeroom for firewood, and this is also where the family keeps their chamber pot. The right side of the house is owned by a man whose father was a younger brother of the man who owns the left side of the house. Thus the left side of the building belongs to the senior line, the right side to the junior line.

In both these examples, the cheng-t'ing represents agnatic solidarity and continuity in the male line and as such contrasts with the stove, which stands for the independence of households headed by individual men. Where the cheng-t'ing is never divided as long as agnates remain in the same house, separate stoves are always established at the time of family division. Typically, the eldest brother inherits the original stove, while his younger siblings build new ones in their own quarters. Because family division involves partition of the parental estate and the creation of separate domestic economies, the division of stoves is a practical necessity, but it is taken as symbolic of the social changes involved in family division. Throughout Taiwan division of the stove is synonymous with family division. The role of affinal ties in distinguishing brothers from one another is neatly illustrated by the fact that at division, their wives' natal families present as gifts the cooking utensils that each of the new households will use in preparing its meals.

In many ways their cheng-t'ing stands in the same relation to the members of a descent group as the graves of their common ancestors. It is never divided and is thought of as capable of affecting individual fortunes through the agency of *feng-shui* (geomancy). Because it is joint property, repair of the cheng-t'ing must have the approval of all the owners, but because the cheng-t'ing is also thought of in terms of feng-shui, agreement is not easily reached, particularly if the residents of the house are on bad terms. To repair or rebuild a cheng-t'ing one must choose an appropriate time, which in turn requires calculations based on the horoscopes of the individual owners. What may be a propitious time for one man is often an unlucky and even dangerous time for another, and as a result the cheng-t'ing often becomes the focus of family tensions. Thus we can see the cheng-t'ing as expressing, on the one hand, the solidarity of descent groups who gather there to worship their common ancestors, and, on the other, the tensions that always threaten group solidarity.

The expressive side of Chinese architecture is also evident in the differences between the houses typical of farming communities and those most commonly found in fishing villages. For primarily economic reasons, agnatic solidarity is more important in farming communities than in fishing villages.[4] This is expressed by a difference in architecture that favors the development of large residential groups among farmers and discourages them among fishermen. Whereas the type of expandable house found in farm areas encourages agnates to remain in the same house and worship their common ancestors in a shared cheng-t'ing, the physical constraints imposed by the house style found in fishing villages make the development of large groups impossible. In the village I studied on Kuei-shan Island, most families had their own cheng-t'ing and worshipped their ancestors independently.

The use of space in Taiwanese houses also reveals something of the relationships within the family and between family members and outsiders. When a member of the family is about to die, he is moved from the bedroom to the cheng-t'ing, where he breathes his last. This privilege is extended to all male members of the family and their wives, but is never granted to anyone who is not a member of their line. Other residents of the house, such as servants and farm laborers, are never allowed to die in the cheng-t'ing. Not even their coffins may pass through the cheng-t'ing or the courtyard in front of it. They are carried out through a back door, or, if there is none, through a hole cut in the wall.

The status of a woman who dies as an unmarried member of her father's family in some ways resembles that of a servant or hired hand. She is not allowed to die in the cheng-t'ing, and her coffin cannot pass through its door. People do not ordinarily prepare an ancestral tablet for an unmarried daughter or make regular offerings to her soul. These dead are only remembered if a *tang-ki* (a type of spirit medium) attributes

---

[4] This point is discussed in some detail in Wang 1971.

an illness or some other misfortune to their agency. When this happens a wealthy family will usually arrange a "ghost marriage" for the girl and thereby pass the responsibility for her soul to another family.[5] Poor families who cannot afford to arrange such a marriage commonly make a tablet for the girl and worship her in a corner of the kitchen or under the eaves of the house. I know of no circumstance in which a daughter who died before marriage would be given a place in her natal family's cheng-t'ing.

The social significance of the cheng-t'ing is also evident in people's attitudes toward beggars. They are allowed to beg at the door of the kitchen, but not at the door of the cheng-t'ing. Of unwelcome guests it is often said, "He can enter my house through the kitchen, but not through the cheng-t'ing." The cheng-t'ing is reserved for members of the line and for their welcome guests. An example I collected on Kuei-shan Island argues that affines have no more right to a place on the altar in the cheng-t'ing than servants, hired hands, or unmarried daughters; they are all outsiders:

A woman, A, had a brother, B, who was past thirty but had not yet married. Because A thought it would be very difficult to find a wife for her brother, she gave him her granddaughter, C, in adoption. Sometime after this B strangled himself on the Taiwan mainland and was buried there. When they learned of this, A and her granddaughter C tried to call B's soul home. They set an ancestral tablet devoted to B on a table outside the house, and, facing the mainland, called B's name, urging him to return. This completed, they started to move the table and the tablet into the house, at which point A's husband insisted, "Don't come in through the cheng-t'ing. Don't come in through the cheng-t'ing." So they brought B's tablet in through the kitchen door and thereafter worshipped the tablet in the kitchen. (Wang 1967: 72.)

By the part of the house in which they are worshipped, all the supernatural beings of Taiwan are divided into two major categories. The gods and one's own ancestors are worshipped in the cheng-t'ing and the courtyard in front of it; the dead of other descent lines and the *kuei* (ghosts) are worshipped in a back room of the house or outside the back door. Prominent among the latter are what are known in Taiwan as the Ti Chi Chu, a class of supernatural associated with the foundations of the house. If the house was built by the present inhabitants' agnatic ascendants, there are no Ti Chi Chu. One needs to make offerings to this class of supernatural only if one is living in a house formerly inhabited by people of another descent line. In this case the souls of outsiders who died in the house may still inhabit the site and must be worshipped on

[5] For further details, see Jordan 1972: 140–55.

the first and fifteenth of each lunar month lest they cause one's children to be ill or bring other misfortunes to the family. The Ti Chi Chu are usually propitiated as a category rather than as individuals, but occasionally a spirit classified among the Ti Chi Chu is known by name and it is then worshipped as a particular person. This was the case with one family whose rites I observed on Kuei-shan:

A bench and chair were set outside the house, and on each of these the family placed several dishes of cooked food and a bowl of rice. I asked the head of the house why they had prepared two sets of offerings. He just smiled and said, "One is for the adults, and the other for the child." His wife explained: "The offerings on the bench are for the Ti Chi Chu proper; the offerings on the chair are for a child of the people who used to live in this house. This child's soul did not follow his parents when they moved to the Taiwan mainland. He is always asking for something to eat, and so we make an offering to him when we worship the Ti Chi Chu."

A large, decorated cheng-t'ing with a long history is sometimes referred to as a *chia-miao,* a "family temple." More commonly, the term *miao* is reserved for buildings especially constructed as the residence of supernatural beings who are considered far more powerful than one's own ancestors. The great majority of these are the deified spirits of notable people, represented in their temples by images dressed in official robes. But this is not always the case. A temple may also be built to house the corpse or bones of a person who died an unnatural death. The missionary George Leslie MacKay (1896: 127) furnishes a vivid example:

In 1878 a girl living not far from Tamsui [the old port at the mouth of the Tamsui River in northern Taiwan] wasted away and died, a victim of consumption. Someone in that neighborhood, more gifted than the rest, announced that a goddess was there, and the wasted skeleton of the girl became immediately famous. She was given the name Sien-lu-liu ("Virgin Goddess"), and a small temple was erected for her worship. The body was put into salt and water for some time, and then placed in a sitting position in an armchair, with a red cloth around the shoulders and a wedding cap upon the head; and seen through the glass, the black face, with the teeth exposed, looked very much like an Egyptian mummy. Mock paper was burned and incense-sticks laid out in front. Passers-by were told the story, and as they are willing to worship anything supposed to have power to help or harm, the worship of this new goddess began. Before many weeks hundreds of sedan-chairs could be seen passing and repassing, bringing worshippers, especially women, to this shrine. Rich men sent presents to adorn the temple, and all took up the cry of this new goddess.

Shrines of this kind are very popular on Taiwan. The body of a person who drowned or hanged himself is considered dangerous but at the same time powerful. People believe that if they bury the body and make offerings to it, these potentially dangerous spirits may use their power to help those who treat them with respect. If the spirit proves responsive to requests from the living, its devotees build a shrine and give the spirit a dignified title, for example, Chu T'ou Kung (Sir Bamboo) for a drowned corpse found in a bamboo grove, or Ch'en Ku Niang (Lady Ch'en) for a girl surnamed Ch'en who hanged herself. The most common shrines of this type are those which serve as depositories for bones turned up during plowing and for remains of children no one cares to worship. These dead are known collectively as Yu Ying Kung. *Kung* is the honorific used in addressing all powerful spirits; *Yu Ying* is from the phrase *yu ch'iu pi ying*, "If there is a request, there is a response." The thought behind the name is that if they are worshipped, these neglected dead become responsive to the prayers of the living.

The architecture of shrines for spirits like the Yu Ying Kung differs significantly from that of temples which serve as the residences of such major deities as Ma Tsu and Ch'ing Shui Tsu Shih Kung. The building is usually smaller and less elaborately decorated, and, more important, always lacks what is known as a *miao-mien*, a "temple face," which is to say that the front of the building does not have double-leaf doors painted with life-size representations of divine generals who serve and protect the god. Consequently, these shrines are commonly spoken of as *san-mien-pi*, "three-face-walls," rather than as miao, "temples." Whereas miao are thought of as the residences of posted officials representing a vast supernatural bureaucracy, san-mien-pi are viewed as the homes of a class of supernatural beings who may be powerful but who lack legitimate authority. People say these lesser spirits have no sense of justice and will respond to anyone who makes offerings to them. Popular opinion holds that only lowly types like gamblers and prostitutes worship at these shrines, and that they do so at night rather than during the day.

The supernatural beings worshipped in true miao are the spiritual remains of men and women who were deified and granted official status in recognition of meritorious service to the country or to their native place. Most of them were prominent people in dynastic China, but some of the gods worshipped on Taiwan have much more recent origins, and a few are remembered as particular people. These less remote cases are interesting because they give us a closer view of the circumstances that lead to deification and the status of *shen* (god). The clearest example I know of appears in Seiichiro Suzuki's account (1934: 373–80) of the origins of I Ai Kung, who is worshipped in the Fu-an Miao in Fu-lai Village, Chia-i hsien, southern Taiwan.

I Ai Kung, Sir Uprightness and Kindness, was a Japanese policeman, a Mr. Seijiro Morikawa, who was assigned to a post in Fu-lai in 1900, when he was thirty years old. People who knew Morikawa told Suzuki that he was an exceptionally considerate man, who devoted his life in Fu-lai to helping the local people. He gave money and medicine to poor families and never asked for compensation; he taught Japanese enthusiastically and helped farmers master new agricultural techniques; he served drinks bought with his own money to the men assigned on night watch; and he often risked his own life to save villagers from danger. He died on April 7, 1902, a victim of suicide. Reportedly the Governor-General had recently announced a new tax that would require Fu-lai's fishermen to pay four yen and fifty cents on each of their bamboo rafts. Afraid that many villagers could not afford this tax, Morikawa petitioned the government for a waiver. When his petition was refused, he became very depressed and shortly thereafter shot himself.

Twenty years later, in February 1923, when a contagious disease was spreading through the area, Fu-lai's headman, named Liu Chiu, had a dream in which Morikawa warned him of the disease: "Be careful. There is an infectious disease in the area." When the headman told his fellow villagers of the dream, they were so moved by Morikawa's concern that they made an image of him, dressed in a policeman's uniform, and invited his soul to take a place in the Fu-an Miao. At that point Mr. Morikawa, a Japanese policeman, became I Ai Kung, a shen, noted throughout the Fu-lai area as a god of epidemics.

Note this story's emphasis on Mr. Morikawa's good deeds and on the fact that they benefited the entire community. This appears to be the crucial difference between spirits who are enshrined in miao and those housed in san-mien-pi. Both classes of spirits are conceived of as powerful, but whereas the spirits worshipped in miao are believed to wield just power for the common good, those propitiated in san-mien-pi are considered capable of serving selfish and sometimes evil purposes. Although the spirits of the san-mien-pi are addressed with honorific titles, the fact is that they are kuei, "ghosts," rather than shen, "gods." Though people commonly take incense ashes from a burner in a miao and thereby invite the god into their home, they would never take incense ashes from a san-mien-pi. This would be like inviting a dangerous bandit or beggar into the house. In short, the gods in their temples represent legitimate authority; the ghosts in the san-mien-pi, illegitimate power.

People sometimes refer to their ancestors as *chia-shen*, "family gods," and occasionally speak of their cheng-t'ing as a chia-miao, a "family temple." Although this suggests that ancestors are to be classed with gods, other evidence argues that they belong with the ghosts. Where people burn gold spirit-money in making offerings to the gods, they burn silver money for both ancestors and ghosts. Moreover, if a family dies out, their neglected ancestral tablets are placed not in a miao, but in a san-mien-pi. The dead are told: "We cannot take care of you. Please follow the Yu Ying Kung and someone will make offerings to you." Thus, the ancestor must be seen as representing a third class of supernatural being, midway between gods and ghosts. We can therefore conclude that miao, san-mien-pi, and cheng-t'ing express a fundamental division of all supernatural beings into three distinct types. In a miao people worship those dead who have been deified as representations of legitimate authority; in a san-mien-pi they propitiate those powerful dead who serve selfish rather than community interests; and in their own cheng-t'ing, they worship the dead of their own line to whom they are obliged by descent.

When a Ghost Becomes a God

C. STEVAN HARRELL

Supernatural beings in Taiwanese popular belief are legion; each community, each household, even each person, believes in and worships a different pantheon. But there is order in this other-worldly multitude: some Taiwanese can describe a coherent supernatural social order, roughly corresponding to the real social order on earth. Others are not given to such systematic theology, but even in their cases it is possible to classify supernatural beings in terms of their relationships to those who worship them. Some spirits are private; they are relevant to individual men and women because of their individual kinship relations. These are ancestors, and will not concern us directly here. Those beings who are public, who are relevant to particular persons not because of particular kinship ties but by virtue of their membership in a local community or in Taiwanese society as a whole, are usually divided into two categories, *sin* and *kui*, or gods and ghosts.[1]

Most sin are commonly believed to be deceased persons who have been assigned a rank in the supernatural bureaucracy by Thi: Kong, the Jade Emperor. Kui, by contrast, are spirits not so honored.[2] But most spirits who are ghosts to one person are ancestors to someone else, and as such are relatively neutral and unimportant in the lives of anyone but their own descendants. Those kui who are important as public figures are either spirits of people who have no descendants to sustain them with offerings and must therefore prey on others for their livelihood, or spirits of people who died by drowning, suicide, or other violent means and lurk near the place of their death seeking to avenge themselves upon the

[1] The ideas and some of the examples for this paper are derived from my fieldwork in the southern Taipei Basin in 1970 and 1972–73. Other unpublished examples were kindly furnished by Arthur P. Wolf.
[2] Masuda Fukutarō, *Taiwan hontojin no shūkyō* (Tokyo, 1935), p. 61.

living. As Arthur Wolf says elsewhere in this volume, "Some are angry because they are hungry and homeless, and some are hungry and homeless because they are angry."

As might be expected from these beliefs, behavior toward sin differs greatly from behavior toward kui. In the first place, people's *purpose* in worshipping sin differs from their purpose in propitiating kui. People usually worship sin in order to gain their assistance, and only rarely in order to forestall harm that they might cause. If the gods are given offerings on the regular holidays, it is not necessary to worship them at other times unless one seeks their help with particular problems or crises. On such occasions, people ask the gods to use their powers on behalf of the supplicant, and promise rewards if the intervention is successful. Only when a god has been somehow offended or insulted do Taiwanese consider that he might be the cause of some problem and seek to propitiate him. Kui, on the other hand, are malicious, and all sorts of misfortunes are attributed to their agency. Instead of asking them for positive favors, people propitiate ghosts in order to buy them off, giving them offerings on regular occasions to forestall their random malice and at times of crisis to persuade them to desist from the harm they are causing.

Sin and kui also differ in the *places* where they are worshipped. Sin are worshipped publicly in temples built for them and privately in the honored place, at stage left of the ancestors, on the domestic altar. Kui, by contrast, receive their public offerings in the outer courtyards of temples or in dangerous places where they are thought to lurk, and are propitiated privately outside the door of the home or somewhere in the open fields.

The *occasions* on which Taiwanese hold regular festivals for sin and kui are also different. Although there are times when both categories are given offerings, the greatest festivals in honor of sin come on their respective birthdays, which may occur at any time of year except during the seventh lunar month. Kui, however, are thought to be abroad during the seventh month, and most festivals in their honor are held at this time.

Nor are the *offerings* made to sin and kui the same. Meat offerings to gods almost always take the form of *sieng-le*—a large piece of pork, a whole chicken or duck, and a whole fish. Sieng-le are given to kui only when the whole mass of wandering ghosts, or "good brothers," receive offerings on the fifteenth day of the seventh lunar month. At other times, when people worship ghosts because of specific problems, the offerings always take the form of *chai-png*, i.e. prepared foods, including cooked rice with chopsticks. The spirit money people burn to gods is always gold; that for ghosts is always silver, and often includes *kieng-i*—paper clothing for the ghosts to use.

Finally, the *organization* of worship is different in the two cases. Most gods choose a *lo-cu,* or Master of the Incense Burner, to take charge of community festivals given in their honor, making their choices known by means of divining blocks. Ghosts do not ordinarily do this, and the leadership of their festival falls upon whoever feels like taking the responsibility. On the whole, then, these two categories of supernatural beings are clearly distinguished, sin representing the yang and kui the yin among Taiwanese popular spirits.

Some spirits, however, have an intermediate status. Though originally kui, in some circumstances they take on characteristics of sin, often achieving a status that contains both kui and sin elements, and occasionally even changing their nature entirely and becoming full-fledged gods. Since the status of these beings is unclear and flexible, it is not surprising that individual Taiwanese often differ on whether particular spirits are sin or kui, whether one can ask favors of them or merely try to keep them away, or whether they should be offered gold or silver money. Furthermore, it is often people whose own social status is questionable, such as racketeers, gamblers, or prostitutes, who are especially attached to these spirits, sometimes going so far as to build and maintain shrines for them.[3]

Such spirits are numerous in Taiwan, and can originate in either of two ways. Some are associated with unknown bones accidentally unearthed during gravedigging, construction, or quarrying operations. The bones are usually placed in a small shrine resembling a Tho Te Biou (earth-god shrine). Over its entrance is often hung a red drapery bearing the inscription *iu-kiu pit-ieng* (ask and you shall be answered); thus many but not all such spirits are called Iu Ieng Kong. When there are more bones, a larger shrine is built, often called Tua Bong Kiong, Ban Siong Tong, or one of several other names. Others of these spirits are people who met violent ends, either in battle or as a result of illicit activity, or people who died with no descendants. Spirits in this category may be housed singly or in small groups in small shrines known by a variety of names; larger shrines, like those containing unidentified bones, are often called Tua Bong Kiong or Ban Siong Tong.[4]

Some of these spirits begin as kui and remain kui. People ask them to stay away, not to help; when shrines are built to house them, they are built in out-of-the-way places that ghosts are known to frequent, not in prominent or scenic spots like those usually chosen for temples to gods. Either there is no regular occasion for their worship, or there is a festival sometime during the seventh month. When people do make offerings,

[3] Tseng Ching-lai, *Taiwan shūkyō to meishin rōshū* (Taipei, 1938), p. 111.
[4] See *ibid.,* pp. 98–108, for numerous brief examples.

they always include chai-png and silver money. Everyone admits these spirits are kui and treats them accordingly. Others have acquired some characteristics of sin. Some people ask them favors as they would gods; some of them are worshipped on birthdays outside the seventh month; some people burn gold money along with, or instead of, silver. When questioned about the status of such spirits, people say that the spirits are really kui but that some people treat them as sin, or that they were originally kui but have been partially transformed into sin. Many of the spirits in this intermediate category rise to prominence overnight and then gradually decline again. They begin either as unknown bones or as violent deaths, somehow acquire reputations as powerful deities and attract large followings of worshippers, then decline in importance until few people pay them any attention anymore. Finally, some intermediate spirits are transformed entirely; they lose their intermediate status and become full-fledged sin. People think of them as potentially helpful rather than harmful; their temples are indistinguishable from those of other gods, displaying the spirits' images prominently; people worship them on birthdays and burn gold money to them. Only their names and their histories reveal that they were once kui.

A few case studies will both demonstrate the range of variation in these spirits and help illustrate the social situations in which they arise. The great majority of such spirits are kui with few pretensions. In Chu-lun, in the mountains outside San-hsia in the southern Taipei Basin, there is a small shrine called the Ban Siong Tong that houses bones dug up when a road into the area was being constructed. That the spirits enshrined here are kui is indicated by the fact that after it was constructed, a Tho Te Biou was built a short distance down the road so that visitors to the area would see sin (Tho Te Kong) before they saw the kui housed in the Ban Siong Tong. Similar shrines can be found by roadsides and in cemeteries throughout Taiwan.

Another spirit, the Cu Hieng Kong, whose shrine is located in Khei-ki:- chu, a rural district between San-hsia and the neighboring town of Shu- lin, is also probably more kui than sin. But it is especially interesting because different residents of the area differ on both its origin and its status. The spirit housed in this shrine is that of one Tan Tong, a local lo-mua: or racketeer who flourished in the latter decades of the nine- teenth century and was killed in 1894. Four informants told me four different versions of his story, but it is probably fair to say that their accounts fall into two classes: those which portray Tong as an unmiti- gated scoundrel, and those which portray him as a sort of Taiwanese Robin Hood. One of the advocates of the first version was Mr. Li, a mem-

ber of a former small landlord family but now rather poor, whose home
is situated across a cart-path from Cu Hieng Kong's shrine. Mr. Li said
that Tong was a notorious character, feared and hated by everyone, who
made his living by extortion and enforced his demands by means of a
long knife, which he carried concealed in a bamboo tobacco pipe. One
day in 1894, when the inhabitants of Khei-ki:-chu were gathered for an
outdoor opera performance, a local band headed by one Tan Sim decided to strike back. They somehow managed to relieve Tong of his
pipe-knife, whereupon the whole band set upon him, beat him up, and
gouged out one of his eyes. After consultation among themselves, they
decided to try to sell him as a slave to the wealthy Lim family in nearby
Pan-ch'iao. But the Lims wanted no part of a one-eyed slave, so his captors took him to a nearby place called Lau-chu-po, where they set upon
him again and killed him. He was buried there, dying with no descendants.

Nothing happened for a while, according to Mr. Li, until the family
of Tan Sim, the leader of the gang that captured Tong, suddenly began
to experience all sorts of misfortunes. All of them took ill, and two died
within a short time of each other. In addition, the wife of the man who
had put out Tong's eye had remained barren since the incident. Those
afflicted called in a shaman in order to ask the god Sieng Ong Kong about
the cause of their troubles, and the god replied that it was Tan Tong
taking revenge upon his attackers. Thereupon they built a shrine in
order to propitiate Tong, calling him Cu Hieng Kong and erecting a
stone tablet to him. Puppet shows were presented when the shrine was
built, and it remained popular for a short time. But now people have forgotten the story of Tan Tong and the temple is largely neglected, though
every once in a while someone comes to worship, and Mr. Li's family
still offers a little food when they are having a festival for some other
spirit anyway.

Another informant was Mr. Ong, an old man with a little literary education who lives nearby. He told the story of Tan Tong somewhat differently. Tong, he said, was one of those lo-mua: who spend their time
robbing the rich to help the poor. Many of his activities were directed
against the Lim family of Pan-ch'iao, and eventually the Lims decided
to put a stop to them. They ordered their agents to post notices of a reward for Tan Tong's capture, and some less scrupulous racketeers in the
area decided to go after the bounty. As in Mr. Li's story, they tricked and
captured him during an outdoor opera performance, but instead of beating him up and gouging out his eye, they took him directly to the Lim
estate, where the leaders of that powerful family ordered his eyes put

out. Since the Lims, having taken their grisly revenge, now wanted nothing more to do with Tong, his captors took him to the local yamen. But Tan Tong, like most lo-mua: before and since, had connections among the yamen underlings. These men took pity on the blind and helpless Tong and beheaded him with his consent, asking him to promise that his spirit would not take revenge on them for this act of euthanasia. Tong's soul, who had descendants to worship him, was true to his promise, and did not bother his executioners, but instead avenged himself on the plotters who had captured him at Khei-ki:-chu. Mr. Ong stated that only those men who actually took part in the plot were bothered, and even their close relatives were left alone. So those of Tong's captors who remained built him a shrine in the middle of the fields. Since he had not held an imperial degree, they could not place his image in the temple, so they erected a tablet instead. There were always a few people who made offerings at the shrine, but it never became very popular and is now largely neglected.

Cu Hieng Kong's status is certainly equivocal; though some informants speak of him as a kind of kui, it is clear that in earlier times, when puppet shows were presented for his entertainment and people came to ask favors, he possessed some characteristics usually associated with sin. Moreover, different people view his status differently. In the first version, in which the earthly Tan Tong was portrayed as an undesirable character, his spirit is a malicious ghost who takes revenge not only upon his captors but upon their families as well. Since he had no descendants, he is forced to prey on others, and besides, he died violently and is angry about it. In the second version, however, where the earthly Tong is depicted as benevolent if not exactly upright, his spirit acts somewhat differently. Having descendants to worship him, he need not resort to extortion to assure himself of sustenance in the other world; rather his spirit righteously and selectively avenges itself on those directly responsible for his death. Here he is acting much more like a god. Besides, the only thing that prevented him from having his image placed in the temple, thus acquiring another characteristic of a true sin, was the fact that he held no imperial degree.[5]

Neither of the shrines described so far is sociologically very important, but there are other intermediate spirits whose role in community religious affairs is greater. These spirits, some of whom originated as unknown bones and some as violent deaths, typically exhibit characteristics of both sin and kui, and it is often difficult for both informants

---

[5] Lack of a degree has not, of course, kept other spirits from being deified, but it was a relevant factor in Mr. Ong's explanation.

and anthropologists to classify them. The Pueq Lang Kong shrine at Lei-ci-be, near San-hsia, is an example. It contains the bones of eight men who were killed by the Japanese occupying forces in 1895. Three of the men are worshipped as ancestors by villagers in Lei-ci-be, a fourth's descendants all moved to central Taiwan, and the other four are unknown to anyone in the village. I have heard villagers refer to the Pueq Lang Kong both as kui and as sin, but most often as kui. This is probably because the story of the men enshrined is known to most villagers; they were men of questionable character who died violent deaths. And indeed many people do treat the Pueq Lang Kong as ghosts, offering them prepared food and silver money in the seventh month.

But other aspects of people's behavior toward the eight spirits is more suggestive of sin than of kui. Everyone in Lei-ci-be agreed that the Pueq Lang Kong were very *sia:*, or spiritually powerful, and that their power was usually benevolent. When I contributed money toward the reconstruction of the Pueq Lang Kong shrine, several people told me that the spirits would thenceforth protect me. People often went to the shrine to seek medical or other kinds of help, and despite leading questions, I was never told that the Pueq Lang Kong could make anyone ill. Also, while some people still offered chai-png and silver money at the shrine, others offered sieng-le and gold money. When I asked A-tit-a and his mother what offerings one should present at the shrine, the two answered simultaneously, the mother saying chai-png and the son sieng-le. When I asked about paper money, the mother suggested silver and the son gold. When I mentioned these discrepancies to other people, they usually said that it was up to the worshipper; either chai-png and silver or sieng-le and gold were acceptable. And when the Pueq Lang Kong shrine was reconstructed, the ceremony was to include a Taiwanese opera, an honor rarely accorded ghosts. Thus if the Pueq Lang Kong were ever purely ghosts, and it seems probable that they were, they have already advanced a considerable distance along the road to godhood.

The southern Taipei Basin also contains several larger shrines of this intermediate sort, all known as Tua Bong Kiong. The largest and best known of them is located at T'u-ch'eng, and houses the bones of people killed in the nineteenth-century battles between immigrants from the two Fukien prefectures of Ch'üan-chou and Chang-chou. A large festival is held at the shrine every year in the seventh month, and responsibility for organizing the festivities falls upon a lo-cu selected in rotation from the three townships of Pan-ch'iao, T'u-ch'eng, and Chung-ho, all of which are inhabited primarily by people of Chang-chou origin. People from surrounding districts come to make offerings, Taoist priests perform

rituals, and operas are presented. Informants differ greatly in describing
the status of the spirits enshrined here. One, a Ch'üan-chou man, the
Mr. Li who told the story of Cu Hieng Kong, said that after the Ch'üan-
chou people had driven their Chang-chou oppressors from the southern
Taipei Basin, the Chang-chou people gathered up the bones of their
dead and built this shrine. The spirits housed there are ghosts, he said,
and worshipping them is equivalent to worshipping the "good brothers,"
or wandering ghosts, at home on the fifteenth day of the seventh month.
Another informant, also a Ch'üan-chou man, thought that the men whose
spirits were enshrined at T'u-ch'eng had been killed by the Japanese
rather than in civil wars, and said that while they were probably kui in
the beginning, the spirits were surely sin now. People Wolf encountered
during the festival held at this temple in 1970 said that the vault contained bones of both Chang-chou and Ch'üan-chou people. Most of them
agreed that worshippers should burn silver money, with one saying that
it would be best to mix in a little gold. Nonetheless, many people at the
festival in fact burned not silver money but gold. What everyone seemed
agreed upon was that the spirits (called Tua Bong Kong) of this temple
were very sia:, very powerful. One informant said that whereas Chieng
Cui Co Su, the god of the large temples in nearby Ting-p'u and San-hsia,
was a high, distant being, difficult to reach or influence, Tua Bong Kong
was lower, closer, and easier of access. This comparison implicitly places
Tua Bong Kong squarely in the category of sin.

What are we to make of this Tua Bong Kong? Some people say it is
kui; some say it is sin; most are probably not sure. Some burn silver
money, some gold. Its festival comes in the seventh month, when ghosts
are usually worshipped, but the selection of a lo-cu to head the festivities suggests that the spirit is a god. In short, nobody really knows exactly what Tua Bong Kong is; his status is intermediate and ambiguous.
But everyone knows his reputation for being sia:, and that is enough to
attract people to the shrine to seek favors and participate in the annual
festivities.

There are two other Tua Bong Kiong located in the southern Taipei
Basin, and both share some characteristics with the larger shrine just
discussed. One is located at Kan-yüan, between San-hsia and Shu-lin,
and houses the bones of lo-mua: killed fighting the Japanese. The other,
situated at Ciam-sua:-po in Ying-ko, was originally built to contain the
numerous bones dug up during the construction of the Taipei–T'ao-yüan
railroad, but people still bring bones to be inserted when they find them
during construction or brick-making. Despite their diverse origins, the
spirits of these two shrines are very similar. Although informants generally describe them as kui, they still come to ask favors (I talked with

a woman at the Kan-yüan shrine who had just been to San-hsia to worship Chieng Cui Co Su and now was making offerings to Tua Bong Kong), and the operas that are presented each year are paid for by people who have promised them to the spirits in return for favors that Tua Bong Kong has granted. Again, a crucial element in people's relationship to these spirits is the belief that the Tua Bong Kong are sia:, that it pays to ask them for assistance.

Since Taiwanese society holds an ambivalent attitude toward many of these spirits, seeing them as effective but often not quite legitimate, it is fitting that many devotees of the Iu Ieng Kong and similar spirits are people whose place in earthly society is similarly equivocal. Tseng describes Iu Ieng Kong as the god of gamblers and of the unemployed and destitute, citing many supporting examples.[6] Success in gambling is said to be one of the wishes most often granted worshippers of many of the Iu Ieng Kong and similar spirits that he discusses.[7] Because of their low and semi-illegitimate status, it is often thought better to ask these spirits for favors of a slightly unethical nature than to take such requests to an upright, official god. For example, Tseng discusses the case of a shrine to Ban Siong Ia built in Kuan-hsi, in north-central Taiwan, to house the bones of pioneers who died of malaria or were killed by aborigines while opening up the area for Chinese settlement.[8] In 1883, people working in this area, along with local gamblers, contributed money to build a bone vault beside the temple. Every day, hundreds of people came to ask assistance in matters of gambling, marriage proposals, and other affairs. Until the Japanese occupation, says Tseng, this continued to be a place where "gamblers, fugitives, illicit lovers, people seeking revenge, and all other types who were engaged in illicit activity" came to carry out their worship.

Another such temple, originally built in the late eighteenth century to house spirits of men killed in an aborigine ambush while opening up the area of Wai-p'u in central Taiwan, once came to the aid of a shady character and thus indirectly saved a whole community. A former militiaman, known as Tua-chun, was smoking opium near the shrine by himself late one stormy night when he was suddenly interrupted by a voice calling "Tua-chun, flee, flee!" Thinking this was ominous, he woke the people nearby and told them to flee to nearby T'u-ch'eng. Even though all the buildings in the immediate area were destroyed by a flood, the inhabitants all managed to gain safety, and attributed their escape to the spiritual power of Iu Ieng Kong.

The status of all the spirits so far described has been ambiguous, and

---

[6] Tseng, p. 111.   [7] *Ibid.*, pp. 98–108.   [8] *Ibid.*, p. 100.

as such is probably even more susceptible to change over time than that of ordinary gods, who still by no means present a fixed and unchanging image in the eyes of the community. But there are other intermediate spirits whose rise to prominence is dramatic and whose decline into oblivion is also precipitate. Perhaps typical of such spirits are the Cui Lau Kong described by Masuda:

Bodies that have been found floating on the ocean or rivers and then are buried are the same as Iu Ieng Kong, but when some kind of rumor starts that they have spiritual power, the people in the vicinity call them Cui Lau Kong and gather in great numbers to ask favors. They offer small flags with the characters Cui Hua Sien Kong (Revered immortal transformed by water), Cui Tik Lau Kong (Revered one flowing with the water's virtue), and so forth, and it can be said that [the phenomenon] becomes fanatic.[9]

Tseng describes such a shrine located at Keng-fang, near Chin-shan on the north coast of Taiwan.[10] The temple was built during the Tao-kuang period (1820–50) to enshrine the spirits of bones that were found on the shore. The local inhabitants built a temple at the roadside, and the bones soon proved to be powerful and remarkable. They attracted a large number of believers, with people coming from far and wide to worship. It was said that the power of the spirit was limitless, and that he would answer any request made in good faith. But the phenomenon did not last very long, and the number of worshippers soon diminished greatly.

Another shrine, located at Ta-an-hai in central Taiwan, seems to have experienced two cycles of rise and fall. Built in 1815, it contained not beached bones but the remains of Ch'üan-chou fighters who died in a battle with Chang-chou forces around 1815.[11] In 1889, by which time the temple had collapsed and was lying in ruins, many people were killed in an epidemic. The pestilence was said to be the work of the neglected spirit housed in the shrine, so the temple was rebuilt. Soon after its reconstruction, it attracted a large following, including many prostitutes. But by the time Tseng was writing in the 1930's, the number of worshippers had again fallen off markedly. It is interesting that whereas the spirit first regained prominence by causing illness, a malicious action characteristic of kui, it soon acquired a reputation as spiritually powerful, a large following, and regular opera performances, all attributes much more characteristic of sin.

Finally, we come to those intermediate spirits who have "arrived" or seem close to doing so, who have lost much of their uncertain status and

[9] Masuda, p. 62.   [10] Tseng, p. 99.   [11] Ibid., p. 104.

become sin or something barely distinguishable from sin. The best described of these are the Tai Ciong Ia. Their temples are typically larger
than those to Iu Ieng Kong, Tua Bong Kong, or similar spirits, so that
Tseng says that many of them are indistinguishable from great temples.[12]
They typically contain an image of the deity.[13] Tseng says that Tai Ciong
Ia is the designation for the spirit or bones of a great official or someone
who has made a contribution to society, who afterward becomes a king
or general among kui. But nowadays, he says, even ordinary Iu Ieng
Kong are sometimes called Tai Ciong Ia. He also says, however, that
these Tai Ciong Ia have left the original characteristics of Iu Ieng Kong
so far behind that they have changed into gods who exercise control over
a lot of lonely ghosts.[14] An example of how this can happen is provided
by Masuda:

Looking at the history of the Tai Ciong Ia temple in Pa-li, . . . about 160
years ago [c. 1775] a lot of bones washed up on the beach and formed a pile
in front of [what is now] the temple. Because nobody worshipped them and
they were buffeted by wind and rain, it came to the point where fire issued
from them in the middle of the night. The local people then built a Tai Ciong
Ia temple to quiet them down, and they say that the fire that used to issue from
them has been extinguished.[15]

Another Tai Ciong Ia is located in Chi-chi, southeast of Nant'ou, in
central Taiwan. In 1863, when the corpses of the defeated rebel army of
Tai Wan-sheng were left scattered around Chi-chi, the local people
gathered them up into a temple, installed a wooden image, and called it
Tai Ciong Ia. It was said that the god was honest and upright and would
not tolerate rudeness, but that if one prayed as sincerely as possible to
him he would grant any favor. He was especially revered as a deity who
protected domestic animals, and was also thought effective in curing
illness and bringing commercial success.[16] Tseng's account of this case
offers little detail, but the characteristics he does describe are those of
sin. The positive favors people ask, the insistence on correct form, and
the wooden image are all attributes of a god, not a ghost.

How are we to account for the presence of intermediate spirits in
Taiwanese folk belief? Their existence is, of course, made possible by
the basic nature of Chinese folk religion, an eclectic system that draws
beliefs simultaneously from Buddhism, Taoism, and the Official-Con-
fucian tradition, and thus inevitably contains varying explanations for
the same phenomenon. But Chinese folk belief is not merely syncretistic;

---

[12] *Ibid.*, p. 92. [13] Masuda, p. 61, plate 54. [14] Tseng, p. 92.
[15] Masuda, p. 62. [16] Tseng, p. 105.

it is flexible and individualistic in the sense that there is no one authority, no church or theocratic state, that establishes dogma and determines belief. The systems of thought worked out by religious specialists such as Taoist priests, Buddhist monks, and Confucian bureaucrats have always influenced, but never dictated, popular belief. Thus the individual Taiwanese is free, within limits set by these great traditions and by the beliefs prevailing in his own community, to form his own system of religious beliefs and practices. But most Taiwanese, like most people anywhere, are not by nature theologians or philosophers, and thus never formulate a perfectly coherent system of religious thought. There are, of course, people who practice no religious specialty but who still have worked out internally consistent sets of religious beliefs, but they are probably a small minority. The great majority turn to religion when tradition or crisis makes it seem advisable. They are concerned less with the logical coherence of their religion than with its practical efficacy. The concern with efficacy is closely connected to the idea of spiritual power. If a spirit, be it a god, a rock spirit, one of the intermediate spirits, or anything else, is proven to be sia: or *hieng*, that is, if he answers requests and grants favors, then it matters little what his origin is or what a religious specialist might say about his position in the supernatural social order.

The fact that efficacy means more to most people than logical consistency does means that change in religious beliefs is common and relatively easy to bring about. It means there is nothing wrong with treating a spirit who was originally or properly kui as if he were sin; if he acts like a god and people fare best by treating him as they would a god, then he must be a god. The importance of efficacy also means that it is easy for different people to hold different views about the same spirit—some of them may have found a particular spirit helpful and efficacious and therefore treat it as a god, while others, having had nothing to do with the spirit, might adhere to the etiological explanation and regard the spirit as a ghost. Thus a system of religious beliefs like the one found in Taiwan, where individual differences are given relatively wide latitude and beliefs are shaped and changed by experience and consensus as well as by theology, allows for the kind of intermediate spirits discussed in this paper.

But though the nature of such a religious system makes possible both individual disagreements and change based on consensus, it does not suffice to explain the intermediate status of the particular spirits in question. Despite the theoretical possibility, no Taiwanese would ever maintain that Chieng Cui Co Su was a ghost, or that the "good brothers" were actually gods. It is only ghosts with recognizable identities who become intermediate spirits and whose status is susceptible to rapid change. The great majority of potentially dangerous ghosts lack any individual identity—when one or several are determined to be the cause of some misfortune, they are propitiated, usually without knowing whose ghosts they are, and when the crisis is past, they are reabsorbed into the great mass of dangerous ghosts who can cause nothing but harm. When ghosts or groups of ghosts are enshrined as separate entities, however, they are not so easily incorporated into the category of anonymous ghosts, and people begin making offerings to their particular shrines. They may at first simply propitiate them when it seems probable that they are causing misfortune, but it is a short step from there to asking them to assist in crises of which they are not clearly the cause. Once this happens, they are no longer pure ghosts; they have become intermediate spirits.

Another reason why such ghosts often acquire an equivocal, easily alterable status is the unknown or socially marginal position of the persons whose ghosts become so enshrined. When bones are dug up, exposed by flood, or washed ashore, no one knows whose they are. Because they are not at rest and have no descendants to tend their graves, they are potentially dangerous. But because properly cared for they might gain favor with heavenly bureaucrats (no one knows, after all, whether their earthly lives merited this or not), they are also potentially powerful. The safest thing to do is build some sort of shrine so that they are cared for and will be less likely to make trouble. Once a shrine is built, the spirit has acquired an individual identity. Offerings are made, stories are told, and consensus begins to form.

Those who have died violent deaths, on the other hand, were usually on the fringes of the social order when they were alive, characters both despised and respected. Many of these are spirits of lo-mua: like Tan Tong. As lo-mua: they are undesirable characters to be feared and avoided, people with no definite status in the legitimate social order, but as Robin Hood types they are clearly beneficial to certain segments of society. As spirits they retain this dual nature, and this contributes to their flexible supernatural status. Soldiers who died in local feuds have a similar double nature. On the one hand, they are dangerous because, as soldiers, they are not entirely respectable, but on the other hand they have made a significant contribution to the community by fighting for it and are considered capable of doing so again. Only experience and consensus can determine whether they will be supernaturally helpful or harmful.

Also important in understanding these spirits is their association with conflict and crisis. Civil struggles, resistance to occupying armies, aborigine raids, floods that uncover buried bones or wash them ashore, all are occasions of great uncertainty and concern to the average Taiwanese. It is especially at times when rational calculations and actions are insufficient to understand or cope with the situation that people are likely to turn to the supernatural, both as an explanation for otherwise inexplicable events and as a source of help. And since the Taiwanese supernatural order is to a great extent a reflection of the earthly social order (as Wolf shows elsewhere in this volume), it appears likely that uncertainty about natural events leads to uncertainty about supernatural events as well. Not only are people likely to be more concerned with the supernatural in times of conflict and crisis; they are also more likely to have doubts about it. It is not surprising, then, that the status of spirits who appear in such circumstances is especially susceptible both to great differences in individual evaluation and to rapid and significant changes in public opinion.

One final question remains to be answered: If ghosts can so easily turn into gods, why is it that gods cannot degenerate into ghosts? The answer seems to be that because gods are thought of as capable of causing harm only when they are somehow offended, any misfortune attributed to a god must ultimately be traced to someone's wronging that god, not to any malicious intent on the part of the god himself. If a sin is known to have helped many people, his reputation as sia: increases and he becomes more popular; if his help is thought to be ineffectual, he is simply ignored and his temple falls into disrepair. The downward road from godhood leads to oblivion, not to ghostliness.

Cantonese Shamanism

JACK M. POTTER

Although they are an important aspect of life in Cantonese villages, the *mann seag phox,* "old ladies who speak to spirits," have been neglected by most students of Chinese society. The only references I have found to them are J. J. M. de Groot's description of similar female shamans in Amoy at the turn of the century (De Groot 1969: VI, 1323–33), and a brief account of Cantonese female mediums in Alan J. A. Elliott's *Chinese Spirit Medium Cults in Singapore* (1955: 71, 135–38). In this paper I shall describe the three female shamans I observed in 1961–63 in Ping Shan, a Cantonese lineage comprising eight villages in Hong Kong's New Territories. Whether the practices I observed there are characteristic of other regions of China, I cannot say.[1]

The mann seag phox (alternatively, *mann mae phox;* see below, p. 219) act as intermediaries between the villagers and the supernatural worlds of heaven and hell.[2] Assisted by their familiar spirits, the seag phox send their souls to the supernatural world, where they communicate with deceased members of village families. They also know how to recapture the kidnapped souls of sick village children, and they can predict the future. They care for the souls of girls who die before marriage, and protect the life and health of village children by serving as *khay mha,* fictive mothers.

[1] I wish to thank the Ford Foundation's Foreign Area Training Fellowship Program for financing my research in Hong Kong, and my wife, Sulamith Heins Potter, for many useful suggestions. See Potter 1968 for a general account of Ping Shan.

[2] The other important religious practitioners in Ping Shan were the Buddhist nuns and priests, and the Taoist priest or Naam Mo Sin Shaang, also called the Naam Mo Lhoo, who served as master of ceremonies for many village rites. See Potter 1970 for a general discussion of Cantonese village religious beliefs and practices and the relation between them.

The Group Seance

In 1962, at the time of the Moon Cake Festival on the fifteenth day of the eighth month, the three spirit mediums of Ping Shan held their annual free group seance open to all the villagers. At dusk the villagers, young and old, men and women, gathered on the cement rice-threshing floor in the open area west of Ping Shan's central ancestral halls. As darkness fell and the full moon filled the sky with light almost as bright as day, the most accomplished shaman of the three, known as the Fat One, took her place on a low stool before a small, improvised altar table. As the incense sticks on the altar burned down, the Fat One, her head covered with a cloth, went into a trance. She jerked spasmodically and mumbled incoherent phrases. Then she started to sing a stylized, rhythmic chant, as her familiar spirits possessed her and led her soul upward, away from the phenomenal world into the heavens. Their destination was the Heavenly Flower Gardens.

Many of the villagers were less interested in the Fat One's destination than in the ghosts (*kuei*) she met along the way. These were the souls of their deceased relatives and neighbors, who took advantage of this opportunity to communicate with the living. They asked for news, gave advice, and sometimes voiced complaints.

The first ghost the medium encountered spoke as follows: "It was not time for me to die. My head was severed by a Japanese sword. I am angry and lost because my bones are mixed with those of other people." The assembled villagers immediately recognized this as the voice of Tang Tsuen's younger brother, who was one of ten villagers executed by the Japanese for smuggling during World War II. The villagers believe that anyone who meets such an unnatural death has an understandable grievance against the living, and his ghost is greatly feared. Tang Tsuen's wife, who was attending the seance, beseeched the ghost in a frightened voice to "protect the luck and safety of my husband." Tang Tsuen and his wife had worried for years about this ghost. To pacify him, they had planned to buy a silver plaque with the brother's name engraved on it, place it in a *kam taap*, a ceramic funerary vessel, and bury it in a permanent tomb where, they hoped, the brother's spirit would rest in peace.[3]

The ghost of the dead brother, speaking through the medium, told Tang Tsuen that a costly permanent tomb was unnecessary because he had died unmarried and an elaborate burial was therefore inappropriate. All Tang Tsuen and his wife had to do, the ghost said, was to write

[3] *Ibid.*, pp. 145–47.

his name on a piece of silver paper and hang it beside their ancestral altar. "If you do this," the ghost said, "I will try to help you, my brother, and your wife to have good luck and many children." As an afterthought, the spirit mentioned how pleased he was that his elder brother's wife had burned so much gold paper for him to spend and had offered him such excellent fruit during festival worship.

Later, while discussing the seance with a villager, I learned that the matter went much deeper than I had realized. Shortly after the war ended, Tang Tsuen's mother had, in fact, been bothered by the restless ghost of her younger son. As the villagers explain it, people accept death without resentment if they have lived a full, normal life and their death mandate is entered in the King of Hell's book in the usual fashion; this is fate, and nothing can be done about it. Executed in his youth by the Japanese, Tang Tsuen's brother had been deprived of the normal balance of his lifespan. The result was a troubled ghost, who could neither find peace himself nor leave his family any. Plagued by her son's ghost, Tang Tsuen's mother became physically and mentally ill, and died less than a year after her son's execution. Convinced that the ghost had driven the old lady to her grave and fearing for their own lives, Tang Tsuen and his wife tried to placate this restless family spirit. On the first and fifteenth days of every month, they made elaborate offerings in the doorway of their house, calling out to the bothersome ghost, "We are giving you money and offerings; take them and be satisfied! Don't come back to bother our family." Tang Tsuen also had gone to the expense of having his brother's spirit exorcised by a famous Taoist priest in the nearby market town during the Hungry Ghost Festival, when great quantities of food and paper money were offered the wandering ghosts of the countryside in hopes of appeasing restless spirits and driving them away.

Nothing seemed to work, however. The ghost continued to haunt the couple's household, causing Tang Tsuen and his wife to fall ill repeatedly, and, they believed, to remain childless. Trips to spirit mediums confirmed that the couple's tragic barrenness was the work of the dead brother's jealous ghost. Tang Tsuen's wife was terrified when she heard the family ghost begin to speak through the medium that night.

Then, suddenly, the voices of children were heard through the medium, quarreling and fighting over the orange and peanuts that were part of the offering. One child's voice said, "These are mine"; another, a little girl's, screamed angrily, "No! These things are not for you; they were purchased as an offering!" Shrilly she continued, "These things belong to my parents and you stole them." The village women shouted in reply, "No, money was spent for this food; go away and don't bother us." By this time all the villagers had recognized the stubborn little girl as the deceased daughter of Tang Kau, the shopkeeper from whom Tang Tsuen's wife had purchased the offerings.

Suddenly the ghost of the girl spoke again: "When I took sick you did not call a doctor; after I became seriously ill you finally called one, but by then it was too late and I died." Speaking through the medium, the voice repeated this accusation again and again. Finally the women of the village grew angry and scolded the ghost, saying, "We don't want to hear any more of this; you are too young to know about things like this." The little girl had, in fact, died four years earlier, when she was two years old.

Tang Kau and his wife, the dead girl's parents, stood among the villagers without saying a word. They were ashamed to have the circumstances of their daughter's death rehearsed before the entire village, and they now feared that the girl's unhappy ghost would return to make her brothers and sisters ill. From the night of the seance on, Tang Kau and his wife dutifully burned silver paper for her on the first and fifteenth of every month. If the family's luck turns bad, they will blame their misfortune on their daughter's angry ghost. Resentment at their failure to call a doctor in time and jealousy of her surviving brothers and sisters are considered sufficient grounds for her returning to haunt the family.

The interview with the child's ghost ended as her final plaintive words drifted across the darkened village: "My parents were careless. When I died, they hired someone who buried me so shallowly that my body was not completely covered and the dogs got at me. I cannot rest."[4]

The other villagers believed that the Fat One had deliberately brought up the case to frighten the guilt-ridden Tang Kau into placing the soul of his dead daughter under the medium's care. The villagers predicted that Tang Kau would wait and see if ordinary ritual procedures pacified his revengeful child's spirit. At the first sign of illness in the family or financial reverses, he probably will ask the Fat One to take charge of his daughter's spirit, a service for which she would of course charge a sizable fee.

The next village spirit the Fat One encountered on her heavenly voyage was Tang Mok-leung's father. The old man had died years earlier, when he was over sixty years old. He was, in the terminology sometimes used by the villagers, an old ghost. Young ghosts, i.e. ghosts of the newly dead, are very powerful beings; if dissatisfied, they usually return to harry people. Like an aging person, the ghost grows progressively weaker as he ages, and he also becomes increasingly disposed to

---

[4] Young children are not given an elaborate funeral like older people. Usually they are perfunctorily buried in a makeshift coffin.

help rather than harm the living. Once a person has been dead more than sixty years, his ghost no longer inspires much fear; he may even be born again as a different person. Occasionally spirit mediums are unable to locate an aged ghost because it has been reborn into another life. Thus supernatural potency diminishes as the personality of the ghost dims in the minds of the living.

Tang Mok-leung and his aged mother were present at the seance. They heard the old man speak through the medium: "Everyone is well; my eldest son, I see, has sent $1,000 from abroad to help the family." Tang Mok-leung remained silent at this, so everyone present assumed that he had in fact received such a sum from his elder brother, who had emigrated to Europe. The old ghost continued speaking in a good-humored vein, now addressing his wife: "You, old 'ghost' [kuei], are very lucky, aren't you? Now that our son has sent you all this money, you have money to gamble with every day." The conversation represented an affectionate exchange between an old married couple; the old man was clearly pleased that his wife and family were doing so well. The good fortune of the family, until now just unsubstantiated gossip, was publicly confirmed, and the fortune and status of the aged woman recognized. In such cases the annual seance served to take stock of the gossip about villagers that has accumulated during the year and deal with it in a public manner.

The interview ended with the old ghost counseling his son and daughter-in-law: "Daughter-in-law, obey your mother-in-law; son, obey your mother. Be careful in doing things; do not quarrel," he said as his voice faded away. Benevolent old family ghosts typically give their families such advice during these seances. Their message affirms the society's normative structure.

The next spirit the medium encountered was the younger brother of Tang Soo's father. Through the medium he admonished his widow: "No matter how much money you make working for your nephew, you always give it to your daughter. You must keep some back for yourself." The old woman would have none of this, and scolded her husband's ghost: "Don't tell me what to do! If I'd known you were going to die so young, I wouldn't have married you because now I am left alone and have to work as a servant to support myself." Good-naturedly the old ghost replied, "But you are very happy now. Your nephew lets you stay with his family and so you have a new house to live in." The old woman scolded her husband again and he riposted. The dialogue continued for some time, until the entire audience was laughing at this incongruous quarrel between the old woman and her husband's ghost.

The shaman continued on her trip to the Heavenly Flower Gardens, describing the beautiful scenery she saw along the way. As she traveled on, she suddenly met a woman's ghost holding three children's souls in her hands. The medium asked the ghost who the three souls belonged to and why she had stolen them. The ghost replied that she was starving and had kidnapped the three children's souls in hopes of receiving ransom money for them. The medium summoned her tutelary spirits—the souls of her own dead children—to question the children's souls in hopes of eliciting their identity. When the spirits asked the children who their fathers and mothers were and how many brothers and sisters they had, the answers made it plain to all that they were the souls of village children whose mothers were in the audience. The mothers berated the woman ghost. "You must be crazy! Why have you stolen our children's souls?" The women asked the medium to send spirit soldiers to recover their children's souls. The ghost, unintimidated by this prospect, defiantly insisted on ransom money before she would release the souls.

The three mothers ran back to their homes to fetch gold paper to burn as ransom, and an article of their child's clothing to be used in retrieving its soul. Once home they examined the children and found they were not well. Their complexions were yellowed, their appetites gone—symptoms of soul loss. If the souls were not recovered, the children would sicken and eventually die.

The three mothers rushed back into the arena and burned the gold paper as an offering to the ghost. After the ransom was paid, the ghost released the children's souls, and the medium's tutelary spirits brought them back down to earth with a loud, whistling sound. The medium then placed the soul of each child in its garment, which the women clutched tightly as they ran right home. As they ran they called their child's name, urging the rescued souls not to worry, they would soon be home and be given sweets to eat. The mothers rushed into their houses still repeating these assurances. Then, after hurriedly bowing before the ancestors, they each laid the garment beside the child it belonged to, so that the soul would easily recognize and reenter the body.

It turned out later that most of the villagers knew from the ghost's description that it was the notorious wife of Bean Curd Jong. Many years earlier, Bean Curd Jong married an evil young woman. From the beginning, the household was unhappy because the wicked daughter-in-law worried and scolded her mother-in-law night and day. Finally, the old lady could bear no more, and hanged herself dressed in a bridal costume. The villagers believe that a woman who dies dressed this way will become a fierce and powerful ghost; perhaps Bean Curd Jong's mother had this in mind. After her death—as the daughter-in-law learned when she consulted a spirit medium about an illness—the old lady complained to the King of Hell about her daughter-in-law's wickedness, and she and the King of Hell together plotted the untimely death of the whole family.

First the ghost of the old lady stole the soul of her son, who had violated his filial obligations by supporting his wife against her. Bean Curd Jong died shortly after his mother. His daughter was the next to die, then the evil daughter-in-law, and finally the son. Although the old lady had killed off the entire family, the villagers said the root cause of the family's troubles was the wickedness not of the mother, but of the daughter-in-law. As a ghost she has been even more ferocious than her mother-in-law, repeatedly bringing harm to the villagers, who are still terrified of her. Her favorite haunt is her family's old house. After the family died out, it was rented to outsiders because no village family would live there for fear of the ghost.

After the children's souls had been ransomed and returned to their owners, the medium and the village women scolded the ghost. "Don't do this again. If you do, spirit soldiers will be sent to catch and beat you. All those children have their own parents, why do you bother them? You must stop doing these evil things."

The evening wore on, with the spirit medium continuing her travels until well past midnight. She continued to run across the villagers' family spirits. Rather than identifying them directly by name, she questioned the spirits, asking such questions as how many daughters-in-law they had, how many siblings, how many children. Given a few general clues, the villagers were able to guess the spirit's identity. Among the spirits there was much quarrelsome jockeying for the opportunity to talk with their families. The questions typically asked of the spirits were the same as those that would be asked in a private consultation with the medium. The most common questions were about the dead person's well-being. This is a matter of great concern because if family spirits are not content and comfortable, their descendants will not prosper.[5]

Finally, after an eventful journey through the heavens, the spirit medium passed through the portals leading to the four Heavenly Flower Gardens, where every living person is represented by a potted flowering plant. The East and South Gardens are large, the North and West Gardens small. When a woman conceives a child, a heavenly flower is planted in one of the small gardens, and a seed is sent down from heaven into the uterus of the woman. The villagers liken the uterus to a flower that begins to enlarge and open after conception. The growing life

[5] See Potter 1970: 147.

flowers remain in the small gardens until the people they represent are between twelve and sixteen years old, when they are transplanted into one of the large gardens. When a person's plant is moved to a large garden, it is placed alongside that of his or her future spouse. The villagers believe that the old, arranged marriages were fixed in heaven in this manner.

Two female deities, Lee Paak and Zap Yih Nae Neung, tend the flowers while they are in the small gardens. The two deities watch over all the world's children, deciding which shall flourish and which shall die. They also decide which women shall have children and which shall remain barren. Understandably, they are very important deities to Cantonese women. There is an image of Zap Yih Nae Neung in the Hang Mei Village temple of Ping Shan. Women pray to it that they may have children and that their children may be protected from harm.

The medium journeys to the Heavenly Flower Gardens in order to inspect the villagers' flowers. This "inspection of the flowers," or *chan fa*, is a form of fortune-telling. The medium examines the condition of a person's flower: are there yellowed leaves or spider webs on the plant, does the flower seem in poor condition? The medium examines the flower to see how many red flowers (representing daughters) or white flowers (representing sons) are in bloom; unopened buds on the plant represent future offspring. If the pot contains bamboo, a woman will be barren; if it holds tangerines, she will have many children. The condition of a villager's flower tells the medium important things about that person's future.

When she had reached the Heavenly Gardens, the Fat One began to tell the villagers' fortunes by chan fa. One of the many villagers whose flowers she inspected was Tang Soo-kwai, a 48-year-old man. Soo-kwai did not attend the seance, but his mother and his wife were there. Soo-kwai's mother gave the Fat One the eight characters denoting the year, month, and day of her son's birth. This was necessary so the medium could locate Soo-kwai's pot, which has the same eight characters written on it. Soo-kwai's plant, the Fat One reported, had one white and three red flowers, representing his three daughters and one son, plus an unopened white bud, indicating that eventually he would have another son.

Suddenly, the Fat One called out that she saw a woman's ghost hovering around Soo-kwai's plant, an announcement that riveted the villagers' attention. Speaking through the medium, the ghost informed the spectators that this flowerpot belonged to her husband. Everyone then knew that the ghost was Tang Soo-kwai's deceased first wife. From the look on the face of Soo-kwai's second wife, this was a bad omen.

The ghost assured her, however, that she would not bother her husband or his family and was merely visiting his plant because she was lonely. Soo-kwai's second wife relaxed a bit. The ghost conversed with several women in the audience. She expressed anxiety about her son and daughter, and admonished the second wife to take good care of them and see that they were well brought up and properly educated. Soo-kwai's younger brother's wife was also at the seance, and the ghost told her that since they had known and liked each other in life, she had nothing to fear. "Now I am a ghost [kuei]," she said, "but I have a good heart and will not bother you. When I was alive we were good friends, and now we are still like sisters." This was a relief to the brother's wife, and Soo-kwai's second wife was also pleased to hear the ghost expressing good will rather than malevolence.

The final event of the seance was a remarkable attempt by the spirit medium to preserve traditional religious beliefs and practices among the younger generation, which is increasingly affected by modern secular ideas. A young couple had just built a modern-style house in the village without installing the paper images that represent the traditional guardian deities of village houses. The spirits of the new household spoke through the medium. They said they had nothing to eat and no permanent place of their own, and so had to flit around restlessly. The spirit generals of the doors, the guardian spirit of the house, and the kitchen god all said that if a suitable resting place and proper worship were not arranged for them, the household would soon meet with disaster. So effective was this warning that the modern young couple installed the traditional deities and began to worship them the very next day.

The Regular Duties of the Spirit Medium

The dramatic group seance takes place only once a year, during the eighth month, which is an especially propitious time for communicating with spirits. Throughout the rest of the year the spirit mediums cure illness, converse with villagers' family spirits, tell fortunes, and care for their fictive children.

The professional headquarters of the spirit mediums are their altar houses or shrines, *pay dhaan*. Each pay dhaan contains an altar on which the medium's special tutelary deities are enshrined, sometimes along with the souls of girls who died unmarried, other spirits entrusted to her special care, and assorted religious paraphernalia. It is here that people come to consult the spirit medium, and it is here that she customarily goes into trances and communicates with the supernatural world. When the medium's altar house serves as a repository for the souls of unmarried village girls as well as the medium's tutelary spirits, it is called a *dsox zan dhaan,* or "shrine where spirits reside."

In 1963 there were two dsox zan dhaan in Hang Mei Village, belonging to Kao Paak-neung and the Fat One, the two spirit mediums of Hang Mei; and there was a pay dhaan in the adjacent village of Hang Tau, which belonged to the elderly spirit medium from China proper. The altar houses of the Fat One and the Old Woman from China were dingy lean-tos, built against walls of their houses. Kao Paak-neung's altar house was a recently built little one-room shrine, situated between the fish pond and the Hang Mei Village temple. Kao Paak-neung had formerly practiced in a lean-to like those of the two other mediums, but in 1957 Tang Nai-men, in gratitude for her efforts on behalf of his many children, had built her a new one.

Kao Paak-neung's altar house was sparkling white inside and out, with colorful testimonial banners given her by Tang Nai-men hanging on the wall. The most striking feature of the shrine was the altar itself, a large piece of orange-red paper, which was affixed to the wall and had written on it in bold black characters the names of the spirits and deities who aided Kao Paak-neung in her profession. Before the altar was a large table, which held a variety of ritual objects: vases of plastic flowers intended to brighten the shrine and please the spirits of the altar; mirrors to gratify the souls of the young girls who dwelled in the altar; tea and fresh fruit for the spirits to eat along with the incense that the villagers considered the spiritual equivalent of rice; a bowl of fresh water so the spirits could wash their hands before eating; and a copper incense burner and candlesticks used in the medium's ritual performance.

Alongside the altar hung five dresses, belonging to five young girls whose spirits dwelled in the altar. These were placed there because the villagers are uncertain how to treat the spirits of women who die before marriage. The spirit tablets of adult men and married women are kept on their family's ancestral altar, and those of unmarried men are placed either on the altar or on a wall beside the altar (cf. the case of Tang Tsuen's unmarried brother, p. 208). Women who die before marriage present a problem because they have no husband and are not members of their father's lineage. People are afraid to put their tablets in the home because they might haunt the family. The solution is to put the spirits of unmarried daughters under the shaman's charge. The medium has the names of her spiritual charges written on her altar, where she worships them twice daily and on festival days. When village parents place a daughter's spirit under the medium's care, they usually bring one of the deceased child's garments to hang near the altar so the child's spirit knows the shrine is her home. Parents visit their dead daughters' spirits during the Spring and Autumn Festivals, when the villagers worship the spirits of their dead kin.

On Kao Paak-neung's altar are written the names of seven deities, the names of her dead son and two dead daughters, who serve her as spirit helpers, the names of six young female spirits entrusted to her care, and the name of Tang Fang-cheung, her husband's younger brother, who died before marriage. Fang-cheung's name appears on the altar because he ended an unhappy life as an opium addict by committing suicide in his lineage's ancestral hall. His spirit was presumed to have been made so unhappy by his unfortunate way of life and manner of death that it was greatly feared. Kao Paak-neung propitiated it daily.

The six powerful *poo-sat*, deities whose names are on the altar, are Yok Waang Daay Tay, Laan Sio Tzex, Cau Kong, Dsann Kux Loo Ye, Kun Iam Mha, and Wa Dho.

Yok Waang Daay Tay is the Jade Emperor, who according to the medium rules over all the spirits and deities of heaven. He is the most powerful deity, commanding the obedience of all the heavenly officials. Because she considers the Jade Emperor a good deity who helps people, Kao Paak-neung always invites him to come down and help her.

Laan Sio Tzex, Miss Laan, is a deity unknown to anyone else in Ping Shan. She is Kao Paak-neung's familiar spirit. Before Kao Paak-neung became a spirit medium, this spirit entered her body and made her ill. Kao Paak-neung had no idea who was making her ill until her children's spirits told her she was being possessed by Miss Laan of heaven. They instructed her to write Miss Laan's name on her altar, and promised that this new spirit would always respond to their mother's request for help. Kao Paak-neung followed her children's instructions, and now Miss Laan is her familiar spirit. The medium knows that Miss Laan is a good friend of her two dead sons because when she calls her sons' spirits down, Miss Laan always accompanies them. She suspects that Miss Laan is a maidservant of Kun Iam, the Goddess of Mercy, but is not certain.

Cau Kong is a well-known Chinese deity who is famous for his invention of the Chinese divination blocks, the *pok kwah*. A pair of wooden blocks shaped like tortoise shells, convex on top and flat on the bottom, the pok kwah are used for divination by spirit mediums and other religious practitioners. The diviner, whether a spirit medium, a Taoist priest, or a fortune-teller, first has to invoke Cau Kong. Then the blocks are thrown, and their position gives a positive or negative answer to a query. Cau Kong assists the spirit medium in her divinations and fortune-telling.

His Excellency Dsann is, according to Kao Paak-neung, a mountain spirit, *saan zan*, who helps and protects people. When a child or adult becomes ill, the medium can call on Dsann to cure the illness.

Kun Iam Mha, Mother Kun Iam, is the famous Buddhist Goddess of Mercy, one of the most popular deities in all China, a deity who embodies all the warm, tender, and merciful female virtues. Strangely enough, Kao Paak-neung claims to know little about Kun Iam except that she protects and helps people. When ghosts see Kun Iam, who is very powerful, they run away in fright.

Wa Dho is the major deity on Kao Paak-neung's altar; he is her teacher and helper, and she is his disciple. Before Kao Paak-neung became a spirit medium there was a struggle between her daughter's spirit, who wanted her to become a spirit medium, and her son's spirit, who wanted her to become a Wa Dho curing specialist. A compromise was finally reached; she became both a spirit medium and a Wa Dho curer.

According to Kao Paak-neung, Wa Dho was the first famous doctor of China. He lived in the third century A.D., in the age of the Three Kingdoms. When Kwan Kong, China's renowned general of the period, fell ill, Wa Dho cured him. Then Tsao Tsao, the famous rival and enemy of Kwan Kong, became ill with a terrible headache, and he consulted the famous doctor. Wa Dho reportedly told him that something was wrong with his brain, and that to cure him it would be necessary to cut it out and wash it before replacing it. Tsao Tsao quite naturally suspected Wa Dho of being in league with Kwan Kong, and had him killed. Kao Paak-neung says this was a disaster, because all of Wa Dho's knowledge died with him. Had he lived longer, the Chinese could have learned a great deal from this famous physician. It is said he was so able that he could cure people simply by blowing on them. After his death, he became the patron saint of Chinese doctors and religious curers.

Alongside Kao Paak-neung's altar hangs a magic horsetail brush like the one Wa Dho supposedly used. When someone is ill because an evil ghost has possessed him, Kao Paak-neung drives the malicious spirit away by waving the brush over and around the sick person. She then brushes the patient all over from head to foot, to rid his body of the intrusive spirit.

The final entry on Kao Paak-neung's altar reads "all Tang ancestors." All altars in the village, the spirit medium said, have this entry because the Tang lineage ancestors always protect their descendants. Not written on her altar but still important in her practice are two other local spirits. One specializes in caring for sick children and the other helps the medium mobilize spirit soldiers to fight recalcitrant ghosts.

Kao Paak-neung's rival, the Fat One, is a more successful medium with a more elaborately equipped altar house. The Fat One's altar has face powder and feather fans for the spirits of little girls, as well as mirrors for them to use. It also has a bowl of pomelo leaf water—the standard purifying agent for the Cantonese—which the Fat One uses to cleanse herself of pollution before dealing with the spirits.

The Fat One also has two wooden buckets, one of which holds lighted candles stuck in rice, the other rice and an egg. The rice is essential for a medium's contact with the supernatural. After the medium has gone into a trance with her head covered by a cloth, the spirit that possesses her tosses handfuls of rice around the room at any of its relatives that are present, thus helping to identify itself. Because of this practice, one of the common names for a spirit medium is *mann mae phox*, "ask-rice woman."

The altars of the three spirit mediums—Kao Paak-neung, the Fat One, and the Old Woman from China—all have different deities inscribed on them, having in common only Kun Iam and Wa Dho. Each shaman has her own ancestors and dead relatives and children to serve as her familiar spirits. Since the names of the altar deities are dictated by the spirits who make a person become a medium (more on this below), and since the Chinese have many deities of rough functional equivalence, the variation in altar deities is not surprising.

When a sick person or a concerned relative comes to the altar house to seek the spirit medium's help, she begins by ascertaining the patient's home village and eight characters. Because the supernatural world is organized bureaucratically, the spirits need the name of the person's village so they know where to start their investigations. The eight characters help them identify the specific soul that is lost. If the patient is seriously ill, the medium then throws the divination blocks to determine whether a cure is possible; if the blocks say the illness is mortal, there is no use proceeding further.

A village woman who was an apprentice shaman told me about one of Kao Paak-neung's untreatable cases. A man from Mai Po Village fell ill, and his wife asked Kao Paak-neung to come to their house and treat him. When Kao Paak-neung called down her tutelary spirits, they told her that the man was dying and there was nothing she could do for him. The ailing man refused to accept this verdict. Speaking through Kao

Paak-neung, he promised her tutelary deities that he would establish a fictive kinship relation with them if they restored his health. But the spirits reiterated that his case was hopeless: his sister in hell had prepared his coffin and he was doomed. The sick man and his family still doubted Kao Paak-neung, but soon afterward she learned that he had died as predicted. (Kao Paak-neung attributes the man's death to his evil sister. Married off to a very poor farmer, she had had a hard life. When she fell sick her husband had no money for a doctor, and she died. After her death her husband did not worship her. Her lonely, dissatisfied soul returned to her father's house, where her brother lived. She caused her brother to die so that his soul would keep her company.) An able spirit medium like Kao Paak-neung should always know whether or not a person can be treated. Kao Paak-neung claimed that of the many cases she had treated over the previous decade, only about ten of her patients had died, and that in each case she had predicted the outcome beforehand with the aid of her tutelary spirits.

If the divination blocks indicate that treatment is possible, the spirit medium proceeds to go into a trance, call down her familiar spirits, and begin a search for the ghost who has stolen the sick person's soul. First she lights two ritual candles and burns three sticks of incense. Then she settles herself in front of her altar. She covers her head and face with a scarf because when she sings she opens her mouth very wide. The scarf spares onlookers the painfully ugly sight of her distorted face.

Usually by the time the three incense sticks have burned down, the medium is already entranced and has called down her familiar spirits to enter her body. She always calls the spirits of her dead children first because she is powerless without their help. They are the intermediaries through whom she contacts the more powerful deities on her altar. Sometimes the children's spirits refuse to enter their mother's body, in which case she can do nothing. The children's spirits are very young and sometimes would rather go off and play. They also may be uncooperative or even vindictive when they feel slighted. For example, about five or six years earlier two women came to play cards with Kao Paak-neung. Her guests arrived early, and Kao Paak-neung, who had not had time to buy party food, took some cakes from the altar to offer them. A few minutes later her eyes suddenly turned glassy and she went into a trance. The souls of her children had retaliated for the misappropriation of their cakes by possessing the medium. For several days she either stared fixedly without speaking or talked gibberish, giving nonsensical answers to questions put to her. She had no appetite, her head ached, and she was always exhausted. She recovered only after she had propitiated the spirits with special offerings.

Usually, however, the medium is on good terms with her tutelary spirits and is able to go into a trance whenever she holds a curing seance. She begins to shake and her body grows cold—signs that the spirits are entering her. As she trembles, she cries out the names of the spirits on her altar, asking them to find the soul of her patient. In searching for the patient's soul they follow a route much like the route to the Heavenly Flower Gardens followed in the annual group seance. Almost always the lost soul is discovered in the hands of a ghost that has kidnapped it. The spirit medium tries to learn the identity of the malevolent ghost and its relation to her client. She asks leading questions, drawing upon her intimate knowledge of village families. The client searches his memory for family ghosts with reason to bother their living relatives. Usually he has a good idea who the ghost might be and helps the medium in her search. At other times, the medium puts leading questions to the client until he cries out, "It must be —." The medium outlines the steps necessary to achieve a cure. If the illness is not serious and the ghostly kidnapper not very powerful, the medium tells the child's mother or some other female relative the kinds of food and amount of paper money required to ransom the ailing person's soul. She uses her divination blocks to find out how long the patient will take to recover. The medium ends the session by scattering rice around to feed her tutelary spirits, and giving her callers rice to take home to the patient.

If the illness is serious or the offending ghost exceptionally powerful, the medium arranges for a ceremony at the patient's home. Lasting from nine in the evening until four in the morning, such a ceremony is very expensive and is usually a last resort. For a ceremony at a patient's home, the medium arrives in the evening. Incense, candles, offerings, and so on have been prepared for her use. She goes into a trance and calls on her spirit helpers to wrest the soul away from the ghost and return it safely home. The battle is often prolonged and difficult. The medium calls on powerful deities, spirit soldiers, and spirit policemen to help her rescue the soul. If she has not located the lost soul in earlier sessions, much of the evening is devoted to the quest. If she already knows where the lost soul is and who has taken it, she concentrates on wresting it away from the kidnapper. By midnight the medium has found the patient's soul and secured its release with offerings of paper money; from then until about 4 A.M. the medium escorts the soul home through the heavens.

In many of these elaborate home seances, the medium places a wooden container holding burning incense, red flags, and lighted candles on her head, invites spirits to possess her, and while possessed marches around in this makeshift headdress. Her purpose is to attract the souls of frightened children, or, less often, of adults. Mediums sometimes perform spectacular feats at these special seances. People say they climb ladders that are unsupported by anything more material than the medium's tutelary spirits, and make eggs stand upright on the floor and then split them exactly in half.

Kao Paak-neung can cure with the help of Wa Dho as well as in her own capacity as a spirit medium. Wa Dho is an ugly, angry-looking spirit, with a long beard. When Kao Paak-neung calls on Wa Dho's spirit to possess her, she shakes almost uncontrollably as he enters her body. She waves Wa Dho's horsetail brush wildly to frighten off evil spirits. She then turns to her patient, brushing intrusive spirits out of his body. Wa Dho also enables Kao Paak-neung to write out magical protective and curative charms. With Wa Dho moving her arms (she is illiterate without his aid), she writes out strange-looking characters in red ink on yellow paper with a Chinese writing brush. The written charms, called *vu*, are burned; the patient then drinks the ashes in tea, so that he will absorb the characters' curative power and suffer no more from intrusive spirits. After Kao Paak-neung has retrieved a soul and returned it safely to the patient's body, she has Wa Dho write a vu, which is placed on the patient's body or given him to drink in water as protection against further attacks by ghosts. This is important in cases of soul loss because the mere fact that a person's soul has been kidnapped shows him to be suffering very bad luck; a ghost cannot steal the soul of a lucky person.[6]

Cantonese villagers attribute most children's illnesses to soul loss. The souls of small children are loosely attached, and are easily frightened out of the child's body, making the child ill. Or a hungry or malicious ghost may enter a person's body and steal his soul. Usually the ghost holds the soul for ransom, releasing it in return for offerings of food and money. Sometimes the assistance of deities and spirit soldiers is needed to force a powerful and determined ghost to release a kidnapped soul. Intrusion of a ghost into a person's body is a third possible cause of illness. Because children are such easy prey for malicious spirits, sick children constitute most of the spirit medium's caseload.

One means of making a child less vulnerable to soul loss is to establish a fictive kinship relationship, known to the Cantonese as *khay*, between the child and a lucky person or beneficent deity. Parents are most likely to establish such a relationship if the child's future health and safety seem particularly doubtful. For example, a few weeks after a

[6] *Ibid.*, p. 150.

child is born, the mother usually goes to the market town to consult a fortune-teller, who may also be a Taoist priest. On the basis of the exact time of birth, the fortune-teller tells the mother such things as the names of the child's "flower mother" and "flower father," i.e. its mother and father in its previous existence, and which of the Heavenly Flower Gardens it has come from. Then the baby's fortune is told. If it is inauspicious, if there is some fear for the child's life, the fortune-teller will recommend the establishment of a protective fictive kinship relation with a person or deity. A couple that has had demonstrably poor luck in raising children to maturity is also likely to establish a fictive relationship for subsequent children—usually with a woman who has raised many children to maturity and whose husband, too, is lucky and prosperous—in the hope that the luck of the new parents will be extended to their fictive children. The same rationale applies when the fictive parent is a deity. The deity protects his human godchild as it grows up.

Fictive kin relationships may also be established out of gratitude to a deity who helped a child recover from illness. Kao Paak-neung once participated in the establishment of such a relationship. A two-year-old boy in Hang Tau Village was seriously ill. He had no appetite and vomited what little he ate; then he started refusing all food. At night he lay awake, crying. The boy's mother blamed his suffering on the jealous ghost of his deceased elder brother, who could not bear to see the living boy loved and cared for. The old spirit medium of Hang Tau Village confirmed the mother's suspicion; she had seen the ghost of the elder brother entering the family's house. Then the sick child began refusing even his mother's breast. It was as if the dead son was so jealous that he was preventing his brother from nursing. The mother tried expressing milk from her breast and putting it in a cup outside her door, as a propitiatory offering to the jealous ghost. But the ghost was not appeased, and the child seemed near death. Kao Paak-neung was called in. Once entranced, she confirmed that the deceased elder brother was the guilty party. Before the sick child's soul was finally retrieved and returned to his body, Kao Paak-neung and her tutelary spirits had to dispatch spirit soldiers and policemen. She then threw the divination blocks to learn how long the child's convalescence would take, and predicted that he would recover in three or four days. The grateful parents promised to make the boy a fictive son of Wa Dho, Kao Paak-neung's master, if the child recovered as predicted.

The child did recover, and his parents kept their promise. After the divination blocks assured Kao Paak-neung that Wa Dho would accept the child as his fictive son, a lucky day was selected from the almanac for the ceremony. When the day came the boy's parents brought him to Kao Paak-neung's shrine. They brought with them as an offering fresh fruit, pork, chicken, rice wine, rice, a ceremonial wooden box full of sweets, and some candles. Then the boy knelt before the altar and bowed three times to show respect. Kao Paak-neung addressed the deity: "Help the child to grow up quickly and in good health; and let him bring fortune to his parents and his brothers and sisters." Then the medium gave the boy a new pair of trousers, a pair of wooden shoes with a plastic strap, a bowl of rice, a pair of lucky red chopsticks, and a packet of lucky red money. She also gave him a red string to wear for luck.

From this day on, Wa Dho was the boy's *khay kong*, or fictive father, and he was Wa Dho's *khay jair*, fictive son. On all major holidays the boy's family had Kao Paak-neung worship Wa Dho on their son's behalf. If the child fell ill his family had her worship the deity again, with a special request for protection against the illness. The fictive kinship relationship does not end until just before the child's wedding. At this point the child comes to the altar and worships (*dsaau zan*) to repay the deity for his protection during childhood and youth. After the young man or woman worships and bows before the deity for the last time, the relationship between them is formally at an end. It is believed that anyone who failed to thank his spiritual godfather at this time would be most unlucky for the rest of his life.

One of the shaman's major duties, then, is to protect her clients' children by establishing and maintaining fictive kinship relations between them, herself, and appropriate deities. Both boys and girls can establish fictive kinship ties, although the practice is more common with boys because they are valued more highly by their families. A spirit medium who gains a reputation for successfully raising children to adulthood may acquire dozens of fictive children from families in her village and the surrounding countryside. Such relationships bring the medium both prestige and profit. It was, for example, the parents of Kao Paak-neung's fictive children, guided by the local political leader, who helped pay for her new altar house.

Another duty of spirit mediums is the questioning of family spirits. Cantonese burial practices and beliefs about the afterlife make it important to ensure the comfort of family spirits and to seek their advice when problems arise. A person's remains are buried three times, and on each occasion a ghost, if made unhappy, may bring his family grief. When a person dies, he is first placed in a wooden coffin and interred in a burial hill near the village. Five to ten years later, the bones are dug up, ritually washed with wine, and placed in a *kam taap*, a ceramic funeral pot. The pot is buried in a hill, where it remains for several years, pending reburial in an elaborate permanent tomb. The villagers believe that the location of an ancestral spirit's tomb profoundly affects the lives and fortunes of his descendants for generations, and the whole process of burial, disinterment, and reburial is fraught with danger and uncertainty.[7]

To assure themselves that they are handling matters properly, the villagers have the spirit medium contact their deceased relatives to discuss the ghost's wishes with respect to burial. The consultation takes place in a private ceremony attended only by the family members concerned and the shaman herself. The family asks if the dead person is comfortable and content in his grave, and if it is time for them to disinter his bones and place them in a permanent tomb. They do as the spirit directs (see the consultation with the spirit of the man executed by the Japanese, p. 208 above).

When the bones have been placed in a permanent tomb (its site chosen in careful accordance with geomantic principles), the ancestral spirits are asked if the tomb is satisfactory and comfortable. An ancestral spirit who is not comfortable in his tomb will become troubled and restless, and his living descendants will suffer for it. If the ancestral spirit says he is unhappy and dissatisfied, a family may even destroy the tomb and move the ancestral remains to another location to ward off misfortune.

Becoming a Shaman

The Ping Shan mediums share the ability to be possessed by spirits and go into trances. The villagers explain this gift by saying the mediums have *sin kwat*, "fairy bones," and *sin low*, a "fairy road."

An unborn child is connected to the Heavenly Flower Gardens by thirty-six ethereal bones. The bones are usually severed when the child is born, but sometimes one bone is not severed, which alters the child's spiritual outlook gravely. During the Ching Ming Festival in the spring, the Dragon Boat Festival, and other major holidays, the child with fairy bones loses his appetite and becomes ill. During these festivals the spirits of adults with fairy bones roam around heaven, to their mortal danger. Since the souls of people with fairy bones move freely and easily from their bodies to heaven, they are particularly vulnerable to attack by malicious ghosts. And if the fairy bones are not severed before marriage,

---

[7] *Ibid.*, p. 145.

marriage itself may cause death. People with fairy bones live in special danger.

The shamans of Ping Shan are not in agreement on fairy bones and the fairy road. The Fat One and Kao Paak-neung refer only to fairy bones. The Old Woman from China, a woman of some eighty years who has been a shaman for over fifty of them, distinguishes between the two concepts. A thread that connects a person to heaven, she calls a fairy road. Fairy bones also link a person's soul to the spirit world, but in less easily definable ways. Whereas a person with fairy bones can go into trances, a person with both fairy bones and a fairy road is easily possessed by spirits and is better able to travel to heaven with the aid of supernatural beings. The Old Woman from China says that only women with both fairy bones *and* a fairy road can become shamans.

Women having this capacity only become shamans if events in their personal lives drive them to it. The lives of the three spirit mediums of Ping Shan follow a remarkably consistent pattern. In each case the woman became a shaman only after a severe crisis—the death of several children, of her husband, or both. After her traumatic loss, each of the women was visited in her dreams by her children's spirits, who urged her to become a shaman. (Deceased children, who mediate between their mother and the supernatural world, are essential to a career as a spirit medium.) In each case the woman resisted, and in the case in which the husband was alive, he opposed his wife's becoming a spirit medium, not out of jealousy of the spirits who would possess his wife, but because shamans are low in status and viewed with distrust. Usually the struggle between the unwilling woman and her insistent children goes on for some time. As the pressure on the woman increases, she suffers attacks of seeming madness, during which she jumps around the house, leaps on top of tables, answers questions nonsensically, and so on. Finally, the reluctant candidate appears to die, and she must choose between becoming a spirit medium and dying permanently. The experiences of the three shamans of Ping Shan all follow this pattern.

The Fat One, considered the best spirit medium in the lineage, had five daughters and two sons, all of whom died very young. Soon after the death of her last child, her husband also died. Her losses left her grief-stricken, depressed, and continually ill. Every night she dreamed of visits from her dead children's souls. They taught her to "sing" in the rhythmic fashion characteristic of all professional shamans during conversations with the spirits, and then they asked her to become a spirit medium so she could help others and also earn extra money for herself. They knew that she had fairy bones because they had seen her call up spirits during the eighth month. They told her they had connections with other spirits and deities and would use their influence to help her deal with the supernatural world.

The Fat One resisted her children's advice, but they persisted in possessing her and forcing her to sing. She became ill, and they made her appear to die many times. Finally she agreed to become a spirit medium.

After making this decision, she sought the aid of an older spirit medium, and together they erected an altar in a shed alongside her house. She had written on her altar the names of her dead children and the names of powerful deities dictated by the children's spirits. After she had worshipped before her altar for many days, her health was restored and she was convinced of her supernatural powers. Parents began to bring sick children to her to be cured, and gradually she won a sizable following as a shaman and curess.

The experience of Kao Paak-neung, the second shaman of Ping Shan, was similar. As a young woman she had three daughters and one son, but they all died while very young. A year after her third daughter died, the daughter's soul entered Kao Paak-neung's body and asked her to become a spirit medium. But her dead son possessed her simultaneously, insisting that she become a curing specialist under the guidance of Wa Dho. The struggle between the two spirits made her continually ill and almost drove her mad. She wandered around the countryside worshipping at all kinds of temples and altars in an attempt to free herself from their demands. Neither she nor her husband wanted her to become a spirit medium and curer.

After a time the spirits of her daughter and son compromised, deciding that she should become both a spirit medium and a curing specialist following Wa Dho. Her husband continued his opposition to the spirits' demands until one day her daughter's spirit entered Kao Paak-neung's body and took her soul up to the heavens, making her appear to die several times during one long evening. Finally, at two in the morning, the husband relented and said she could become a shaman. Kao Paak-neung went wild with joy, jumping on tables and chairs, eating silver paper, incense, and candles, and singing loudly.

Shortly thereafter, she established an altar in her house. On the altar a Taoist priest wrote the names of her children, of Wa Dho, and of deities whose names were given her by her children's spirits. The priest reportedly addressed the deities as follows: "Here is a woman who, with the aid of her children's spirits, wishes to become a spirit medium. Please help her." After worshipping at the new altar, she was cured of her illnesses. The villagers heard about this, and began coming to her for help when their children were ill.

The history of Ping Shan's third shaman, the Old Woman from China, follows the same pattern. Her most important tutelary spirit is that of a son who died at age nine. After his death, she was ill for three years. During this period her son's spirit visited her many times, repeatedly kidnapping her soul and making her appear to die. This ended when she finally agreed to become a shaman. She learned the profession from her father's mother's sister, a woman who lived to be 120 years old and practiced as a spirit medium for almost a century.

The Old Woman from China claims that when she was younger, before World War II, she was famous throughout the countryside and had been consulted by people from many villages, including some quite distant ones. "I was popular," she says, "not only because of my ability, but because I charged less than the going rate for my services." When she was in her prime, many New Territories people established fictive kinship relations with her and her tutelary deities, and she now has over one hundred fictive sons in Ping Shan alone.

The personal tragedies each medium suffered were psychic shocks of the first magnitude. Their profession gives these women a useful and important social role that replaces their aborted family relationships. Perhaps the spirit mediums find sustenance in their contact with the spirits of the children who would have been of such emotional and social importance to them had they lived to adulthood.

The Shaman and Village Society

The supernatural world of Cantonese villagers is divided into two parts, which reflect the two aspects of their social world. One part belongs to the benevolent ancestral spirits who represent and celebrate the valued goals of lineage existence and the powerful and lucky deities who fill the imposing temples. These spirits and deities bring success and fortune to some of the villagers. The second part is the realm of the malevolent ghosts who bring the villagers sorrow and misfortune. These ghosts represent the unsuccessful, the unfulfilled, the jealous, the angry. The Cantonese shaman contributes to village society by controlling the dark side of the supernatural world.

The lineage of Ping Shan consists of most of the inhabitants of eight villages, all situated around a central ancestral hall. The men of the lineage, surnamed Tang, are descended in a direct line from a common ancestor, who founded the lineage over eight hundred years ago. Seen from outside, the lineage appears to be a highly solidary, unified social group, which struggles for power, status, and wealth with other such social groups. In the ideal view of the villagers, too, the lineage is a unitary group of brothers and kinsmen who enjoy equal status and a common social identity. Seen from within, however, the lineage is a hatchwork of competing families and sublineages. The ideal of fraternal equality is undermined by a drive for achievement that pits brother against brother. After death men who fail to rise in village society join the ranks of malevolent ghosts who populate the dark supernatural world of the spirit medium. Cantonese villagers believe that a person should be born into a nurturing family, grow to maturity in good health, prosper, have sons, and live to an advanced age. Anything that upsets this normal sequence is considered unlucky, and the person who dies young, who suffers particularly dire poverty, or who in some other way fails to taste the fruits of what the villagers consider a successful life has received less than his due. When such a person dies, the dissatisfied spirit becomes a malevolent ghost.

That most malevolent ghosts are female is surely no accident. Ground down by the lineage and family system, women may not join the competition for power, wealth, and prestige except vicariously, through their husbands and sons. They are the most downtrodden group in village society. When they marry they leave their parents' home and all their friends in the village of their birth. In their husband's village they must defer to their mother-in-law, to their husband, and to their husband's family. In many cases they are mistreated. Often they must endure the humiliation of seeing their husband take a mistress or a second wife. The frustrations of Cantonese women from one village could supply enough discontented, angry, revengeful ghosts to populate ten village hells.

A third group of malevolent ghosts are products of the conflicts, rivalries, and jealousies inherent in Cantonese family structure. Most malevolent ghosts are those of close kinsmen, usually members of the immediate family. Although the solidarity of brothers is a keystone of family and lineage structure, brothers compete for their parents' love and favor while they are growing up and for their property after their father's death. In Ping Shan numerous ghosts of brothers came back to haunt their living brothers and their families, a reflection of the ambivalence of fraternal relationships in village families.

Another common theme in the cases treated by shamans is the return of a sister's ghost to bother her living brother. Sometimes the sister's ghost is jealous of her brother and is malevolent, but usually the sister's ghost longs for her brother, who stands for the lost world of her natal family. This reflects the reluctance of many women to leave their parental home when they marry. Women pay a heavy psychological price for the Chinese patrilineal system. They do not really belong to their father's and brothers' family while they are growing up, and when they marry they are wrenched away from their parents and siblings to spend the rest of their lives among strangers.

In the case of unmarried females returning to haunt their family, the theme of sibling jealousy is evident. These ghosts are particularly dangerous because they are social anomalies; they do not belong to their father's family, yet they have no husband to care for their soul after death. So dangerous are these abnormal ghosts, they must be placed under the special care of the spirit medium. Ghosts of deceased first wives are also considered dangerous by the villagers, because they are so jealous of their successor. As might be expected, the tensions inherent in the notoriously difficult relations between mother-in-law and daughter-in-law find frequent expression in cases handled by spirit mediums. Daughters-in-law come back to seek revenge on a cruel mother-in-law; and mothers-in-law return to punish rebellious daughters-in-law for unfilial disrespect.

Village society is dominated by rich and successful males, the heads of successful families and sublineages. It is they who reap the rewards of Chinese society. It is the ancestors of these successful men who fill the ancestral halls of the lineage and are buried in impressive tombs. Only the rich and successful are immortal in China because it is only their descendants who can afford to build tombs and ancestral halls to house tablets and remains and to carry out the yearly ancestral rites. Even after death, the rich in rural China flaunt their wealth and status within the village, making the failure of the less fortunate members of village society even more galling than it would otherwise be.

Like villagers in many parts of the world, the inhabitants of Ping Shan share the image of limited good (Foster 1965). Because all good things in life are in short supply, if some members of the community attain wealth and success, it must be at the expense of others who are deprived of their rightful share. The poor people of Ping Shan hate their successful kinsmen with passion. Deprived of their share of life's fruits when alive, they form a mirror image of village society when they die. The most unsuccessful villager in life becomes the most powerful malevolent ghost after death. By kidnapping the souls of the living, by possessing their bodies and making them ill, the aggrieved ghosts blackmail the living into giving them gold and silver money and succulent food—all beyond their reach when they were alive. They so often attack children because they are not only the most vulnerable, but the most valued possessions of the living.

The spirit medium is the high priestess of this black half of the villagers' supernatural world. She rules over the dark world inhabited by the malevolent ghosts of the unsuccessful, the discontented, the abnormal, and the exploited. Her major function in village society is to deter these discontented and dangerous beings from wreaking their vengeance on the living villagers.

Cosmic Antagonisms: A Mother-Child Syndrome

MARJORIE TOPLEY

The period immediately following the birth of a baby is a time of biological and emotional adjustment for mother and child, when, in the Chinese view, a variety of difficulties can be anticipated. The child, for example, may refuse to nurse and gain little weight; it may have skin, bowel, or digestive disorders. It may be easily agitated and may respond poorly to the mother's management. The mother, too, may have difficulties: in establishing her milk, in dealing with her own weakness and depression, in developing affection for the child. But such difficulties are expected to be temporary; if they persist, they call for diagnosis and treatment. During an exploratory child-rearing study conducted in urban Hong Kong in 1969, I discovered that my informants—twenty illiterate and semiliterate mothers of small children—sought different explanations and treatments when any one or two such difficulties persisted.[1] But when they all persisted together, the women all thought that there must be a causal connection, that the difficulties of both mother and child formed a pattern, or syndrome. This syndrome is the subject of my essay.

Fifteen of the twenty women were immigrants from rural and semi-rural Kwangtung province; two others came from Hong Kong's rural New Territories. All lived in government-owned, low-cost, high-rise housing developments, mostly in one-room apartments, and were relatively poor, coming themselves from poor families.

Their explanations of the syndrome rest on cosmological assumptions.

[1] The study was sponsored by the Hong Kong Child Development Project, which is supported by the Nuffield Foundation and other organizations. Nineteen of my informants were Cantonese; none spoke any English. The data were gathered during several in-depth interviews I held on a variety of topics, all conducted in Cantonese in the mother's home.

Although two of the women were Christians, they not only shared the others' belief that all the symptoms were connected, they suggested the same immediate cosmological explanation for the syndrome itself, and the same ritual treatment, rejecting only certain underlying explanations and related treatments that by implication conflicted with their Christian beliefs.

Postnatal Adjustment

To understand my informants' conceptions of maladjustment, we must first look at what they thought to be happening in the period of postnatal adjustment. Traditionally the period is one hundred days, the same span Chinese consider necessary for many biological and social adjustments —to measles, for example, to marriage, and to death. During the whole period mother and child should stay quietly at home; no visitor should call before the end of the first moon, the point when the child is accepted into the family.

My informants believed that during the hundred days, a woman is still polluted from her pregnancy and is gradually purifying herself. While polluted, she is "strange," *k'ei.* Pregnancy and childbirth were classified with a group of disorders considered "poisonous" (*tuk*) that fall into two phases, first incubation and then eruption or purging. To fall victim to such poisonous disorders a person must be *kwaai,* which also means "strange." Indeed, *k'ei-kwaai* is a Cantonese compound for strange; one element complements the other. But the two words k'ei and kwaai have different definitional relations to disorder, and so to distinguish them in this essay, I use "strange" for k'ei and "queer" for kwaai.

Poisonous disorders include cholera, dysentery, smallpox, measles, bubonic plague, and epilepsy—all regarded as very dangerous and difficult to cure. One can get poisonous disorders by encountering things which are kwaai or queer, and which belong to either society, or the physical universe, or (for the non-Christians) the world of the spirits; to use Chinese classifications, to Man, Earth, or Heaven. Parts of the theory of what might be called "strangeness" are familiar to many other Chinese I have questioned, including traditional doctors. But Chinese medical theory in Hong Kong is in a complex state of transformation. Many concepts are shared by all traditional doctors, but applied and even described in varying ways. Thus the more Confucian-minded doctors do not talk about "strangeness" because "Confucius did not talk of strange things." Where my informants spoke of queerness, these doctors spoke of "polarization": some people or things were polarized either in the direction of *yeung* (mandarin *yang*) or in the direction of *yam* (mandarin *yin*). They also rejected the idea that the social or spiritual realm, as opposed to the physical, could be a source of disease. Other traditional specialists, however, were willing to entertain the idea that social and spiritual phenomena might be relevant to disease, and that polarized conditions could be termed queer.

One other observer, writing about child-rearing among Hokkien-speaking villagers in Taiwan, refers to ideas that seem related to my own informants' theory of "strangeness," and I will touch on them presently. But there is no comprehensive account of the theory in the literature on popular traditional cosmology, and the finer points appear to derive from the esoteric knowledge of the diviners and priests my informants consulted. Thus I have an insufficient basis for understanding all the logic of "strangeness," but must say what my informants believed because of its relevance to parts of the following analysis. Some of my insights were obtained from traditional doctors.

I said just now that one gets a poisonous disorder from contact with things that are queer. My informants' examples of things that are queer included brides, mourners, striking features of the landscape, demons, and gods. A bride is queer because she has "double happiness." Mourners are queer because they are "empty" or "sad." Some things in the landscape are queer because, like funerals, they are inauspicious—a petrol station was queer because it looked "like a coffin." Other queer things are, like marriage, auspicious—e.g., a huge boulder in the New Territories, famous to tourists as Amah Rock, which looks like a woman and child. The examples accord with the Confucian doctors' examples of polarization toward yin or yang. Demons and gods are phenomena "of Earth and of Heaven," and Earth and Heaven are further classified in classical literature as yin and yang. Furthermore, demons are popularly termed *kwai*, a yin characteristic in Chinese philosophy, and gods are *shan*, which is a yang characteristic. Even the Confucian doctors' concept of polarization is also implicit in the concept queer. In popular Cantonese speech kwaai means "extremely," and queerness is an extreme condition: happiness is not balanced by sadness, shan is not balanced by kwai, or yang by yin.

Being queer does not necessarily result in either poisonous or non-poisonous disease. Not in itself bad, and at times even necessary, queerness does, however, predispose an entity to disease. To contract a disease one has to meet (touching is not necessary) another entity that is also queer. Doctors say that a person polarized toward yin who meets an entity similarly polarized will get a yin disease, and a person polarized toward yang who encounters a similarly polarized entity will get a yang disease. My informants said that when two brides meet, each may give the other a similar disease; similarly two mourners at different funerals who met would catch similar diseases from each other. But these diseases are not poisonous. Poisonous diseases result when two people polarized in opposite directions meet each other, or a polarized person encounters some social, physical, or spiritual entity that is polarized in the opposite direction. Some women referred to this state as k'ei-kwaai.

A meeting between opposed polarized entities has a catalytic effect. The two entities emit a powerful "wind." This is ts'e-fung, ts'e also meaning "extreme" in some dialects (cf. Mathews 1961: 390). When the two opposed entities clash, a poison is generated and a poisonous disorder incubated. During the erupting or purging phase of the disorder, the sufferer can give a normally balanced person a disease. Such diseases are known as k'ei-peng, "strange" diseases. Some doctors in Hong Kong specialize in curing these almost incurable diseases; one is leprosy.

In the situations described thus far, two separate entities are involved. But a poisonous state can exist within a single universe, as can an extreme state. As we have seen, some things are permanently polarized in a given direction (a demon or god, a feature of the landscape), whereas others (a mourner or bride) are polarized only temporarily. Still others, however, are polarized in two directions simultaneously. They are locked in eternal conflict, permanently k'ei-kwaai. An expression in popular speech in Hong Kong for something k'ei-kwaai is "not three, not four" (m-saam, m-sz)—that is, neither one thing nor another. Things like this are anomalous. Examples given me include eels ("scaleless fish"), which are both "fish" and "snake," and a kind of spirit called iu-kwaai, iu being another term for strange, not common in Cantonese, but a homophone for agitated or disturbed. Iu-kwaai are something like a god, something like a demon. All such things are poisonous and dangerous to both normal and polarized people, but have curative properties for persons afflicted with poisonous disorders. The Cantonese say "poison drives out poison" (i-tuk, kung-tuk). The poisonous entity drives a poisonous disorder into its eruptive stage. By contrast, a queer but not poisonous, i.e. yin or yang, disorder is cured by something of the opposite polarization, along with some ingredient that prevents a catalytic effect—a "pure" or balanced phenomenon. So yin, which in physical substances has the humoral characteristic of coldness, may be cured by yang foods or medicaments with the humoral characteristic of hotness, and vice versa, but always with something balanced added. My informants talked not of yin and yang, but of "cold" and "hot" foods and medicaments, and those that were of "peaceful ethers" (tsing-hei).

For poisonous conditions, however, one takes poisonous medicine. Traditional doctors differentiate between yin and yang medicaments as "noble" and poisonous medicaments as "ignoble." The sufferer must at the same time avoid foods with the polarization he or she was experiencing when the poisonous disease was contracted, and take foods with the opposite polarization, i.e., that of the entity which transmitted the disease. Thus a bride who encounters a mourner and becomes poisonous or kʾei-kwaai takes a poisonous cure. She must avoid hot or yang foods (marriage is a yang affair) but eat cold (yin) foods. I will return to these points in due course, but first let us look again at pregnancy and the postnatal period in the light of these explanations of strangeness and balance.

A pregnant woman is temporarily like a poisonous entity: forces pulling in opposite directions are contained in one body. She is described as "four-eyed"—having two eyes in the head, two in the belly. The whole entity, so to speak, is kʾei-kwaai. She herself is polarized in the direction of cold and the fetus in the direction of hot. The woman is considered cold because internally she is losing blood to the fetus. Each month women move from cold toward hot, which they reach in the middle of the month, and then back to cold when blood is passed as menstrual fluid. Because the woman and the fetus have opposite polarizations, "wind" is generated and poison condenses in the womb. Because of this condition, which is like the incubation phase of a strange disorder, the fetal soul (tʾoi-shan) wanders around outside the mother's body to avoid danger. The pregnant woman should avoid poisonous foods or her "disorder" will erupt, i.e. she will go into labor prematurely and lose the child. She should also avoid foods that are definitely either cold or hot, for they will polarize the two entities further, generating more poison and wind. Her ideal diet is very restricted: no vegetables, and little meat besides pork, which is regarded as neither hot nor cold but perfectly balanced. Chicken is barred because it is hot, and fish because it is either cold or poisonous. Some informants also believed that pregnant women should avoid all places of worship.

In the postnatal period the mother gradually returns to a normal balance. She is purified of poison and the wind subsides. Special medicines and diet assist the natural processes: wines to dry up the wind (which is "wet"); hot foods that now will help her move back to normal; and special soups to improve her milk. She should not wash her hair for the hundred days because this aggravates wind, and she should eschew poisonous foods because they will pollute the milk and irritate the vagina and womb. She should not have intercourse with her husband or he will catch a "contagious" disease (kʾei-peng) of the lung. It is natural for her to be weak and depressed while these adjustments are in progress.

All infants are born k'ei-kwaai, but normally the condition is temporary. During the postnatal period a root medicine is given to reduce the
baby's heat; the poison is not finally eliminated until it has measles (cf.
Topley 1970: 425). Traditionally cow's dung was rubbed on the um-
bilicus to reduce wind, and tranquilizing medicines are given to inte-
grate the baby's soul and body.[2] The infant is agitated because its soul
is reluctant to be born. The non-Christian women attributed the soul's
reluctance to boredom with past lives in the world, the Christian women
to its disappointment at leaving Heaven. The infant does not know why
it is agitated, but the soul is seen as some sort of social, hence moral,
entity. For example, in a ritual for curing "injury by fright," the soul
is told to "be a man," i.e. a person, and "obey people's instructions"
(Topley 1970: 432). During the first hundred days of life, until its soul
settles, it is natural for a child to be nervous. It must be protected from
further poisons (e.g., from its mother's milk) during this period or its
own poison may erupt in a dangerous disease; it might, for example,
contract measles too early. Anything polarized in the same ("hot") direction may keep it from getting measles, which it must have eventually
to be purged of poisons.

For a particular infant, however, even polarizations toward cold may
be harmful, for every person has a different constitution, i.e. a different
natural balance of "elements"—fire, water, metal, earth, and wood—as
shown by his horoscope. The mother's horoscope also has an effect on
a child, through her "flower fate" (fa-meng), which relates to the element predominating in her own horoscopal blueprint. (The term relates
to a belief that children are "flowers" on maternal "plants" growing in
a garden tended by Mother and Father Gardener, fa-wong foo-mo.)
Elements are mutually destructive or creative. You add up and subtract
(or hire a diviner to do so) to arrive at the element to which you basically "belong" (shuk). "Flower fates" are listed in the Chinese almanac
for women belonging to each of the five elements. Each year the tem-
peraments of all a woman's children change: one year, for example,
"fire" women's children are placid and "metal" women's lively, and the
next year the position may be reversed.

If, then, a mother and child experience prolonged maladjustment,
many explanations are possible. An ailment might be explained by the

---

[2] From the standpoint of the modern medical practitioner, many of the precautions taken to ensure the infant's health are tragically misdirected: the heat-reducing
root medicine is now thought to cause jaundice and possible permanent liver damage; the past high mortality rate of measles is now attributed to the toxicity of the
"curative" purge; cow dung applied to the navel can cause tetanus; and the tranquilizing medicines were recently discovered to have a toxic ingredient.

mother's failure to observe all the correct food avoidances during pregnancy (few claimed to do so) or all the restrictions of the postnatal period. Only one of my informants claimed to have stayed in for the full hundred days; most women in urban Hong Kong have to go out because they have nobody to do their marketing for them. Such cases may be cured by medicine and diet. In other cases a diviner will ascertain that a woman's "plant" needs attention, a ritual watering, perhaps, or fertilizing. This may help in cases where the mother is unable to feel affection for the child; perhaps the father wanted a son and the child is a girl; perhaps there is no cash for another child, or not enough space; or perhaps the mother wants to go out to work but has nobody to care for the infant at home. It was thought that with the help of a diviner, such feelings of resentment or disappointment would soon fade away and natural affections be established.

The matter is more serious, however, if the horoscope shows the child to have a kwaai or queer fate (*meng*). All children have rather more hot in their balance until they are seven, and they have poison until they have had measles, so they are regarded as a little bit kwaai and a little bit k'ei-kwaai. After age seven they move toward a normal adult state, i.e. not hot or cold or poisonous. Their peculiar balance during the first seven years makes them prone to many disorders. Children with different horoscopes are predisposed to different diseases upon encountering different things at different periods. The almanac shows when children of different horoscopes are likely to get a particular disease if they encounter a particular entity, thus enabling them to avoid such encounters. A child born with a queer fate, however, is more severely polarized and hence likely to be fractious and susceptible to many diseases. Such children are usually intelligent, however, and if one can get them over this difficult period of seven years, it will have been worth the effort. Some of the factors determining their constitutions begin to adjust, and their queerness will probably subside. Margery Wolf describes a village in Taiwan where difficult, ailing children are spoken of as *kui khi* (Hokkien), and children continually ailing but likely to be prosperous and happy when they grow up, if they do, are spoken of as *kui mia:*, having a *kui* fate (Wolf 1972: 63–64). Although Wolf translates kui mia: as "expensively fated" and kui khi as "expensive," i.e. difficult to raise, it may be noted that the sound of kui khi resembles the Cantonese k'ei-kwaai in reverse. I will have something to say about these linguistic differences later. According to my informants, children with queer fates sometimes continue to be queer even at maturity. Then their lives are shot through with restrictions. If, for example, they are basically hot, they should eat only cold and balanced foods, and preferably become a vegetarian, perhaps taking up a religious profession appropriate for a vegetarian, e.g. as a Buddhist nun.

The constitutional imbalance of a child with a queer fate may also involve other parties. First, the child may be polarized in the same direction as someone with whom it has a continuous relationship. Then both parties may suffer from continual illness. This may be corrected by adding an element to the child's name so it is compatible with that of the other party; for example, a radical may be added to the character with which the name is written. Or, if child and mother are involved, something may be gained by attention to the latter's "plant." In such cases, because of the similarity of fates, the mother is likely to feel too much affection for the child rather than too little—i.e., to be overanxious about it.

When mother and child have opposite polarizations in their fates, the consequences are more serious. Both parties will be k'ei-kwaai, they will always be getting poisonous diseases, and they will feel no affection for each other. Moreover, the trouble starts in the womb. In cases of polarization in the same direction during pregnancy, the mother will be too cold or not cold enough, but this can be corrected with medicine. But if the polarizations of mother and fetus are opposite, more poison will be created, and the mother may get toxemia. Symptomatic of opposite polarizations are a complicated pregnancy, difficult labor (perhaps a breech birth), or some peculiarity surrounding the birth, such as the child's being born with a thick coating of vernex (thought to protect the mother and child from each other), the waters' being discolored when they break, or the child's having a bowel movement or urinating as it is born.

When mother and child are k'ei-kwaai in respect of each other, then they are antipathetic; both will suffer from a variety of poisonous ailments, and they will feel no affection for each other. Some cases described to me suggested that the child or mother in fact had some physical abnormality. One child could not move its arms and legs; another was always weak and eventually proved to have a hole in its heart; another had a large birthmark on its face, and one had frequent convulsions. In the last case the mother had suffered from a toxemic condition during pregnancy.

If the syndrome deriving from antipathetic fates is suspected, one should first of all visit a diviner, for a problem related to the horoscopes of the two parties can affect the general luck of the whole family. Let us see how this cosmic clash is explained and treated.

Unmatched Horoscopes and Methods of Adjustment

All the women said that a person's horoscope contained eight characters: two for the lunar year, two for the month, two the day, and two the period of the day (*shi-shan*) that one is born. These characters determine one's fate. One woman explained that each pair of characters has something of Heaven, which affects one's social relationships, and something of Earth, which relates to material success (*wan*). Both aspects are somehow related to health because they determine the four elements in one's constitution. But most of the women thought these four pairs of characters also related to four important relationships— with one's ancestors, parents, children, and spouses (most of the women knew their eight characters and those of their husbands and children). The pair relating to spouses differs from the others because one character stands for the person in question and one for his or her spouse; the spouse is one's "other half."

Now, except in the case of adopted children, the spouse is the only person of this group about whom one has any choice. But marriages are made in Heaven. This belief is symbolized in Cantonese marriage rituals by the red cord given as part of the gifts of the bride's side. The cord, which "ties" the couple together in Heaven, is called *t'in-shing*, "heavenly thread," a term closely related to *t'in-sing*, "heavenly instincts." Such feelings are given people by Heaven to assure them of a harmonious relationship. As one informant said, "*t'in-sing* makes you know inside how to treat people. If there is no *t'in-sing*, there is no affection." One assures a compatible relationship by comparing the couple's horoscopes before betrothal. If the horoscopes are compatible, the parties will balance each other, flourish in health and wealth, and feel heavenly instincts. If this does not happen, then the horoscopes were not correctly matched by the diviner (Freedman 1970: 128–29).

With the other relationships, however, such assurances are not available. One cannot match the horoscopes of mother and child in advance and make sure the right child is born. Nor can one choose the time of a child's birth to ensure a horoscope compatible with its mother's. One of my informants said that sometimes a midwife was asked to either hasten or delay a birth so the child would arrive at an auspicious time (*shi-shan ho*). But this, she added, was useless as well as dangerous because a child decides its own time to arrive (cf. Tsay 1918: 535; Thompson 1890: 189). If the horoscopes of mother and child clash, the difficulties of early infancy will persist, the child as it grows up will be disobedient and unfilial, and the mother will find herself disliking it intensely. In the absence of t'in-sing, disaster (*ts'aam*) will strike the family. One woman blamed the growing crime rate among young people in Hong Kong on the absence of t'in-sing between parents and children: the absence of t'in-sing means the absence of morality; people do not behave correctly toward one another. Yet how can you blame either mother or child if they have a horoscope clash? It is an intolerable situation. The mother finds it *ho-naan tso-yan*, "difficult to act as a person."

One solution, provided the child is not manifestly abnormal, is adoption. This is also the best way of handling the matter if the child is expendable, of the undesired sex, or an impossible financial burden on a poor family. Otherwise one can try bonding the child to another, a relationship known as *k'ai-kwoh*. What does this relation achieve? Let me remind the reader that only things that are k'ei-kwaai can purge k'ei-kwaai conditions: "poison drives out poison." And something k'ei-kwaai is neither one thing nor another, but anomalous. Second, we have a problem not only of health but also of morality—i.e. the absence of heavenly instincts. Finally, the clash involves one person who is supporting the other. I want to see how these three factors are acknowledged in the ritual symbolism of bonding, and then what the relationship itself is thought to achieve.

A child may be bonded to another person or to a god, stone, or tree. As my informants perceived, aspects of the bonding ritual resemble aspects of the marriage rituals. At betrothal, as we saw, a "heavenly cord" of red silk thread is given by the bride's side, along with a bolt of cloth and a pair of shoes. At bonding these gifts are given by the party to whom the child will be bonded, the bonder, although in this case the cord is referred to as a "trouser cord" (used in traditional dress to tie round the waist). At betrothal the man's side gives pork, beef, chicken, and wine. At bonding these gifts are given by the child's parents. If the child is being bonded not to a person but to a god or natural feature, the food is placed on an altar and the other gifts are made of paper and burnt.

The trouser cord may suggest "incorporation" (Van Gennep 1960: 132) and the establishment of a new relationship. But the cord also suggests that the relationship will be a harmonious one. The child will flourish in health as a result, and feel affection for the bonding party; in short, t'in-sing will be established. But the fact that the gifts given by the bonder resemble those given by the family of the bride-to-be might also suggest that the bonder is allied with the family of the child, rather than the child with the bonder's. And in fact the child does not have to leave home and live with the bonding party, although as we shall see it may do so. In the latter case the bonding party may be seen as a parent rather than a bride. The parent aspect is further symbolized by the bonder's gifts to the child of a pair of chopsticks and a bowl, suggestive of support. Indeed, a person bonded to a child is known as *k'ai-ma,* bonded mother, if a woman, or *k'ai-ye,* bonded paternal grand-father, if a man. The child is called *k'ai-tsai,* bonded son, or *k'ai-nui,* bonded daughter. Moreover, the relationship lasts, theoretically at least, for the period that intimacy was traditionally expected to last with one's parents; for a daughter it terminates with her marriage (when she leaves home) and for a son it lasts throughout life (he may continue to live with his parents).

The symbolism of bonding, then, is ambiguous; it includes both ideas about spouses and ideas about parents and other lineal kin, pulling in opposite directions. In popular speech the terms k'ai-ye and k'ai-tsai refer to another relationship that Chinese in Hong Kong certainly re-gard as ambiguous—that between homosexual lovers. The term *k'ai-tai* (*tai* meaning younger brother) may alternatively be used. The English word "queer," also used for this relationship, has as a verb the meaning "to put out of order," and thus appears to coincide with the Chinese meaning.

The ambiguity symbolically expressed in bonding ritual is paralleled by expectations of the relationship itself. Certainly a cosmic reaction is anticipated. It is hoped that mother and child will both improve in health and even in affections—that the bonder will drive out the k'ei-kwaai condition. Bonding is sometimes arranged for children with a kwaai fate resulting from internal imbalances or with some abnormality or unusual feature. In such cases it may be hoped not only that the child will feel affection for the bonder, and vice versa, but that other social and economic duties will be acknowledged between the bonder and the child's parents. Other things may be hoped of the relationship; the range of expectations varies with the nature of the parties.

A popular god for bonding in Hong Kong is Wong Taai Sin, Great Sage Wong, whose temple gives its name to a large resettlement area in Kowloon where many of my informants lived. This god is noted both for improving health and curing "strange" diseases and for giving good tips at the races. He brings the family both material benefits and good luck. The stone most women mentioned as suitable for bonding is a prominent rock on Hong Kong Island known as Yan-uen Shek, Marriage Affinity Rock, because it is also appealed to when marriages do not work; it corrects any nonaffinity diagnosed after the event. It is appealed to frequently when a child has a kwaai fate, particularly a kwaai fate that clashes with its mother's. The dual function of Affinity Rock underlies the parallel between cosmic affinity in marriage and cosmic affinity in other relationships. Trees selected for bonding are usually pines, said to be strong and to have long roots suggestive of long life. Children who clash with their mothers are not expected to live very long unless their fates are modified.

Two kinds of people were considered suitable for bonding relationships: rich people with many children, who are obviously lucky, and devout vegetarians, usually women. The latter are usually childless, and may be rich or poor. A rich person with many children is expected to bring good fortune (in a transcendental sense), and a devout person is said to improve everyone's destiny. There seems to be nothing ambiguous about such persons. But it may be relevant that a lucky person can be seen as polarized in an auspicious direction, and that a religious profession is considered appropriate for a person with a queer fate. It may be that within the relationship of bonding, where ambiguities appear to be ritually underlined, the bonder is ideally someone also polarized in an appropriate direction—to prevent the neutralization of the "poisonous" (and hence for those with a queer fate, curative) effect of the relationship itself. Diviners were said to recommend the type of person or entity to which a particular child should be bonded; i.e., the choice is not a random one if an expert is consulted.

Not everyone consults a diviner, however, and other factors may influence the choice. Certain basic obligations are incurred, first by the mother and later the child. A god must be worshipped regularly, especially at its chief festival; a rock or tree must have regular offerings of paper money and food. If the bonder is a person, the child should visit him or her on all occasions when Chinese visit paternal kin and should come armed with gifts. The child should attend the person's funeral as a kinsman and the bonder the child's wedding. A rich person may additionally be expected to help the family in general and the child in particular by securing its admission to a good school, paying for schooling and medical care, and buying presents. If the child and mother are hopelessly at odds, the child may be brought up by the bonder. One of my informants said she had been brought up by her bonded mother and had emigrated with her from China. A childless, unmarried woman might be expected to treat the bonded child like a son or daughter, taking it out and buying it things. On the other hand, one woman told me her relative's son's bonded mother was poor and was always seeking financial help from the family. Because he feared such demands, one woman said, her husband did not like her to bond their children to people, only to gods.

Financially, then, the child's family may be either assisted or bur-
dened by a bonding relationship. Socially, too, the relationship is an
ambiguous one: beyond the ceremonial observances, the rights and
duties are not stated very precisely, so many permutations are possible. Much depends, for example, on the precise socioeconomic status
of the family, and on the particular difficulties experienced by mother
and child.

Former Resentments and Role Adjustment

Theoretically the bonding relationship will ameliorate the cosmic position of both mother and child; their health and emotional responses
should improve. Sometimes this does happen, perhaps because the
bonder pays for medical care or removes the child to his or her own
home. But suppose the syndrome persists and the relationship with the
bonder does not take hold? A mother may ask why she has been saddled
with such a child, why do their horoscopes clash? One of my two Christian informants, who belonged to a Protestant fundamentalist sect,
thought it could be "the sins of the fathers visited on the children."
The other, a Catholic, said it was just fate, and all one could do was
to pray for a miracle (she also suggested that bonding to the Virgin
Mary might help). The non-Christian women suggested that, in the
absence of any obvious cause, the syndrome might result from wrongs
committed in a previous existence, *ts'in-shai,* "former generations." (Con-
fusingly, this term was also used by the Christian woman who spoke of
"sins of the fathers," quite a different concept.) To demonstrate the
effect of ts'in-shai, one woman described a rich but childless maternal
aunt. The aunt had been told by an old woman specializing in knowledge of the past that in a former existence she had spent much money
on Buddhist ceremonies and charity but had once stolen from her husband's family. This explained why she was rich but childless: her social
problem was caused by her former social failings.

Several women thought that if one had behaved very badly toward a
particular person, his soul would come back in the body of one's own
child. The possibility that souls come back and work out their credits
and debits with people they formerly knew—wreaking vengeance, for
example, on their family—is fully explored in Cantonese folklore. This
argument was used to explain why a woman might continue to produce
difficult, even abnormal, children. And of course if there is a family history of congenital defects, a mother might be predisposed to see a particular child as having the soul of a deceased relative who also had that
defect and for that very reason had been badly treated. Such a child is
a *loh-kwai tsai,* "child drawing a spirit of the dead." This is suggestive

of another expression, *loh-chaai tsai*, meaning a child who dies before "repaying his parents." Although it is accepted that a mother may deserve her fate, it is also considered very wrong of a soul to exact revenge in this way. So one does not have to accept all the blame for the situation.

A resentful soul may do many things to harm either the mother or its own infant body. For example, it may refuse to wander outside its mother's body during gestation. This wandering around itself leaves the fetus susceptible to accidental injury, but the almanac shows where the soul is at different stages of pregnancy, so people can take care to avoid it. The soul's failure to vacate the mother's body can make the mother swell up (toxemia?) during pregnancy and suffer dangerous difficulties during childbirth. Numerous peculiarities of childbirth were interpreted to me in terms of a resentful fetal soul. A child with thick vernex is a "good child," one woman said, because it is trying to protect both its mother and itself from any clash. But a bowel movement at birth shows a soul resentful of its father, and urination resentment of its mother. Such an infant might even cause the eventual death of the resented parent. I was told that in the past, a mother-in-law supervising the birth who diagnosed resentment would immediately dispose of the child: a boy would be given away, a girl "thrown on the rubbish heap." But the baby must not be allowed to see its mother or father, or it will eventually seek them out and take its revenge. An ordinary adoption was not always a solution; if the child is not disposed of immediately and is indeed a loh-kwai tsai, it might later seek out its parents and exact revenge. Moreover, an obviously abnormal child might find no takers. If the child is expendable, one might consider giving it to a monastery or nunnery, where the atmosphere of continual prayer might help neutralize its aggression.

There is no real solution if such a child remains with its mother, but one could try to redefine the problem, adjusting the role to the behavior rather than behavior to the role. By changing the term of address, one suggests that the mother is not really the mother. The child is taught to call her either *a-tse*, "elder sister," *a-so*, "brother's wife," or *a-naai*, "wet-nurse."

What appears to be argued by the use of these terms? When I asked for other instances of such a switch in kinship terms, I was given the example of a young concubine (*ts'ip*) and children of her fellow-consort who were approximately the same age as she. The concubine should theoretically be addressed as "mother" and has some of a mother's duties, but the children address her as "elder sister" because "it is difficult for children to treat people the same age as if they were senior" (in generation). The concubine's generation is made to match her age. In the case of mother and child, of course, there is already a difference in both generation and age. Putting the mother into the same generation as the child (elder sister; brother's wife) appears to anticipate a difficult relationship. I was told that when the term of address for mother was modified, the child should not really treat its mother as elder sister or brother's wife, but the mother need not feel so bad if the child who did not call her mother was difficult to control.

What of the term wet-nurse? Informants said the term implies familiarity. It also suggests that the milk the child drinks is not the mother's, and mothers with antipathetic children are believed to produce milk harmful to them. The term also evokes a deity who helps with children's problems. Children are believed to be in the charge of a goddess called Golden Flower Mother, Kam Fa Mo, whom informants likened further to Mother Gardener. Her attendant deities are twelve "wet-nurses," who appear in temples as smaller images than the mother goddess and are subject to her authority. The role of wet-nurse is also ambiguous. In one way she is superior to a mother—she performs one of her most important functions—but in another she is inferior, for she is subject to the mother's authority.

A similar element of conflict is implicit in the other substituted role terms. Elder sister, for example, has an important role in the rearing of younger brothers and sisters in village society, which entitles her to respect and obedience. She plays an even greater role in urban Hong Kong, where in many cases she goes out to work and pays for her younger siblings' education—an education often superior to her own. Though entitled to respect and obedience, however, she is ultimately subject to her mother's authority, and her decisions may be countermanded; her authority is ambiguous. Like the wet-nurse and the concubine, an elder sister has substantial authority over another woman's children, and, again like the concubine, is ultimately subject to the greater authority of the children's mother. One can also infer potential conflict between a woman and her brother's wife. If, for example, the sister is older than both brother and brother's wife, and if the sister is unmarried and living at home, what is her relationship to the new daughter-in-law? She is senior in age, but in some ways socially inferior, at least in traditional society, where these terminological changes were worked out. She is supposed to leave the family, not contribute children to it, a role reserved precisely to the daughter-in-law. Because of this potential conflict, in some areas of Shun Tak, in Kwangtung province, elder sisters had either to marry or to signal their intention of remaining unwed before younger brothers could take a wife.

More narrowly linguistic considerations are also important. I referred earlier to the suggestiveness of homophones, noting that Cantonese- and Hokkien-speaking people have some of the same ideas about unusual fates and troublesome children, and used different terms with similar sounds. Such transformations can take place from one linguistic group to another, particularly among nonliterate people.

Conclusions

My informants were all poor and illiterate, and they lived in crowded conditions. Most came from poor families in rural areas, where there had been high rates of infant and maternal mortality. Poverty, customs affecting the pregnant woman and both mother and infant after childbirth, delivery by midwives who were sometimes trying either to hasten or to delay births—all these factors may have increased the number of difficulties in childbirth, the incidence of birth defects among the newborn, and mortality rates among both mothers and children. Given these high mortality rates, and the importance of children in traditional society, one might anticipate considerable anxiety at any sign of abnormality. And strong resentment against an abnormal child.

For any family, a child who is sickly and fractious, particularly one who seems to suffer a serious abnormality, is a heavy burden. And a mother unable to cope because she herself is ailing from a complication of childbirth would be an additional burden. In crowded households harmony is essential, and a child who is hard to manage will create disharmony. A difficult or abnormal child would require special nurturing—a need perhaps reflected in the Hokkien term "expensive." And at the end of the rearing one might have a son unable to marry and beget children or an unmarriageable daughter. For a family such an outcome could be disastrous. It is not surprising, then, that a mother-in-law might want to dispose of a sickly child immediately, before the mother has seen it. Heaven expects affections to develop between mothers and children, but it by no means ensures that this will happen. And supposing one resents a child, any child, because one cannot support it or it is of the undesired sex? One might be predisposed to perceive a syndrome that justifies such feelings, to see all the symptoms when only one or two—or even none—exists.

My informants, none of whom were committed exclusively to any one cosmological system, went for an explanation first to the theory of "strangeness," "poisonous conditions," and horoscope incompatibility.

Poisonous conditions are usually dangerous, and sometimes difficult to cure. A horoscope clash that produces a poisonous condition helps justify one's anxieties over the symptoms. Horoscope clashes also prevent natural affections from spontaneously developing, making an adoption an acceptable solution if somebody is willing to adopt. Bonding is another possible solution for horoscope clash. It can drive out the poisonous condition, and offers other potential benefits.

If all else fails, one can always fall back on the explanation that the syndrome is punishment for wrongs committed by the mother in an earlier existence. Even this explanation takes some of the sting out of a painful situation: it explains the absence of affection, and relieves the mother of responsibility for controlling the situation in the present. Moreover, it places some of the blame on the child: in exacting revenge for earlier wrongs, the child is acting in a blamably unfilial fashion. Perhaps now the child can be given to a monastery or nunnery. Or, if it is to remain in the family, a terminological device can be used that reflects the mother's difficult role position by implying a difficult relationship and, by replacing the term mother, suggests that "this is no child of mine."

I have not dealt here with all the possible problems of newborn children and their mothers. I have not touched upon the relationship queer people have with spirits—the possibilities of spirit possession or of antipathy to an ancestor. Nor have I considered the implications of a horoscope clash or lack of affinity between child and father. But when problems arise between a mother and her newborn child, they may well result from gestation or childbirth. I have discussed a set of beliefs that addresses itself to this possibility.

Ancestor Worship and Burial Practices

H. G. H. NELSON

This paper reports on some aspects of the fieldwork that I carried out in the New Territories between April 1967 and October 1968.[1] The paper asks what use people make of the biological facts of birth, death, and descent, and what interpretation they put on them. The proportion of data to theory is high, and I must ask the reader to accompany me through a labyrinth of genealogical detail. My excuse is that so far as I know, no other fieldworker has gone around a Chinese village copying down every available domestic ancestral tablet and compared the results with every other available record of the village's past.[2]

That I was able to do this derives naturally from my choice of a small, poor, and relatively insignificant village. Thus the present paper, as well as the fuller study I am working on, serves as a complement to the earlier studies by Baker (1968) and Potter (1967) of the large, rich, and influential villages of Sheung Shui and Ping Shan. The particular question to be discussed here is not raised by either Baker or Potter, and I hope that my detailed analysis of events in a small lineage may acquire a more general relevance in throwing light on, and raising questions about, the

[1] From 1967 to 1969, I was employed as a Research Officer of the London School of Economics, on a project financed by a grant made to Professor Maurice Freedman by the (British) Social Science Research Council. The assistance in the field of my wife, Janet Nelson, was invaluable; her fare to Hong Kong was provided by the London-Cornell Project for East and Southeast Asian Studies, financed jointly by the Carnegie Corporation and the Nuffield Foundation. I am glad to acknowledge their generosity.

[2] Not all the anthropological guile in the world would have persuaded some residents of Sheung Tsuen even to talk to the fieldworker, let alone allow him to copy the family ancestral tablet. A further excuse for going into great ethnographic detail is the exceptional interest of the ethnography itself: the length of domestic tablets, for example, must raise questions about the relation between domestic and hall worship.

nature of similar events in the lineage's larger and better organized counterparts, in both Hong Kong and Taiwan.

The paper is very much a detailed study of the interaction between ritual behavior and social reality—a respectable theme for an anthropologist, although my treatment may contrast oddly with some recent approaches to the same phenomena. I should like to see this paper as in some sense a link between the first volume in this series (on family and kinship in Chinese society; Freedman 1970) and the present one. Ancestor worship is the ritualization of kinship ties, and if I seem to lay more stress on kinship than on its ritualization, I shall be doing no more than the Chinese would have me do; and if, moreover, in the process I raise the question of whether ancestor worship is a religious activity in the same sense as other forms of Chinese ritual behavior, this will be no bad thing. I am attempting, in other words, to draw together some of the major behaviors focused on the dead, and to see them as a single phenomenon: a phenomenon which may as well be termed ancestor worship, but which manifests itself only partly in ritual.

The Site

Sheung Tsuen is a Cantonese-speaking village of approximately 150 households situated roughly in the center of Hong Kong's New Territories.[3] Local legend (confirmed by such archeological evidence as remained visible to my untrained eye) has it that there was originally a small walled and moated settlement called Wing Hing Wai on the site where Sheung Tsuen's primary school now stands. The village expanded immediately outside the walls at some stage in the unremembered past to form a heterogeneous collection of dwellings now known as Tung Sam Tsuen (Central Village); from this nucleus, groups and families have hived off at various times, so that Sheung Tsuen now consists of a number of discrete hamlets scattered over a radius of about half a mile.

Eight surnames are represented in the village. The Leis are the largest and most influential group, with about half the households; they are followed by the Wus, the Leungs, the Chaus, and the Wongs, and then by very small groups of Maks and Laus (four households each). Within living memory, a few families of Yuens have moved out of the village, and a single family of Lams has moved in. Tung Sam Tsuen is a mixed-surname hamlet, with as many as three different surnames represented in a single row of nine houses. People still say they dislike living cheek by jowl with people of different surnames, and the movement out of Tung Sam Tsuen seems to be continuing: it has more empty and tumble-

[3] I.e. native-born households; the study did not touch the immigrant population.

down houses than any of the outlying hamlets, all of which are inhabited by people of a single surname.[4]

This paper is concerned exclusively with the Leis, some of whom live in Tung Sam Tsuen and who together own outright four of the outlying hamlets. Their distribution raises interesting questions about the relationship between genealogical divisions and residence, questions I cannot explore here. The Leis own three ancestral halls; only two of the other surnames had even a single supra-domestic ancestral structure.

The Problem

The problem that most engaged me both while I was in the field and ever since was the fit between the high- and low-level structures of the Lei lineage (and, by extension, of any Chinese lineage). There appeared to be a number of connected practices, which were all focused in some way on the dead forebears of the present members of the lineage, but whose interrelation was far from clear. Two contrasts in particular stood out. First, despite the apparently tender concern of the Chinese, at the domestic level, for the welfare of their immediate ancestors, the Leis nevertheless adopt burial practices that seem to expose those ancestors' bones to the absolute maximum danger. Second, although genealogies seemed to be recorded in meticulous detail, the relations between groups in the village appeared confused in the extreme. The two contrasts merged into the more general problem of just how lineage segments emerge from the men in and on the ground. Then I was led to hypothesize that the paradoxes just described in fact concealed a more or less deliberate attempt to get rid of all but a highly selected number of ancestors; to obscure all but a few crucial, high-level genealogical relationships; and to merge other, closer relationships into the generalized status of "village brother." I set out, therefore, to test the hypothesis that just as in non-literate ancestor-worshipping societies, the structure of the localized Chinese lineage is determined by the political and economic relations of the men on the ground; and that burial practices, and certain recurrent inefficiencies in the system of recording ancestral links, provide mechanisms whereby in a literate society the often inconvenient facts of biological descent can be bent to suit the changing needs of the living. In other words, it looked very much as if the domestic tail might be wagging the ancestral dog.

---

[4] Unfortunately, data are lacking to test the interesting question, raised by the discussant of this paper, Emily Ahern, whether multi-surname settlement (as in Sheung Tsuen) tends to heighten or diminish a lineage's concern with internal segmentation. Professor Ahern suggested that the more predominant the lineage's position in the community, the greater its tendency to segment.

When I set out to test this hypothesis, however, I found myself faced with a number of problems: an absence of records of the Lei lineage's past, an extreme vagueness on the part of nearly all my informants about the details of their genealogy, and a great deal of apparently contradictory information. The day was saved by my realization that the absence of records was rather a proliferation of very incomplete ones; that I had just enough informants who could give me precise information; and that even though most information given me was misinformation, nobody actually lied.

To prove the hypothesis that there is major structural significance in the apparent discrepancy between high- and low-level lineage records, my attempt to reconstruct the lineage on the basis of all the information available to me would have had to fail; to prove it conclusively, I should have had to find positive evidence of contradictions between those two kinds of records. The way would then have been open for an exploration of the gap's functional significance. In the event, however, my attempt to reconstruct the history and structure of the Lei lineage has been successful, and I am confident that the lineage records, scattered and patchy though they are, are consistent and accurate. The conclusion of the study has therefore to be somewhat negative, in that I have discovered simply that people are doing precisely what they say they are; on the more positive side, the exercise has value for proving that internal segmentation (at least in a small Chinese lineage) is not of such great significance that people resort to genealogical fictions to maintain segments in any sort of political or economic balance. They are content, in the final analysis, to let the facts of biological reproduction control their social structure.

What follows is a detailed report on the reconstruction of the Lei lineage, in the course of which I point to certain mechanisms that appear to effect the emergence of lineage segments. It is a totally nonideological presentation of one aspect of Chinese ritual activity. Just who are the ancestors who get "worshipped"?

The sources of lineage history available to me were:

1. Such general information about the lineage's past as was recorded in oral tradition, and in the occasional written record.[5]

2. The written genealogy of one sub-branch of the lineage,[6] all others having been lost during the Japanese occupation.

---

[5] E.g. Li Hsiang, "Wei Yüan-lang Shang-tsuen Li-shih tsung-tz'u chung-hsiu lo-sheng ching-kao tsung-ch'in shu," in *Li-shih tsung-ch'in hui sheng-li shih-i chou nien chi-nien t'e-k'an* (Hong Kong, 1961).

[6] The title page of the manuscript volume I was shown is missing.

3. The ancestral halls and the tablets they contained.

4. Domestic ancestral tablets.

5. The lineage tombs.

6. The land records in the local District Office, which record holdings and every transaction from about 1906 to the present.

Early History of the Lineage

The earliest record of the lineage's remote past is contained in the first sections of the sub-branch genealogy just mentioned. This genealogy is somewhat like an hourglass in shape: its narrowest point is the founding ancestor of the localized lineage; the part above him serves to place him and his ramifying descendants in the widespread structure of the Lei clan of Kwangtung province. The record begins in the Sung dynasty with one Lei P'eng, who graduated as a Hanlin scholar in 1164, and who moved from Kwangsi to Kwangtung. He is referred to as the *t'ai-shih-tsu* or great original ancestor: his six sons are said to be the founders of the six major branches of the clan.[7] Only his third son is included in this genealogy; he founded the branch at Pak Sha in Pok Lo hsien, Kwangtung, and is regarded as the first-generation ancestor.[8] A further division in the fourth generation brought one man to Wong Chung village in Tung Kun hsien, also in Kwangtung, which the Leis of Sheung Tsuen still regard as their "native place."

From this point, the focus of the genealogy seems to shift from the overall structure established by the original ancestors of the clan to the Sheung Tsuen branch; the view is from below rather than from above. The son of the man who moved to Wong Chung (the fifth generation from Lei P'eng) is again called first generation (and all subsequent generations are numbered from him). The genealogy bears the subtitle "of the Tung Kun Wong Chung branch"; and five generations later appears the subtitle "Genealogy of the Pat Heung Sheung Tsuen branch of the Tung Kun Wong Chung branch," although the move to Sheung Tsuen did not occur till eight generations later.

[7] The genealogy says merely that the six sons of Lei P'eng all came to Kwangtung and dispersed. I owe this information on their status (and their names) to a man who, though not a member of the Sheung Tsuen branch, had managed to buy a house in the village on the strength of his descent from another of the six sons. He had been a lineage official in his home branch in Tung Kun hsien, Kwangtung, and was now an active member of the Lei Clan Association in Hong Kong; a useful informant, therefore, on the province-wide structure of the clan.

[8] The incompleteness of the record at this point, coupled with the linking of the first ancestor to a "great founding ancestor," makes me suspect a high-level genealogical fiction here. Either six unrelated groups came together, or (more likely) this group attached itself by this means to an existing group.

The genealogy of the Sheung Tsuen branch proper begins with a man of the eleventh generation; it is here that the genealogy approaches its narrowest point. Only one man is recorded in the twelfth generation, and his only son, Wui-wan, of the thirteenth generation, is recorded as having actually made the move to Sheung Tsuen. The genealogy says simply, "He moved from Kam Tin and settled in Sheung Tsuen; for this reason he is the founding ancestor [k'ai-chi-tsu]." There is no reference to any earlier move, but village oral tradition has it that Wui-wan first moved to Kam Tin, and being badly treated there, moved up the valley to Sheung Tsuen.[9] He must have arrived about 1600.

In 1950, a Lei Clan Association was formed in Hong Kong, and it provides a focus for many members of the Kwangtung Lei clan who now regard themselves as exiles. Ten years after its founding, the Clan Association had become sufficiently large and well organized to feel the need for a ritual center—specifically, an ancestral hall. The hall in Sheung Tsuen, now about a hundred years from its last restoration, was the only one of this surname in the Colony, and overtures were made; in the end, the Clan Association contributed generously (HK $7,345 to Sheng Tsuen's HK $5,620) to a further restoration and expansion of the hall. Three interior halls were built where before there had been one. The central hall is devoted to the tablets of the villagers' ancestors, and one of the side halls is given over to the Clan Association.[10] Since this early flowering, relations between the villagers and their urban brethren have cooled, but the essay by the Clan Association's president commemorating the rebuilding of the hall, published in the Association's yearbook for 1961, contains the only other written history of the Leis of Sheung Tsuen. Some of the information in the president's essay was unquestionably derived from the same branch genealogy that was made available to me, and it adds relatively little to what I was able to glean from my informants. Only on the subject of the history of the hall does it add to the information I already had.

[9] One suspects, in view of the subsequent hostility between the Tangs of Kam Tin and the surrounding villagers, that the bad treatment is a fiction. It seems more likely that Wui-wan came to the area controlled by the Kam Tin Tangs, and became a tenant farmer on the edge of their territory.

[10] The urban members of the Clan Association used their section of the hall in a markedly different way, which called to mind the shrines in Buddhist monasteries devoted to the tablets of pious laymen and laywomen. Whereas the villagers' tablets go back many generations, can be installed only at a restoration of the hall, and once installed are largely ignored except as a collectivity, the Clan Association tablets are those of the recently dead and fondly remembered; they are installed shortly after a person's death, and are picked out for the individual attention of their descendants.

Structure of the Local Lineage

The hall has a social significance quite apart from the information its tablets hold for the anthropologist; for the present, I propose to confine myself to the topic of the links between Wui-wan's descendants recorded in the hall and in the one surviving branch genealogy.

The central chamber of the main ancestral hall holds seven rows of tablets.[11] The one in the center of the top row is an elaborately ornamented general tablet to the founding ancestor of all the Leis. Following this, reading in the traditional order of precedence (starting from the left, facing out from the tablets, and then taking alternate sides) are large green tablets to:

1. The men of the eleventh and twelfth generations, mentioned above as forming the neck of the hourglass. Lineage tradition has it that when Wui-wan came down from Wong Chung, he brought his father's and grandfather's tablets with him to install in the new community.[12]

2. Lei P'eng of the Sung, the earliest ancestor recorded in the genealogy. Why he is regarded as less senior than his Ming dynasty descendants is unexplained.

3. Lei Wui-wan himself, the Ming thirteenth-generation ancestor, who gives his name to the hall.

4. Two men of the fourteenth generation, Yut-wai and Nim-wai. The genealogy confirms one's logical supposition that they were brothers, the sons of Wui-wan. However, Yut-wai, the younger son, is placed in a higher position than his elder brother.

These tablets are clearly the core of the lineage. They form a charter, which provides a statement of the four fundamental facts about the Leis of Sheung Tsuen, namely:

(a) that they are related by common descent to all the Leis in China;

[11] No distinction is made between man and wife; each couple is accorded a single tablet. As far as the hall is concerned, a woman's genealogical personality is totally subsumed in her husband's.

[12] Either this story—surely standard; cf. the Sheung Shui Wan Shih T'ang, which similarly records a single line of ancestors leading to the one in whose name the hall is built (Baker 1968: 55–56)—is teleological, or Chinese views of emigration have changed. The former seems more likely. The proverb "Where men go, spirits go" exists to support a definitive move from one's old home; uprooting one's ancestral tablets and reestablishing them elsewhere is a positive statement of one's intention not to return. Few modern Chinese, however, seem to do this. Most emigrate without their tablets, leaving them in their home village as a symbolic statement of their intention to return. It seems probable that when an emigrant community has been established for several generations and is prospering sufficiently to stay put, the myth of the founding ancestor's having brought his tablets with him is put about to justify his descendants' otherwise unfilial behavior in failing to return.

(b) that they are part of the Kwangtung clan of the Leis, by virtue of their descent from Lei P'eng;

(c) that all descendants of Lei Wui-wan have a particular stake in this hall; and

(d) that the local lineage is divided into two major branches (focused on the two sons of the founding ancestor; for convenience I refer to them throughout as the senior and junior branches).

These seven central tablets are distinguished from the remainder not only by their position, but also by their style. They are elaborately carved and ornamented, whereas all the other tablets in the hall are simple affairs of white painted wood, with black characters painted on.

With the change in style comes a change in the quality of the information given. Logic alone serves to interpret the relations between the ghosts behind the central tablets, and hence their significance for their living descendants, but the hall gives absolutely no further information on the structure of the lineage it represents. Including the remaining six tablets in the top row, the generations are represented as shown in this table:

TABLETS IN THE LEI ANCESTRAL HALL

Generation	No. of tablets	Died by	Generation	No. of tablets	Died by
15	3	1666	21	21	1826
16	2	1693	22	9	1853
17	6	1719	23	1	1879
18	8	1746	24	21	1906
19	17	1773	25	24	1933
20	11	1799	26	5	1959

From the fact that Wui-wan and his sons are described on their tablets as ancestors of the Ming (and the president's essay says that Wui-wan arrived in the area "at the close of the Ming"), and the fifteenth-generation men are described as ancestors of the Ch'ing (although the gravestone of one of them says Ming), one can be fairly certain that the fourteenth generation gave way to the fifteenth about 1640. That five men of the twenty-sixth generation were dead by 1960, when the hall was last rebuilt,[13] provides another fairly fixed date; and from these two points, one can establish the chronology for the lineage given in the table. Further, using the method suggested by Baker (1968: ch. 2, *passim*), one can identify moments at which the hall was probably re-

[13] I infer that the custom of placing one's own tablet in the hall, covered with red paper until one's death, was not much followed in 1960, because many men known to have been actively involved in the restoration and who were still alive in 1967–68 had not installed their tablets.

built (more on this below). One is struck most forcibly, when presented with the undistinguished mass of tablets in an ancestral hall, by the paradox that for a genealogy-conscious people, so little information is given by the hall to the lineage members on their relationship to one another. In the hall at least, the ancestors are merged into a common mass; the hall may be said to stress the unity of the lineage as a whole rather than the tension between its component parts. If one did not know that in tombs and on domestic shrines individual ancestors are selected for particular attention, and thus segments distinguished, one could dismiss segmentation in the lineage as insignificant. If the reverse situation prevailed—if segments were so prominent as virtually to exclude any centralizing focus—the situation would not be problematic. But it is precisely the existence, side by side, of systems that interpret the facts of having ancestors in radically different ways which creates the problem this paper attempts to resolve. What is the relation between the two systems, and which, in the final analysis, is the more important?

We have to turn to the written genealogy of the local sub-branch for an elaboration of the basic information given by the hall, and even this does not get us very far. Nim-wai, Wui-wan's elder son, is mentioned only once; for his family we are merely told "see volume 1." The senior branch of the lineage clearly at one time had its own genealogy, but this was lost long since. The surviving volume specifically confines itself to the descendants of Yut-wai, Wui-wan's younger son (see Fig. 1). Yut-wai had three sons; the names of two of them, Pun-yuen and Wing-fu, correspond to two of the three fifteenth-generation tablets in the hall, but of the third, Wing-cheung, who apparently had five sons, there is no further trace. He is indeed only the first of several men who appear in the genealogy, but have no descendants recorded there. Such dead ends are common in New Territories genealogies; they are presumably evidence of a fairly steady rate of out-migration.[14] The third of the three fifteenth-generation men recorded in the hall does not appear anywhere else. He can be tentatively ascribed to the senior branch.

One of the two sixteenth-generation tablets in the hall belongs to Mo-tin, who also figures at the top of a domestic tablet and can be ascribed with confidence to the senior branch. The early history of the senior branch must, without a genealogy, remain a little mysterious; but that of the junior, and now much larger, branch is better documented.

---

[14] We know from other sources of pressure on local land resources, political upheavals, and (since the middle of the last century at least) opportunities to make a living elsewhere. Faced with evidence of the continuous and substantial paring down of the lineage, one is led to speculate that it may have been the shedding of members in each generation which, paradoxically, enabled the core to survive.

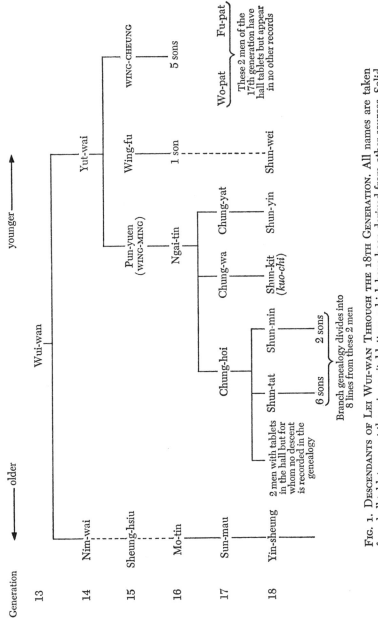

FIG. 1. DESCENDANTS OF LEI WUI-WAN THROUGH THE 18TH GENERATION. All names are taken from hall tablets except those in capital letters, which have been derived from other sources. Solid lines represent confirmed links, dotted lines suppositions on my part. All the men in the senior line from the 16th generation down to the 26th generation are listed on a single domestic tablet.

Yut-wai's eldest son, Pun-yuen, had one son, Ngai-tin. Yut-wai's second son, Wing-fu, is recorded as having had a single son, but there is no further written trace of his descendants; only oral tradition now serves to identify them. This fact—for as it turned out, the sub-branch descended from Wing-fu is one of the most important in the village—was a further spur to my inquiry. Why should the descent of what is nowadays the most influential segment of the lineage (albeit of only relatively recent prosperity) be the most poorly recorded?

For the seventeenth generation the genealogy confines itself to the descendants of Ngai-tin. He had six sons; the genealogy records only the descent of the eldest, Chung-hoi, and tells us merely that Chung-hoi's fifth and youngest son was adopted (*kuo-chi*) to the second of Ngai-tin's sons, Chung-wa. Of Chung-yat, Ngai-tin's third son, there is evidence from other sources, but of Ngai-tin's last three sons there is no further trace; they may have died young, they may have emigrated. That they had disappeared completely by the time of their father's entombment is suggested by the fact that Chung-hoi, Chung-wa, and Chung-yat are recorded on Ngai-tin's gravestone, but no other sons are mentioned.

The hall contains the tablets of all these three, together with three others of the seventeenth generation. Of these, one figures on the domestic tablet that also includes his father, Mo-tin, and he can therefore be placed in the senior branch. The remaining two names occur nowhere else. That they were brothers is suggested by the fact that they share a generation name, and they may represent a flowering in the senior branch of which no trace now remains.[15] Alternatively, they may belong to Wing-fu's branch.

In the eighteenth generation Chung-hoi had five sons (the fifth being adopted by his brother Chung-wa).[16] All five appear in the hall. Of the

[15] One is on shaky ground with generation names. Although they appear to have been widely accepted—even across most of the twenty-seventh generation in the junior branch—there is no guarantee either that a given person will prefer to be known by the form of his name that contains the generational element, or that this name form will be chosen for the ancestral record, or, indeed, that the same name form will be used in all the written records. Pun-yuen of the fifteenth generation, for example, is buried under his "style" (*tzu*), Wing-ming. The two apparently unaccounted-for men of the seventeenth generation whose tablets are in the hall may well be men who are recorded by different names in the genealogy. The problem is not very great at this stage of one's interpretation of the lineage's past because only a few men are involved. The difficulty in marrying the land records to domestic ancestral tablets is very much greater. The New Territories Chinese were (and still are) quite canny enough to appreciate the advantages of being known by one of their names to their friends and relatives and by another to the government (cf. note 27 below).

[16] In general, I lay little emphasis on *kuo-chi* in this paper, which aims to present the genealogical history of the lineage as it is perceived by its members. In the

remaining three tablets for this generation, one (the only one with a different generation name) belongs to the senior branch (he appears on the same domestic tablet that identifies his father and grandfather); the second is identified as the son of Chung-yat by the tablets in a subsidiary hall (the Sai-yip hall, discussed below); while the third, once again, is not recorded. I ascribe him tentatively to Wing-fu's branch. Of Chung-hoi's four sons (assuming the fifth, Shun-kit, to belong now to Chung-wa), the two eldest must have moved away from Sheung Tsuen; the genealogy reports that they married, but does not record any sons. The other two, Shun-tat and Shun-min, continue their father's line.

At the nineteenth generation, the genealogy divides into eight sections. It records as separate lines the descent of Shun-tat's six sons and Shun-min's two. Seven of the eight lines cease variously at the twenty-fourth and twenty-fifth generations; one stops at the twenty-second. During my sojourn in the village, the lineage headman (as often, the oldest man in the senior surviving generation) was of the twenty-fifth generation, and there were very few others of this generation still alive; generally the older men were of the twenty-sixth, and the majority of the adult men were of the twenty-seventh. There were therefore no living men recorded in the genealogy. It must have been last revised a full three generations ago, at a time when only the youngest children were of the twenty-fifth generation (the young children of the village now are of the twenty-eighth). The last revision must have taken place about 1890. The difficulty I experienced when I tried to link the living with the dead confirmed my belief in a gap between such high-level records of the lineage as the genealogy and the evidence of the people on the ground. My conviction was strengthened by the kinds of information the living could and could not give me. Whereas they could tell me with no hesitation which of the two major branches, senior or junior, they belonged to, their uncertainty increased as they approached the present. Disarmingly precise about the broad outlines of their relationships, they became infuriatingly vague about the details.[17] I became convinced that they were doing it on purpose.

figures I present, there are several cases of filiation that are treated simply as such, although in fact an adoption was involved. Adoption generally takes place during the lifetime of a man who lacks sons or very shortly after his death. As a genealogical fiction, adoption is too low-level to be of importance here.

[17] At one time I assumed that "modern change" had made people lose interest in such traditions as their genealogy, but a wise informant pointed out scornfully that genealogical ignorance is not a recent development; did I really imagine that a village of illiterate farmers would have been more painstaking about their genealogy than today's village of semi-literate manual laborers?

On one point, however, my informants generally agreed. There were five branches—of equal status vis-à-vis the founding ancestor—in the lineage. Try as I might, I could not extract from anyone any satisfactory explanation of the relation between the two major branches and these amorphous five. The impasse we have now reached will be clarified by reference to Figure 1, which sets out the genealogy of the founders of the lineage, from the thirteenth to the eighteenth generation. Only by bringing in evidence from other sources can we answer the question of how, from this root, five balanced branches have grown.

Ancestral Halls and the Development of the Lineage

I mentioned earlier that the Lei lineage had two other ancestral halls. I was firmly and consistently told, however, that they were not the same as the main hall, which was called the *tz'u-t'ang*; the subsidiary halls were *shen-t'ing*.[18] The two shen-t'ing were located in parts of the village that differed from the rather amorphous remainder in being occupied by clearly defined, self-conscious, closely related groups of kin. Only two of the houses in these two areas had domestic ancestral tablets, and it was explained to me that the shen-t'ing fulfilled the functions of domestic altars for the households in each area. Nowhere in the village did I find domestic tablets to which younger brothers, although economically divided, returned to worship; when families divided, the younger brothers set up identical copies of the eldest brother's tablet and worshipped independently. Nobody lived in the shen-t'ing, but they appeared to be functioning precisely as a ritual center for groups of kin who were divided in every other respect. As one informant put it: "The *cheng-wu* is the house with the ancestral tablets.[19] You could say that the shen-t'ing is the cheng-wu for all those who install their ancestors there, rather than in their own houses." The smaller of the two Lei shen-t'ing—the Sai-yip hall—was in fact a normal domestic structure, undistinguished externally from the neighboring houses, and it is possible that at one time it was the home of an early member of this branch. It has clearly not been used for domestic purposes, however, for a long time. The other shen-t'ing—the Tsoi-sin hall—is an enormous building, outshining in size and magnificence the main ancestral hall itself. It was built in the early years of this century, and clearly was intended from

[18] Elsewhere in the New Territories, shen-t'ing may refer to a small temple devoted to the worship of gods rather than ancestors. The people of Sheung Tsuen were quite clear about the usage followed in this paper.

[19] Strictly speaking, the cheng-wu is the house which contains that version of the ancestral tablet that has been passed down the eldest-son line.

the outset for purely ritual purposes. Most of what follows is based on the smaller Sai-yip hall.

Consistent with the absence of domestic tablets in the households attached to the shen-t'ing is the fact that the dead can be installed there immediately. There is no rule, as there is for the tz'u-t'ang, that tablets can be installed only when the hall is restored—and then for a price. In houses with domestic tablets, there are frequently small pieces of paper on the right-hand wall (facing out from the altar, i.e. the junior side); these are *shen-t'ai-tzu*, little ancestral altars, containing the names of members of the household head's own generation or those junior to his, who have predeceased him. Such early departed spirits are allowed to ascend the main altar when their generational turn comes (in the interim incense is lit before the shen-t'ai-tzu at the same times as before the main altar). Similarly, in shen-t'ing–owning groups, shen-t'ai-tzu are placed on the houses' side walls, and I was told that the names on them could be transferred to the shen-t'ing "after quite a long time."[20] I was also told, though this seems to me unlikely, that in the past, young men's names could not be transferred from shen-t'ai-tzu to the shen-t'ing. The implication would be that only genealogically significant men could enter the hall, but both shen-t'ing in Sheung Tsuen contain a preponderance of men who clearly died young. It seems more realistic to see this as a hint of the dual function of the shen-t'ing: they occupy a place halfway between tz'u-t'ang and domestic altars.

In the Sai-yip hall, the large central tablet is a red board, on which are carved the names of a single line of ancestors, from Chung-yat in the seventeenth generation to Sai-yip in the twenty-second. The central line is devoted to the founding ancestor of all the Leis in the same words as the equivalent tablet in the main hall, and the remainder of the board clearly functions for this segment in the same way as the core tablets in the main hall function for the lineage as a whole: it is the segment's charter, locating its focal ancestor unequivocally in his place in the overall structure of the lineage. One of the lines shown in Figure 1 is therefore extended, to the twenty-second generation at least. All the ancestors on this central board also appear in the main hall, with the sole exception of Sai-yip himself. Although we cannot be certain which member of this line established its fortunes on a secure enough basis to make differentiation of this segment appropriate, we may infer that it was either Sai-yip himself or his son. It looks as though the tablets already in the main hall were duplicated to establish the segment's charter; it seems less likely that each member of the line should have

---

[20] Daughters' names cannot be placed even on the shen-t'ai-tzu.

been installed in the main hall at a rebuilding that took place after the establishment of the Sai-yip hall.

After Sai-yip, however, this hall lets us down badly. No men of the twenty-third generation are included at all.[21] Two larger paper tablets, one on either side of the central board, carry the names of five men in the twenty-fourth generation, nineteen in the twenty-fifth, nine in the twenty-sixth, and two in the twenty-seventh. Of the thirty-five men represented, twenty appear not to have married, and can therefore be presumed to be genealogically insignificant. More important, no indication is given of the relationships that existed among these men. Again, the shen-t'ing is fulfilling for this segment one of the functions of the tz'u-t'ang for the lineage: after stressing the segment's differentiation from the rest of the lineage, it blurs to the point of concealment any internal differentiation. It stresses only the segment's unity vis-à-vis the outer world.

One house attached to the Sai-yip hall has a domestic tablet, which includes generations from the twenty-second to the twenty-seventh. The man of the twenty-second generation is given merely the familiar form of his name, a single character prefaced by *A-*, and no link with the tablets in the shen-t'ing appears anywhere. The old widow living in this house told me that her deceased husband, a man of the twenty-sixth generation, was the brother of a man whose tablet does appear in the shen-t'ing. The remainder of my information on the structure of this segment comes from conversations with its members and inferences from the land records. The picture remains pretty unclear, even though, while I was in the village, the segment consisted of just four households. My informants' inability to describe clearly the structure of a segment only five generations deep and four households wide shows the sort of problem I confronted: precision down to a certain level and thereafter ignorance, even of relationships that *must* have been close.

Several interesting questions arise with respect to shen-t'ing. First, when do people start establishing domestic tablets again to differentiate themselves from the remainder of their segment? Why do they, when they do? Is some part of the impetus derived from the very absence

[21] Cf. the main hall, which has but one tablet of the twenty-third generation (which belongs, I was told, to a man who came down from Wong Chung to work as a sedan-chair carrier in Hong Kong, and, having prospered, attached himself to the Sheung Tsuen branch). At several other points, the twenty-third generation proved a stumbling block, but I am at a loss to explain why. Its members died by about 1880. In the case of the main hall, it looks as though they just missed out on the 1860 rebuilding and had been mostly forgotten by 1960, when their chance next came. It may even be that the one man installed only got in *because* he was an outsider, and his descendant was determined to legitimize his own position in the village.

of differentiation in a hall or shen-t'ing? When does a shen-t'ing become a tz'u-t'ang? Can the two processes be said to coincide? Let us return now to the main hall of the lineage for clues to the evolution that must have occurred.

No one, coming alone to a new place, with or without his ancestors' tablets on his back, begins by building an ancestral hall. When he arrived in Sheung Tsuen, more immediate considerations must have occupied Wui-wan, as well as the first few generations of his descendants. Only after several reasonably prosperous and prolific generations had passed are they likely to have been in a position to signify their status by constructing a full-fledged ancestral hall. In all likelihood a shen-t'ing was established very early on, probably in a house (Wui-wan's own cheng-wu?) that was vacated for the purpose. Like the present shen-t'ing, it would have served as a repository for the tablets of all members of the group. If these suppositions are correct, the early tablets in the hall would provide a record of all the Lei men who lived and died in Sheung Tsuen. And in fact the numbers of tablets for each generation from Wui-wan to at least the eighteenth generation represent a realistic rate of increase in a newly founded but thriving community.

We then have a sudden peak in the number of tablets for the nineteenth generation. By the time of the eighteenth generation, the Lei community of Sheung Tsuen consisted of at least six separate households, some of which were quite prolific (in Chinese terms, this is generally synonymous with prosperity). Shun-tat alone is recorded as having had six sons. It seems reasonable to suggest that over the period of the eighteenth to the twentieth generation, the Lei shen-t'ing became a tz'u-t'ang.[22] Members of the group wanted to give expression to the social differentiation that had arisen within the group, and were by now in a position to establish something more imposing than a shen-t'ing. The peaking of tablets in the nineteenth generation may occur because it was the twentieth who built the original hall. As the table on p. 258 makes clear, a peak in the number of tablets is followed by a trough. The rule that tablets can be installed only at a restoration of the hall means that those who restore stand the least chance of being installed themselves: the restorers install the tablets of the most recently dead, and by the time the hall is restored again, they are the most distant of

---

[22] The president of the Clan Association dissents. He says that the hall was first built four generations after the founding ancestor—i.e. by members of the seventeenth generation. His evidence seems to be no better than mine, but his assertion may indicate that some sort of differentiation took place four generations after the founder, in about 1720. The shen-t'ing itself may not have been distinguished from a private house until this point, if the analogy with the Sai-yip hall is sound.

the eligible ancestors, and therefore the least likely to be remembered. It therefore looks as if the hall was first built about 1780. The next peak in the number of tablets occurs at the twenty-first generation, the next trough at the twenty-second and twenty-third generations. Informants could not tell me anything about the initial building of the hall, but did report a restoration in the Hsien-feng period (1851–62), which fits with the chronology given in the table. Apparently the members of the twenty-second and twenty-third generations (because branches develop at different rates, it is increasingly likely that generations will overlap) installed the tablets of the twenty-first and possibly some of the twentieth. When restorations follow one another at relatively short intervals, one can expect some overlap in the generations installed, which would tend to fill in the troughs of forgotten ancestors. The most recent restoration, in 1960, is of course not in question; we know that members of the twenty-sixth and twenty-seventh generations installed the tablets of their fathers and grandfathers, causing peaks in the number of tablets representing the twenty-fourth and twenty-fifth generations. Only five men of the twenty-sixth generation had died by 1960; assuming another century before the hall is again restored, one can predict that the twenty-sixth and twenty-seventh generations will be poorly represented.

Much of the foregoing is undeniably speculative. No anthropologist has been around, let alone been around long enough, to observe the development of a house into a shen-t'ing and then into a tz'u-t'ang. I offer my description of the process as a reasonable hypothesis. I had hoped, before considerations of time and space overtook me, to flesh out the hypothesis by a case study of a second shen-t'ing–owning segment in Sheung Tsuen, in which the ascent to prosperity, followed by the construction of a magnificent shen-t'ing and then by a gradual decline into poverty and disunity, was both recent and very much in evidence.[23]

Domestic Ancestral Tablets: The Link Between High- and Low-Level Records

The ancestral tablets kept in people's houses should provide the vital link between the high- and low-level records of the lineage. The high-level records, as we have seen, are arranged in such a way as to stress the unity of the whole; do the low-level records complement the hall and the genealogy by lending precision to segmentation, or do they supplement them by blurring the issue still further?

---

[23] The hypothesis posits a similarity between the evolution of a community developing at a distance from its home base and that of a segment differentiating itself within a localized lineage. Is there necessarily any difference?

With few exceptions the domestic tablets in Sheung Tsuen all took the same form: a single sheet of red-orange paper pasted onto the partition that divided the house into living and sleeping quarters. Above, there was a representation of the goddess Kuan Yin, with two attendants; she was, however, completely associated with the ritual for the ancestors, and distinguished from them in no way, even on her birthday. In a few cases the names of the ancestors were recorded not on paper, but on a piece of red-painted glass, which was then installed in a rather more elaborate wooden surround. This modern innovation made my task easier, for it meant I was not in competition with the local rats for the information the tablets contained.

There are numerous references in the literature to domestic tablets made of wood; some speak of younger brothers who copy their eldest brother's stock of inherited wooden tablets onto paper sheets when families divide. None of these sources provides an explanation for the almost exclusive use of paper tablets in the New Territories, or for my informants' general agreement that the change from wooden tablets to paper ones is fairly recent. Among the less satisfactory explanations is one Baker reports from Sheung Shui (1968: 62): the wooden tablets were removed because "the children were frightened of them." Only one of the explanations I was given seems sociologically significant: wooden tablets took up too much space. The length of some of the paper tablets in Sheung Tsuen tends to confirm this explanation. The length also suggests that any system of removing the most senior of the domestic ancestors, either to the hall or to oblivion, has long since fallen into desuetude.

The widespread use of lengthy paper tablets, indications that shorter lines of wooden ones were used in the fairly recent past, and the practice of installing individual ancestors in more than one place,[24] combine to suggest that what I observed represents a change—some would say a decline—from an earlier, more rigid system. Here I must leave open the questions of whether another system once prevailed, and if so, how it related to the ideal system of domestic ritual described in the literature; why any change that may have occurred took place; and whether the present system represents a development or a decline.

Members of the family were added to the tablet in their turn, but no one, it seems, was eliminated on the occasions when the tablet was renewed (at the New Year following a death in the family, or at a re-

---

[24] The record was three: one man appears in the main hall, in the shen-t'ing of his segment, and on a domestic altar.

building of the house).[25] One extraordinary tablet, as indicated in Figure 1, began at the sixteenth generation and ended at the twenty-sixth; another, even more remarkable, ran from the twelfth to the twenty-fifth; yet another, from the seventeenth to the twenty-eighth. Tablets of six to eight generations were common; tablets covering less than six generations were the exceptions. The tablets that went back furthest had in common the recurrence in the ancestral hall of their earliest recorded names. The duplication extended to the twenty-first generation in the first case mentioned, and to the nineteenth in the second and third. Thereafter, only the occasional name recurs in the hall. This tends to confirm my earlier suggestion that a shen-t'ing, taking all tablets, became a more selective tz'u-t'ang around the time of the nineteenth generation; it also suggests that along with the change went a tendency to copy from the hall the names of one's individual ancestral line in order to establish a domestic tablet.

At first sight, it would seem that such lengthy records would make it relatively easy to reconstruct the lineage, but despite their length, domestic tablets left much of the story untold. In the first place, they share the hall's failure to specify the links between persons on the same tablet; in the second, they give no indication of the links between persons on different tablets. Obviously, one looks for the occurrence of the same name on different tablets in order to identify related lines, but such recurrences were remarkably rare. Within a single tablet, one could safely assume a direct father-son link only when there was only one man in each generation recorded. (Kuo-chi, involving as it does the complete transfer of a man from one line to another, makes no difference here; the tablets record social, not biological, filiation, and it is the former that we are exploring.)

Analyzing every tablet and attempting to fit it and the family owning it into the structure of the lineage is difficult and fascinating work. Here I shall confine myself to a single example, beginning with the descendants of Lei Chung-hoi, of the seventeenth generation. I have selected this line because the only surviving genealogy relates to this branch and, by coincidence, I lived in the part of the village largely occupied by members of it. Two sons remain filiated to Chung-hoi: Shun-tat and Shun-min. Shun-tat had six sons, and seven families in the village still identified themselves as members of the *liu-wu* or six-households branch; Shun-min had two sons. The genealogy divides into eight branches at

---

[25] How to dispose of the tablets of uxorilocally married men is a problem that does not arise, since this form of marriage does not occur in Sheung Tsuen, nor, I believe, anywhere else in the New Territories.

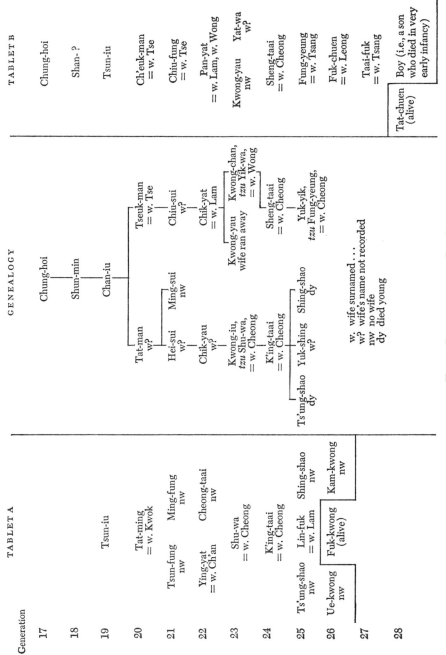

FIG. 2. DESCENDANTS OF LEI SHUN-MIN

the nineteenth generation, each based on one of these eight men, and continues the lines to the twenty-fourth and twenty-fifth generations. Of Shun-tat's six sons, however, I was able to trace the descent of only three, and to account for the position of only five of the seven households claiming membership in the liu-wu branch. The remaining two households were unable to spell out for me their precise relationship to Shun-tat, and at no point did their domestic tablets tie in with the genealogy.

The most complete and interesting example I have comes from the Shun-min branch; only two lines have survived, and these are recorded as shown in Figure 2.

The following correspondences and contrasts emerge:

Eighteenth generation. Tablet B has Shan-? for the genealogy's Shun-min; the question mark stands for a nonexistent character closely resembling the character for *min*. Thus the tablet has both a phonetic error (Shan for Shun) and an orthographic error.

Nineteenth generation. Both tablets have Tsun for Chan. Local dialect tends to turn *u* and *i* into *a*.

Twentieth generation. Tablet A has Ming (locally pronounced *man*) for Man. Tablet B has Ch'euk for Tseuk, but the wife's name corresponds.

Twenty-first generation. Fung is the generation name on the tablets, Sui in the genealogy; it is difficult to say why. Is it right to assume that Chiu-sui is Chiu-fung, and that Ming-sui is Ming-fung? How are we to explain Hei-sui and Tsun-fung? Too few wives' names are given to provide further clues.

Twenty-second generation. Again, is Chik-yat the same man as Pan-yat? Both are shown as having wives named Lam.

Twenty-third generation. The genealogy is annotated with the tzu ("style") of Kwong-iu and Kwong-chan, which appear on the tablets (with the variant Yat for Yik, locally Yak, on Tablet B). Kwong-yau corresponds exactly. I cannot explain why one brother is recorded by his *ming* (given name), the other by his tzu.[26]

Twenty-fourth generation. The correspondence is exact, although Tablet A uses an abbreviated form of K'ing.

Twenty-fifth generation. Fung-yeung of Tablet B and the tzu Fung-yeung of the genealogy appear to be the same man, although the wife's name differs (there is only a minor orthographic difference between the two characters pronounced *yeung*). In the other branch, two men who died young correspond exactly, though a variant form for Shao is used in the tablet. I take it that Lin-fuk was the tzu of Yuk-shing.

---

[26] The genealogy records that Kwong-iu was born the son of Chik-yat, and was adopted to Chik-yau.

Twenty-sixth generation. The last names on Tablet A were those of deceased brothers of the present household head, Fuk-kwong.

Twenty-seventh and twenty-eighth generations. Taai-fuk was still remembered: his dead wife's mother still lived in another part of the village. Tat-chuen is currently working in a restaurant in London.

The correspondence between the two sets of records is therefore very close, and requires little further comment. (In other cases, points of similarity are much more rare.) One is struck by the narrowness of the descent lines: Fuk-kwong, his two sons and one nephew, and Tat-chuen in the other branch (who probably will not return to Hong Kong) are the only members of a segment that is now nine generations deep. Genealogically, Fuk-kwong and Tat-chuen are related only through an ancestor who is seven generations back from the former and nine from the latter (the adoption in the twenty-third generation produces a slightly closer biological link, but strictly speaking, this is genealogically irrelevant). Fuk-kwong and Tat-chuen were on the closest terms: they were described to me as uncle and nephew; they exchanged gifts of money and food; Fuk-kwong takes care of Tat-chuen's house while the latter is in England, and had cared for him when he was orphaned as a small boy. I knew of the close social relationship before I had worked out the genealogical details, and was genuinely astonished to discover them. Given the conditions of life in such a village until very recent times, the pattern here—the bare survival of descent lines, and behavior appropriate to the closest kinship ties between families that are in fact very widely separated when no closer kin exist—is probably widespread.[27]

This would explain at least in part my informants' vagueness about their precise kin relationships to one another. In the first place, the relationship of seventh cousins, twice removed, is extremely hard even for a competent genealogist to describe. In the second, the details scarcely matter when no intervening kin survive. One can understand why the categories "own brother" and "village brother" are allowed to merge.

[27] It might be of interest to draw in the land records at this point, to complete the documentary evidence on this line. Kam-cheung and Kwong-yat are recorded as having inherited, in 1961, the joint and separate property of Lung-po and U-sham. They sold two-thirds of the joint estate a few days later (it is clear that it was only the desire to sell the land that prompted them to obtain *de jure* recognition for a longstanding *de facto* succession); it had evidently been a minor *tsu* estate which had never been recorded as such. This example illustrates just the sort of difficulties that arise over names. Lung-po must be another name of K'ing-taai or of Lin-fuk; and U-sham was definitely Fung-yeung. He was, as it turned out, an influential figure at the time of the British arrival in the New Territories, and he appears, as U-sham, in the list of village councillors appointed by the British in 1901.

So much for my conviction that a deliberate effort is made to obliterate the details of all relationships between the closest (and most inevitable) and the most distant (and least demanding)!

Figure 2 presents the most detailed evidence I have of the link between the ancestors and their descendants. It covers only the descendants of Chung-hoi, however. I also have fairly detailed evidence for the structure of the senior branch; the descendants of Chung-yat are covered by my earlier description of the Sai-yip shen-t'ing group. Chung-wa adopted one of Chung-hoi's sons, and the descendants of this man, Shun-kit, identify themselves by reference to his name. (*Tsu* property, i.e. ancestral land, exists in the names of Chung-hoi, Chung-yat, and Shun-kit.) Most of Shun-kit's descendants now occupy a hamlet with pronounced left-wing feelings, and they would not talk to me; I therefore have only the sketchiest evidence for the structure of this branch. The descendants of Wing-fu provided my final headache; the following section of this paper describes its resolution.

Burial Practices

So far I have shown that, with luck and sufficient data, one can trace the precise ancestry of present-day inhabitants of the village and fit them into the overall structure of the lineage. It remains to discuss the place of tombs in the overall scheme, their value where other records are incomplete, and the reason why burial practices early aroused my suspicions. My treatment of these subjects is cursory; neither I nor my informants were inclined to pursue the details.

The three-stage burial process (around Hong Kong, at least) is familiar enough: coffin burial for a period of about seven years; exhumation of the bones and their placement in a pot, which is left on the open hillside for an indefinite period; and finally, for some of the dead, permanent entombment of the pot. At first these practices seemed to me calculated to expose the ancestors' precious bones to the maximum possible risk: even the principles of *feng-shui* (geomancy) do not require three burial locations for every ancestor. I wondered if this paradoxical treatment of the ancestors' bones—to reach the final stage of entombment, they must survive exposure to the elements, passing cows, and even dogs, on the hillside—concealed another more or less deliberate attempt to pare down the ancestral record, in order to make that record easier to fudge.[28] On closer inspection, something more straightforward seems to be involved.

[28] The carelessness of the New Territories people with the bones of their ancestors contrasts with the apparent assiduity of the Taiwanese. Emily Ahern assures

Two areas of uncertainty interested me most: the first was on what principles the rows of pots on the hillside are made up; the second was how treatment of close and distant ancestors differed. I asked informants what determined the siting of pots on the hillside, and received conflicting answers. Some informants insisted that father and son are so closely related that their pots have to be placed together; others denied the logical inference from this, that brothers' pots should be placed together; still others merely said that a geomancer is consulted in every case.[29] Not surprisingly, my attempts to test theory against practice by asking just who was inside each pot elicited the vaguest possible answers. The vagueness was heightened in response to my enquiries about final entombment. My informants generally agreed that a number of pots are collected and placed together in a single tomb, but were quite unable to supply any rules about which pots might be regarded as belonging together. Once the pots are entombed, however, at least one can try to deduce principles of selection by reference to the gravestones; while the pots are on the hillside they are identified only by the name inside the lid.

In practical terms, individual circumstances and desires determine which pots are placed together, and when or whether pots are assembled into a single tomb. Theoretically, every ancestor is eventually accorded a three-stage burial, but in practice what happens to a dead person's remains varies with the fortunes of his descendants and the relationships among them. The circumstances under which individual ancestors achieved rapid entombment were instructive. One man who had prospered entombed his own parents, but left his grandparents on the hillside; his father had been one of several brothers, and their descendants' fortunes had differed considerably. In another, slightly less recent case, a wealthy man had selected for entombment a single line of ancestors going back to his great-grandfather; investigation revealed that his father and grandfather had been only sons, but that the great-grandfather had

---

me that there was a great furor in her village if any pots were lost. On the other hand, Myron Cohen tells me that among the Hakka, unattended pots are collected by the pot collector, and the bones placed in a common grave for people without descendants.

[29] I found no evidence in Sheung Tsuen of the separate treatment of women's bones; a man's wife or wives seemed generally to be placed alongside him, and eventually entombed with him. The only foreseeable exception to this was the sixth wife of the village's most wealthy man in this century. She had outlived her husband by some fifty years, and all her co-wives had died in time to be entombed with him about five years ago. She, perforce, would be buried separately, and the geomantic considerations affecting her own descendants' fortunes might well control the siting of her pot and tomb.

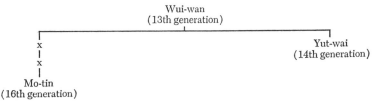

FIG 3. TOMB OF LEI WUI-WAN

had a brother, from whom another line descended. When descendants are poor, their ancestors' pots are allowed to accumulate on the hillside. The geomancer, if he is indeed consulted in every case, has only to gauge the family's current fortunes to decide where the most recent pot should be placed.

There is no clear line between the worship of close ancestors and of distant ones; nor, as will be evident from the preceding paragraph, is there any line corresponding to a distinction between ancestors in pots and those in tombs. The search for an upper limit to "personal" ancestors and a lower limit to "senior" ancestors—which might correspond to a similar distinction between high- and low-level records in the village—founders on the realization that here, too, we are dealing not with two self-contained categories, but with a continuum. Poor fortunes may lead to the scattering of a line of ancestors' pots, and the consequent loss of the older ones; without sufficient prosperity to ensure entombment, no more than two or three generations of pots are likely to survive at any one time.

It remains to discuss the tombs in the possession of the Lei lineage, and their relation to the ancestral record. Wui-wan, the founding ancestor of the local lineage, shares a tomb with two other men as shown in Figure 3.

No record has survived of the tomb's original construction; the stone says only that it was restored in 1861 by representatives of "the two major branches." The tomb thus appears to provide a charter for the basic twofold division of the lineage, with unity provided by the single focal ancestor, Wui-wan. When the lineage visits its ancestral tombs at the Chung-yeung festival, however, the worship does not take place in Wui-wan's name. Wui-wan tsu provides the pork that is shared at Chao-fen, when the lineage assembles for a feast in the ancestral hall, but at Chung-yeung, the two branches of the lineage assemble on either side of the tomb (senior branch on the left, facing out from the tomb, junior branch on the right). Yut-wai tsu is much the more prosperous: each male member of the branch who attends the tomb-worship is given a pink printed ticket that he later exchanges for a share of pork. The members of Mo-tin tsu, however, receive only a handful of fruit.[30]

The senior (Mo-tin) branch is small and relatively undifferentiated. The junior (Yut-wai) branch has two more senior tombs: of Pun-yuen in the fifteenth generation, and Ngai-tin in the sixteenth. Both these tombs were restored in 1910 by representatives of the "three branches," i.e. descendants of the three sons of Ngai-tin. The junior branch thus has three men in consecutive generations in tombs, which argues against any selection of men for entombment for the purpose of providing foci for tsu segments in later generations. It is more likely that a period of prosperity shortly after their time (possibly the same period that saw the first construction of the ancestral hall) enabled their close descendants to see them all through to final entombment. Other, less crucial, graves follow down the lines of the junior branch.

We now return to the problem of the five branches, for despite the apparent unity of the senior branch, and the tripartite division of the junior branch, I discovered that responsibility for the Chao-fen feast in the ancestral hall (provided by the tsu of the founding ancestor himself) rotated among five men: four I could ascribe to the four branches just listed, but the fifth, who was the richest and most influential man in the village, did not seem to fit in anywhere. I assumed that he was related, possibly distantly, to one of the three segments of the junior branch, and was only included in the cycle because of his wealth and position. However, a verbal hint that he might be descended from Wing-fu, a fifteenth-generation member of the senior branch (see Fig. 1), was confirmed when I realized that his father, who was even wealthier and more influential than he and who had died in 1914, had had no part in the restoration of the graves of Pun-yuen and Ngai-tin in 1910; and this despite the fact that he was actively entombing his own immediate ancestors at the time. The son manages the Yut-wai tsu, but has no share in the property of the Ngai-tin tsu; therefore he can only be the representative of a branch that also goes back to a fifteenth-generation ancestor, but to someone other than Pun-yuen.

Conclusion

The answer to the problem of the five balanced branches, and the result of my exploration of the apparent gap between the high- and low-level structure of the lineage, must be that there is a gap, and it is exploited, but that both the nature of the gap and the way it is exploited

---

[30] Little has been said here about the custom of ancestral or tsu estates because tsu property counted for very little in Sheung Tsuen. So far as I could gather, no

differ from what I had anticipated. The lineage records are accurate; it is the interpretation put upon them that defines the political and economic balance of the lineage. Asymmetric segmentation in fact is countered by a symmetric ideal conception of the lineage: the five branches of the lineage differ in level of segmentation, but are roughly equal in size and status. Thus the senior branch is focused on an ancestor of the fourteenth generation, the three Chung- branches on ancestors of the seventeenth, and the Wing-fu branch on a man of the fifteenth. Any genealogically balanced interpretation of the lineage's structure would reveal great demographic and economic imbalances. Groups on the ground can thus be seen as the starting point: the relations between them can to some extent be governed by choosing points of reference which divide branches that get too big, and reunite those that would otherwise be too small.

Two questions arise from this conclusion. First, how widespread is this pattern, in which the otherwise inescapable fact of asymmetric segmentation is counterbalanced by a symmetric interpretation of lineage structure? Second, if my conclusion is sound, it should follow that the interpretation of the ancestral record will change, albeit very slowly, with changes in the economic and demographic circumstances of lineage segments. We can discount deliberate falsification of the record, which means we must look all the harder for evidence of its more or less conscious manipulation. Time and the paucity of written evidence are against us. We can only speculate that in the case of the Leis, the five-branch conception of the lineage is relatively recent. The Wing-fu branch prospered and multiplied only around the turn of the century,[31] but by the time the land records begin (ca. 1906), a member of the branch is already included among the trustees of the Wui-wan tsu.

Insofar as the ancestral record is laid down as events occur, and is not (or only very rarely) thereafter subjected to deliberate falsification, it is a historical document. But a selective approach to the evidence in that document means that it is a charter only to the extent that it is appropriate to the circumstances of the living.

---

estate had ever been large enough to provide its members with more than an annual share of pork. In larger and wealthier lineages, tsu estates have an important role in the political structure of the lineage.

[31] The segment hived off about 1900, to found a new hamlet on the edge of the village. Its physical separation from the remainder of the lineage may have made more pressing the need to perceive it as genealogically independent as well.

Affines and the Rituals of Kinship

EMILY M. AHERN

The relationship between affines in China has been the subject of much contention. Two recent commentators, Maurice Freedman and Arthur Wolf, have taken opposing positions, with Wolf claiming that between families related by marriage, the relationship is "essentially one of equality" (1970: 199), and Freedman holding that the affinal tie "leaves the girl's family ritually and socially in a relationship of inferiority with the boy's" (1970: 185). In at least one small pocket of Chinese society, the village of Ch'i-nan, in northern Taiwan, the relationship between affines conforms to neither description. Contrary to Wolf, affines in Ch'i-nan are not equal; contrary to Freedman, marriage creates a ranking in which wife-givers are distinctly superior to wife-takers. From the time of betrothal the bride's family is defined as ritually superior to the groom's, irrespective of the previous economic and social positions of the two families.

Ch'i-nan is located in the southwestern part of the Taipei Basin, about ten miles southwest of Taipei City. The ancestors of Ch'i-nan's approximately one thousand residents first arrived in Taiwan from Fukien province in the mid-eighteenth century. Over the years they built settlements of sturdy brick farmhouses and cleared land for rice growing, both on the flat plains along the river that flows in front of the village and in the valleys between the mountains that embrace it. Most families still own some of the paddy land cleared by their ancestors and a few plots of mountain land planted with tea or fruit trees. Few live entirely off the land; income is commonly supplemented by wage labor in nearby factories and coal mines. The village is now organized into four lineage settlements, each clustered around an ancestral hall. The settlements are spatially distinct but nearly contiguous, ranged in a line at the foot of

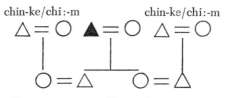

FIG. 1. REFERENTS OF THE TERMS CHIN-KE AND CHI:-M

the mountains. Although the settlements are inhabited by four separate agnatic groups, each of them strongly identifies with the territorial unit that includes them all. Because of a stand of bamboo that grows in front of the village, the traditional name for the area is "within the circle of bamboo"; the name emphasizes the territorial unity of the four settlements.

The Rites of Betrothal and Marriage

The key to understanding the rites of marriage and the relationships between affines "within the circle of bamboo" was given to me by an articulate elderly informant.[1] He methodically explained,

We call the father of our daughter's husband "chin-ke" and his mother "chi:-m." In the same way, our daughter's husband's parents call us "chin-ke" or "chi:m." So you can see that each family has two sets of people they call "chin-ke/chi:-m," that is, the parents of their daughters' husbands and the parents of their daughters-in-law. [See Figure 1.] But these two sets of chin-ke/chi:-m are not the same at all, and even more important, they are not equal. The parents of our daughters-in-law are chin-ke/chi:-m who have given wives to us, whereas we have given a wife to the chin-ke/chi:-m who are the parents of our daughters' husbands. We are ranked higher [khaq-tua] than the chin-ke/chi:-m to whom we have given wives, but lower [khaq-sue] than the chin-ke/chi:-m who have given wives to us.

He went on to say that the positioning of cloth given to the bereaved family at funerals shows the ranking of affines. Before the procession leaves for the graveyard, lengths of brightly colored cloth are marked with the giver's name and kinship relation to the deceased, hung on bamboo poles, and displayed in the ancestral hall. My informant pointed out, "The lengths of cloth are hung in the ancestral hall so that cloths given by chin-ke who have given wives to the bereaved family are in

---

[1] In this essay I refer only to the most prestigious form of virilocal marriage, in which the bride joins the groom's household as a young adult. What I say about engagement and wedding rites does not apply either to virilocal marriages in which the girl is adopted as a young child and raised by the family of her husband-to-be, or to the uxorilocal form of marriage.

the place of highest honor.[2] They must be hung so that they occupy a higher place than the cloths given by chin-ke to whom the bereaved family has given wives." When I protested that I had expected the ranking to be just the opposite, he replied,

Of course wife-giving chin-ke are superior to those who take a wife from them. If I give a daughter to be another family's daughter-in-law, she will bear them sons and give them descendants to carry on their line. What greater gift could we give them? They owe the means of obtaining descendants to us who have given them a daughter-in-law. It's a debt greater than all others, and one they can never pay off. Naturally we are ranked higher than they.

There was no reason to think he was giving a biased account from the point of view of either wife-givers or wife-takers. Rather, he was making general descriptive statements about marriage customs in the community.[3]

Although other informants were less systematic, they expressed basically the same view. In discussing affines, people referred to the higher *ritual* status of the wife-giving group, rather than a higher social status based on superior wealth or social standing. These two kinds of status are separable; I shall try to show that wife-giving affines are ritually superior to wife-taking chin-ke whatever the two families' prior social standing. It is worth noting, however, that many people in Ch'i-nan considered the ideal relationship between affines to be one in which the wife-giving family is socially, and especially economically, superior to the wife-taking group. This is the direct opposite of what is considered ideal elsewhere. Many published ethnographies report that because a girl from a family of higher social and economic standing than the groom's will find the harder conditions in her new family difficult to accept, parents of sons seek brides from families that socially and economically are equal or inferior to their own (see, for example, Yang 1965: 107). People in Ch'i-nan fully recognize that absorbing a girl from a wealthier family is difficult; they are inclined to prefer a wealthy daughter-in-law nevertheless because of the larger dowry she will bring her husband's family. As one informant put it, "Most people think that,

[2] The term chin-ke is often used to refer to the whole wife-giving or wife-taking family.

[3] I use the terms wife-givers and wife-takers as shorthand translations of the longer Chinese expressions: chin-ke to whom we have given wives or from whom we have taken wives. I do not thereby imply that in Ch'i-nan there are marriage classes, between which brides pass in a predictable direction. As I note below, that interesting issue remains unsettled. The terms wife-givers and wife-takers apply only with reference to a specific marrying couple.

ideally, a daughter-in-law's family should be richer. They think this even though they know it will increase the daughter-in-law's ability to have her own way in her new family. The reason they want a richer daughter-in-law is so they will get a big dowry [ke-cng]."

I do not know the actual percentage of marriages in which the bride comes from a wealthier family than the groom. In some weddings I witnessed in the village she clearly did; in other cases the two families were said to be equal in wealth. Nonetheless, people's attitudes clearly conveyed their view that ideally the bride's family should be the wealthier. In what follows I shall omit discussion of the actual social or economic status of wife-giving affines, considering only whether they acquire an automatic superiority expressed in ritual, and, in certain contexts, in the authority they wield. This superiority would complement superior status based on wealth or prestige in cases where wife-givers were initially the social superiors; where they were not, it would exist despite their prior social inferiority or equality.

The exchanges of goods and cash during the betrothal and marriage ceremonies show the strong obligation the wife-takers have toward those who have given them a bride. Betrothal ceremonies, held at the girl's home, begin with the boy's family bringing the *phieng-le*—many gifts of food and drink, substantial amounts of cash, and personal gifts for the girl. Acceptance of the gifts marks the beginning of affinal relations between the two families. Although some exchanges of gifts between the two families are symmetrical, others place the greater burden on the boy's family. During the betrothal ceremonies, for example, the boy's family must present the girl's with many "red envelopes" containing money to pay for services rendered them. Each of the wife-taking affines must give the girl a red envelope for the tea she serves them; another red envelope given her family must contain enough cash to completely cover the cost of the betrothal feast; other envelopes are given to the people who cook the dinner and those who perform such services as bringing pans of water for washing after the feast. With the visit of the girl's family to the boy's house at the time of the wedding feast, the one-sidedness of these payments becomes manifest. Even though a sumptuous dinner is served and many courteous services are provided the bride's family, they give out no red envelopes at all. It is as though the wife-takers must seize every opportunity to whittle away at the enormous debt they owe the wife-givers; the wife-givers, under no such obligation, simply accept what is their due.

On the surface, the exchange between the phieng-le given to the bride's family at the betrothal and the ke-cng (dowry) sent to the groom's home before the wedding is more even-handed. In fact, however, most families who have given away a daughter in marriage do not see it that way. One woman whose daughter had married out a short time before I interviewed her enumerated over and over the costs of the dowry. She estimated that they had spent NT $16,000 (about two years' income) on the dowry and related expenses.[4] Indignantly she exclaimed, "Do you know we had to use all the money the groom's family gave us and more to pay for the wedding? There was nothing at all left over." Her feeling was consistent with the worth that we have seen is vested in the bride. The money given to the bride's family is compensation for her loss. If it is used up in the efforts of her family to provide an impressive dowry, they feel cheated. They have lost not only the girl, but the cash that was partial recompense for her loss. The feeling of the wife-givers that they have been robbed of a valuable commodity without sufficient recompense is the reciprocal of the heavy obligation the wife-takers feel toward those whose daughter they have taken.

A further manifestation of the obligation felt by the wife-takers is the deferential treatment they give the bride. Her special treatment during the wedding ceremonies takes two forms. First, she is waited on, served, as an honored person. Second, she exerts control over people from whom she will shortly be taking orders. During the betrothal rites, for example, the girl is seated on a chair with a footrest beneath her feet to symbolize the comfort and ease she will enjoy in her husband's home. Then, while her feet are resting on the stool, her prospective mother-in-law places the wedding ring on her finger. I was told that girls are advised beforehand to crook their ring finger while the mother-in-law is putting on the ring so that she cannot slide it past the second knuckle; if she does, the villagers say, she will be able to dominate her daughter-in-law in the future. The assumption is always that the girl can keep the ring from being forced on, even if some mother-in-law is obstinate enough to try. One girl told me, "Most mothers-in-law wouldn't dare try to force the ring on all the way. Even if one tried, she'd never succeed because the girl would make sure her finger is crooked." Every time I observed this part of the ceremony, the mother-in-law merely slid the ring up to the second joint and desisted. There was no struggle at all.

The girl's privileged treatment is continued in the marriage rites. For the first three days of her marriage she is literally waited on hand and

[4] In 1969–70 the exchange rate was NT $40 = U.S. $1.

foot by her husband's family and accorded many special favors. After she has arrived at her new home, she expects her mother-in-law to serve her by opening her wardrobe and laying out a change of dress for her when she wants it. At the wedding feast somewhat later, a footstool is again provided for her. In addition one of her husband's relatives, perhaps his father's brother's wife, must wield chopsticks with her own hand and feed the bride bits of chicken and rice. The next day pans of hot water and clean towels are brought to the bride's door so that she can wash in privacy.

In my view a bride is provided with material comforts and allowed to resist her mother-in-law because she is a priceless gift, but one might argue instead that this treatment reflects her liminal position between being a daughter and being a daughter-in-law. Perhaps what looks like honorific treatment is instead a manifestation of what Victor Turner (1969: 109) calls "the powers of the weak." Indeed, some of the ritual proscriptions in the wedding itself lend credence to such an interpretation. There are restrictions on what can and cannot be done at the bride's house on the day of the wedding; the ancestors should not be worshipped, for example, and pregnant women should not come into the bride's presence. Other restrictions regulate who can safely meet the bride in the groom's house. People often say that the bride is very powerful and potentially dangerous. "The bride should always keep her eyes averted, because if she should look at someone, he might be struck blind." Is the bride's position between well-structured states the source of her ominous power? As Turner has suggested, persons who do not fit into well-structured positions, even temporarily, are regarded as "dangerous and anarchical, and have to be hedged around with prescriptions, prohibitions, and conditions" (1969: 109).

The deferential treatment shown the bride begins, however, at the betrothal ceremony, before the girl has entered the crucial transitional phase. Furthermore, practices characteristic of other transitional states are absent from betrothal ceremonies. In other contexts, when a person undergoes an important change in status, he or she is prevented from "seeing heaven" (khua:-thi:) by being covered with an umbrella. At funerals, for example, the paper tablet representing the deceased is covered by an umbrella as it is carried to the grave. At this point the dead as corpse is separated from the dead as resident of the tablet; the transition makes the umbrella necessary. Later, when the corpse is disinterred and the bones transferred to a ceramic pot, they are covered with an umbrella. At this juncture, the dead man loses the malevolent powers he possessed as a corpse; because he can no longer be transformed into a dangerous monster, he can safely be moved from place to place. Again, his changing condition means that he must be covered by an umbrella. At betrothals, however, the girl requires no such protection; she can walk about outside as she pleases without being covered. At her wedding, by contrast, someone must hold an umbrella over her whenever she steps outside. It is said that she is a "new person" (*sinlang*) and hence cannot view the sky.

Again, transitions are characteristically scheduled for a propitious time carefully selected by a geomancer. This requirement holds for almost any kind of change in status or place: transfer of a corpse to the graveyard; disinterment of bones; groundbreaking for buildings; moving into a new house; weddings. In all such cases, a propitious day and, within the day, a propitious two-hour period, must be selected beforehand. The crucial transition is carefully timed to occur within that two-hour period. Yet although a propitious day is selected for betrothals, no two-hour period is set for the girl's ring ceremony. The betrothal ceremonies are held on a propitious day because they mark a change in the relations between the couple's families. The ring ceremony is a transaction between the two families (a pledge that the girl will be transferred in the future), and as such does not constitute the crucial transferral of the girl from one status to another. Hence it need not be scheduled during a propitious two-hour period. In contrast, when a girl prepares to enter her husband's house as a bride, great care is taken to ensure her stepping over the threshold during the preselected two-hour interval. The absence of careful scheduling for the betrothal ceremony that most involves the girl, together with her freedom to walk about under the open sky, suggests that at betrothal the girl is not yet in a dangerous liminal phase, and therefore the deferential treatment shown her on this occasion cannot be explained on that account.

The wedding ceremonies themselves hold further evidence that the girl's crucial transition is made at that time, rather than at the betrothal. When the bride appears dressed in her wedding gown, she must hold two fans in her hand. As the car that will take her to her husband's home pulls away, she drops one fan but retains the other. The fan she drops represents the role of daughter she is leaving behind. The fan she keeps represents the role of daughter-in-law she will shortly acquire. This is when the bride begins her crucial transition from one role to another; the explanation for the deference with which she is treated at the betrothal ceremony lies elsewhere, in her value to her husband's family as guarantor of their line.

For a short time the bride is accordingly treated as an honored guest.

Yet her position is not permanent; it derives only from her association with her natal family. Once she ceases to be considered a precious gift from another family and becomes instead a daughter-in-law, once her position is defined in relation to the other members of her husband's family rather than in relation to an outside gift-giving group, the tenuousness of her new status becomes apparent. Her special status lasts but three days. Waited on by her husband's family, she does little but sit in state in her room, wearing new dresses and offering sweet tea to anyone who comes to call. Her mother-in-law does not request her help with housework, and indeed she scarcely ventures outside her room.

This period of grace ends abruptly on the third day following the wedding, when the newlyweds pay their ceremonial visit to the bride's natal home. The name of this visit, *cue-kheq*, "being a guest," underlines its significance for the bride's status. From this day on she is a full member of her husband's family, a daughter-in-law, and therefore an outsider, a guest, in her natal family. The completion of the "guest" visit means that both families have recognized and approved the incorporation of the bride into her husband's family. When the bride returns to his family, she must begin to assume her tasks as daughter-in-law. The transition between statuses is now complete; the girl is an outsider in her mother's house and a daughter-in-law in her mother-in-law's house. Her close association with her natal family now severed, she will no longer be the beneficiary of the obligations her husband's family owes hers. She need no longer be treated as a precious gift provided at great cost; she can be required to fill the low-status role of daughter-in-law.

Another facet of the wedding ceremonies demonstrates that the basis of the bride's value to the wife-takers is as a source of future descendants. The importance of her ability to bear sons is strikingly expressed in a ritual that occurs just after the dowry has been transferred to the groom's house, sometime after the betrothal but before the wedding. The one time I saw this ritual, the young groom emerged from the house as soon as the furniture and other goods in the dowry were unloaded. His brother accompanied him, holding an open umbrella over his head. The two proceeded directly to the large chest of drawers that was part of the dowry. Still covered by the umbrella, the groom brought out a key with which he unlocked the small upper-right-hand drawer of the chest. He pulled it open, looked in, and immediately closed it again. After he locked the drawer, the two men (still covered by the umbrella) returned to the house. The go-between for the marriage told me later that this rite (called *khui-hue*, "opening the flowers") is performed so that the bride will bear sons quickly. Other informants said the groom was "looking at the flowers." No one I asked could give me any further exegesis. Only if we look at the elements of the rite in other contexts can we make sense of it.

The flowers referred to in the phrase "opening the flowers" are on one level actual paper or plastic flowers in various colors designed to be worn in a woman's hair. The bride purchases a dozen or so of these and stores them in the top right drawer of her chest. On her wedding day she removes these flowers from their locked compartment and gives them to her husband's female relatives. In other contexts the symbolism of flowers is intimately connected with childbirth. In a well-known legend, a young girl disguises herself as a boy and leaves home to attend a university. She swears she will remain virtuous and, as proof, predicts that a certain plant will not flower all the while she is gone. The flowering of the plant would mean that she had borne a child. Likewise, people believe that each person has a kind of "double" in the underworld. Men are represented by a tree, women by a flowering tree. The flowers on a woman's tree represent the children she will bear in the future; those that have matured and fallen off represent the children she has already borne. Tying the images together, the afterbirth is referred to as "the flower" (*hue*).

In view of these connotations, the rite of "opening the flowers" is clearly related to conception and childbirth. The drawer that the groom unlocks is the only locked and private place the bride will have after her wedding. She retains the key to this drawer; only she has access to it. In this dark compartment she may keep her most precious possessions —whatever cash she owns, jewelry, souvenirs of her wedding, pictures of her natal family. In "opening the flowers" the groom violates this private place. He inserts a key, opens the drawer, and thereby "opens the flowers" or, according to some informants, "looks to see if there are flowers there." A phallic key opens a feminine receptacle; the sexual connotations are obvious. But is the rite best interpreted as a public, symbolic impregnation of the bride, or as a verification of fertility? My evidence is inconclusive. Perhaps the rite expresses both meanings; alternatively, different informants may interpret it differently. The paper flowers in the drawer represent the bride's fertility, the children she will bear. The groom opens the drawer and thereby ritually "opens the flowers," impregnates the womb, and starts the fetus's development. Alternatively or simultaneously, he makes sure the bride has flowers and is, therefore, capable of bearing children.

Two aspects of the ceremony support the interpretation that the groom is ritually impregnating the bride. First, an umbrella is held over the groom's head while he performs the rite. As we have seen, people are protected from "seeing heaven" only during a significant change from one state to another. If an umbrella is held over the groom when he opens the bureau drawer, we may expect that he, too, is undergoing an important change. If he is merely verifying his bride's fertility, no change in his status is involved. If, on the other hand, he is ritually impregnating his bride, symbolically beginning her first pregnancy, then he might be said to be undergoing a change from being merely a son to being both son and father. Second, it is said that an umbrella is held over the groom's head during this rite so that T'ien Kung (the highest god in the supernatural hierarchy) cannot see what is happening. If this implies an element of embarrassment, then we should probably interpret the rite as a symbolic sexual act, for the sexual act is embarrassing and requires concealment in a way that a symbolic fertility test does not. In the eyes of the larger kinship group present at the ceremony (the groom's direct ascendants and close collaterals), the most important aspect of his role as husband is his fertilization of the bride. He publicly "opens the flowers" or fertilizes her in sight of the group that hopes to have its numbers increased and its future guaranteed by the sons the bride will bear.

Relations Between Affines After the Wedding

The end of the marriage rites is by no means the end of social interaction between the affines. Their relationship after the wedding has several components, which I will illustrate by describing in chronological order the occasions on which they interact. The most important occasions on which the families encounter each other are events involving change in the wife-taking family, such as births or funerals. At these times, the wife-givers are expected to perform services for the wife-takers and present them with lavish gifts. This may be surprising in view of the heavy obligation wife-takers owe wife-givers. One might expect wife-takers to find occasions to send gifts to the wife-givers to reduce their indebtedness. This sometimes happens: if the wife-giving family celebrates a wedding or a birthday, their wife-taking chin-ke will certainly send them the best gift they can afford. But more important, at other times the wife-givers must bestow even more expensive gifts on the wife-takers. The rationale for this seeming contradiction is that the wife-givers must validate their superior status by acting in a superior manner, both economically and socially. Hence, as we shall see, the contacts between affines after the marriage ceremonies provide a setting in which wife-givers may do precisely this. Another important factor in relations between the two families is the authority that wife-givers exercise over the heavily indebted wife-takers. In addition, we will see emerging from affinal interactions the belief that wife-giving affines possess strong ritual power to make things happen, a power that can be used to either help or harm the wife-takers.

This last element, the ritual efficacy of the wife-givers, appears soon after the wedding rites in events that involve the birth of the couple's first child. At several points, the wife-givers are expected to send objects to their affines that are intended to ensure an early first pregnancy. The most lucid example occurs at the bride's "guest" visit to her natal family. When she leaves, her parents send along a basket of goods. Included in it are some sweet cakes that will be arranged on the marriage bed and offered to the bed mother (a minor goddess). The basket must also include six eggs that are about to hatch. These are placed under the marriage bed and allowed to hatch there. The hope is that children will follow the chicks' example. If the first chick to hatch is a male, the bride's first child will be a boy; if it is female, the bride will bear a girl.

When, with the ritual help of the wife-giving chin-ke, the bride gives birth, another element of the affinal relationship comes to the fore. As soon as a child is born, the groom's family notifies the bride's family by sending them a special kind of glutinous rice dish cooked in oil, along with a pot of soup made of chicken, sesame oil, and rice wine. The wife-givers then offer these items to their ancestors, as if to inform them that the promise of the engagement and wedding rites—that the wife-takers were to be provided with an heir—has been fulfilled. Following this, the newborn child is virtually deluged with gifts from his mother's natal family. They immediately give him a suit of clothes, gold jewelry, a red quilt, and a long strip of cloth the mother will use to tie the child on her back. On his one-month, four-month, and one-year anniversaries, they give him money, more jewelry, and clothes.

Since the birth of this child, if it is a male, marks the beginning of the mother's brother's special relationship with his sister's son, one might surmise that the gifts given the child represent a display of affection by an indulgent maternal uncle. Yet my informants' explanations emphasized the ranking of the two affinal groups (the wife-givers and the wife-takers) rather than the relationship between two particular members of those groups (the mother's brother and his sister's son). For example, two proverbs were often quoted to me in explanation of the many gifts a child receives from his mother's family: "Eating the things of mother's brother is like eating bean curd, eating the things of sister's son is like eating iron nails"; and, "In heaven T'ien Kung is highest, on earth mother's brother is highest." On first hearing, the two proverbs seem contradictory. The first seems to say that just as it is easy to eat soft bean curd, so it is easy to obtain the things of mother's brother; just as it is difficult to eat hard iron nails, so it is hard to obtain the things of sister's son. But if, as the second proverb states, mother's brother is highest of all, then how could it be so easy to gain access to his belongings? One of my informants replied,

Our mother's brother occupies the position of highest rank because he is a representative of the family that has given us a wife. They are our wife-giving chin-ke, so in relation to us they rank very high. Because of this they want to give us as many expensive gifts as they can, to show their superiority. Since it's so easy to get things from them we say it's "like eating bean curd." Whenever we visit them they provide the finest food and drink because they would be embarrassed not to put on an impressive show. But, on the other hand, when they come to our house, although we do provide the best we can afford, they wouldn't want to eat any fine food or accept any gifts at all because it would show they were in need of something. Since they seldom can accept anything in return from sister's son, we say it's like "eating iron nails."

Thus the relationship between mother's brother and sister's son in the first proverb is interpreted in terms of the relationship between affinally related groups. The wife-givers try to validate their high status by providing generous gifts that show their wealth and resources. They refuse gifts from their wife-taking chin-ke to show they have no unfilled needs.

The next incident in the family cycle that involves affines might well be the division of property. In Ch'i-nan, division of the father's household and estate commonly takes place in two stages. In the first, brothers may set up separate economic households, with each brother's wife cooking food for her family on a separate stove. In the second, which may occur several years after the first, usually after the father's death, the father's land and goods are divided. The two stages are the primary concern of different affinal groups. The first phase, the separation of stoves, involves all the affinal groups that gave wives to the dividing brothers. If the full ritual takes place, the natal family of each brother's wife is expected to attend, bringing as gifts an entire set of kitchen utensils and dishes. They provide what amounts to another installment on the dowry, additional economic undergirding for the unit formed when they gave their daughter in marriage. It also provides one more occasion for the wife-givers to dazzle their affines with the splendor of their gifts.

When the time comes for the brothers to divide their father's estate, their mother's brother, representative of the affines who gave their father his wife, may arbitrate the division. Once called in, he has absolute authority; no one may dispute his decisions. The superior position of the wife-givers is reinforced by virtue of the mother's brother's being, in relation to the dividing brothers, the representative of a group that gave a wife to a higher generation. In this instance the status difference between wife-givers and wife-receivers is strengthened by the generational difference. Wife-giving affines, then, are instrumental in bringing both phases of the division to a successful conclusion. In the first phase they provide a partly tangible, partly symbolic, basis for the new-formed economic units. In the second phase, they ensure an equitable division of the brothers' inheritance with a minimum of ill feeling. Their authority is invoked for the specific purpose of overcoming dissension so that division can take place.

The next occasion on which the wife-givers must interact with their wife-taking chin-ke is the marriage of one of the original couple's children—that is, a child born to the girl they gave away. When a daughter of the original couple is about to marry, it is said that to be assured of prosperity after her wedding, she must eat a meal with her mother's brother. Shortly before the wedding she must appear unannounced at her mother's natal home, whereupon she must be served a meal of at least six separate dishes. The proverb "Unless you eat with your mother's brother, you won't have anything" (i.e., any material possessions) explains this practice. We meet here with familiar themes. First, the unannounced visit of the bride-to-be emphasizes the inexhaustible beneficence of the mother's brother toward his sister's family. So wealthy and generous is he that he can produce a six-course feast on a moment's notice. Second, as with the birth of the first child, members of the mother's family are thought to have powerful efficacy. The chicks they sent with the new bride helped her to conceive a child; now the meal the daughter of the bride eats with them helps her prosper after marriage.

A woman's natal family has a role in the weddings of her sons as well, though it is subsidiary to that of the son's bride's family, the affines most directly involved. At a wedding the family of the groom may be simultaneously attached to three different wife-giving groups (see Figure 2). If these affines all attend the wedding feast, they are all seated at the table of honor. The highest seat goes to the father or brother of the bride because he is most directly involved. Next highest should be a representative of the groom's paternal grandmother's natal family if

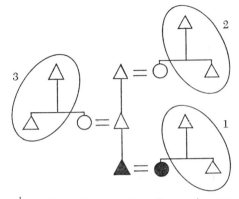

FÍG. 2. THREE SETS OF WIFE-GIVING AFFINES

connections with them are still maintained. (The duration of affinal ties is discussed below.) Finally, still at the table of honor, would come the representative of the groom's mother's natal family.[5]

Thus the three families who have given wives to the groom and his direct ascendants are singled out for honored seats. The wife-taking chin-ke, the groom's sister's husband or his father's sister's husband, may attend the feast, but they do not sit at the table of honor. To emphasize how important it is to pay proper respect to wife-giving chin-ke, I was told the following story about a wealthy physician:

Quite a few years ago Dr. Ong was giving a feast for his son's wedding. Either because the doctor was too busy, or because he didn't know about the correct procedure, he failed to seat his mother's brother at the table of honor. So, halfway through the feast, the slighted mother's brother grabbed the tablecloth at his table, pulling it and all the food and dishes off onto the floor. The doctor couldn't say anything to him at all. By pulling off the tablecloth the uncle meant to say to the doctor: you have so much money you look down on me, but I'm your mother's brother and that won't do.

Wife-giving affines must also be given a place of honor at the birthday feasts given once each decade from the fiftieth birthday on. When the celebration is for a woman, representatives of her natal family must be given the highest place of honor at the feast. I was told another story illustrating the consequences of failing to pay proper respect to these affines:

A member of the Li lineage [one of the four Ch'i-nan lineages] was giving a birthday feast for his mother. He naturally invited his mother's brother. But

---

[5] The honored position given the mother's brother at wedding feasts is well documented. See Gallin 1960: 639.

since he and his mother's brother didn't get along well, the mother's brother sent his young son in his stead. The host, seeing his mother's brother's son arrive instead of his mother's brother, and thinking that he was only a young boy, felt it was unnecessary to give him the seat of honor. So the seat of honor went to another guest. Later, when a whole steamed chicken was brought to the table, the server set it down according to custom, with the chicken's head pointing toward the man in the seat of highest honor. But the host's mother's brother's son was not dumb. He knew that he was sent to the feast as a representative of his father and that he was entitled to the place of honor. So as soon as the chicken was set down facing someone else, he reached out and grabbed the chicken's head, wrenching it off and saying, "This was raised by my father's sister; I ought to receive it."

On formal occasions such as feasts and weddings, clearly, wife-giving affines must be shown special respect. Yet even on less formally structured occasions, the relationships between affines can vary only within limits. This is illustrated by the case of a man named Tan who lives in Ch'i-pei, the market center across the river from Ch'i-nan. His son married a girl from the Ong lineage of Ch'i-nan. One day, my landlady in the village, an Ong herself, was chatting with Tan and an elderly, respected member of the Lou lineage. Tan began discussing his relations with his daughter-in-law's natal family. "My daughter-in-law's father looked down on all of us. Just because we had less money he despised us. He was always saying that his daughter wasn't cared for and had to work too hard. He cursed us bitterly whenever we went to his house, and all this only because we weren't rich. So now we don't have anything to do with them at all. I didn't even attend the funeral of my daughter-in-law's father." On hearing this outburst my landlady and old Mr. Lou began castigating Tan severely. "How can you act that way? You have to respect your daughter-in-law's father and the rest of his family *no matter what they do or say*. No other way is allowable. Never before in all the history of Ch'i-nan or Ch'i-pei has there ever been a case of a fight between a man and the chin-ke who gave him a daughter-in-law." My landlady added later that there are never any fights between affines because the groom's family always defers to the wife-giving group. Relations between affines are always outwardly harmonious because wife-takers never take offense, never argue back. If, like Tan, they should do so, they would be subjected to severe public criticism. Later I heard several other people, both Ongs and others, say that Tan was a "bad man" because he fought with his daughter-in-law's father. Hence, even apart from feasts and formal occasions, under ordinary circumstances wife-receivers are expected to defer to their wife-giving chin-ke no matter what abuses they suffer.

Similarly, pressure on the wife-givers to show generosity toward the wife-takers is not limited to such occasions as births and marriages. Two of the Ch'i-nan lineages, the Lis and the Lous, consider themselves to have been affines for several generations because the daughter of the first Li settler was given in marriage to the first Lou settler. I was told that a few years ago the Lis and the Lous owned pieces of land separated only by a cleft in the river bank. One spring, after a severe flood, earth was thrown up so that it filled in the cleft in the river bank, making the Li and Lou plots contiguous. Invoking their affinal relationship, the Lous said to the Lis, "Eating the things of mother's brother is like eating bean curd...; what about that land of yours?" The Lis realized they had no choice; they made over their land to the Lous. To validate their superior status as wife-givers, they had to show they were so wealthy they could even give away land.

The long duration of this affinal tie between Lis and Lous is unusual; ordinarily wife-takers could not make demands on wife-givers so many years after the original marriage. The Li-Lou tie has been maintained partly because the two groups have continued to be next-door neighbors. In addition, because the first Li settler gave a wife to the first Lou settler, the two descent groups that trace their ancestry to these men regard each other as wife-givers and wife-takers. That is, all Lous regard Lis as their wife-giving affines, because they are all descended from the woman the Lis gave to their founding ancestor. Usually affinal relationships last only about three generations, or until the woman whose transfer established the tie and her husband are dead. This means that after their funerals, the two sets of affines will probably no longer interact.

Funerals, besides marking the end of affinal ties, also reveal most clearly the power and authority of the wife-giving chin-ke. It has been held that the personal tie of affection between a woman and her brother or father is the primary reason for her natal family's participation in her funeral. Affection may be an element in their participation, but a man plays the same role in the funeral of his sister's husband as he does in hers, even if she is already dead—a fact that is hardly accounted for by affection between brother and sister. The affinal tie and the authority of wife-giving affines extend to situations in which the welfare of the original bride is not involved. The following account of funeral ceremonies, in which I discuss only those events that illuminate the relationships between affines, therefore applies to funerals of both men and women.

The arrival of wife-giving chin-ke at a funeral is announced as soon as they come into sight. As the cry *"gua-ke!"* (i.e., affines; usually applied only to wife-giving affines) spreads through the mourning family, the direct descendants of the dead man or woman don their mourning dress and wait at the gate to the compound or at the edge of the settlement. As soon as the chin-ke approach, the mourners fall to their knees, wailing. The senior male among the chin-ke, usually the brother or brother-in-law of the deceased, more rarely the father or father-in-law, asks the group to stand. They resist, are urged again, then finally stand and lead the gua-ke up to the house.

The first acts the gua-ke perform are of great significance for an interpretation of their role in the subsequent funeral ceremonies. Before their arrival, a special table, called the *gua-co-touq* (affines' table), is prepared for their exclusive use. First, the table is covered with a brightly colored embroidered hanging turned inside out. Then it is placed in the courtyard in front of the house so that the gua-ke will pass it before they reach the coffin. On the table is placed a tin can, half filled with raw rice, which serves as a holder for three unlit sticks of incense. Both the can and the incense are wrapped in strips of red paper. When the gua-ke reach this table, the senior male among them does two things: he picks up a corner of the hanging and folds it back onto the table, right side out, securing it there by placing the incense can on top of it; then he picks up the incense sticks, turns them upside down, and replaces them in the can, still wrong end up.

The rite seems to express a distinction between the role of the bereaved descendants and that of the affines. For the descendants, the event is one that requires mourning. Hence for them it is fitting that the hanging on the table (which is hung on such joyful occasions as weddings or New Year's feasts) should be turned inside out. When the senior gua-ke turns up a corner so that the red and gold colors show, it is as if he is saying "I am not a bereaved descendant, I am under no obligation to mourn the dead." That is, he is not under the social obligation to mourn that juniors owe their deceased seniors. Similarly, lighting incense sticks and placing them right side up in a holder is characteristically performed by juniors on behalf of deceased seniors. All the descendants of the deceased perform this act on his or her behalf both at the funeral and thereafter. When the gua-ke places unlighted incense upside down in the can, he is again demonstrating that he is not there as a descendant mourning a senior kinsman. Finally, the red wrapping on the incense and its holder again underlines the distinction between affines and descendants. Arthur Wolf has demonstrated that the color red has a prophylactic function in funeral ceremonies, protecting those, such as affines, who are not direct descendants of the deceased (1970: 193). The gua-ke, not obligated to the deceased as descendants, are entitled to the protection of red. At the beginning of the rite, the hanging is inside out and the incense is right side up, as they should be for the mourning descendants. In turning the cloth right side out and the incense upside down, the senior gua-ke establishes his position—and by extension the position of all the gua-ke—as non-mourners in contrast to the descendants.

Thus the keynotes of the gua-ke's role in the funeral are established within moments of their arrival: they are owed obeisance and respect, and they are not mourners come to worship the deceased. Extreme respect is shown them, especially the all-important mother's brother, throughout the funeral ceremonies. Soon after the rite at the gua-co-touq, a son of the deceased prepares a tray, on which he lays the funeral costume for his mother's brother. The son kneels before his uncle, and, holding the tray over his head, asks him to accept the costume. Then a relative of the deceased in the same generation as the mother's brother arranges the robe for him and sees that it is tied properly. Later, when the mother's brother and his family leave, a group of the deceased's descendants again kneel before them. No one else at the funeral is honored with such respect, but it is absolutely obligatory for the gua-ke. A man explained to me, "Almost everyone is scared to death of his mother's brother because he has so much power. Once a man in this settlement didn't show the proper courtesy to his mother's brother at a funeral. The mother's brother got angry and beat him terribly. He has this power because his family raised a daughter and gave her to us as a gift to carry on our lines of descendants."

Wife-giving affines have the authority to demand respect. They also have the authority to act as disciplinarians of their sisters' sons. Many informants recalled incidents in which they had seen a young man beaten by his mother's brother at the funeral of his mother or father. If the mother's brother feels that the boy has been unfilial or disrespectful toward his parents, he has complete license to beat him. In this fashion, the gua-ke continue to protect the welfare of the woman they gave away and her husband.

In a similar way, the mother's brother is entitled to assurance that the death of his sister or brother-in-law was not brought on by mistreatment. In earlier times, the coffin was left unsealed until the mother's brother had inspected the body. Informants told me that although the mother's brother was permitted to look at the body, under no circumstances could he touch it. "If relations are bad between the two families, the mother's brother could say some bad words [*kong phai:-ue*; curse] as he touched the body. Whatever he said would come about." Again we meet with the powerful efficacy of the wife-givers' words and deeds. In this case, unless precautions are taken, the mother's brother's words can affect the family adversely, even bringing about their destruction.

Nowadays this is not a serious concern because the coffin is sealed before the affines arrive. Nonetheless, a ritualized mock coffin-nailing ceremony is still performed at the funeral. It is said to give the mother's brother a chance to satisfy himself that the death was natural; until he performs this ceremony, burial cannot take place. Shortly before the ceremony is to begin, a son of the deceased prepares a tray, laying on it a hammer and a single nail, both wrapped in red paper to protect the affines. Once again the son kneels before his mother's brother with the tray raised above his head. His uncle accepts the tray but usually hands it over to a Taoist priest, who completes the ritual in his stead. If the mother's brother performs it himself, he must pretend to hammer the nail into the coffin at all four corners, each time uttering a good-luck phrase such as, "May the family have many sons." The sons and other direct descendants of the deceased kneel until he is finished. Then a son removes the nail (actually hammered part-way into the coffin at the last corner) with his teeth, thus showing extreme respect for his mother's brother; pulling the nail out by hand would be more casual, and show less care for an object touched by his mother's brother.

In this ritual, the authority of the wife-giving affines is again underlined. A family can do as they wish with a daughter-in-law, but only within certain limits: they cannot treat her so badly that she dies as a result. Her brother will always have a chance to act as final arbiter over the cause of her death. The rite also shows once more the potency of the mother's brother's words. The good-luck phrases he utters while sealing the coffin are considered very powerful. "Whatever the mother's brother says will come about." In return for this service, the bereaved family must present him with several hundred NT dollars in a red envelope, far more than red envelopes usually contain.

The final ritual that delineates the relationship between the affines takes place just before the coffin is removed to the graveyard. Preparations for this ritual are elaborate: several offering tables are arranged in front of the coffin and laden with dishes of food; the gua-co-touq is moved in front of the offering tables; mats are arranged in front of the gua-co-touq. A small bowl containing a green sprout stuck into a few inches of dirt is placed under the affines' table. When all is ready the male gua-ke are asked to come forward. Then, two by two, they stand before the table, kneel, and touch their foreheads to the floor, repeating this sequence three times. Meanwhile the dead person's descendants are huddled under the table, kneeling to show respect for the gua-ke. While the gua-ke are still kneeling, a kinsman or high-ranking acquaintance of the deceased faces them, also kneeling, and reads a document that announces to the deceased exactly how much food has been offered and how much paper money will be burned for him. Finally he hands each of the gua-ke a small cup of wine, which they raise as in a toast and then empty into the bowl with the green sprout. After doing this three times, they make way for the next pair of affines, who repeat the entire performance.

The villagers say this ritual accomplishes two things. First, it establishes communication with the dead, so he can be informed of the services his descendants have provided for him. People say that just as officials are promoted one rank at death, so ordinary men gain one generation at death. Hence it is fitting that the wife-givers, the highest ranking among those at the funeral, should communicate with him. The purpose of the communication seems to be to ensure the deceased's satisfaction with the offerings made him. To this end the gua-ke bring a rich plate of offerings for the deceased. Their high status, it is thought, makes an offering from them especially impressive. In return, the dead person's family must see that the gua-ke return home not only with the offering they brought, but also with a red envelope containing enough money to cover its cost.

The second purpose of the ritual is more complex. I asked many informants why, if the gua-ke rank so high, they must kneel before the coffin of the deceased. Some seemed puzzled by the question; all denied that the gua-ke were kneeling to show obeisance to the dead. Most people held that the kneeling was part of a ritual designed to get rid of the dead. They said the sprout under the table represents the deceased. The affines who pour wine on the sprout were said to be applying the maxim "When you weed, get out the roots." One man said, "It means you must get rid of the dead entirely, not let him become a hungry ghost or come back to do bad things to the descendants." By this interpretation, the gua-ke are carrying out their most difficult task: to exorcise the dead man so he will not return to harm the living. Their initial communication with the deceased is intended to assure him that he has received all he is due; the pouring of wine is to remove the dead man once he has been satisfied. In other contexts as well, the application of wine is designed to make things go away: in the rites of second burial held six or seven years after death, if the flesh on the body has not decayed, wine is spit onto the corpse to make the flesh rot. In the funeral ceremony, wine is applied to eradicate the presence of the dead as a corpse among the living, for the rite of pouring wine immediately precedes the removal of the coffin to the graveyard. If all goes well, the corpse and its potential maleficence are removed entirely. This is not the place to analyze precisely why people feel they need rituals to facilitate the removal of the corpse. For our purposes it suffices to note that the extrication of the corpse from among the living is problematical, and requires the ritual help of powerful, wife-giving affines.

Interpretations

In thinking about the social correlates of the ritual ranking of affines, one obvious question comes immediately to mind: does a group that has given wives to another ever take wives from that group? Unfortunately, I cannot pursue this intriguing line of inquiry here because the necessary data are not yet available.[6] Instead, I will turn to an analysis of the ritual role of affines, in an effort to explain why it is appropriate for them to behave as they do.

By one reading the exaggerated ritual deference shown the wife-givers is an expression of their actual low social status.[7] Secure in their superiority, the wife-takers can afford to make a ritual show of politeness and respect. Similarly, the costly dowry and the many gifts showered on the wife-takers are attempts by the wife-givers to compensate for their social inferiority by a show of lavishness. One difficulty with this interpretation is that wife-givers in Ch'i-nan are sometimes socially superior to wife-takers; more important, many people regard the acquisition of a daughter-in-law from a wealthier family as ideal. Under these circumstances, it is difficult to see why the rituals surrounding marriages would require wife-takers to treat socially inferior wife-givers with such deference. At least in those instances in which wife-givers are socially superior, it would be equally reasonable for wife-givers to show ritual deference to wife-takers. In some societies, to be sure, ceremonial deference can be an expression of social superiority, and there may be instances of this in Chinese society. Yet there seem to be no grounds for interpreting deference in these marriage ceremonies as an expression

[6] On cross-cousin marriage in China, see Gallin 1963 and Hsu 1945. Until I obtain detailed information on the transfer of women between lineages, lineage segments, and families in Ch'i-nan I prefer not to comment on the relationship between the ritual ranking of affines and the pattern that the transfer of women between families actually follows.

[7] I am grateful to Maurice Freedman for making this suggestion during the conference. I am of course responsible for the use I have made of his suggestion here.

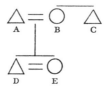

FIG. 3. THE WOMAN'S CONJUGAL FAMILY AND THE AFFINES

of superiority. Informants explicitly interpret the position of the wife-takers as inferior to that of the wife-givers. So hopelessly indebted are the wife-takers that they remain inferior in this sense whatever their social standing before the marriage. There is no hint that people believe that the ceremonial deference and lavish gifts extended to wife-givers signify their social inferiority. Moreover, in other Chinese rituals, those who receive ceremonial respect are in no sense inferior to those who give it. For example, the gods, who are always treated with great respect, unquestionably rank much higher than ordinary people.

Another possible interpretation is that the respectful politeness shown wife-giving affines is an attempt to create distance between the daughter-in-law and her natal family, to totally absorb the bride into her husband's family. The relative familiarity shown wife-taking affines, on the other hand, expresses a family's desire to maintain close ties with daughters who have married out by treating their husbands and the husbands' families like close relatives rather than strangers.[8] Although the data allow this interpretation, I am disinclined to accept it in part because none of the actors in these rituals offered it as an explanation, in part because the explanation they did offer seems to account for aspects of the marriage ritual that this interpretation does not. Although a family's desire to fully absorb women it takes in and retain connections with women it gives out would account for the politeness shown to wife-givers, how can it explain the authority and power wife-givers wield over wife-takers? I will try to show below that by pursuing the implications of the interpretation offered by informants in Ch'i-nan, we can explain these puzzling aspects of marriage ritual.

Before I begin, I must define a kinship category important to the following analysis. This is the family group formed by a woman, her husband, and the children she bears (A, B, D, and E in Figure 3).

The affines (C and his family) who originally gave the woman (B) remain interested in the others until the woman and her husband die and her children marry. Thus, this kinship category is formed by a

---

[8] Sung Lung-sheng advanced this hypothesis at the conference.

woman and those of her primary kin who share involvement with her natal family. She and her children are most centrally involved; her husband is most peripherally involved. I will hereafter refer to this group of people as the woman's conjugal family, and to the woman's natal family simply as the affines.[9] Although other members of her family can play the ceremonial role required of wife-giving affines, it usually falls to her brother, her father being too august, her brother's children usually too young. Her brother plays the affines' ritual part only as a representative of her family. As we have seen, he can send one of his sons in his stead.

The affines' relationship with the woman's conjugal family begins with the engagement and marriage ceremonies. Thereafter, wife-giving affines play a critical role in the lives of the woman and her husband at the births of the couple's children, the weddings of their daughters, the separation of their household from those of the woman's husband's brothers, division among their sons' households, and at their deaths. These are the occasions on which the roles of the couple and their offspring—that is, their rights and duties—undergo substantial change. They are, further, role changes that involve a major alteration in the relations within a woman's conjugal family. In other words, the change a person experiences on these occasions affects his rights and duties in relation to his immediate kinsmen. These two characteristics apply to all the contexts in which affines act. At birth, for example, a person is for the first time integrated into a kinship nexus, a position with attendant rights and duties. His parents and siblings are also affected, acquiring a set of obligations toward the new member of the family. As we have seen, the affines act to bring about this event with their gift of fertilized eggs. At marriage, a girl breaks her ties to her natal family and establishes new ones with her husband's kin. Here, too, the affines have a role, ensuring a prosperous and comfortable life for her in the future. At the separation of households, economic and social obligations between brothers, between brothers and their parents, and between husband and wife are drastically rearranged. Here the affines play a key role in providing the basis for new households. At death, finally, a person abandons the roles he or she filled in life. As we have seen, the affines also assist in this transition by removing the dead from among

[9] There are striking similarities between what I call "the woman's conjugal family" and what Margery Wolf has called "the woman's uterine family" (1972: 32ff). When the woman's conjugal family is considered together with a representative of the woman's natal family (Figure 3), this group of kin is identical to Lévi-Strauss's "atom of kinship" (1963: 72), "a group consisting of a husband, a woman, a representative of the group which has given the woman to the man."

the living. In each case, clearly, roles change in a way that profoundly affects members of the woman's conjugal family.

Contrasting the transitional contexts in which affines participate with those in which they do not clarifies their function. Sometimes a person undergoes transitions that involve a change in role but not in kinship relations. If the role change does not affect any kinsmen, the affines play no part. For example, several years after his funeral a dead person is first transferred to the underworld and later installed in a house there. For the dead, these transitions entail radical changes, from fearful occupancy of a dangerous realm filled with monsters, to an insecure position at the mercy of potentially punitive underworld officials, and finally to a secure dwelling safe from harm. But his relationship to his living kin is unaffected by these changes. They offer him food, money, and obeisance before, during, and after these moves; his role in their lives continues unaltered. No old ties between him and his kinsmen are broken, no new ones are formed; the changes he undergoes involve only his relationship with underworld officials and residents. As we might expect from the foregoing, the wife-giving affines play no part in these transitions. Their role is confined to a transition that affects the living: the removal of the corpse to the grave. Before this event the dead person is still present among the living, and in some ways must be treated as if he were still alive. Hence, someone must keep him company by sleeping next to his coffin every night until the funeral. Further, he poses a distinct threat to the living because of the capacity of corpses to become terrible monsters. With his removal, that danger is gone. The obligation of the living to treat him as if he were still alive also ends.

Again, the affines play no part in transitions that produce role changes and changes in relations among some kin but do not affect relationships within the woman's conjugal family. Moving into a new house, for example, is a transition hedged about with ritual. Such a move may portend a considerable change in social position; if the new house is luxurious or located in the market town, for example, the family may rise in prestige. If a woman's conjugal family, having already established a separate stove, moves to a new house, social relationships between it and such close relatives as her husband's brother may be changed. If the conjugal family itself does not split in such a move, however, its members continue in the same relationships to one another. It is noteworthy that wife-giving affines play no ritual role in such cases. Unlike the occasions on which they do take part, a change of address involves no significant change in relationships within the woman's conjugal family.

Another conspicuous class of occasions for role change in which the affines usually play no active part is wedding ceremonies for the off-spring of the original couple. Of course, if a son of the couple were to marry a daughter of his mother's brother, the same affines would preside at his wedding as at his father's. But ordinarily a marriage marks the beginning of an affinal tie with a different group, and is thus the concern of another set of affines. Affines who do not play the primary role at a wedding (giving a wife) are merely honored guests; they have no spe-cial role at all. Wife-giving affines have an active part, then, in role changes that affect relationships in the woman's conjugal family, except on those occasions when another set of wife-giving affines has the pri-mary role.

What effect do wife-giving affines have on those occasions when they do intervene? The maternal uncle is often described as a "mediator," largely because he arbitrates conflicting interests in the division of fam-ily estates (Fei 1939: 87). If we recall that the mother's brother is viewed as a representative of his family, the wife-giving affines, and analyze the kind of role he plays in contexts other than the division of estates, "transformer" seems a more accurate description than "media-tor." First, wife-givers are the source of an agnatic group's capacity to grow in numbers. It is their gift that makes the birth of children pos-sible; those children will in turn marry and beget still more children.[10] Thus the wife-givers provide the impetus for the entire sequence. Ob-taining a wife from another group enables a lineage to transform itself from a static set of kin to an expanding group; the wife-givers are seen as the source of the transforming growth. It is perhaps for this reason that wife-givers continue to act as creators of growth and change, a capacity that lies at the heart of their mystical ritual power. The fertile eggs they send with the bride precipitate her first pregnancy, the start of a new life. When households are divided, the goods brought by the natal family of each brother's wife provide the symbolic basis for the new economic and social units being created. When the sons of the original couple divide their parents' estate, the arbitration of their moth-er's brother ensures their successful transformation into separate prop-erty holders. Finally, the offerings and communications to the dead ensure his transformation from a potentially dangerous spirit hovering among the living to a harmless ancestor buried in his grave. In these

[10] Families and lineages can secure mates for the younger generation in other ways. A family can adopt a girl in early childhood with the intention of marrying her to her foster brother when she is old enough. Or a man can marry uxorilocally, allowing some of his children to take his wife's surname. Here I must bypass the interesting question of the nature of affinal ties in such cases.

cases, wife-giving affines perform actions that transform a person from one role into another or create a new role: babies are brought to life; sons are separated from one another and from their father; the dead are taken from the living. The power that wife-giving affines have to initiate growth in a lineage makes it appropriate that they have power to create change in other contexts as well.

The transitions in which the wife-giving affines have a role are those that involve substantial role changes for members of the woman's conjugal family; as we have seen, such changes are accompanied by rituals. Because of the circumstances in which they are enacted, these rituals form a distinguishable class of rituals, and may appropriately be called "the rituals of kinship." On the one hand, this class of rituals obviously differs from what Turner calls "rituals of affliction." Rituals of affliction among the Ndembu attempt to cure persons "believed to be afflicted with illness or misfortune by ancestor-spirits, witches, or sorcerers" (1968: 15). On the other hand, the rituals of kinship include rituals that have in other contexts been classified as life-crisis rituals. Turner defines these as "rituals designed to make the transition from one phase of life or social status to another" (1967: 7). The rituals of kinship and life-crisis rituals are overlapping but not identical categories; a transition occurring after a funeral, for example, might involve a life-crisis ritual, marking a change in the dead person's status, but unless it involved a change in his relations with his immediate kinsmen, it would not be a ritual of kinship.

The foregoing analysis helps explain why the rituals accompanying role changes affecting immediate kin—the rituals of kinship—are presided over by powerful affines. Because of the problematic nature of creating, changing, or breaking ties among primary kin, outside help is considered necessary. Wife-giving affines, having demonstrated with the gift of a bride their capacity to foster desirable changes, are appropriate sources of assistance. When a person must change or eliminate ties in which he is deeply embedded, the rituals of kinship take place. The powerful affines in attendance aid in the transition from one role to another.

One might object that although the debt owed wife-givers accounts for the gratitude shown them, it does not explain their authority. Is that authority not better explained by reference to a brother's responsibility for his sister's well-being? His obligation to see that his sister's children treat her filially gives him the right to call them to account and order them to change their ways if necessary. Unquestionably, this is a crucial element in the relation between a mother's brother and his sister's sons.

It seems compatible with the interpretation offered above, however, and beyond that, subsumable within it.

On the view I proposed, the character of the affinal relationship is determined by the initial act of the wife-givers. It is their role as the givers of the ultimately valuable commodity, a son-bearing woman, that invests them with exceptional capability and power. Their gift creates a hierarchy between the two families, with the wife-givers on top. There are three major instantiations of this hierarchical difference after the initial gift. First, the wife-givers are credited with the ability to promote desired change by intervening in their affines' family whenever the original woman and her conjugal family undergo role changes. This is an extension of the ability to initiate change they already demonstrated by providing for the growth of the lineage. The second ramification of the hierarchical difference between the affines is the wife-givers' ability to produce valuables; this is both an analogy to their initial ability to produce a woman and a reinforcement of it. Third, the authority of wife-givers over wife-takers is an extension of the ability of the former to make things happen in other contexts; if wife-givers have the power and ability to facilitate role changes, then surely they have the power and ability to exercise some control over wife-takers. But the *contexts* in which they exercise control are generally related to a brother's concern for his sister's welfare: at her funeral he inspects her body and may chastise her sons. Thus a brother's concern for his sister is encompassed by the interpretation of the affinal relationship I have offered.

There is still another way of understanding the authority exercised by wife-givers. It is not uncommon in this part of Taiwan for a spiritual being to start being worshipped as a god because he is credited with a great service such as curing a seriously ill person. In the subsequent relationship between the god and the worshipper, the worshipper expresses gratitude toward the god, but the god in turn is usually expected to manifest his power by granting other requests. Beyond this, because of his capacity to harm as well as help, the god will doubtless be feared if he shows anger; he will also be obeyed if he issues a direct command.

The position of the god in such a relationship parallels that of the wife-giving affines. The wife-givers perform an invaluable service by bestowing a wife on the wife-takers. Consequently, they receive the latter's gratitude. But at the same time, the wife-givers are expected to continue exercising their demonstrated ability to create change on numerous ritual occasions. Additionally they are regarded as potential agents of harm: people fear that the mother's brother might say phai:-ue (bad words) at the funeral and bring ruin on the family of the wife-

takers. Any commands they choose to make will be obeyed. Perhaps
this gives us another sense in which the proverb "In heaven there is
T'ien Kung, on earth mother's brother" might be understood. Yet the
power of mother's brother is more restricted than that of a god. In most
cases, his writ extends only to occasions on which his sister's welfare
is at stake, because he is obligated to see that she is cared for. Only
occasionally does his authority extend further: he can punish unfilial
behavior toward his sister's husband as well as his sister; and he can
punish any lack of respect toward himself. Unlike gods, wife-givers
have minor powers, restricted to a few uses. Yet, perhaps because they
wield god-like powers as living men, their capacities are only somewhat
less awesome.

The validity of the interpretations offered here cannot be assessed
fully without further study. For example, *if* it proves to be true that
most women marry into socially superior families, then the interpretation that sees the deference shown wife-givers as a kind of ceremonial
reversal of status (see above, p. 299) will gain credence. Or, *if* it can
be shown that there is in practice no bar to wife-givers in turn taking
wives from their wife-taking affines, then the theory that the ritual
ranking between affines is created by the giving of valuable gifts will
be undermined. Since the giving and receiving of gifts is carried out
over and over again in *public* contexts, it would seem that the ranking
created could not easily be reversed, so that those from whom one received the deference due a wife-giver could demand that deference
themselves. If, however, it is demonstrated that in practice the relationship can easily be reversed, then interpretations based on the relationship between brother and sister or on a family's desire to cut off its
daughters-in-law's relatives while keeping its daughters close would gain
in appeal. Both these explanations attribute the character of the affinal
tie primarily to relations within the family, and hence make public re-
versals of the wife-giving/wife-taking relationship less difficult to explain. Until these questions are resolved, the explanations proposed here
must remain tentative.

One final word can be added, however, to bolster the interpretation
I have favored throughout this essay. In *The Ritual Process* Turner suggests that in kinship-based societies, those who occupy positions on the
"structural" side of society, involving inheritance of property, jural authority, rights to office, and exclusive interests, can fruitfully be contrasted with those who occupy positions involving what he calls "communitas" (1969: 113ff). In brief, such positions emphasize interests
common to all humankind, such as the fertility of man and nature, the

mediation of conflict, the maintenance of peace. Drawing on material from several African societies (the Tallensi, the Nuer, and the Ashanti), he shows that these two aspects of society are often associated with two distinct principles of reckoning kinship. For example, if structural concerns such as rights in land and office flow patrilineally, then a person's ties to matrilateral relatives involve matters associated with communitas. In general the jurally weak side tends to have ritual powers associated with fertility or other life processes.

Such a summary statement of Turner's ideas cannot do them justice; yet even in this truncated form, their relevance to the affinal relationship in Ch'i-nan is clear. No matter how we resolve the problem of the relative standing of prospective affines, in most instances the natal kin of a man's mother hold less jural authority over him than the members of his own patrilineal family. His mother's relatives are also far less concerned with property ownership or political leadership within his family or lineage. In Chinese society, then, patrilineal kin are on the side of structural relationships; the mother's kin, jurally weak, fall on the side of relations associated with communitas. We have seen how the mother's brother encourages fertility and other desired changes in families; in addition, he represents impartial, disinterested authority in making peace between brothers or chastising an unfilial sister's son. The powers allotted to the mother's brother are not uncommonly allocated to the jurally weak side in other societies. To the natal kin of a married woman, herself a fount of natural fertility, is delegated the power to foster change, growth, and life.

The Written Memorial in Taoist Ceremonies

KRISTOFER M. SCHIPPER

In the religious vocabulary of the Taiwanese, the "reading of the memorial" (Hokkien: *thak-so*) denotes a particular solemn rite performed in connection with collective or private worship. In daily usage it means the recitation, by a priest, of a document written in literary language for one of several liturgical occasions. Most commonly the term is associated with rituals for the benefit of the living (whether the whole community or individual families), although the ritual for the dead may also include such a memorial. The memorial in question is a written prayer, addressed to the gods. It states the name and purpose of the ritual worship being performed, names and addresses of the worshippers, the date and place of the reading, and finally the vow, or *yüan* (wish *and* pledge). The use of written prayers in worship is in itself an interesting phenomenon, but it becomes even more intriguing when one looks into the question of who makes use of memorials in current ritual practice and who essentially eschews them.

Defining Taoism

Writing and reading memorials is a Taoist practice. But Taoism is difficult to define in present-day Chinese observance, in part because it is so often confounded with both folk religion and various forms of sectarianism. The function of the Taoist priest, in particular, resists definition. When he serves as a liturgical specialist in such collective rituals as the great community festivals—the *chiao*—his role is clear. After all, such festivals have been part of the liturgical tradition of Taoism since Han times. But the Taoist priest or *Tou-su* in Taiwan is not just a ritual Master. He also acts as an exorcist and healer, expelling and pacifying demons. And it is this aspect of his role that normally is highlighted in literature and art. To compound the confusion, most of the Tou-su's functions are also performed by the *Huat-su* (in this context to be translated as magician). On liturgical occasions the two perform the same rituals, composed of the same, vernacular, incantations. The Tou-su even "borrows" a vestimentary element from the Huat-su: a red turban or headscarf, which he winds around his own headdress. If a Tou-su is ordained as a head priest, he undergoes initiation rites that qualify him as a Huat-su; this is stated expressly in the orthodox ordination liturgy in use on Taiwan. The converse, however, does not occur: a Huat-su is never habilitated to perform the Tou-su's communal chiao ritual, the funeral rites, or wedding ceremonies.[1]

The rites of the Huat-su are incorporated into the solemn Taoist communal liturgy and performed in conjunction with it, either separately by a Huat-su or by a Tou-su. The communal chiao celebration similarly incorporates the Buddhist rite of *p'u-tu*, the Feeding of the Hungry Spirits. The rite is performed either by Tou-su, by Buddhist priests, or by both simultaneously but at different altars. Here again the Taoist, when performing the p'u-tu rites, superimposes a "Buddhist" headdress on his own. The simultaneous performance of rites from different religions has always baffled students of Chinese society.[2] Unfortunately I am not yet in a position to end their bafflement, not having enough detailed information about the different persuasions to draft a synoptic table of rituals performed by the professional specialists of different liturgical systems. For the present purpose it suffices to emphasize that although Tou-su and Huat-su perform the same rites, there is one essential difference between them: a pure Huat-su ritual does not make use of written prayers, whereas the same ritual performed by a Tou-su does.

An example will clarify the difference. In a rite called Presenting Money for the Restoration of Luck, *Cin-ci: po-un*, large sums of paper money are transferred to the Treasury of Fate to offset deficiencies in a person's destiny. The ritual, in vernacular, describes the journey of the divine messenger charged with the transfer. The same text is used throughout Taiwan (and also in the Pescadores), by Tou-su and Huat-su alike. But there is a significant difference in execution: the Tou-su includes a written memorial, which is presented with its own ritual context of several hymns and the libation of wine. The Huat-su, who presents no memorial, often has a medium take his place at the altar, and

---

[1] But a Huat-su may take part in these, either as an exorcist or as a conductor of mediums.

[2] Marcel Granet, *La Religion des Chinois*, 2d ed. (Paris, 1951), pp. 157–64.

it is the spirit of the medium that makes the journey and effects the transfer of funds. For the Tou-su it is the burning of the memorial that effects the transfer. The reading of the memorial, in this instance as in a great many others, may be taken as the hallmark of Taoist practice. The memorials are always written and always read by a Taoist priest.

The evidence suggests that this has always been so. The *Wei-lieh*, one of the earliest official sources we have on the history of the Taoist church, gives few specific facts, but it does mention the salient particularity that the priests offered written memorials to the Agents of the Universe.[3] Without necessarily waxing philological, we must take historical sources into account. For one thing, Taoist memorials are part of a written tradition; today's *shu* are copied from examples in manuscript handbooks handed down from generation to generation of the hereditary priesthood. To ignore this tradition would be to amputate a dimension of the present. Moreover, there is nothing against regarding the past as a series of stages where the pertinent data suffice to reconstruct a possible context. Here, however, I must regretfully confine my discussion to present-day Taiwan. But I do want to stress that the practices flourishing in Taiwan today are not an isolated case, but part of the greater liturgical tradition of China.

The Tou-su is colloquially called *sai-kong*, Master. His position is normally hereditary. Adoption is possible, but it is rare and difficult. In order to become a priest, one has to have the bones, *sai-kong-kut*. Only head priests, *Tou-tiu:*, receive ordination in the Orthodox Church of the Heavenly Master. The rank they thus obtain is expressed in connection with a Register, *Lu*, which in principle is a talismanic list of divine intermediaries who will obey the priest's commands and enable him to communicate with the different spheres of the universe. The more extensive the Lu, the higher the priest's rank. The priest's rank in the Taoist church is specified in the octroi granted by the Heavenly Master, who traditionally resided in the Lung-hu Mountains of Kiangsi province. Pilgrimages to that spot by prospective ordinees from important priestly families in Taiwan were by no means rare. The postwar presence of the 63d Heavenly Master as a refugee in Taiwan has made the number of ordained priests grow, but not significantly. In any case, the intervention by the Heavenly Master only consecrates an initiation that has already taken place. The newly initiated priest receives the ritual corpus, as well as, for instance, the secret contents of the ordination Registers of divine intermediaries, at home. Thus local tradition could be assimilated whenever necessary.

[3] *Wei-lieh*, ap. *San-kuo-chih*, *Wei-shu*, ch. 8, p. 45b (*chien-pen*).

The final and decisive condition for ordination as a Taoist priest is local popular support. One has to be accepted. The ordination ceremony (not to be confused with the granting of the Heavenly Master's octroi, which requires a pilgrimage) is of the solemn chiao type, and involves community participation and consent. Perhaps as little as a century ago, the community bore the expenses of ordination. Nowadays, the priest's own family pays most of the expenses, but the festive ordination ceremonies, sometimes lasting three days, still take place in the local temple and are open to the public. They invariably attract large crowds. The priest is very much a son of the people.

The octroi of the Heavenly Master assigns the priest to a diocese, *chih*, which is not a particular place but one of the twenty-eight mansions of the Chinese zodiac. There is no formal relationship between the priest and his place of residence. His services are sought by those who need them on a contractual basis, for a mutually agreed remuneration. A priest's prestige is enhanced when his services are solicited by people from afar, especially when they are for a communal chiao. For an equal occasion, the services of a Tou-su are generally more expensive than those of Buddhist priests or Huat-su. In postwar Tainan, Taoist funerals were double the price of Buddhist ones, and several times as expensive as those performed by members of vegetarian sects (*chai-yu*). After ordination, the sai-kong is politely addressed as Tou-tiu:. His friends and neighbors will call him by his personal name followed by the suffix *sian*, Master. In his role of master of a large ceremony, he is called popularly *Tiong-cun*, the Worthy in the Center, referring to his position at the altar, where he occupies the center, surrounded by four or more acolytes.[4]

I should like now to examine both kinds of memorials: the ones used in large collective services conducted by a head priest and those used in small individual rites. In emphasizing the distinction between them, I am doing as the priests do. The rites of the communal services, in their canonical aspect, are called "the great ritual." The exorcising and healing rites he shares with the Huat-su, the Tou-su calls the "small rituals."

Memorial for a Collective Service

The memorial for a collective service I have chosen as an example was used at a chiao held in 1969, in the village of A-lien in the north

---

[4] Acolytes are not necessarily younger than the priest. Ordination is a privilege accorded only one son in each generation of a priestly family. Many Tou-su are never ordained, remaining at the rank of disciple all their life. They are nonetheless called sai-kong, and can perform rituals and write and read memorials on their own, but they cannot conduct a group of priests in a ceremony.

of Kao-hsiung hsien. A-lien Village is the administrative center of the similarly named canton. At the turn of the century it became an important sugar-growing area, and much of its relative commercial and administrative importance dates from that time. The village now comprises three hamlets, Ch'ing-lien, Ho-lien, and A-lien, the first two names being derived from that of the village temple, the Ch'ing-ho Kung. The entire agglomeration has about 5,000 inhabitants, according to the census of 1959. Since the end of the war, the three hamlets have collaborated in a Great Communal Sacrifice, *ta-chiao*, every twelve years. Participation of the villagers is near unanimous, with almost 80 percent of them contributing financially to this festival.

A collective memorial such as the one used for A-lien's Great Sacrifice is written in bold *k'ai-shu* on a long piece of high-quality red paper. After the memorial is written, the paper is folded like an accordion, the folds being about three inches apart, and the title of the document is written in large characters on the outer fold. This is the main memorial. As is customary, the A-lien memorial had several annexes, executed on paper of the same size and folded in the same way, which bore names of all the faithful, *sin-su*, i.e., those who had helped finance the festival. The A-lien memorial had three such appendixes, one for each hamlet. The text of the collective memorial, including all the annexes, is copied a second time on a far larger sheet of red paper, one more than three feet high and several yards long. This is the *pang* or placard, posted at the start of the ceremonies on the outer wall of the village temple for everyone to see. The placard is usually written in the special style known as *ta-tzu*, which was used for official announcements by the Ch'ing dynasty.

The following is a somewhat condensed version of the main memorial. I have numbered the sections into which the original document is divided in order to facilitate reference to my commentary, which follows the translation.

1. *Blessed Memorial of the Fragrant Sacrifice of the Golden Register for Thanksgiving and Prayer for Peace in the Ch'ing-ho Kung temple at A-lien, the eleventh month of the year* chi-yu [1969], *the 24th, 25th, and 26th days.*

2. *The Immortal Grand Official of the Canonical Register of the Orthodox Covenant, Holder and Preacher of the Law of the Divine Empyrean, appointed Prefect of the Boards of Heavenly Medicine, Fate, and Thunder, the humble servant Ch'en Ting-sheng,*

3. *with sincere fear and apprehension, bowing and knocking his head in a hundred-fold salute, the aforenamed servant humbly presents this memorial on behalf of*

4. the population of A-lien, Kao-hsiung hsien, Taiwan province of the Republic of China,

5. having all gathered at the Ch'ing-ho Kung temple to profess their faith in the Tao and prepare a sacrifice in thanksgiving and prayer for peace, to protect the territory and cultivate blessings.

6. [Each of the following titles is preceded by a person's name.] *Chief of the Assembly, Chief of the Sacrifice, Chief of the Altar, Chief of the P'u-tu, Head of the Lamp of Heaven; Head of the Lamp of the Three Officials, Head of the Lamp of the Heavenly Master, Head of the Lamp of the Supreme Emperor, Head of the Lamp of Kuan Yin, Head of the Lamp of Prayer for Peace; Assistant Chief of the Assembly, Assembly Coordinator, Assembly Director, Assembly Cantor, Assembly Correspondent [?]; General Manager.* [Here, at the reading, may be inserted the names of the faithful, i.e., the family heads whose names appear in the annexes, followed by a count of their sons and daughters. Sons are counted as *ting*, daughters as *k'ou*. A name may thus read as follows: Chang Ping-ting, five ting, two k'ou (five sons, two daughters). In the three annexes, there were altogether 780 heads of household listed; I did not count up the children.]

7. All these, together with the masses of believers, respectfully, having bathed and lit incense, venture to do obeisance and communicate that:

8. Heaven is high but hears those who are low, the gods can be stirred to answer those who approach them. Thus the Pole Star did away with the calamity about to befall Chao-tzu,[5] and the [god of the] Ni Mountain answered the prayer of Confucius's father. These proofs of ancient times today give us trust. But, considering that we, residing together in our tree-shaded village, while maintaining the countryside's tradition of benevolence, have experienced in former years great natural calamities, as well as periodic epidemics that contaminated our territory, disturbing the peace of people and animals alike; therefore we have, with utmost sincerity, lit incense, bowed our heads, and invoked Our Divine Benefactor Marshal Hsin, as chief of the population, to act on our behalf and transmit to the High Perfect Beings of the Three Worlds and the High Firmament as well as to the multitude of Divine Saints, the sacrificial vows we have pronounced: That epidemics may disappear and calamities may cease to occur in our region; that auspi-

---

[5] This is an allusion to a little-known story, told in a commentary of the Dipper Sutra, the *Pei-tou-ching*, of the Yüan dynasty. The book is extant as a popular catechism in Taiwan. It also figures in the Taoist Canon, vol. 527, *T'ai-shang hsüan-ling Pei-tou pen-ming yen-sheng chen-ching chu*, ch. 2, p. 17a.

cious emanations may herald happiness and that felicitous blessings may be diffused in our community; that each family may prosper, man and animal alike may have peace, grains be abundant, cattle multiply. Having indeed moved [Heaven and Saints with our prayers], *we now evidently must answer.*

9. *Through divination we selected the 24th, 25th, and 26th days of this month to devote ourselves to our religion and gather at the temple, erecting an altar in order to celebrate a great communal fragrant sacrifice of the Golden Register for Thanksgiving and Prayer for Peace, the ceremonies lasting for three days and nights, beginning with the sounding of the drum at the propitious hour* [here follows a list of all the rites performed during the three days of ceremonies].

10. *All this in order to thank the High Perfect Beings above and ask for peace and blessings below.*

11. *The . . . day of the eleventh month of the cyclical year* chi-yu, *the humble servant Ch'en Ting-sheng, prostrated, salutes and with humility presents this memorial.*

1. Collective services for the benefit of the living are now called sacrifices of the Golden Register, *Chin-lu-chiao*, whereas services for the dead are called retreats of the Yellow Register, *Huang-lu-chai*. This distinction, which has developed since the Sung dynasty, is a rather artificial one. It reflects the association of funeral with mortification and of festival with sacrifice and communion. In practice, both kinds of liturgy comprise a retreat as well as a subsequent sacrifice. In the present case of a three-day chiao ceremony, the first day, in terms of the rituals performed, is taken up with preparation for the retreat, the second day (counting from midnight to midnight) constitutes the retreat, and the third day is devoted to the sacrifice, chiao, from which the whole ceremony derives its name. As for the terms Golden and Yellow Registers, they originate in the early Taoist seasonal festivals, the Retreats of the Three Origins, *San-yüan chai*. The first festival, which fell in the New Year period and was called *Shang-yüan*, was dedicated to Heaven. Its divine administration was listed on the Golden Register. Similarly, the festival at the beginning of winter was called *Hsia-yüan*, and was dedicated to the earth and the infernal world. The dignitaries of those regions were known from the Yellow Register.

Thanksgiving, *Hsieh-en*, is a generic term for this class of chiao. Other similar large collective services are: Averting Calamities, *Jang-tsai*; Inauguration (of temples), *Ch'ing-ch'eng*; and Anniversary (of deities), *Chu-shou*. The ritual actually performed varies little from one class to another. Variety is introduced in the memorial and associated written prayers, petitions, and other religious documents. The term Prayer for Peace, *ch'i-an*, figures generally in the titles of all chiao. At the end of the title appears the term *fu-shu*, blessed memorial, with *fu* denoting the propitious action from Heaven anticipated as a result of the sacrifice. Instead of *shu* we often find *chang*, which in Taoist tradition has a slightly more specific meaning. Note that here, as well as at the end of the memorial, the year is indicated by its cyclical number only. This is a Taoist tradition.

2. The long title of the head priest in charge of the ceremonies can only be approximated. This title is given the priest on ordination, and every priest's is slightly different. The first part corresponds to the Lu, a general title signifying the priest's rank. The second part, beginning "Holder and Preacher . . . ," is the *chih*, the office to which the priest has been appointed.

The Lu of the Orthodox Covenant (with the Mighty Beings), *Cheng-yi meng-wei*, is the present-day equivalent of the fifth rank in the hierarchy of the Church of the Heavenly Master headquartered in the Lung-hu Mountains (which had little influence in Taiwan before the arrival of the 63d Heavenly Master). In Fukien and Taiwan, however, the Lu under discussion means much more, as is shown among other things by its association with the term *chi-chiu*, libationer. The chi-chiu, long forgotten by the clerical administration of Lung-hu, was in Han times the headman of the early Taoist communities. The title, borrowed from the Han rural administration, denoted a village elder, the dignitary chosen to make libations to the ancestors and local deities before community banquets. These "wise men" also had the prerogative of memorializing the throne in the event of bad management by local imperial officials. It is interesting that this title should have remained attached to the office of the ordained priest in Fukien and Taiwan while elsewhere it has been completely forgotten. More or less the same situation obtains for the Lu of the Orthodox Covenant. In Taiwan it is not just another rank, but is the highest title a traditional priest can be given at ordination. The point is of some historical interest because *Cheng-yi meng-wei Lu* was also the highest rank possible for a newly ordained priest in the early period of the movement. In later times, as the Han church was diminishing in importance, this title remained a prerogative for all Taoist priests conducting communal services, including those of sects and movements, such as the Ling-pao and Mao-shan sects, that did not belong to the Church of the Heavenly Master. This shows the fundamental importance of the liturgical canon elaborated and established in the early days of the Taoist church.

The second part of the title, corresponding to the "office," was invented by the magically oriented instigators of the New Orthodox Church of the Heavenly Master of Southern Sung times and is of little importance. It denotes nothing specific, and can be chosen individually from several hundred variants, at random or through divination.

3. The expression of apprehension and humility is a standard formula found not only in this kind of Taoist literature, but also in similar documents of the imperial administration. The priest's function is defined as presenting the memorial to Heaven on the community's behalf. This role is not explicitly mentioned in the ordination documents, which instead stress the opposite role: *tai-t'ien hsing-hua,* civilizing (i.e. converting) on behalf of Heaven. The capacity to address memorials stems simply from the priest's status as an official of the divine administration and, as such, a mediator.

4. The population is defined as *chung-hu-min,* all the inhabitants. Geographically, the village is defined as part of the worldly administration. Through the mediation of the priest, however, it also belongs to the divine administration. As we have seen, the time of the festival is mentioned in cyclical characters only, without reference to any official era name. The place is immanent, the time transcendent. Dioceses, along with other administrative units, are invariably expressed in time values.

5. Chiao in Taiwan are invariably held in the local temple. This relationship is a profound one. Newly built temples are consecrated through a chiao, as is every major renovation. This in itself accounts for the regular celebrations of community chiao at intervals of approximately one generation.

All the rites of the first two days in our present example, that is, the retreat part of the service, are held inside the temple, behind locked doors. The greater part of the sacrifice part takes place in the open air, in front of, or near, the temple. The preparations for a chiao require major alterations in both the interior and the exterior of the sanctuary. Inside, the statues of the deities normally worshipped in the temple are removed from their regular niches, situated at the noble side (opposite the entrance), and placed on the exact opposite side, with their backs turned toward the closed doors. In this location, they are said to be "inspecting the sacrifice," *chien-chiao.* Joining them are a host of usually smaller statues brought from the home altars of the faithful (who do not themselves participate in the proceedings), so that the part of the altar established inside the temple is crowded with deities of all possible kinds. Their place, which has a definite liturgical function, is known as *San-kuan-cho,* Table of the Three Officials (of Heaven, Earth, and Water), who represent, theologically, all the higher spiritual beings this side of the Tao. Opposite this table, at the noble side of the sanctuary, are placed five or more votive oil lamps. They are called *tou-teng*, bushel lamps (and in fact rest on pedestals made from rice measures of one bushel and filled with rice grains). These lamps symbolize *fate*: bushel = measure = the Dipper = the controller of Destiny.

6. The memorial next lists the names and titles of the community representatives. There is a connection between them and the bushel lamps, because each lamp represents the destiny of a given representative; together they stand for the fate of the community. The representative dignitaries or "Chiefs" are the only members of the community to participate in the ceremonies. The five main dignitaries, the Chief of the Assembly, et al., are the traditional ones. The title of the last of the five, Head of the Lamp of Heaven, refers to another votive lamp, which unlike the tou-teng is placed outside, in front of the temple, where it hangs on a long bamboo pole. Made of paper and round in form, it bears in large red characters the inscription "Lord of Heaven." A similar bamboo pole with an identical lamp is installed in front of the Head of the Lamp's house. After the chiao, he may keep both lamps, hanging them before his home altar as a token of his dignity.

Similar votive lamps are dedicated to other deities who occupy secondary altars during the festival: the Three Officials, the Heavenly Master, Kuan Yin (associated with the p'u-tu), etc. Before these secondary altars are lamps like the one described above (the one for the Three Officials being hung on the temple ceiling) and similar poles before the dwellings of those responsible for them. All the ordinary faithful also have lamps on bamboo poles in front of their houses. Their lamps do not carry any deity's name, but are simply marked "prayer for peace." They are represented at the ceremonies by a headman. Finally there are several assistant dignitaries, aides to the Chief of the Assembly. In certain rites, the five main dignitaries represent the faithful of the five orients, but in most cases their function is honorific, and very vague. They have the privilege and duty of assisting at all the ceremonies, holding incense sticks, standing when the priest stands, kneeling when he kneels, and having their personal fate lamps receive the most intense impact of the forthcoming blessings. They also have their names on the main memorial, while the names of the ordinary faithful are entered on the annexes, the so-called *ting-k'ou shu.*

Every family that wants its name included in the memorial must pay a certain sum, which is fixed before the chiao at a general community meeting. The basic rate for each family is the same, with increments for each child (the more one is blessed, the more one pays). In A-lien, most families paid NT $20 (U.S. $.50) per household, plus NT $5 for each son. People known to have been successful in business and community leaders are supposed to pay more. It is among the latter that the big contributors who serve as Chiefs and Assistant Chiefs at the ceremonies are recruited. Either a high price for each such post is fixed in advance by common consent, or the offices are distributed through divination, i.e. the throwing of the divination blocks among the largest contributors. The Chiefs are mostly the elderly heads of large and wealthy local families. They are not necessarily the organizers of the chiao. The latter, the *tung-shih, kuan-li,* or whatever they may be called, normally do not have their names entered in a special way on the memorial. But the custom of including them and their functions is gaining acceptance. In A-lien, only the main organizer, called the General Manager, gained the privilege of being mentioned along with the Chiefs.

The precise nomenclature of the dignitaries and representatives varies from place to place and is subject to (more or less precisely recalled) local traditions. In any case the Taoist priest, unless invited to intervene, accepts all titles and names as they are supplied to him by the organizers and enters them on the memorial.

7. This is the standard presentation of all the faithful at the chiao, and serves as the opening formula for the "intention" that follows. The reference to purification is pertinent. At a variable interval before the chiao begins, the entire village starts to observe certain restrictions: meager food, no sexual intercourse, no gambling, etc. The evening before the ceremonies begin, everyone takes a bath.

8. In general, the wording of the shu corresponds to established models and formulas. The text of the so-called intention or *yi,* however, in which the community explains why it is holding the service and formulates its vows, is free. The community, as was the case here, may commission someone to write it. In earlier times, many great men of letters wrote intentions for Taoist memorials, and some examples of their work have come down to us.[6] The priest, too, normally has a manuscript collection of ready-made yi, which he may propose if the community itself lacks the means to produce one. In any case, the yi is considered the literary work of a layman, something outside the scope of Taoist writings, which are all supposed to be divinely inspired.

An intention normally begins with a few cosmological maxims, followed by a summary explanation of the reason for the service. In the

[6] See, for instance, the Collected Works of Ou-yang Hsiu (A.D. 1007–72), *Ou-yang wen-chung kung wen-chi,* ch. 82.

present case, we see that the community has made a vow of a very general nature toward its tutelary saint, the Marshal Hsin, to whom the A-lien temple is dedicated. Hsin Yüan Shuai is a saint of modern Taoism. His cult is reputed to have been brought to A-lien from Foochow, and to have started in A-lien as a semi-private medium cult on a farm just outside the village. The first sanctuary was built around 1860, also outside the village. Only in 1905, ten years after the arrival of the Japanese, was a communal effort mounted to build a temple in A-lien itself, of which Hsin Yüan Shuai became the tutelary saint. Before its own temple was built, A-lien belonged to an association of twelve communities that worshipped at the temple in the neighboring village of T'u-k'u (not to be confused with a place of the same name in Yün-lin hsien). At this temple, dedicated to Hsüan T'ien Shang Ti, the Ruler of the North, exorcising deity and divine protector of the Ming, a chiao involving all twelve communities was held every three years.[7] In A-lien today, it is Marshal Hsin who is in charge of the population (*wei-min tso-chu* says the memorial) and who transfers their prayers (*tai-wei chuan tsou*). The latter function, as we have seen, belongs during the chiao to the head priest, while Marshal Hsin is temporarily reduced to the role of communicant. But the chiao is also intended to be a service of thanksgiving for the blessings received through the Marshal's mediation. He is the divine benefactor of the village. The offerings are in the first place directed to him, as a solemn consecration of the bonds between him and the community.

8. The program of a chiao is fixed by the Taoist priest in accordance with immutable standards, the main variant being one of duration. A five-day chiao includes many more rituals than one lasting two days, but the same rationale underlies all such ceremonies, and they all follow the sequence of preparation-retreat-sacrifice. The sequence and also the time of execution (morning, evening, night) are all predetermined; the memorials preserved over the last two hundred years, from both Taiwan and the mainland, as well as those preserved in the Taoist Canon, show that the system is very traditional indeed and virtually unchangeable. During the three days of ceremonies at A-lien, eighteen different rituals were performed by the head priest and his four acolytes, two (preliminary purification and cloture) were performed by a single acolyte, and the reading of the different sutras and litanies (during the intervals between rituals) was done by one acolyte at a time, on a rotating basis.

----

[7] Among the villages that participated was Kang-shan, now an important town of 25,000 inhabitants on the main railroad line.

The memorial enumerates all the rituals, one by one. Included in the list are rituals that may or may not be executed by the Taoists: the Buddhist p'u-tu and the *siu:-pieng*, a Huat-su ritual. At the A-lien chiao, the Feeding of the Hungry Spirits was done by Buddhists as well as Taoists, and the siu:-pieng by a local Huat-su. Both rituals are performed on the third day of the festival, the day of sacrifice. Both also take place near or during the evening, when in principle the Taoist ritual is already completed. But both figure in the Taoist memorial as an integrated part of the service.

At each of the eighteen major rituals, the memorial is read at least once. Although the document is in the head priest's name, the actual reciting of it is done by an acolyte. During the recitation, the head priest prostrates himself in front of the altar, and the Chiefs, behind him, follow suit. During certain rituals the head priest performs a silent meditation while the reading goes on. His meditation takes the form of a confession of sins, directed to the patriarchs of the Taoist church, notably the original Heavenly Master. In the ritual the head priest is considered the patriarchs' representative, and, while presenting the memorial, he transfers it to the patriarchs for them to transmit higher up, to the Lord of Heaven at the pinnacle of the pantheon. The day date is left open at the end of the memorial because the priest cannot foresee the date at which the patriarchs will effect the transfer. The patriarchs will insert it themselves when the time comes.

Only the main part of the memorial is normally read at all eighteen major rituals. The complete version, including annexes, with all the names of the common faithful, is read on only three occasions. The first is at the very beginning of the service. The second is at the very solemn ritual with which the third day of ceremonies, the day devoted to the sacrifice, begins. A high platform (with an altar table and offerings on top) is erected in the open air, in front of the temple. The head priest and his acolytes ceremonially ascend this altar to present the message of the impending sacrifice to the Lord of Heaven. On this solemn public occasion, the names of all the faithful, along with the numbers of sons and daughters, are recited. While this ritual is taking place, each household prepares, at home, offerings to the Lord of Heaven. Among them is usually a sacrificed pig. The offerings are put on a festively decorated table at the foot of the lamp pole. When the ritual is over, the acolytes visit each home to purify and consecrate the offerings. Their duties include the recitation of a short individual memorial stating the household's exact address, the names and birthdates of all its members, and a general prayer to "the High Perfect

Beings." This part of the communal service is called in the main memorial *ke-chia hsin-hsiang yen men hsüan-shu*. For the Chiefs and other dignitaries, the head priest, surrounded by his acolytes, performs this service. In these cases the individual offerings are very abundant and presented in a special setting, often a temporary "Altar of Heaven" erected in front of or near the Chief's house. These temporary altars, made of bamboo and paperboard, are elaborately painted and ornamented so as to resemble a real temple. They sometimes have two or more stories, making them towers from which to address Heaven. Inside these altars, the Chiefs expose their family's heirlooms and treasures: antiques, silver and gold coins, dwarf trees, etc.

10. All memorials of this kind end with this phrase. The ultimate recipients of the village's request are the High Perfect Beings, i.e. all the gods of Heaven.

In a highly condensed form, the memorial incorporates all aspects of the service. It is read a final time at the solemn presentation of the sacrifice, the real chiao ceremony, the concluding ritual of the entire celebration. After this, the bans are lifted and the Feeding of the Hungry Spirits can begin, to be followed by the festive communal banquets at which the offerings are consumed. Unlike individual memorials and the many other written prayers presented at almost every rite, which are invariably burned as part of the ceremony, a collective memorial such as the one discussed here is preserved. The head priest keeps it at his home altar as a keepsake and a model for future reference. The similarly worded placard, by contrast, is carefully taken down and burned.

Memorial for a Private Ritual

The memorials for the "small" rites do not differ essentially from the one we have seen. Although they are considerably shorter and lack some elements of the collective memorial, they follow the same basic pattern. They are more specific, however, in all cases being addressed to a particular deity.

Today is presented: At [such and such place] *of* [such and such] *hsien of Taiwan province* [etc.], *confessing his Taoist faith and wishing to avert calamities and restore his good fate through the presentation of money, the faithful*———, *born at ... o'clock ... day ... month ... year, his destiny being controlled by the luster of* [such and such] *Stellar Official of the Dipper, he, together with the members of his family, on this day, with a sincere heart, wishes to salute and communicate that: Considering that this person is prostrated by an unhealthy body and by much bad luck, we fear that the mighty planets are having a destructive influence and that obnoxious rays are attacking him; we wish to seek peace and security and particularly pray to avert calamity, hoping that the benevolence of the Jade Emperor from Above and the High Saints may bring forth blessings, that the Pole Star may have an auspicious influence, warding off evil luminaries, bringing back auspicious influences, so that the personal fate-controlling star may shine brightly, his lot may improve, calamities be diminished, health be excellent [etc., etc.], we have chosen, by divination, this auspicious day for a Single Feast of excellent retribution, consisting of all necessary good rites to cultivate blessings. For this we offer respectfully this memorial to the High Beings above, for inspection. On . . . day, . . . month, [cyclical year], by [name of priest].*

The official title of the priest is lacking. This is natural, as most small rites are performed by unordained sai-kong. In the memorial the priest is called simply *shih*, gentleman, or *hsin-shih*, faithful. This does not imply, however, that the memorial can also be presented by a simple layman.

The service is counted not as an assembly (*hui*), but as a feast laid out for the deities. The presentation of money is a rather simple rite. Stacks of cultic paper money of different kinds are offered and burned to resupply the heavenly "treasury," from which the amount necessary for the life luck of each person has to be provided. If through negligence or wasteful or sinful conduct this store has been depleted, then it must be replenished. The text of the ritual that enacts the presentation describes, in vernacular verses of seven characters, the journey of an emissary who passes through mythical regions to the Dipper, where the controlling administration of Fate is located. This type of ritual is entirely the province of the Huat-su, and the reading of the memorial, together with its ritual frame (a hymn, an invitation and invocation of a few abstract Taoist gods, a triple libation, and the burning of the memorial), is an added feature. In Huat-su liturgy, the enactment of this ritual may involve a medium. The latter, in a trance, makes a journey to the Dipper while several attendants chant a description of his journey to the accompaniment of a small drum. In this case the spirit of the medium accomplishes what is done in the orthodox version through the burning of the memorial: the transmission of the prayer.

Why prayers in writing? The remarks of T. H. Hsien in his introduction to *Written on Bamboo and Silk* are instructive.[8] It seems that Chinese writing was invented in the first place in order to communicate with spiritual beings.

For us, the memorial and its use suggest a context that can only be seen as a centralized, orthodox, and highly institutionalized morality religion. The collective ritual embraces in both theory and practice all the inhabitants of a given place. Among other things the memorial is a census of the population—until rather recently, the only one of its kind. The chiao is a sacrifice to Heaven. From the viewpoint of the central government, this was an imperial prerogative. The Ch'ing code formally forbids the burning of chiao memorials by Taoist priests.[9] Of course the practice was never stopped or even interrupted. It simply was ignored in the writings of the bureaucracy, and remained an immensely important factor in the lives of the common people. The periodic chiao sacrifice is nothing less than the constitutional assembly of an autonomous state, during which the Chiefs renew their alliance and infeudation, and a collective covenant is made. This assertion of regional autonomy portends direct conflict with the central authority. But the present-day Taoist church does not represent a rebel ideology. In Taiwan, it is simply *the* church, the church that marries and buries people, that assembles and divides communities. As representative of the divine, as minister to the community, the Taoist priest is undisputed. His power is questioned only from below, by the spirit-medium cults, and his authority by the new sects—the very forces that in the past he has overcome. As to the outcome of the eternal conflict with the state, it remains to be seen.

[8] T. H. Hsien, *Written on Bamboo and Silk* (Chicago, 1962), p. 3.
[9] Guy Boulais, *Manuel du code chinois* (Shanghai, 1924), p. 360.

Orthodoxy and Heterodoxy in Taoist Ritual

MICHAEL SASO

The ritual of religious Taoism is esoteric; that is, it is not meant to be directly understood and witnessed by all the faithful. The esoteric meaning of Taoist ritual and magic is concealed from all but the initiated; only after many years of training and a gradual introduction to religious secrets is the disciple deemed worthy of elevation to the rank of master and full knowledge of the esoteric meanings of religious ritual. For this reason the aspirant disciple tries to join the entourage of a famous master, so he can learn the formulas for ritual performance and gradually gain access to the hidden aspects of ritual Taoism.

The expertise of a Taoist priest is judged by several criteria, the first one being his external performance of ritual. Learning to sing well, to dance the various ritual steps, perform the mudras or hand symbols, memorize the several hundred ceremonial texts and innumerable accompanying formulas, is of course the primary goal of the young disciple in attaching himself to a famous master. Most of the Taoists in Taiwan never go beyond this stage, simply because the ability to perform the standard repertoire of rituals will enable a priest to attract a large enough following among the pious faithful to earn an excellent livelihood. If he can write a stylish *fu* talisman to cure illness, exorcise evil spirits with sword and oxhorn trumpet, perform ritual dances and acrobatic tumbling, climb a blade-side-up sword ladder, and win a reputation for being a powerful magician, the demands for his services will be almost endless. Most disciples therefore study with a master just long enough to learn the external rituals and enough of the esoteric doctrines to lend credence to their ritual performance.

The second criterion for judging a Taoist, which determines his rank at ordination, is his knowledge of the esoteric secrets of the religion, including the ability to perform the meditations and breath-control techniques of internal alchemy (*nei-tan*), and to recite the classical orthodox lists of spirits' names and apparel and the mantric summons found in the Taoist Canon. These lists are called *Lu*, or registers, and appear in the earliest Taoist collections in the Canon. (See Saso: 1972a, chap. 5, and 1972b for a description of some of the registers currently used in Taiwan.) Taoists who call themselves "orthodox" or "orthodox one" (*Cheng-i*) are required to know at least one of the three ancient Lu of spirits' names and apparel. The first of these, the *Cheng-i meng-u ei lu*, appears in Volume 877 of the Taoist Canon. It is the longest of the registers, containing 24 chapters. The second is called the *T'ai-shang cheng-i meng-wei fa lu*, in fourteen chapters, and occurs in Volume 878 of the Canon. The third, known as *Cheng-i fa-wen shih lu*, also found in Volume 878 of the Canon, is the shortest and least prestigious of the three. It contains only ten chapters, and the smallest number of spirits. Taoists who call themselves *San-wu tu-kung* ("Three-five Surveyors of Merit") are supposed to have memorized the names, apparel, and description of spirits given in this register.[1] Taoist priests are assigned a rank and a title at ordination according to the number of esoteric spirits they can describe and summon during the performance of liturgy. A Taoist is called "orthodox" if he or she knows at least one of the three orthodox Cheng-i lists of spirits' names included in the Canon.

There are two crucial problems facing the scholar who would plumb the secrets of Taoist ritual. The first is to gain access to the private documents that reveal a Taoist's Lu with its lists of spirits' names and descriptions.[2] The second is to receive the oral explanation or gloss that accompanies the text, demonstrating the appropriate mudra, mantra, and circulation of breath used in summoning and controlling the spirit during the performance of orthodox ritual.[3] In Taiwan I have not met a single Taoist who does not claim to be "orthodox" or *cheng* (as opposed to "heterodox" or *hsieh*) in his performance of ritual. Furthermore, there are deep rivalries and antagonisms between Taoist masters of different schools, all of whom claim to possess the traditional orthodox registers of spirits' names and summons, deriving from antiquity. Besides the three

[1] Michael Saso, *Taoism and the Rite of Cosmic Renewal* (Pullman, Wash., 1972), ch. 5, and "Red-head and Black-head: The Classification of the Taoists of Taiwan According to the Documents of the 61st Generation Heavenly Master," *Bulletin of the Institute of Ethnology* (Academia Sinica, Nankang, 1972), No. 30, 2: 69–82.

[2] The Taoist's Lu can be found in the manual of written documents called *wen chien*, meant for the Taoist master's private use.

[3] The oral secrets (*k'ou-chüeh*) are often written out in the esoteric rubrical manuals *mi-chüeh*, also meant for the master's private use. The wen chien and mi-chüeh manuals of Taiwan's Taoists are often more complete and systematized than those found in the Taoist Canon.

above-named registers, I have found many other Lu currently used by the "orthodox" Taoists of northern Taiwan, that is, from the Taipei Basin southward through T'ao-yüan, Hsin-chu, and Miao-li hsien. Among these registers are the *T'ai-shang pei-chi fu mo shen-chou sha kuei lu*, found in Volume 879 of the Canon, and the *Kao-shang shen-hsiao yü-ching chen-wang tz'u-shu ta-fa*, in Volumes 881–83 of the Canon. Taoists who know the first of these registers are called Pei-chi (Pole Star) Taoists, and claim origin from Wu-tang Shan in Hupei. Taoists who know the second are invariably called "Red-head" by the people, and claim membership in a variety of orders, including the Ling-pao, Lu Shan, Lao Chün, and San-nai sects.[4] Once one has been accorded permission to see the Lu of these Taoists, it becomes evident that the Taoists of modern Taiwan have preserved far more than the Cheng-i tradition in the performance of religious ritual.

Indeed, it is the practice among Taoists in northern Taiwan to learn as many kinds of ritual from as many sources as possible. There are a number of impelling reasons for doing so, the most obvious one being that the Taoist who knows many rituals can earn a better livelihood for his family than the one who knows but a few. The second reason, even more crucial, is the greater prestige and higher rank at ordination that comes with mastering higher forms of perfection. Since one of the definitive traits of esoteric religion is the assurance of salvation in the present life for the initiated, in the Taoist case the striving for *hsien*-hood or personal immortality by means of internal alchemy takes priority over and sometimes supersedes motives of personal profit. Thus there are a number of Taoist masters in northern Taiwan who practice esoteric forms of internal alchemy, breath control, and meditation on the spirits, and consider Taoist ritual but a means of making the blessings that derive from these practices available to the pious faithful. There are even Taoist masters who perform ritual and refuse remuneration, or practice internal alchemy in private without making their ritual powers known to the public.

It is therefore essential for the researcher not only to investigate the Lu of the Taoist master with whom he chooses to study and to gain acceptance as a student in the school of ritual, but also to win admission to the school of internal meditation. In the esoteric tradition, ritual is

---

[4] In northern Taiwan the term Black-head refers to Taoists who bury the dead, and Red-head to those who do not. In the technical terminology used by the Taoists themselves, the Red-head Taoists all belong to the Shen-hsiao order (dating from the Hsüan-ho reign years, A.D. 1119–26) or the Lu Shan sect. The Black-head Taoists belong to the Cheng-i Lung-hu Shan sect, the Pole Star Wu-tang Shan sect, or the Five Thunder method sect. Most Black-head Taoists practice ritual deriving from all three sources.

but the visible reenactment of the internal meditations that precede and accompany the performance of liturgy. It is in revealing the oral secrets (k'ou-chüeh) connected with his Lu that the Taoist master transmits to his disciples the secrets of internal alchemy, and it is with regard to these secrets that rivalries between the various Taoist masters take an acute form. Taoists are in fact ranked according to the number of registers that they have learned from a number of sources, some of which traditionally are in direct opposition to one another. The opposition extends not only to name-calling ("heterodox" vs. "orthodox"), but to great physical battles for control of a temple or a city, and to magical jousts fought with conjurations, mudras, and spirits. Many stories are told of battles in which the black magic of one Taoist has caused the illness or even death of a rival Taoist with less powerful magic. The magic of Lu Shan, for example, is mortally opposed to the Cheng-i sect of Lung-hu Shan, and both orders fear the powerful magic of Mao Shan. No matter what a Taoist claims to be, or what kind of magic he is supposed to command, the proof of his prowess is to be found in the manuals that list his Lu, and in the gloss put on the manuals by the k'ou-chüeh. The glosses are sometimes written out in manuals called mi-chüeh (esoteric glosses) and like the Lu prove whether or not the Taoist truly is what he claims to be.

In battling the rival magic of the Mao Shan and Lu Shan orders, the Cheng-i Taoists use a kind of magic called "Five Thunder method" (Wu-lei Fa).[5] The method is adequately explained in the Tao-fa hui-yüan, a collection occupying Volumes 884–941 of the Canon. Most Taoists in Taiwan claim expertise in this method, and freely use the Five Thunder Magic rubric when signing ritual documents with their official titles. Of the fifty or so Taoists practicing in or around Hsin-chu City, however, not more than a handful can actually perform the meditation described below for implanting the thunder spirits in the body, and summoning them forth for exorcistic cures. The Taoist masters who know the tradition guard the secrets jealously, and pass them on to but a small number of their trusted disciples.

In the following paragraphs I would like to contrast the methods used by a Red-head Shen-hsiao or Lu Shan Taoist in curing a child's illness, and those used by a Black-head Cheng-i Taoist performing Five Thunder

[5] The Five Thunder method derives from the Ch'ing-wei order, a Taoist sect based in Hua Shan, Sung Shan, and the southern Heng Shan. The registers are very old, dating according to T'ao Hung-ching (A.D. 456–537, the eighth Mao Shan patriarch) to the late-Han period (cf. T'ai-shang ch'ih-wen tung-shen san lu, Taoist Canon, Vol. 324). The Five Thunder method was incorporated into the registers of the Cheng-i sect during the Sung dynasty. The late-Sung Taoist Chin Yün-chung attests in the Shang-ch'ing ling-pao ta fa (cf. Taoist Canon, Vol. 965, chs. 4, 10) to the great secrecy with which the Thunder Magic registers were kept.

Magic. The Lu Shan or Shen-hsiao magic is described in a manual commonly used by the Taoists of Hsin-chu associated with the Taoist master Ch'ien Chih-ts'ai, and in Chung-li and T'ao-yüan by followers of the Taoist Huang. The manual describing the Thunder Magic cure was purchased at Lung-hu Shan in 1886 by Lin Ju-mei, and now belongs to the Cheng-i Tz'u-t'an, a Taoist fraternity in Hsin-chu.[6]

The Red-head rite for curing a child's complaint is both simple and effective. When the worried mother carries the child into the Taoist's front room, he first asks the child's birthdate: year, month, and day. He then computes on the *T'ung-shu* or Daily Almanac whether for the present year, month, and day, the relative influences of yin and yang are auspicious for the child or not. He then lights incense, and while ringing a small handbell, attracts the child's attention. The natural cause of the illness is first determined (e.g., a common cold or some other discernible ailment), and then the supernatural cause (for example, the restless soul of a deceased relative or a demonic spirit).

Having put mother and child at ease with the gentle ringing of the handbell and the quiet chanting of purificatory incantations, the Taoist next summons the spirits at his command, namely the exorcistic Pole Star spirits, the local Ch'eng Huang deity, the spirit of the soil, the virgin goddess Ma Tsu, and the patron of Lu Shan, Ch'en Nai Ma. On a piece of yellow paper he draws a fu talisman (the model for which can be bought in bookshops) and signs it with a special talismanic seal at the bottom. The Taoist then lights a candle at the altar and recites an exorcistic mantra, or conjuration, such as the following:

> I command the source of all pains in the body—
> Muscle pains, headaches, eye sores, mouth sores
> Aching hands and aching feet
> [insert the particular ailment of the child]—
> With the use of this magic of mine,
> Here before this Taoist altar,
> May all demons be bound and captured,
> May they be cast back into Hell's depths.
> "Ch'iu-ch'iu Chieh-chieh"
> You are sent back to your source!
> Quickly, quickly, obey my command![7]

[6] Lin Ju-mei's journey to Lung-hu Shan is noted in the *Hsin-chu hsien chih* (Hsin-chu County Gazette; Hsin-chu hsien, Wen-hsien wei-yüan Hui, 1955), 9: 9–10. The Cheng-i Tz'u-t'an fraternity was founded in 1888 on the return of Lin Ju-mei from the mainland. The Thunder Magic manuals purchased from the 61st Generation Heavenly Master, including those used in the following pages, are in the library of the present head of the fraternity, Chuang-ch'en Teng-yün.

[7] For the text quoted here, cf. the forthcoming *Chuang-lin hsü tao-tsang*, Michael Saso, ed. (Taipei, 1974), pt. 4, ch. 6.

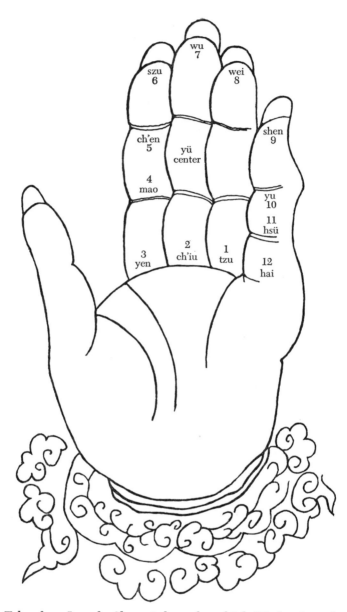

Fig. 1. Taken from *Lung-hu Shan mi-chuan shou-chüeh* (Mudras from the esoteric tradition of Lung-hu Shan; Hsin-chu, 1888), p. 40. Copied by Lin Wen-ta from the collection of Lin Ju-mei, purchased from the 61st Generation Heavenly Master at Lung-hu Shan in 1886, and used as an instruction manual by the Ch'eng-i Tz'u-t'an.

He then casts the divination blocks, i.e., two crescent-shaped pieces of bamboo with one side rounded and one side flat. The flat sides down (yin in ascendancy) is a negative answer. The flat sides up (yang in ascendancy) means "the gods are laughing." One flat side and one round side up (yin and yang in balance) is an affirmative response, an indication that the proper spirit has been exorcised. Once an affirmative answer has been received, the talisman is burned, and a few of the ashes are mixed in a glass of boiled water. A teaspoon of the water is given the child as an exorcistic cure. The Taoist then recommends aspirin, antibiotics, or whatever Chinese herbal medicine he judges an appropriate remedy for the natural cause of the illness.[8]

The cost of a Red-head cure is currently about NT $25, the equivalent of about sixty cents in United States currency. Unquestionably the Red-head cure is both effective and calming, being far more entertaining for the child and more reassuring to the mother than a visit to a doctor's office, where the threat of an injection and the presence of other crying children do little to soothe the mother's frayed nerves. The rite of curing over, the mother returns home with a pacified child in her arms.

The cure of a Black-head Taoist, by contrast, is both far more exacting and more expensive. To be able to perform such a ritual, every year on the first day after the Li Ch'un festival (the first day of spring in the solar calendar) that a thunderstorm occurs, the Taoist must perform a special meditation. At the first thunderclap he must arise, and facing the direction from which the thunder is coming, perform the following meditation.[9]

A. The Taoist imagines the twelve earthly stems to be embodied in the joints of his left hand, as shown in Figure 1.

B. Next, the Taoist touches each of the twelve joints with the tip of his thumb, while holding his breath and envisioning the primordial breath held in the cinnabar field (*Tan-t'ien*, or Yellow Court, the locus of the T'ai-chi in the microcosm) circulating through the corresponding organs:

    1. *Tzu* position, the gall;
    2. *Ch'iu* position, the liver;

---

[8] In all cases I have witnessed in which the child does in fact have a physical ailment, the Taoist, whether Red-head or Black-head, has included western or Chinese medicine with the cure. One of the Black-head Taoists of the Cheng-i Tz'u-t'an, Ch'en Ting-feng, is a licensed practitioner of Chinese medicine and runs a pharmacy. A knowledge of Chinese medicine is required of Taoists who practice ritual cures.

[9] Taken from the mi-chüeh manual *shih chuan ch'ing-wei ch'i chüeh* (The [Lung-hu Shan] Heavenly Master's Transmission of the Ch'ing-wei [Five Thunder

3. *Yen* position, the lungs;
4. *Mao* position, the large intestine;
5. *Ch'en* position, the stomach;
6. *Szu* position, the spleen;
7. *Wu* position, the heart;
8. *Wei* position, the small intestine;
9. *Shen* position, the bladder;
10. *Yü* position, the kidneys;
11. *Hsü* position, the blood vessels;
12. *Hai* position, the three tubes.[10]

C. Facing the direction from which the thunder is coming, the Taoist touches the tip of his thumb to seven joints on his left hand, envisioning the power of the thunder and lightning entering the corresponding organ. As he touches each joint, he recites the mantric word that brings the power of the thunder under his control:

i. Touching the wu position, he brings the breath (ch'i)[11] of the thunder into his heart, saying the mantric word "lei."
ii. Touching the wei he brings the breath of the thunder into the small intestines by reciting the mantric word "wei."
iii. Touching the thumb just beneath the position marked wu on the left hand, he brings the breath of the thunder into the center of the chest while reciting the mantric word "chen."[12]
iv. Touching the position marked yü (jade) in the center of the middle finger, he summons the breath of the thunder into the lower cinnabar field, between the kidneys, while reciting the mantric word "tung."
v. Touching the position marked ch'iu he brings the breath of the thunder into the liver, pronouncing the mantric word "pien."
vi. Touching the position marked tzu he brings the thunder into the gall, reciting the mantric word "ching."

Magic] Secrets (61st Generation Heavenly Master, Lung-hu Shan, 1886). A copy of this manual is in the author's possession.

[10] The term three tubes refers to ducts through which ch'i, or life breath, is thought to flow. The first is the duct into the stomach. The second is the center of the stomach, where breath is held and not allowed to flow away. The third is the entrance to the bladder, where impurities are separated out and allowed to flow away.

[11] "Breath" is to be taken here in the philosophical sense, that is, as a principle of life, "primordial breath." The mantric words used here, seven in number, can be forced to make sense, but in fact the sound of the word itself acts in a sacramental manner to command or summon the life-giving breath of the thunder.

[12] That is, into the Yellow Court in the center of the chest, the center cinnabar field. The upper Yellow Court is in the brain, and the lower Yellow Court is in the belly, between the kidneys, as in the following mantra.

    vii. Finally touching the position marked hsü he brings the breath of the thunder into the blood vessels, reciting the mantric word "jen."

The same process is repeated on the right hand, and he ends the meditation by holding his breath and envisioning the power of the thunder as first entering the microcosmic center of the body, then circulating through each of the five central organs—liver, spleen, lungs, kidneys, and heart—where it is stored and drawn upon until he repeats the meditation the next year.[13]

The Taoist summons forth the five breaths of thunder stored in the five central organs by touching the tips of the four fingers and the thumb of both hands to the palm, in a tight-fisted mudra, while drawing the character "lei" (thunder) with the tip of his tongue on the hard palate of his mouth. The thunder method that I have just described can be used to exorcise malevolent demons, and is an essential part of the rite of curing.

The curing of a child's complaint is from beginning to end quite different for the Cheng-i Black-head and the Lu Shan Red-head Taoist. The Cheng-i Taoist always stands before the altar when performing the rite of curing, and he carries no small handbell. He first lights sandalwood incense, and computes for the month, day, and hour the direction of the "Gate of Life," that is, the direction from which the spirits are to be summoned and blessings obtained for the afflicted child.[14] Next, he inquires after the source of the illness, and if he concludes that the child has a simple cold, prescribes Western or Chinese medicines. If, however, the disease is attributable to a demon or an unattended ancestor, he proceeds with the rite of exorcism.

Standing before the household altar, the Cheng-i Taoist first summons the spirits of his Lu or register. He builds around himself the Mandala (Tao-ch'ang) of the Prior Heavens, envisioning various esoteric spirits unknown to the ordinary faithful and appropriate to his own sect and

---

    [13] The five central organs in which the power is stored correspond to east, south, west, north, and center in the macrocosm, and to wood, fire, metal, water, and earth, the five cosmological principles of gestation. The Five Thunder breaths can be summoned forth through the seven organs as described above, or through the simple two-handed fist mudra described in the following paragraph.

    [14] The Gate of Life is computed, in the Five Thunder method, from the direction in which the handle of the Dipper is pointing. Since the Dipper revolves around the heavens continually, the Taoist is given, as an esoteric secret, a chart showing the Dipper position for any given month, day, and hour of the year. The principle is used both in funeral ritual, to determine the direction in which the soul leaves the earth and enters heaven, and in *chiao* renewal rites, to determine where the Gate of Heaven (the trigram *ch'ien*) is located in the temple area.

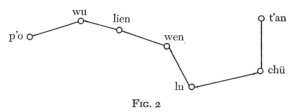

FIG. 2

rank at ordination, notably spirits who can help cure the child's illness.[15] Each spirit is summoned by a mantric word and a mudra. Thus the five organs of the body in which the thunder breath was stored are now called upon to yield forth the breath for ritual use.

Among the spirits that the Wu-lei Fa Taoist may summon to help him in curing a child are the spirits of the *Pei-tou*, Ursa Major—that is, the seven star gods who correspond to the seven stars of the Dipper.[16] Since the breaths of the thunder magic also number seven, the seven Pei-tou spirits are often combined with the seven thunder breaths to effect a cure. The summoning is done in the following manner. The Taoist touches the same seven stems listed above, summoning the thunder breaths with the thumb and fingers of the left hand. He then envisions the Pei-tou constellations in the northern heavens, and in a meditation similar to the one described above, implants the spirits in his body.

The Taoist presses the thumb of his left hand to the tzu position, envisioning a ray of light from the *t'an* star as penetrating the big toe of his left foot (Figure 2). He presses the joint marked ch'iu and sees a ray of light from the star *chü* enter the big toe of his right foot. He presses the yü position in the center of the middle finger, and sees a ray of light from the star *lu* penetrate his right knee. Pressing the point directly above the character tzu, he sees a ray of light from the *wen* star enter his left knee. Pressing the joint immediately below the wei character, he sees a ray of light from the star *lien* enter his navel. Pressing the wei

[15] For the building of the Mandala around the Taoist before the ritual (technically called *fa lu*), see Michael Saso, "On the Ritual Meditation of Orthodox Heavenly Master Sect Taoism," *Journal of the China Society* (Taipei, 1971), 8: 1–21. The use of the rite in curing is very early; cf. T'ao Hung-ching, *Teng-chen yin-chüeh* (Taoist Canon, Vol. 193), Chuan Hsia, 6b–7b, where the meditation is said to originate in Szechwan at the end of the Han dynasty.

[16] The Dipper has been associated with Thunder Magic at least since the T'ang period and the influence of Chen-yen (mantric Sanskrit) on the Ch'ing-wei Taoist sect. It was during this period that the Hindi goddess Marishi was identified with Tou Mu (mother goddess of the Dipper) and made a patron spirit of the Five Thunder method. The texts in the *Tao-fa hui-yüan* (Taoist Canon, Vols. 884–941) describing the association date from the early Sung.

position itself he sees a ray of light from the *wu* star enter his heart. Finally, pressing the wu position with his thumb, he sees a ray of light from the *p'o* star enter his tongue.

Now alive as it were with the purifying rays of light from the Pole Star constellation, the Taoist draws a fu on the hard palate of his mouth with the tip of his tongue. He draws a talisman depicting the character Thunder (lei), and forming the Thunder Magic mudra by closing both hands into tight fists, turns toward the child and breathes on its head. Then, facing the Taoist altar, he repeats the process, this time summoning the Pole Star spirits and purifying the child. As each spirit is summoned, the Taoist envisions its countenance, clothing, and height. Thus the god of the star t'an is ten feet tall, has a red face, a red beard, red shoes, and protruding eyes, and bears a long sword. The mantric summons for the spirit is *"Huo-po."* The god from the star chü is also dressed in red, is eight feet tall, and responds to the mantric summons *"Hung-hsi."* Unquestionably the exorcistic cure of the Cheng-i Taoist is far more stately than that of the rival Red-head Lu Shan orders. The ritual ends with the Taoist bowing before the altar, mentally restoring the spirits to their original positions in the cosmos. The cost for a Cheng-i cure ranges from NT $30 (U.S. $.75) for the simple ritual to NT $50 (U.S. $1.25) for an elegantly drawn fu talisman to be taken home as extra protection.

Since the capacity to invoke Thunder Magic is greatly admired, there is intense rivalry between Taoist masters and between their followers over its secrets. Not only are the meditations described above concealed from opposing schools, but the esoteric secrets are kept from lower-ranking colleagues. The names of the spirits, the mudras and mantras for summoning them, and the meditation with which the Taoist brings them under his control are the most carefully guarded secrets in the master's liturgical repertoire. Most disciples readily master the external performance of ritual, but only a very few are taught the formulas of esoteric meditation. The reason for the restriction, of course, lies in the very nature of esoteric religion; that is, grade or rank at ordination is determined by the aspirant's proficiency, and professional jealousy reinforces the rule of inheritance that restricts revelation of the entire system to one son of a priest's family per generation.[17] But even more crucial than the Taoists' system of inheritance is the rivalry between the various forms of Taoist magic.

Five Thunder Magic is conceded by the Taoist masters of all schools

---

[17] The rule that a master may reveal esoteric doctrines in their fullness to only one son a generation is of very ancient origin. It can be found in the *Hsüan-tu lü wen* (Taoist Canon, Vol. 78), dating to the North-South period, ca. fifth century A.D.

to be more powerful than either Mao Shan or Lu Shan magic. The respect shown to the expert in the Five Thunder method is reflected in the high rank given him or her at the time of ordination. That is, the Five Thunder expert is given the high-ranking Grade Two (*Erh P'in*) title, whereas the non-canonical Mao Shan and Lu Shan experts receive no such grade at the time of ordination.[18] In the mi-chüeh manuals used by the Taoist masters of Hsin-chu City's Cheng-i Tz'u-t'an fraternity, a special mantric conjuration is always used to culminate the rites of curing and exorcistic purification. "Bind the evil spirits and myriad heterodox breaths," the Thunder Magic mantras conclude, "And send them back to Mao Shan and Lu Shan." The magic of Mao Shan and Lu Shan is considered to be harmful to men. The demonic spirits and the evil breaths commanded by its conjurations bring sickness and even death.[19] The Five Thunder method is therefore not just a form of ritual used by Cheng-i orthodox Taoists, as distinguished from their competitors, on the day-to-day professional level; it is also a form of spiritual power that can overcome the influence of heterodox "black magic."

In conclusion, if the magic of Lu Shan and Mao Shan can be used to harm men as well as help them, to both cause sickness and restore health, the magic of the Cheng-i Taoist, particularly the Five Thunder method, is in the last analysis a means to combat heterodoxy, a magic used only for man's good, not to his detriment. Orthodoxy in Taoist ritual is therefore to be judged on two counts. The first is knowledge of the ancient Cheng-i registers found in the Taoist Canon, as enumerated at the beginning of this paper, and the attendant oral secrets. The second is the rejection of harmful forms of black magic, deriving from non-canonical forms of the Mao Shan and Lu Shan sects, and the combatting of such practices with the Five Thunder method.

[18] The distinction between the orthodox Shang-ch'ing or Yü-ching (Highest Purity, Jade Capital) sect, a highly orthodox monastic order deriving from Mao Shan, and the heterodox popular Mao Shan must be carefully observed. Orthodoxy is judged by the registers and by the kind of magic a Taoist uses. The highest grade at ordination (*I-p'in*) is given for knowledge of the Shang-ch'ing registers, which are found in the *Ta-tung chen-ching* (Taoist Canon, Vol. 16).

[19] It is well known throughout Taiwan that the magic of Lu Shan and Mao Shan can be used to harm men, even to kill. The heterodox Mao Shan manuals in particular contain formulas for talismans that can kill an enemy. The talismans include black, bird-like "Five Thunder demons" in imitation of the orthodox Thunder Magic rubric. People who fear that black magic is being used to make them sick summon a practitioner of the Five Thunder method to counteract it. The Cheng-i Tz'u-t'an Taoists of Hsin-chu are frequently called on to exercise their Thunder Magic for this purpose.

Afterword

ROBERT J. SMITH

The discussant at a conference devoted to a topic outside his own field of specialization is faced with several tasks. Lacking an intimate acquaintance with the tradition within which the conferees operate, he must decide for himself why they have chosen the issues they take up. Having come to some understanding of their sense of problem, he must next try to make some judgment of the ways they have gone about answering the questions they have posed themselves. Only then can he turn his attention to the recurrent themes that usually give a conference its shape. Finally if his own interests are not too remote from those of the conferees, he probably will be tempted to explore one or another of these themes comparatively.

As I listened to the discussion of the papers now included in this volume, I was struck by the extent to which the situation resembled a field interview. Each participant seemed to be dealing with all the others as though they were *informants*. Those who had conducted their research in Hong Kong expressed great interest—and sometimes polite incredulity—when informed of practices and beliefs on Taiwan. Those who had worked in the northern part of that island interviewed those who knew the southern part, and often registered surprise at what they learned. And there were others who found all these informants' accounts at such variance with orthodox practice and belief (as they understood them from documents and interviews with members of the vanished elite) as to be offensive and perhaps not even Chinese. The occasion was an exciting one, not least because it turned out that not one participant had conducted field research in both Hong Kong and Taiwan. They were all, in some sense, subarea specialists. Or so I thought then, for I was bewildered by what seemed to be variation of many kinds on a scale entirely unfamiliar to me from my own study of Japanese religion, and thought it must result from the scattered character of the data. Students of Japan are more accustomed than most area specialists to treating the society they study as though it were a virtually undifferentiated aggregation of like-minded people. It is not, of course, and it was during this conference that I began to see a problem in the study of Japanese society that I had given insufficient thought to before.

There is no reason to inflict on the reader a detailed review of the variations of custom and institution reported by contributors to this volume. Some of the material will already have caught his attention; much more was brought out in the discussion of the papers. There may be some utility, nevertheless, in touching on some representative points. In Topley's discussion of the problem of adjustment between mother and newborn child, she tells us that her informants, lacking a common commitment to a single Chinese cosmological system, draw on a variety of sources of knowledge to explain and deal with the problem. Schipper, on the other hand, finds it hard to define Taoism—one of the Chinese cosmological systems—because it is so thoroughly confounded with folk religion and sectarianism. Indeed, the *chiao* he discusses incorporates the Buddhist rite of feeding the hungry ghosts (called *segaki-e* in Japanese) and may be performed by Taoist or Buddhist priests, or by both simultaneously at their respective altars. At the chiao the regular deities of the temple are joined by a great mass of deities of all possible kinds brought from the home altars of the worshippers. Schipper also notes that although there is an immutable written tradition in Taoism, whose memorials and titles are modeled after those of the imperial administration, local tradition has been assimilated whenever necessary. Saso writes of the rivalry among Taoist schools and masters, each with a claim to orthodoxy, and in another connection points out that the registers the Taoists must master are derived from many sources, some of which are traditionally in diametrical opposition to one another.

Wang Shih-ch'ing discusses two kinds of worship unit: one is the community, which worships its tutelary deity; the other is based not on territory, but on kinship affiliation, ethnic identity, or simply devotion to a particular deity. He makes a striking point with respect to the gods on Taiwan when he says that just as some settlers survived to establish the Chinese colony on the island, so did some of their gods. There appear to be a great many reasons for erecting temples, and both Wang and Brim report that some lineages which participate in communal worship of the tutelary deity also maintain independent links with the supernatural. Even the souls of the dead are differentiated. Some are deified as representations of legitimate authority who serve community interests; some are deified as powerful supernatural beings who serve selfish rather than communal interests; some are the ancestral dead, for whom one is committed to performing rites by virtue of descent from them. Feuchtwang offers a fascinating glimpse into the relationship between men and gods in his reference to the deities associated with Buddhism and asceticism, who are offered sweets and fruits, but whose soldiers are offered meat. The character of the offerings appears to be determined by the preferences of the deity, rather than by dietary rules of the living.

The papers by Wolf, Harrell, DeGlopper, and Freedman deal more explicitly with the theme of variation, albeit in very different ways. Wolf's central point is that there are as many meanings in Chinese religion as there are vantage points on the social landscape of its adherents. The complexity of the materials he presents amply justifies his claim that the identification of gods, ghosts, and ancestors is a highly variable matter. As Harrell sees it, each community, each household, and each person on Taiwan believes in and worships a different pantheon. Although some people can describe a coherent supernatural order, others are not given to systematic theology. The latter are able, however, to classify supernatural beings in terms of their relationships to those who worship them. Like Wang Shih-ch'ing, Harrell draws a tripartite distinction among the spirits of the dead: there are private spirits, which are worshipped by their kinsmen, and two kinds of public spirits, those worshipped to gain their assistance (*sin*) and those worshipped to buy them off (*kui*). These two varieties of public spirit also differ with respect to the places where they are worshipped, offerings made to them, and the organization of their worship. To complicate the picture still further, there is also a category of spirits that Harrell calls intermediate, about whom opinions differ. People disagree over whether they are sin or kui, and often differ over the identity of a deity enshrined in a particular place of popular worship. In Harrell's view, because Chinese religion draws on Buddhism, Taoism, and the Confucian tradition, it inevitably contains variant explanations for the same phenomenon. There is no single authority that attempts to establish dogma and doctrine, and though priests, monks, and bureaucrats have influenced popular belief, they have never been able to determine it. In fact, the individual worshipper is free, within unspecified limits, to construct his own system of belief and practice. The overriding consideration is the efficacy of a deity or a practice, and because people have highly variable experiences in this regard, they hold very different views about a given deity or rite. Chinese religion is above all flexible and individualistic.

DeGlopper, too, confronts the issue of diversity of belief and practice on Taiwan. Festivals very popular in one place may hardly be noted a few miles away; deities of enormous importance in one town may be only minor figures in the pantheon of a nearby community. Firewalking, planchette divination, and many other popular ritual practices may be central to the religious life of one place and hardly known in another. Even the dates of major festivals vary considerably. It is, DeGlopper suggests, not really difficult to abstract from all this a general pattern and call it Taiwanese popular religion. The variations are then easily explained, for "Taiwanese popular religion" is nothing more than a blanket term that refers to the multitude of practices, cults, and customs which have in common only that they are found on Taiwan. Like Harrell, DeGlopper says that in the absence of elaborated doctrine and dogma, the individual worshipper has great latitude in what he chooses to believe and do. But, he cautions, one feature of religion on Taiwan is very hard to understand: it is not the fact of variation, but rather the absence of systematic, readily explained variation. If we compare communities of the same type, we find great variation of religious belief and practice. This is all the more difficult to understand given the considerable homogeneity of other aspects of culture on this small island, settled in the last 250 years largely by people from Fukien. Even now, despite exposure to island-wide uniform influences, public communal ritual remains unstandardized. How shall we approach this problem?

DeGlopper believes that three courses are open to us. If we assume the existence of a system, or if we assume that we can construct a system, then we can dismiss the issue of variation as trivial. If we stress the common core of communal ritual, we can dismiss local variation as superficial, contingent glosses on some basic structure, but are left with the problem that there are no obvious differences among the communities that correlate with the ritual variations. If we assert that local customs are simply traditions brought in by the early settlers from different parts of Fukien, then we have only pushed the question back 250-odd years to that province, and the variability found there at the time of the beginning of emigration requires explanation.

It is Freedman who comes down most heavily on the side of system. Despite all appearances to the contrary, he writes, Chinese religious ideas are not a congeries of randomly assembled elements. Behind the superficial variety there must be order of some sort. Ideas and forms need not be uniform to be common; they may be reflections or transformations of one another. Indeed, Freedman suggests that a society like the Chinese, so differentiated by social status and power, will allow differences in beliefs and practices to complement one another, permitting religious similarity to be expressed as though it were religious difference. It seems to me equally likely that this society may instead have treated religious differences as though they were religious similarities, a possibility I will explore further below. And once again we encounter the theme that Chinese religion is a polymorphous system that permits variation within the religious life of the individual worshipper and within social classes as well. Freedman has added the contention that for all the variability, Chinese religion has represented a single community of ideas.

There was more, but I need pursue the issue no further. Some of the conference participants seemed mildly disturbed by the overwhelming evidence of diversity of religious practice and belief, but for the most part they were willing to pass it off as resulting somehow from the absence of a central authority that sought to establish orthodoxy. Had there never been, I wondered, occasions when some central authority moved to suppress heterodoxy? What were the limits set for the individual Chinese in choosing what he would believe and do? Was the same lack of specificity of required behavior found also at the community level? This was heady stuff, and I was beguiled by the notion that, in the face of such tolerance, the Chinese had nonetheless maintained a community of ideas for a very long time over a vast territory.

When in the presence of authorities on Chinese society, the Japan specialist is wont to present a low profile, particularly if the subject being discussed is religion. In comparison with China's, Japan's history is short and her territory minuscule, and her religious beliefs and practices are heavily indebted to Chinese Buddhism, Confucianism, and Taoism. We are also accustomed to saying that the Japanese readily adapt cultural features borrowed from elsewhere, fitting them into indigenous patterns of belief and practice. Not unnaturally it occurred to me to wonder whether what we had been calling an indigenous pattern with reference to Japan might be the same as the notion of the single community of ideas that had been under discussion with reference to China. If we had been operating on the assumption that an otherwise chaotic diversity must be reduced to a pattern, what had been lost by essentially ignoring the issue of diversity?

I think now, with respect to the issue of variation in belief and practice, that it is intrinsically important. Instead of dismissing such variations—or condescending to the folklorist who delights in them—we must examine them closely. The result of such an exercise might well be to clarify the nature of Japanese religion, demystifying its analysis by forcing us to look once more at the variation in what people say and

do, what they say they believe and why they believe it, and how they
have come to have available to them the options among which they make
their choices. With the possibility that such a clarification might be a
worthwhile goal, I wish now to turn to the issue of variation in belief
and practice in Japanese popular religion.

It is a commonplace that almost all Japanese Buddhists are Shintoists
as well. Like most commonplaces, this one is accurate in only the most
restricted sense. The character of Japanese Buddhism has been a source
of puzzlement, or even despair, to many of its students, with the result
that the Japanese are often credited with an unusual propensity to syn-
cretism or a rare indifference to orthodoxy or both. This view fails to
take into account the nature of Buddhism and the fact of the long history
of its spread through northern Asia. After all, the Japanese are at the
easternmost terminus of the great sweep of Mahayana Buddhism across
the continent through China and Korea. They were the last great Asian
population to learn of that religion; the court embraced it only in the
fifth and sixth centuries, and another five or six hundred years passed
before a second major wave of Buddhism, carried by Japanese zealots
trained in China, lodged it firmly among the populace. In seventeenth-
century Japan, to be a Buddhist meant little more than that one would
be buried with Buddhist rites and that one's soul became a buddha
immediately upon death or very shortly thereafter. Have we an example
here of the Japanese ability to adapt borrowings to the indigenous pattern referred to earlier, or might it be that the Buddhism they borrowed
from China already contained many of the ideas that the Japanese are
credited with adding later? The question can be answered in part by
reference to the state of Chinese Buddhism when the Japanese encountered it. Having endured a very long passage through time and space,
it was neither pristine nor a unity. We can, then, understand some aspects
of the Japanese interpretation of Buddhist doctrine and practice only
if we know what these had already become at the time the Japanese
in effect learned their Buddhism. At least two central conceptions of
Chinese Buddhism were to have an enormous impact in Japan. They
were the notion of Buddhism as protector of the state, and the importance of filial piety and the care of ancestral spirits. Pseudo-sutras
extolling the virtue of filial piety, all of Chinese origin, were received
by the Japanese as a central part of the canon.

But there were also in Japan indigenous practices and beliefs that
had no generic name until Buddhism was introduced, when the native
religion began to be called Shinto (the way of the gods) as opposed
to the newly imported "way of the buddhas." And, as had happened in

all societies influenced by Mahayana Buddhism, the local deities of Japan (the *kami*) came to be regarded as avatars of the buddhas and bodhisattvas. The unification of the gods and buddhas, as the Japanese called this process of identification, endured for more than a thousand years, until the Restorationist government of the 1870's set about separating the two once more, for very good political reasons of its own.

There is a wealth of information about what was happening in Japanese religion from the seventh century on. Sects rise and fall. Ideas are expounded, take hold, remain current here but disappear there. Gods who were initially conceived to be avatars of buddhas become later and and in some places buddhas who are avatars of gods. The state exploits, rejects, alters, suppresses, and reinterprets anything it finds expedient to have its way with. Different sections of the country are the targets of proselytizers of very different persuasions at different times, and some isolated areas remain to this day untouched by Buddhism in any form. The thesis that Buddhism is the protector of the state was rejected out of hand by one school in the medieval period, but has been pressed to extravagant new heights by another in our day. Ancestors are deified in one place; deities are "ancestorized" in another. It is not even the case that all Japanese households are Buddhist. Today some 10 percent of households in Japan worship their ancestors in Shinto rites. Of these only a fraction represent households of Shinto priests, who until about 1890 were in any event given Buddhist funerals. The rest are in part families from former feudal domains whose lords decreed in the seventeenth century that all households should abandon Buddhism. Still other families followed the urging of the nineteenth-century Meiji government to shift to Shinto worship of the ancestors as an earnest of patriotic sentiment.

It is often said that today Buddhism, Shinto, and Confucianism do in fact represent three rather distinct emphases in Japan. Buddhism, a universal religion, features deities whose preeminent capacities are compassionate assistance, the salvation of the individual soul, and the soul's conveyance into paradise. The Japanese have accorded Buddhism the major role in providing ways to achieve harmony in this world and in mortuary rites for the souls of the dead. Shinto, a parochial religion, has deities of place and of social group, each of them the tutelary god of a territory and its people, or of a category of persons, such as a group of artisans. To it has been assigned the major role in the rituals of life—birth, marriage, the New Year, planting, and harvesting. Confucianism, in Japan an ethical system that is rarely embodied in temple or practitioner, affirms the filial duties of the child to its parent and the loyalty of subject to sovereign. All three systems have warred, been variously combined, and waxed and waned at certain times and in certain areas for over a thousand years. The contemporary effects of this history are not far to seek. What has resulted is a layering of coexistent practice and belief, a variability of both even within small communities, and the setting out of genuine contradictions that may be subscribed to even by a single person. By this bald statement I mean to suggest that the totality cannot be reconciled into a systemic whole, and later I will try to say why I think this is so for Japanese materials of many other kinds as well.

Yet there are thresholds that will not be crossed. There is a general outline, a framework if you will, within which certain variants will not occur. It is almost impossible, for example, to imagine an instance of blood sacrifice, real or symbolic, in Japanese religion. But within that framework I think it is essential to examine the degree to which there is specificity of requirement in religious behavior. For purposes of illustration, let me take up selected aspects of ancestor worship in Japan.

It is clearly set out in the Civil Code that ancestral rites shall be observed. The domestic altar in a household will usually contain memorial tablets; these are the most common objects of worship in ancestral rites. But there is no rule specifying whom the tablets shall represent. The current Civil Code requires that one child shall assume responsibility for the care of the tablets upon the death of the family head, but it is not stated that other children may not do so as well. What in fact do we find? In some households and in some communities, any given altar may contain the tablets of senior ascendants and a great variety of other ancestors. In the house next door or in some houses in the next community down the road, tablets may be limited to agnatic kin. In some regions only one child (the successor) is accorded the right and duty of caring for the ancestors, and none of the other children make copies of the tablets for their own domestic altars; in other places all sons may receive a copy of a parent's tablet; and in still others a copy is given to all children, sons and daughters alike. In still other places all altars in effect hold bilateral tablets of the kin of both husband and wife.

In a single village one finds that the souls of children of the household are held by some to require special treatment of a kind elsewhere given only to the wandering ghosts of strangers, while their neighbors reject out of hand the notion that the spirit of one's own dead child could be potentially harmful. All households in the community I am referring to belong to the same sect of Buddhism, are longtime residents of the village, and do not differ markedly in occupation, economic status, or ethnic origin. In most rural communities, people say that the ancestral

spirits are passively benign or altogether powerless, but we have accounts of some places where they are regularly charged with causing
misfortune. For most Japanese households the aim of the ancestral rites
is to comfort the spirits, to express gratitude to them for past favors, and
to ask them to protect the family. But at least one of the popular, syncretic New Religions teaches that one must sever all karmic links with the
ancestors in order to avoid an evil fate. Another of the New Religions
urges the faithful to collect as many memorial tablets as possible, regardless of the kinship bond between the worshipper and the deceased,
and to offer prayers on behalf of the spirits represented by the tablets.

Now it may be that all these attitudes are nothing more than superficial variations on a common theme or core, which may be simply
stated: the Japanese believe that the living and the dead are linked
in such a way that the one can affect the fate of the other. Surely we
lose a great deal by moving to such a level of generality. Is it really of
so little importance that for some people and for some sects (and, inci-
dentally, more commonly in some historic periods than in others) the
spirits of the dead are malign, whereas for other people and sects (and in
other times) they are either benign or passively dependent on the living?
It is of great importance, of course, but we have done little to analyze
these differences because they seem to covary with other phenomena
in unexpected ways. It is not, I think, that they make no sense, but rather
that we have abandoned the search for the meaning of variation.

Variations in religious practice and belief other than ancestor worship
are equally great, and there is ample evidence that many of them are
mutually contradictory. It is time to return to an examination of the
question why people hold different beliefs, what the sources of their
beliefs are, and how they reconcile flat contradictions if indeed they try
to do so.

Even one person's opinion about so fundamental a matter as the fate
of the soul may prove unexpectedly complicated. A great many people
say that the spirits of the dead inhere in their memorial tablets *and* in
their graves, *and* that at midsummer they are annually summoned back
to the house from the mountain "where the spirits are," *and* that they
are then sent back to the sea "where the spirits go," *and* that they are
in paradise. The observer cannot doubt a person who offers all these
statements about the location of the soul of the dead, for his behavior
shows clearly that he is acting on the assumption that all the statements
are true. He prays to the tablets, and at the grave, and goes to the mountain and to the sea at midsummer, and speaks of paradise.

At the levels of household and community rituals and pantheons, we find the same kinds of diversity reported for Taiwan by DeGlopper and Harrell. How shall we explain the coexistence of so many variants? One important consideration surely is that, for the most part, the religious acts of the Japanese have traditionally been limited to the context of a specific social group—household, kinsmen, and community. Furthermore, the chief officiant in a ritual involving a particular group is its head, not a religious practitioner. These lay officiants are often assisted by a priest—Shinto or Buddhist, depending on the context—who is not regarded as essential to the conduct of the ceremony. Indeed, priests often are not summoned at all, or are accorded only very marginal status at a rite. There are no congregations of the faithful, and therefore very few occasions on which doctrine can be expounded and dogma affirmed. As a consequence of the absence of serious pressures to orthodoxy, traditions of worship and attitude are felt to be the concern of the individual Japanese, the household, the kin group, and the community, and are not the business of the larger public. Many Japanese are accustomed to referring to the extreme tolerance of the system; many foreigners judge it to represent almost a limiting case of apathy. John Embree wrote of the people of Suye-mura in the 1930's that many said that a person's soul goes to the afterworld he believed in during life. Given such an attitude, where shall we expect variability to end?

It is well to recall that the diversity of religious belief and practice in Japan occurs in a society where the grosser diversities are minimal, as DeGlopper has suggested is the case for Taiwan. But Japan is not a small island, lately populated by migrants from a nearby province. Particularly since the Meiji Restoration, the government has sought to standardize Japanese life in many ways. The various programs have resulted in a population that is in some respects extraordinarily homogeneous. How then shall we deal with the persistence of diversity in religious practice and belief?

We can confidently expect to find social, political, economic, educational, occupational, or demographic correlates for some of the variations in religious behavior. We will not, however, be able to account for them all by this means. An alternative strategy would be to ferret out the limits within which all variations fall and to offer as the product of our analysis a large framework—a newer term now much in vogue is paradigm—which specifies the thresholds of behavior and belief that are never crossed. We could then relegate the internal variations to the limbo of discarded, because troublesome, detail. Or we could construct a system completely extrinsic to the phenomena that can account for the entire range of behavior and belief, employing paradox to dissolve contradictions that threaten the elegance of our construct.

Any or all of these strategies will produce analyses of interest, but at the moment my preference is for still another approach. It has to do with history. What has been called Japanese religion is at one level only those practices, beliefs, customs, rites, doctrines, and texts that have *survived*. According to Harold Rosenberg,

> The culture of any society at any moment is more like the debris, or "fall-out," of past ideological systems, than it is itself a system, a coherent whole. Coherent wholes may exist, but human social groups tend to find their openness to the future in the variety of their metaphors for what may be the good life and in the contest of their paradigms.*

Of all the innumerable examples of practice and belief that we know to have been introduced into Japan or to have been developed there over the centuries, only the ones we observe today survive. Many enjoyed only brief favor; others were carried into some parts of the country but never into others; some have been continuously rephrased and set into new contexts; a few are almost certainly the result of outright misunderstandings of orthodoxy; many are of recent origin but credited with extreme antiquity; others are current in some age groups but not in others.

As I see it, the problem of variation is of particular interest here because it occurs in a society that by its own account is remarkably uniform in most ways that other nations are not. It is a society whose members will generally tell you that the Japanese way of doing a thing is thus and so, often with considerable specificity. When confronted with evidence of contrary behavior, the response is likely to be "Well, that's not the Japanese way," but with absolutely no implication that it should therefore be stopped. A man's religious convictions and practices are, in short, no one else's business; his observance of social obligation, on the other hand, is everyone's business.

Where this line of investigation will lead I cannot be sure. Perhaps it is only a kind of revisionist reaction against what I think to be an overgeneralized picture of Japanese society, but I hope there is more to it than that. Nothing would be easier than to dismiss variability as a nonproblem, the better to concentrate on the larger picture. But most people live out their lives in a very little picture indeed, and the important question is what shall we make of the fact of variability, rather than how

---

* Cited in Victor W. Turner, *Dramas, Fields, and Metaphors: Symbolic Action in Human Society* (Ithaca, N.Y., 1974), p. 14.

shall we get around it. Perhaps we shall find that the more readily people can produce an ideal phrasing of an institution or set of behaviors—unaccompanied by rigid imperatives beyond those of the most general sort—the less concerned they will be with idiosyncratic or group-linked variations. In such a society, where prescription of behavior does occur it will be closely followed, but where the content of a required form is left unspecified, which is more often than not the case in Japan, we can expect to see the exercise of freedom of option, continuity of historically fixed practices endlessly reinterpreted in contemporary terms, and variable behavior that draws down upon itself no sanctions.

Reference Material

References

Introduction

Ahern, Emily M. 1973. *The Cult of the Dead in a Chinese Village.* Stanford, Calif.

Elliott, A. J. A. 1955. *Chinese Spirit Medium Cults in Singapore.* London.

Fortes, Meyer, 1949. *The Web of Kinship Among the Tallensi.* Oxford.

Freedman, Maurice. 1958. *Lineage Organization in Southeastern China.* London.

————. 1967. "Ancestor Worship: Two Facets of the Chinese Case." In Maurice Freedman, ed., *Social Organization: Essays Presented to Raymond Firth.* Chicago.

————. 1970. "Ritual Aspects of Chinese Kinship and Marriage." In Maurice Freedman, ed., *Family and Kinship in Chinese Society.* Stanford, Calif.

Geertz, Clifford. 1972. "Deep Play: Notes on the Balinese Cockfight," *Daedalus,* Winter, 1–37.

Saso, Michael R. 1972. *Taoism and the Rite of Cosmic Renewal.* Pullman, Wash.

Schipper, Kristofer M. "Religious Organization in Traditional Tainan." In G. William Skinner, ed., *The City in Late Imperial China.* Stanford, Calif., forthcoming.

Skinner, G. William. 1964. "Marketing and Social Structure in Rural China (Part I)," *Journal of Asian Studies,* 24: 3–43.

Wolf, Margery. 1974. "Chinese Women: Old Skills in a New Context." In Michelle Zimbalist Rosaldo and Louise Lamphere, eds., *Woman, Culture, and Society.* Stanford, Calif.

On the Sociological Study of Chinese Religion

Balazs, Etienne. 1965. *Political Theory and Administrative Reality in Traditional China.* London.

Bodde, Derk, and Clarence Morris. 1967. *Law in Imperial China, Exemplified by 190 Ch'ing Dynasty Cases.* Cambridge, Mass.

Chan, Wing-tsit. 1953. *Religious Trends in Modern China.* New York.

Ch'en, Ta. 1939. *Emigrant Communities in South China: A Study of Overseas Migration and Its Influence on Standards of Living and Social Change.* Ed. Bruno Lasker. London and New York.

De Groot, J. J. M. 1881–82. *Jaarlijksche Feesten en Gebruiken van de Emoy-Chineezen.* Verhandelingen van het Bataviaasch Genootschap van Kunsten en Wetenschappen, Deel 4. Batavia.

———— 1885. *Het Kongsiwezen van Borneo.* . . . Koninklijk Instituut voor de Taal-, Land- en Volkenkunde van Nederlandsch-Indië. The Hague.

———— 1886. *Les Fêtes annuellement célébrées à Emoui (Amoy): Etude concernant la religion populaire des Chinois.* Trans. C. G. Chavannes. Annales du Musée Guimet, vols. 11 & 12. Paris. (French translation of De Groot 1881–82.)

———— 1892–1910. *The Religious System of China.* Vols. I–VI. Leiden. (Individual volumes are cited in text as De Groot I, De Groot II, etc.)

———— 1893. *Le Code du Mahâyâna en Chine: Son Influence sur la vie monacale et sur le monde laïque.* Verhandelingen der Koninklijke Akademie van Wetenschappen te Amsterdam, Afdeeling Letterkunde, Deel 1, no. 2. Amsterdam.

———— 1903–4. *Sectarianism and Religious Persecution in China: A Page in the History of Religions.* Verhandelingen der Koninklijke Akademie van Wetenschappen te Amsterdam, Afdeeling Letterkunde. New series, Deel IV, nos. 1 & 2. Amsterdam.

———— 1910. *The Religion of the Chinese.* New York.

———— 1918. *Universismus: Die Grundlage der Religion und Ethik, des Staatswesens und der Wissenschaften Chinas.* Berlin.

Diamond, Norma. 1969. *K'un Shen: A Taiwan Village.* New York.

Doré, Henri. 1970. *Manuel des superstitions chinoises, ou petit indicateur des superstitions les plus communes en Chine.* Introduction by Michel Soymié. Paris–Hong Kong.

Dunstheimer, Guillaume. 1972. "Some Religious Aspects of Secret Societies." In Jean Chesneaux, ed., *Popular Movements and Secret Societies in China, 1840–1950.* Stanford, Calif.

Eberhard, Wolfram. 1971. "Studies in Chinese Religion: 1920–1932" (originally published in German in 1933). In Eberhard, *Moral and Social Values of the Chinese: Collected Essays.* Taipei.

FitzGerald, C. P. 1969. "Religion in China." In Guy Wint, ed., *Asia Handbook.* Harmondsworth.

Freedman, Maurice. 1962. Review of C. K. Yang's *Religion in Chinese Society, Journal of Asian Studies,* vol. 21, no. 4.

———— 1963. "A Chinese Phase in Social Anthropology," *The British Journal of Sociology,* vol. 14, no. 1.

———— 1969. "Geomancy." In *Proceedings of the Royal Anthropological Institute of Great Britain and Ireland, 1968.* London.

———— 1974. "The Politics of an Old State: A View from the Chinese Lineage." In John Davis, ed., *Choice and Change: Essays in Honour of Lucy Mair.* London.

Gernet, Jacques. 1968. *Ancient China from the Beginnings to the Empire.* Trans. Raymond Rudorff. London.

Giles, Herbert A. 1882. *Historic China and Other Sketches.* London.

Granet, Marcel. 1919. *Fêtes et chansons anciennes de la Chine*. Paris. 2d ed., 1929.

————— 1922. *La Religion des Chinois*. Paris. 2d ed., 1951. Translated into English as *The Religion of the Chinese People*. Trans. Maurice Freedman. Oxford, forthcoming.

————— 1926. *Danses et légendes de la Chine ancienne*. 2 vols. Paris.

————— 1929. *La Civilisation chinoise: La Vie publique et la vie privée*. Paris. Translated into English as *Chinese Civilization*. Trans. K. E. Innes and M. R. Brailsford. London, 1930.

————— 1932. *Festivals and Songs of Ancient China*. Trans. E. D. Edwards. London. English translation of Granet 1919.

————— 1934. *La Pensée chinoise*. Paris.

Harvey, Edwin D. 1933. *The Mind of China*. New Haven, Conn.

Hsiao, Kung-chuan. 1960. *Rural China: Imperial Control in the Nineteenth Century*. Seattle.

Hsu, Francis L. K. 1952. *Religion, Science and Human Crises: A Study of China in Transition and Its Implications for the West*. London.

————— 1971. *Under the Ancestors' Shadow: Kinship, Personality, and Social Mobility in China*, rev. ed. Stanford, Calif.

Kulp, Daniel Harrison, II. 1925. *Country Life in South China: The Sociology of Familism*. Vol. 1, *Phenix Village, Kwangtung, China*. New York.

Levenson, Joseph R., and H. Franz Schurmann. 1969. *China: An Interpretive History, From the Beginnings to the Fall of Han*. Berkeley and Los Angeles.

Lévi-Strauss, Claude. 1949. *Les Structures élémentaires de la parenté*. Paris. Revised and translated into English as *The Elementary Structures of Kinship*. Trans. James Harle Bell and John Richard von Sturmer; ed. Rodney Needham. London, 1969.

Levy, Marion J., Jr. 1949. *The Family Revolution in Modern China*. Cambridge, Mass.

Li An-che. 1938. "Notes on the Necessity of Field Research in Social Science in China," *Yenching Journal of Social Studies* (Peking), vol. 1, no. 1.

Lyall, Sir Arthur C. 1882. "Relation of Religion to Asiatic States," *Fortnightly Review* (London), Feb. 1882.

————— 1907. "On the Relations Between State and Religion in China." In Lyall, *Asiatic Studies, Religious and Social*, Second Series, 2d ed. (part of this essay had appeared in the First Series of 1882). London.

Mote, F. W. 1972. "China's Past in the Study of China Today—Some Comments on the Recent Work of Richard Solomon," *Journal of Asian Studies*, vol. 24, no. 1.

Muramatsu, Yuji. 1960. "Some Themes in Chinese Rebel Ideologies." In Arthur F. Wright, ed., *The Confucian Persuasion*. Stanford, Calif.

Shirokogoroff, S. M. 1942. "Ethnographic Investigation of China," *Folklore Studies*, vol. 1.

Shryock, John. 1931. *The Temples of Anking and Their Cults: A Study of Modern Chinese Religion*. Paris.

Skinner, G. William. 1964. "Marketing and Social Structure in Rural China, Part I," *Journal of Asian Studies*, vol. 24, no. 1.

————— 1971. "Chinese Peasants and the Closed Community: An Open and Shut Case," *Comparative Studies in Society and History*, vol. 13, no. 3.

Smith, Huston. 1970. "Transcendence in Traditional China." In James T. C. Liu and Wei-ming Tu, eds., *Traditional China*. Englewood Cliffs, N.J.

Stein, R. A. 1957. "Les Religions de la Chine." In *Encyclopédie Française*, vol. 19. Paris.

Tambiah, S. J. 1970. *Buddhism and the Spirit Cults in North-East Thailand*. Cambridge, Eng.

Thompson, Laurence G. 1969. *Chinese Religion: An Introduction*. Belmont, Calif.

Topley, Marjorie. 1967. "Some Basic Conceptions and Their Traditional Relationship to Society." In *Some Traditional Chinese Ideas and Conceptions in Hong Kong Social Life Today*. Hong Kong.

Van der Sprenkel, Otto. 1964. "Max Weber on China," *History and Theory, Studies in the Philosophy of History*, vol. 3, no. 3.

Wakeman, Frederic, Jr. 1966. *Strangers at the Gate: Social Disorder in South China, 1839–1861*. Berkeley, Calif.

Ward, Barbara E. 1965. "Varieties of the Conscious Model: The Fishermen of South China." In M. P. Banton, ed., *The Relevance of Models for Social Anthropology*. London and New York.

Weber, Max. 1951. *The Religion of China, Confucianism and Taoism*. Trans. and ed. Hans H. Gerth. Glencoe, Ill.

———— 1965. *The Sociology of Religion*. Trans. Ephraim Fischoff. London.

Welch, Holmes. 1970. "Facades of Religion in China," *Asian Survey*, vol. 10, no. 7.

Yang, C. K. 1957. "The Functional Relationship Between Confucian Thought and Chinese Religion." In John K. Fairbank, ed., *Chinese Thought and Institutions*. Chicago.

———— 1961. *Religion in Chinese Society: A Study of Contemporary Social Functions of Religion and Some of Their Historical Factors*. Berkeley, Calif.

Religious Organization in the History of a Taiwanese Town

Chu-lo hsien chih. 1968. Taipei: Reprinted by the Kuo-fang Yen-chiu Yüan and the Chung-fa Hsüeh-shu Yüan. Vol. 12.

Saso, Michael R. 1972. *Taoism and the Rite of Cosmic Renewal*. Pullman, Wash.

Tan-shui t'ing chih. 1968. Taipei: Reprinted by the Kuo-fang Yen-chiu Yüan and the Chung-fa Hsüeh-shu Yüan.

Wang Shih-ch'ing. 1972. "Min-chien hsin-yang tsai pu-t'ung tsu-chi i-min te hsiang-ts'un chih li-shih," *T'ai-wan wen-hsien*, no. 23, pp. 1–38.

Village Alliance Temples in Hong Kong

Baker, Hugh D. R. 1968. *A Chinese Lineage Village: Sheung Shui*. Stanford, Calif.

Barrow, J. 1959(?). *Report on the New Territories for the Year 1950*. Hong Kong.

Brim, J. A. 1970. "Local Systems and Modernizing Change in the New Territories of Hong Kong." Ph.D. dissertation, Stanford University.

Blau, Peter M., and W. Richard Scott. 1962. *Formal Organizations: A Comparative Approach*. San Francisco.

Dispatches, 1899. *Dispatches and Other Papers Relating to the Extension of the Colony of Hong Kong.* Hong Kong Sessional Papers, 1899.

Freedman, Maurice. 1966. *Chinese Lineage and Society: Fukien and Kwangtung.* New York.

Groves, R. G. 1969. "Militia, Market, and Lineage: Chinese Resistance to the Occupation of Hong Kong's New Territories," *Journal of the Hong Kong Branch of the Royal Asiatic Society,* 9: 31–64.

Hayes, James W. 1962. "The Pattern of Life in the New Territories in 1868," *Journal of the Hong Kong Branch of the Royal Asiatic Society,* 2: 75–102.

—————— 1963. "Cheung Chau 1850–1898: Information from Commemorative Tablets," *Journal of the Hong Kong Branch of the Royal Asiatic Society,* 3: 88–106.

—————— 1964. "Peng Chau Between 1798–1899," *Journal of the Hong Kong Branch of the Royal Asiatic Society,* 4: 71–96.

Hong Kong Government. 1962. *Report of the Census, 1961.* Hong Kong.

Lin Huo. 1964(?). *Ta-shu-hsia T'ien-hou miao ho-tan-jih ch'iang-p'ao yen-pien.* In *Yüan-lang shih-pa-hsiang ch'ing-chu T'ien-hou pao-tan hui-ching hsun-yu t'e-k'an.* Hong Kong.

Lockhart, J. H. Stewart. 1900. *Report on the New Territory during the First Year of British Administration.* Hong Kong Sessional Papers, 1900.

Lott, Albert J., and Bernice E. Lott. 1965. "Group Cohesiveness as Interpersonal Attraction: A Review of Relationships with Antecedent and Consequent Variables," *Psychological Bulletin,* 64: 259–309.

Parsons, Talcott, Robert F. Bales, and Edward A. Shils. 1953. *Working Papers in the Theory of Action.* Glencoe, Ill.

Potter, Jack M. 1968. *Capitalism and the Chinese Peasant: Social and Economic Change in a Hong Kong Village.* Berkeley, Calif.

Report 1898. *Extracts from a Report by Mr. Stewart Lockhart on the Extension of the Colony of Hong Kong.* Hong Kong Sessional Papers, 1899.

Sung, Hok-p'ang. 1935. "Legends and Stories of the New Territories," *Hong Kong Naturalist,* vol. 6, no. 1.

Teng Yu-chung. 1965 (?). *Hsia-ts'un-hsiang chien-chiao ching-kuo.* In *Yüan-lang Hsia-ts'un-hsiang shih-nien i-chieh t'ai-p'ing ch'ing-chiao chien-chiao t'e-k'an.* Hong Kong.

Tratman, D. W. 1922. "Report on the New Territories for the Year 1921, Northern District," *Hong Kong Annual Reports, 1921.*

Wakeman, Frederic, Jr. 1966. *Strangers at the Gate: Social Disorder in South China, 1839–1861.* Berkeley, Calif.

Wang, Ch'ung-hsi, et al. 1891. *Hsin-an hsien-chih.* (Twenty-four *chuan.*)

Wodehouse, P. P. J. 1911. *Report on Census, 1911.* Hong Kong Sessional Papers, 1911.

Domestic and Communal Worship in Taiwan

Feuchtwang, Stephan. 1974. "City Temples in Taipei under Three Regimes." In Mark Elvin and G. William Skinner, eds., *The Chinese City Between Two Worlds.* Stanford, Calif.

Ino Yoshinori. 1928. *Taiwan bunkashi* (Cultural history of Taiwan).

Jordan, David K. 1972. *Gods, Ghosts, and Ancestors.* Berkeley, Calif.

Kataoka Iwao. 1924. *Taiwan fūzoku shi* (Taiwanese customs). Taipei.

Li T'ien-ch'un. 1962. "T'ai-pei ti-ch'ü chih k'ai-t'o yü ssu-miao" (Temples and the development of the Taipei area). In *T'ai-pei wen-hsien* 1 (June 1962).

Liu Chi-wan. 1963. "Ch'ing tai T'ai-wan chih ssu-miao" (Temples in Taiwan during the Ch'ing period). In *T'ai-pei wen-hsien* 5 (September 1963).

Gods, Ghosts, and Ancestors

Addison, J. T. 1925. *Chinese Ancestor Worship: A Study of Its Meaning and Relations with Christianity*. Shanghai.

Ahern, Emily M. 1973. *The Cult of the Dead in a Chinese Village*. Stanford, Calif.

Ayscough, Florence. 1924. "Cult of the Ch'eng Huang Lao Yeh," *Journal of the Royal Asiatic Society, North China Branch*, 55: 131–55.

Bryson, Mary. 1900. *Child Life in China*. London.

Ch'ü, T'ung-tsu. 1962. *Local Government in China Under the Ch'ing*. Cambridge, Mass. Paperback ed.: Stanford, Calif., 1969.

Coltman, Robert. 1891. *The Chinese, Their Present and Future: Medical, Political, and Social*. Philadelphia.

Cormack, Mrs. J. G. 1935. *Everyday Customs in China*. Edinburgh.

Day, Clarence Burton. 1940. *Chinese Peasant Cults: Being a Study of Chinese Paper Gods*. Shanghai.

Diamond, Norma. 1969. *K'un Shen: A Taiwan Village*. New York.

Doolittle, Rev. Justus. 1865. *Social Life of the Chinese*. New York. 2 vols.

Fabre, P. Alfred. 1935. "Avril au pays des aieux," *Catholic Church in China: Commissionis Synodalis*, 8: 111–31.

Fei, Hsiao-tung. 1939. *Peasant Life in China*. New York.

Freedman, Maurice. 1966. *Chinese Lineage and Society: Fukien and Kwangtung*. London.

———— 1967. "Ancestor Worship: Two Facets of the Chinese Case." In Maurice Freedman, ed., *Social Organization: Essays Presented to Raymond Firth*. Chicago.

Giles, Herbert A. 1915. *Confucianism and Its Rivals*. London.

Hsu, Francis L. K. 1952. *Religion, Science and Human Crisis*. London.

———— 1963. *Clan, Caste and Club*. Princeton, N.J.

Johnston, R. F. 1910. *Lion and Dragon in Northern China*. New York.

Jordan, David K. 1972. *Gods, Ghosts, and Ancestors: Folk Religion in a Taiwanese Village*. Berkeley, Calif.

MacKay, George Leslie. 1895. *From Far Formosa: The Island, Its People and Missions*. New York.

Pruen, Mrs. William L. 1906. *The Provinces of Western China*. London.

Schipper, Kristofer M. "Religious Organization in Traditional Tainan." In G. William Skinner, ed., *The City in Late Imperial China*. Stanford, Calif., forthcoming.

Shen, Chien-shih. 1936–37. "An Essay on the Primitive Meaning of the Character *Kuei*," *Monumenta Serica*, 2: 1–20.

Shryock, John. 1931. *The Temples of Anking and Their Cults*. Paris.

Smith, Arthur H. 1899. *Village Life in China*. New York.

Wang Sung-hsing. 1973. "Ancestors Proper and Peripheral." Paper presented at the Symposium on Ancestor Worship, IXth International Congress of Anthropological and Ethnological Sciences. Chicago.

Taiwanese Architecture and the Supernatural

Dillingham, Reed, and Chang-lin Dillingham. 1971. *A Survey of Traditional Architecture of Taiwan.* Taichung, Taiwan.

Jordan, David K. 1972. *Gods, Ghosts, and Ancestors: Folk Religion in a Chinese Village.* Berkeley, Calif.

Kajiwara Michiyoshi. 1941. *Taiwan nōmin seikatsu kō* (Peasant life in Taiwan). Taipei.

MacKay, George Leslie. 1896. *From Far Formosa.* New York.

Suzuki Seiichiro. 1934. *Taiwan kyūkan: Kankonsōsai to nenjū gyōji* (Taiwanese customs: The life cycle and the year cycle). Taipei.

Wang Sung-hsing. 1967. *Kuei-shan tao: Han-jen yu-ts'un she-hui chih yen-chiu* (Kuei-shan Island: a study of a Chinese fishing village). Taipei.

———. 1971. "Pooling and Sharing in a Chinese Fishing Economy: Kuei-shan Tao." Unpublished Ph.D. diss., University of Tokyo.

Cantonese Shamanism

De Groot, J. J. 1969. *The Religious System of China.* 6 vols. Taipei. (Originally published 1892–1919.)

——— 1912. *The Religion of the Chinese.* New York.

Doolittle, J. 1966. *Social Life of the Chinese.* Taipei. (Original publication: New York, 1865.)

Elliott, Alan J. A. 1955. *Chinese Spirit Medium Cults in Singapore.* London.

Foster, George M. 1965. "Peasant Society and the Image of Limited Good," *American Anthropologist,* 67: 293–315.

Potter, Jack M. 1968. *Capitalism and the Chinese Peasant: Social and Economic Change in a Hong Kong Village.* Berkeley, Calif.

——— 1970. "Wind, Water, Bones and Souls: The Religious Life of the Cantonese Peasant," *Journal of Oriental Studies* (Hong Kong), vol. III, no. 1, pp. 139–53. (Reprinted in Laurence G. Thompson, ed., *The Chinese Way in Religion,* Belmont, Calif., 1973.)

Cosmic Antagonisms: A Mother-Child Syndrome

Doolittle, J. 1865. *Social Life of the Chinese.* Vol. 1. New York.

Freedman, Maurice. 1970. "Ritual Aspects of Chinese Kinship and Marriage." In Maurice Freedman, ed., *Family and Kinship in Chinese Society.* Stanford, Calif.

Gennep, Arnold van. 1960. *The Rites of Passage.* Trans. Monika B. Vizedom and Gabrielle L. Caffee. London.

Mathews, R. H. 1961. *Chinese-English Dictionary.* Rev. American ed. Cambridge, Mass.

Thompson, J. C. 1890. "Native Practice and Practitioners," *China Medical Journal,* vol. 4.

Topley, Marjorie. 1970. "Chinese Traditional Ideas and the Treatment of Disease: Two Examples from Hong Kong," *Man* (n.s.), vol. 5.

Tsay, Queenie. 1918. "Chinese Superstitions Relating to Childbirth," *China Medical Journal,* vol. 32, no. 6.

Wolf, Margery. 1972. *Women and the Family in Rural Taiwan.* Stanford, Calif.

Ancestor Worship and Burial Practices

Baker, Hugh D. R. 1968. *A Chinese Lineage Village: Sheung Shui.* Stanford, Calif.
Freedman, Maurice, ed. 1970. *Family and Kinship in Chinese Society.* Stanford, Calif.
Potter, Jack M. 1968. *Capitalism and the Chinese Peasant: Social and Economic Change in a Hong Kong Village.* Berkeley, Calif.

Affines and the Rituals of Kinship

Fei, Hsiao-tung. 1939. *Peasant Life in China.* London.
Freedman, Maurice. 1970. "Ritual Aspects of Chinese Kinship and Marriage." In Maurice Freedman, ed., *Family and Kinship in Chinese Society.* Stanford, Calif.
Gallin, Bernard. 1960. "Matrilateral and Affinal Relationships of a Taiwanese Village," *American Anthropologist,* vol. 62, no. 4.
———— 1963. "Cousin Marriage in China," *Ethnology,* vol. 2, no. 1.
Hsu, Francis L. K. 1945. "Observations on Cross-cousin Marriage in China," *American Anthropologist,* vol. 47, no. 1.
Lévi-Strauss, Claude. 1963. *Structural Anthropology.* New York.
Turner, V. W. 1967. *The Forest of Symbols: Aspects of Ndembu Ritual.* Ithaca, N.Y.
———— 1968. *The Drums of Affliction.* Oxford.
———— 1969. *The Ritual Process: Structure and Anti-structure.* Chicago.
Wolf, Arthur P. 1970. "Chinese Kinship and Mourning Dress." In Maurice Freedman, ed., *Family and Kinship in Chinese Society.* Stanford, Calif.
Wolf, Margery. 1972. *Women and the Family in Rural Taiwan.* Stanford, Calif.
Yang, Martin C. 1965. *A Chinese Village: Taitou, Shantung Province.* New York.

Character List

Entries are categorized as follows: Mandarin (M), Cantonese (C), and Hokkien (H). When the same term appears in more than one language or in different romanizations of the same language, the characters are given for one entry only. The entries without characters refer the reader to the one with characters. He is thereby reminded that *fu* (M) is the same as *hu* (H) and *vu* (C). Personal names and names of provinces, countries, and major cities are excluded.

A-lien (M) 阿連
a-naai (C) 阿奶
a-so (C) 阿嫂
a-tse (C) 阿姊
am-hang (H) 暗行
an (M) 安
Ang Kong (H) 尪公

Ban Siong Ia (H) 萬善爺
Ban Siong Tong (H) 萬善堂；萬善同
bou sun e kui (H) 無孫的鬼

Cau Kong (C) 周公
ce (H) 祭
chai-png (H) 菜飯
chai-yu (H) 菜友
chan fa (C) 診花
chang (M) 章
Chang Kung-kuan (M) 張公館
Ch'ang-fu Yen (M) 長福岩
Chao-fen (C) 酒飯
Chau Wong Temple (C) 周王廟
Ch'e Kung (M) 車公
chen (M) 震
chen-yen (M) 真言

Ch'en Ku Niang (M) 陳姑娘
Ch'en Nai Ma (M) 陳奶媽
Ch'en Sheng Wang Hui (M) 陳聖王會
Cheng (M) 正
Cheng-i (M) 正一；正乙
Cheng-i Tz'u-t'an (M) 正一嗣壇
cheng-t'ing (M) 正廳
cheng-wu (M) 正屋
Ch'eng Huang (M) 城隍
Ch'eng Huang Yeh (M) 城隍爺
chi (M) 祀
Chi-an Kung (M) 濟安宮
Chi-chi (M) 集集
chi-chiu (M) 祭酒
chi:-m (H) 親姆
ch'i (M) 氣
ch'i-an (M) 祈安
Ch'i-chou (M) 溪州
Ch'i-nan (M) 溪南
Ch'i-pei (M) 溪北
chia (M) 甲
chia-miao (M) 家廟
chia-shen (M) 家神
Chiang-tzu-liao (M) 猪仔寮

ch'iang-p'ao (M) 槍炮
chiao (M) 醮
chien (M) 間
chien-chiao (M) 鑒醮
chien-jen (M) 賤人
chien-ts'o (M) 簡厝
ch'ien (M) 乾
Chieng Cui Co Su (H), *see*
    Ch'ing Shui Tsu Shih Kung
Chih (M) [priestly office] 職
chih (M) [diocese] 治
ch'ih-fu-hui (M) 吃福會
Chin Hua Fu Jen (M) 金花
    夫人
chin-ke (H) 親家
Chin-lu-chiao (M) 金籙醮
Chin-shan (M) 金山
ching (M) 驚
Ch'ing-ch'eng (M) 慶成
Ch'ing-ho Kung (M) 清和宮
Ch'ing-lien (M) 清連
Ch'ing Ming (M) 清明
Ch'ing Shui Tsu Shih Kung (M)
    清水祖師公
Ch'ing-wei (M) 清微
Chu-kan-ts'o (M) 竹篙厝
Chu-lun (M) 竹崙
Chu-shou (M) 祝壽
Chu T'ou Kung (M) 竹頭公
Chun-an-chiao (M) 圳安腳
Chung-chuang (M) 中莊
Chung-ho (M) 中和
chung-hu-min (M) 眾戶民
Chung-li (M) 中壢
Chung-p'u (M) 中埔
Chung-yeung (C) 重陽
chung yüan (M) 中元
Ch'ung-hsing Kung (M) 重興宮
Chut mng, ciaq Tho Te Kong (H)
    出門食土地公

chü (M) 巨
ci: (H) 錢
Ciam-sua:-po (H) 尖山埔
cieng-sin (H) 正神
cin-ci: po-un (H) 進錢補運
ciok-pik siu-kim (H) 祝百壽金
ciou (H), *see* chiao
co-kong (H) 祖公
Cu Hieng Kong (H) 自興公
cue-kheq (H) 做客
Cui Hua Sian Kong (H) 水化
    仙公
Cui Lau Kong (H) 水流公
Cui Tik Lau Kong (H) 水德
    流公

dsaau zan (C) 酬神
Dsann Kux Loo Ye (C) 陳古
    老爺
dsox zan dhaan (C) 坐神壇

erh-fang (M) 二房
Erhlin (M) 二林
Erh P'in (M) 二品

Fa-lu (M) 發爐
fa-meng (C) 花命
Fa-shih (M) 法師
fa-wong foo-mo (C) 花王父母
Fan-tzu-p'u (M) 番仔埔
fang (M) 房
fen (M) 分
Feng-kuei-tien (M) 風櫃店
feng-shui (M) 風水
fū (M) [a sage] 夫
fú (M) [evil charm] 符
fú (M) [propitious action
    from Heaven] 福
Fu-an Kung (M) 福安宮
Fu-an Miao (M) 福安廟

Fu-hsing Kung (M) 福興宮
Fu-lai ch'un (M) 福來村
fu-shu (M) 福疏
Fu Te Cheng Shen (M) 福德
　正神
Fu-te Kung (M) 福德宮

gou-ci: (H) 高錢
gua-co-touq (H) 外祖桌
gua-ke (H) 外家
gua-sin (H) 外神

Ha Tsuen (C) 廈村
Hai-shan chuang (M) 海山
Hang Mei (C) 坑尾村
Hang Tau (C) 坑頭村
hap-kang-e (H) 闔港的
Heng-k'eng-tzu (M) 橫坑仔
Heng Shan (M) 衡山
hi-su (H) 喜事
hieng (H) 興
hiong-su (H) 兇事
Ho-lien (M) 和連
ho-naan tso-yan (C) 好難做人
hok-kim (H) 福金
hok-sai (H) 服事
hong-cui (H), *see* feng-shui
hou-hia:-ti (H) 好兄弟
Hou-ts'un-tzu (M) 後村子
Hou-t'u (M) 后土
Hsi-sha-lun (M) 西沙崙
Hsi-sheng (M) 西盛
Hsi-tzu T'ing (M) 惜字亭
Hsia-ch'i-chou (M) 下溪州
Hsia Hai Ch'eng Huang Temple (M)
　霞海城隍廟
Hsia-shan-chiao (M) 下山腳
Hsia-shan-tzu-chiao (M) 下山
　子腳
hsia yüan (M) 下元

hsiang (M) 鄉
hsiao-tsu (M) 小租
hsieh (M) 邪
Hsieh-en (M) 謝恩
hsien (M) 仙
Hsien Kung Temple (M) 仙
　公廟
Hsin-chu (M) 新竹
hsin-shih (M) 信士
Hsin-tien (M) 新店
hsin-t'u (M) 信徒
Hsin Yüan Shuai (M) 辛元帥
Hsing Fu Wang Yeh (M) 邢府
　王爺
hsing-hsiang (M) 行像
Hsüan T'ien Shang Ti (M) 玄天
　上帝
hu (H) [court or prefecture] 府
hu (H) [a sage], *see* fū
hu (H) [evil charm], *see* fú
hu-a-sian (H) 符仔仙
Hua Shan (M) 華山
huan-kan (H) 凡間
huan-shen (M) 還神
Huang-lu-chai (M) 黃籙齋
Huat-su (H), *see* Fa-shih
hue (H) 花
hui (M) 會
hun (M *and* H) 魂
Hung-hsi (M) 吽? 咴?
Hung Sheng (M) 洪聖
Huo-po (M) 吷嗳

I Ai Kung (M) 義愛公
I-p'in (M) 一品
i-tuk, kung-tuk (C) 以毒攻毒
im (H), *see* yin
im-kan (H) 陰間
iong (H), *see* yang
iong-kan (H) 陽間

iu (c) 妖
Iu-ieng Kiong (H), *see*
  Yu-ying Kung
Iu Ieng Kong (H), *see*
  Yu Ying Kung
Iu-kiu pit-ieng (H), *see*
  Yu-ch'iu pi-ying
iu-kwaai (c) 妖怪

Jang-tsai (M) 禳災
je-nao (M) 熱鬧
jen (M) 人
jen-ch'ing-wei (M) 人情味

ka-be (H) 甲馬
K'ai Chang Sheng Wang (M)
  開漳聖王
k'ai-chi-tsu (M) 開基祖
k'ai-kwoh (c) 契過
k'ai-ma (c) 契媽
k'ai-nui (c) 契女
k'ai-shu (M) 楷書
k'ai-tai (c) 契弟
k'ai-tsai (c) 契子
k'ai-ye (c) 契爺
kak-thau-e (H) 角頭的
kak-thau-sin (H) 角頭神
Kam Fa Mo (c) 金花母
kam taap (c) 金塔
Kam Tin (c) 錦田
Kam Tin Pak Pin (c) 錦田
  北邊
Kan-yüan (M) 柑園
Kang-shan (M) 岡山
ke-chia hsin-hsiang yen-men
  hsüan-shu (M) 各家行香
  沿門宣疏
ke-cng (H) 嫁粧
ke-kieng (H), *see* kuo-ching

k'ei (c) 奇
k'ei-kwaai (c) 奇怪
k'ei-peng (c) 奇病
khan-bong-hun (H) 牽亡魂
khaq-sue (H) (較)小
khaq-tua (H) (較)大
khay (c) 契
khay jair (c), *see* k'ai-tsai
khay kong (c) 契公
khay mha (c), *see* k'ai-ma
Khe-ki:-chu (H) 溪墘厝
kheq-thia: (H) 客廳
kho-ci: (H) 厙錢
kho-kun (H) 犒軍
khua:-thi: (H) 看天
khui-hue (H) 開花
kiat-su (H) 吉事
kieng-hong (H) 敬奉
kieng-i (H) 供衣
kim (H) 金
kim-ci: (H) 金錢
ko-niu-biou (H) 姑娘廟
kong-ma (H) 公媽
kong phai:-ue (H) 講歹話
kong-thia: (H), *see* kung-t'ing
kong-tik (H) 功德
k'ou (M) 口
k'ou-chüeh (M) 口訣
ku (M) 股
ku-hun (M) 孤魂
kua-kim (H) 刈金
kuan-hsi (M) 關西
Kuan-li (M) 管理
Kuan Ti (M) 關帝
Kuan Yin (M) 觀音
Kuan Yin Fu Tsu (M) 觀音
  佛祖
Kuan Yin Kuo-t'ou (M) 觀音
  過頭

kuei (c *and* м) 鬼
Kuei-lun Ling (м) 龜崙嶺
Kuei Shan (м) 龜山
Kuei-shan Tao (м) 龜山頭
kui (н) [expensive] 貴
kui (н) [ghost], *see* kuei
kui khi (н) 貴氣
kui mia: (н) 貴命
kui-sin (н) 鬼神
kun-cua (н) 銀紙
Kun Iam Mha (c) 觀音媽
kung (м) 公
kung-t'ing (м) 公廳
kuo-chi (м) 過繼
kuo-ching (м) 國慶
kuo-huo (м) 過火
kwaai (c) 怪
kwai (c), *see* kuei
Kwan Kong (c) 關公

Laan Sio Tzex (c) 蘭小姐
Lan-ts'o (м) 藍厝
Lao Chün (м) 老君
Lau-chu-po (н) 劉厝埔
Lau Tua Kong (н) 老大公
lau-ziat (н) 鬧熱
Le-ciq-be (н) 犂舌尾
Lee Paak (c) 李伯
lei (м) 雷
Li Ch'un (м) 立春
li-hai (н) 厲害
lien (м) 廉
lieng (н), *see* ling
Lieng Cui Khi: (н) 冷水坑
lieng-hun (н) 靈魂
lieng-kam (н) 靈感
ling (м) 靈
Ling-pao (м) 靈寶
lo-cu (н), *see* lu-chu

lo-mua: (н) 流氓
loh-chaai tsai (c) 攞債仔
loh-kwai tsai (c) 攞鬼仔
lu (м) [name of a star] 祿
Lu (м) [Register] 籙
lu-chu (м) 爐主
Lukang (м) 鹿港
Lu Shan (м) 盧山
Lung-hu (м) 龍虎
Lung-hu Shan (м) 龍虎山
Lung-shan Ssu (м) 龍山寺

m-saam, m-sz (c) 唔三唔四
Ma Tsu (м) 媽祖
Ma Tsu Hui (м) 媽祖會
Mai Po (c) 米婆
man kwai p'o (c) 問鬼婆
mann mae phox (c) 問米婆
mann seag phox (c) 問醒婆
Mao Shan (м) 茅山
meng (c) 命
Mi-chüeh (м) 祕訣
miao (м) 廟
miao-chu (м) 廟祝
Miao-li (м) 苗栗
miao-mien (м) 廟面
ming (м) 命
Mu-cha (м) 木柵

Naam Mo Lhoo (c) 南無佬
Naam Mo Sin Shaang (c) 南無
　先生
nei-tan (м) 內丹
ngo-kui (н) 五鬼

Ong Ia (н) 王爺
Ong Ia Kong (н) 王爺公

Pa-li (м) 八里

pai (H *and* M) 拜

Pai Hsing Kung (M) 百姓公

pai-luan (M) 百亂

pai-pai (H) 拜拜

Pak Sha (C) 白沙

Pan-ch'iao (M) 板橋

pang (M) 榜

Pao Sheng Ta Ti (M) 保生大帝

Pat Heung Sheung Tsuen (C) 八鄉上村

pay dhaan (C) 拜壇

Pei Chi (M) 北極

Pei Ti (M) 北帝

P'eng-ts'o (M) 彭厝

Peq Ho (H) 白虎

phieng-le (H) 聘禮

pho-sat (H) 菩薩

Pho To Kong (H) 普渡公

pien (M) 便

Ping Shan (C) 屏山

p'ing (M) 坪

P'ing-ho (M) 平和

P'ing-ting (M) 坪頂

p'o (M) 破

P'o-chiao (M) 坡角

P'o-nei-k'eng (M) 坡內坑

pok kwah (C) 卜卦

poo-sat (C), *see* pho-sat

P'u-li (M) 埔里

p'u-tu (M) 普渡

Pueq Lang Kong (H) 八人公

pun-cau (H) 分灶

pun-mia-ci: (H) 本命錢

put-co (H) 佛祖

put-kong (H) 佛公

Saan Zan (C) 山神

sai-kong (H) 師公

sai-kong-kut (H) 師公骨

Sam Kai Kong (H) 三界公

Sam Kuan Tai Te (H) 三官大帝

San-chiao-p'u (M) 三角埔

San Chieh Kung Hui (M) 三界公會

San-chung-p'u (M) 三重埔

San-hsia (M) 三峽

San-kuan-cho (M) 三官棹

san-mien-pi (M) 三面壁

San-nai (M) 三奶

San Shan Kuo Wang (M) 三山國王

San-wu Tu-kung (M) 三五都功

San-yi (M) 三義

san yüan chai (M) 三元齋

shan (C), *see* shen

Shan-chiao (M) 山腳

Shan-tzu-chiao (M) 山子腳

Shang-ching (M) 上清派

Shang Ti Kung (M) 上帝公

shang yüan (M) 上元

Shap Pat Heung (C) 十八鄉

shen (M) 神

Shen-hsiao (M) 神霄

Shen-kang hsiang (M) 神岡鄉

shen-ming (M) 神明

shen-ming-hui (M) 神明會

shen-t'ai-tzu (M) 神柸子

shen-t'ing (M) 神廳

Sheung Shui (C) 上水

Sheung Tsuen (C) 上村

shi-shan (C) 時辰

shi-shan ho (C) 時辰好

shih (M) [scholar, official] 士

shih (M) [weight unit] 石

Shih-hui-k'eng (M) 石灰坑

Shih Pa Shou Kuan Yin Hui (M) 十八手觀音會

shu (M) 疏

Shu-lin (M) 樹林

Shu-te Kung (M) 樹德宮

Shu-yüan (M) 書院

shuk (C) 屬

Shun Yi Kung (M) 順義宮

Shun Yi Wang Yeh (M) 順義 王爺

sia: (H) (神)

Sia: Ma (H) 聖媽

sian (H) 先

sian-si:-ma (H) 先生媽

sieng-le (H) 牲禮

Sieng Ong Kong (H) 聖王公

sim-pua (H) 新婦仔

sin (H), *see* shen

sin-bieng (H), *see* shen-ming

sin kwat (C) 仙骨

sin-lang (H) 新人

sin low (C) 仙路

sin-su (H), *see* hsin-shih

Siong-pieng (H) 賞兵

siou-gun (H) 小銀

siu-kim (H) 壽金

siu:-pieng (H) 賞兵

So Tua Ong (H), *see* Su Ta Wang

song-su (H) 喪事

su (H), *see* shih

Su Fu Ta Wang Yeh (M) 蘇府 大王爺

Su Ta Wang (M) 蘇大王

Sun Gi Ong Ia (H), *see* Shun Yi Wang Yeh

Sung Shan (M) 嵩山

Szu-ku Ma (M) 四股媽

Ta-ch'i (M) 大溪

Ta Chiang Yeh (M) 大將爺

ta-chiao (M) 大醮

Ta Chung Yeh (M) 大眾爺

ta-fang (M) 大房

Ta Tao Kung Miao (M) 大道 公廟

ta-tsu (M) 大祖

ta-tzu (M) 大字

tai (C) 弟

Tai-an-hai (H) 大安海

Tai Ciong Ia (H), *see* Ta Chung Yeh

tai-lang (H) 代人

Tai-t'ien hsing-hua (M) 代天 行化

tai-wei chuan tsou (M) 代為 轉奏

T'ai-chi (M) 太極

T'ai-p'ing-ch'iao (M) 太平橋

t'ai-shih-tsu (M) 太始祖

Tan-shui (M) 淡水

Tan-t'ien (M) 丹田

t'an (M) 貪

T'an-te Kung (M) 潭德宮

T'an-ti (M) 潭底

tang-ki (H) 童乩

t'ang (M) 堂

Tao-shih (M) 道士

T'ao-yüan (M) 桃園

Te-an Kung (M) 德安宮

te-cu (H) 弟子

te-gak (H) 地獄

Te Ki Co (H), *see* Ti Chi Tsu

thak-so (H) 讀疏

thau-ke (H) 頭家

thi:-kau (H) 天狗

thi:-kim (H) 天金

Thi: Kong (H), *see* T'ien Kung

thia: (H) 廳

thia:-thau (H) 廳頭

Tho Te Biou (H) 土地廟
Tho Te Kong (H), *see* T'u Ti Kung
Ti Chi Tsu (M) 地基主
Ti Ts'ang Wang (M) 地藏王
tien-teng (M) 點燈
T'ien Hou (M) 天后
T'ien Kung (M) 天公
T'ien Shang Sheng Ma (M)
　天上聖媽
T'ien Shang Sheng Mu Hui (M)
　天上聖母會
t'in-shing (C) 天繩
t'in-sing (C) 天性
ting (M) 丁
Ting-chiao (M) 頂郊
ting-k'ou shu (M) 丁口疏
Ting-p'u (M) 頂埔
Tiong-cun (H) 中尊
t'oi-shan (C) 胎神
Tou Mu (M) 斗母
Tou-su (H), *see* Tao-shih
tou-teng (M) 斗燈
Tou-tiu: (H) 道長
ts'aam (C) 慘
Tsao Chün (M) 灶君
ts'e (C) 疾
ts'e-fung (C) 疾風
ts'in-shai (C) 前世
tsing-hei (C) 靜氣
ts'ip (C) 妾
tso-fu (M) 作福
tsu (M) 祖
Ts'un-te Kung (M) 村德宮
T'u-ch'eng (M) 土城
T'u-k'u (M) 土庫
t'u-ti (M) 土地
T'u Ti Kung (M) 土地公
T'u-ti-kung-p'u (M) 土地公埔
Tua Bong Kiong (H) 大墓宮

Tua Bong Kong (H) 大墓公
tua-gun (H) 大銀
Tua Ong Ia (H) 大王爺
tua pai-pai (H) 大拜拜
t'uan-lien (M) 團練
tuk (C) 毒
Tun Men K'ou-chiao Miao (M)
　屯門口角廟
Tun Mun (C) 屯門
tung (M) [a form of military
　alliance] 動
tung (M) [a mantric word] 洞
Tung-kua-shan (M) 冬瓜山
Tung Sam Tsuen (C) 東心村
tung-shih (M) 董事
T'ung-shu (M) 通書
tzu (M) 字
Tzu-chih T'ing Hui (M) 字紙
　亭會
Tz'u Pei Ssu (M) 慈悲寺
tz'u-t'ang (M) 祠堂

ui-lo (H) 圍爐

vu (C), *see* fú [evil charm]

Wa Dho (C) 華佗
Wai-p'u (M) 外埔
wan (C) 運
Wan-hua (M) 萬華
wang hsiang t'ai (M) 望鄉台
Wang Yeh Kung Hui (M)
　王爺公會
wei (M) 威
wei-min tso-chu (M) 為民
　作主
wen (M) 文
wen chien (M) 文檢
Wen-ping She (M) 文炳社

Wen-wu Miao (M) 文武廟
Wing Hing Wai (C) 永慶圍
Wong Chung (C) 凰涌
Wong Taai Sin (C) 黃大仙
wu (M) 武
wu-chien-wei (M) 五間尾
wu hsing (M) 五行
Wu-lei Fa (M) 五雷法
Wu-tang Shan (M) 武當山

yam (C), *see* yin
Yan-uen Shek (C) 姻緣石
yang (M) 陽
Yang Hou Wang (M) 楊侯王
yeung (C), *see* yang
yi (M) 意
yin (M) 陰
yin-ssu (M) 陰司

Ying-ko (M) 鶯歌
Yok Waang Daay Tay (C)
　玉皇大帝
Yu-ch'iu pi-ying (M) 有求必應
yu ying (M) 有應
Yu Ying Kung (M) 有應公
Yu-ying Kung (M) 有應宮
Yung-hsing Kung (M) 永興宮
yü (M) [strange simian creature] 禺
yü (M) [jade] 玉
Yü-ching (M) 玉京派
Yü Huang Ta Ti (M) 玉皇
　大帝
yüan (M) 願
yüeh (M) 約

Zap Yih Nae Neung (C) 十二
　奶娘

Index

acolytes, Taoist, 17, 312, 320–25 *passim*

adoption, 152–53, 166, 261, 269. *See also fictive* relationships

Africa: ancestor cults in, 168, 304, 306

Ahern, Emily M.: cited, 12ff, 149, 161, 164, 167n, 181–82, 253n, 273n; paper discussed, 13–15

altars: domestic, 13, 106ff, 114ff, 120, 131, 133, 148, 158, 184, 194; communal, 158; lineage, 158, 264; spirit mediums, 215–19, 227; Japanese, 344. *See also* domestic worship

am-hang festival, Lukang, 47–48

Amoy: mourning rites, 29

ancestor worship: Marcel Granet on, 33–34; as common element in Taiwanese belief, 44; and village alliance temples, 103; ritual seasons of, 114; motives for, 117, 146–47, 155–56, 159ff, 168; claims to, 147–48, 150f; and inheritance, 155–56, 16of; in Japan, 342–45 *passim*. *See also* ancestors

ancestors: character, 8, 117, 119, 160–68 *passim*; and domestic worship, 107, 188; place in supernatural order, 107, 192; kinds of offerings to, 111, 177, 180f, 289; in Japanese perception, 344–45. *See also* altars: domestic; ancestor worship

ancestral property, 149n, 155–56, 275–76, 277

An-ch'i: as place of origin, 73, 79, 89f, 105f, 132

Ang Kong, 125, 141

animism, 23n

anthropology: as distinct from sociology, 36–37; and Chinese studies, 36–38

architecture, 183–92; temples, 98, 190; San-hsia compounds, 154–55; principles of, 183; diagrams, 185, 186; economic influence on, 187

Ayscough, Florence: cited, 140

Baker, Hugh D. R.: cited, 268

Ban Siong Ia, 201

Ban Siong Tong, Chu-lun, 196

bandits: associated with ghosts, 8f, 170–75 *passim*, 179

Bed Mother, 289

beggars: associated with ghosts, 8f, 127, 134, 170–75 *passim*, 179, 181

benevolence, 122. *See also* "character" under ancestors; ghosts; *and* gods

Black-head Taoism, 17, 327n, 328–29, 331–33

bonding, *see* fictive relationships

branch temples, *see under* temples

breath-control, *see* Taoist priests: techniques

brides: qualities desired in, 281–82, 299

Brim, John A.: paper discussed, 6, 338

brotherhoods, 126–27, 128

Bryson, Mary: cited, 147

Buddhism 23, 34f, 40, 111; in Japan, 18, 342–43

Buddhist priests, 40, 49, 118. *See also* ritual specialists

bureaucrats: gods as, *see* gods: as metaphor

divination, 43ff, 52, 119, 123, 214–23
passim, 238–44 *passim*, 315, 319, 331,
333n. *See also* geomancy
domestic altars, *see under* altars
domestic worship: relationship to communal worship, 107–8, 111, 116, 122–
23; focuses of, 110, 114–16, 145,
153–54, 157f, 188; daily acts of, 131.
See also altars: domestic; *cheng-t'ing*
donations to temples, 50–58 *passim*, 62,
64–65, 76ff, 80f, 83f, 101, 108
Doolittle, the Rev. Justin, 143, 171, 175
Dragon, the, 123
Dsann Kux Loo Ye, 217f
Durkheim, Emile, 31ff

Earth God, *see* T'u Ti Kung
economic status and religious organization, 84f
elite: aspects in religion, 16, 23, 28, 38–
40; role of, in Lukang, 50, 51n, 54f
Elliott, A. J.: cited, 10
Embree, John: cited, 346
Emperor, Pearly (Jade), *see* Yü Huang
Ta Ti
Erhlin, 3, 44–45, 59f, 61f
ethnicity: role of, in Taiwan, 44, 73, 81,
86, 90, 92
exorcism, 125, 209, 218, 309, 328–36.
See also curing; mediums; Taoist
priests

Fabre, P. Alfred: cited, 149
fairy bones, fairy road concept, 225–26
familiars, 207, 217, 220. *See also*
mediums; possession
family: as expressed in architecture,
184, 186–87; divisions in, 290; social
relationships of, 279–307; conjugal,
300–304 *passim*
fa-shih, 48, 50
feasts and festivals, 43, 48, 54, 61–62,
76–78, 81–88 *passim*, 111–12, 126,
317; Moon Cake Festival, Ping Shan,
9, 208; Ch'ing Ming, 43f, 225; *am-
hang*, 47–48; and rotation, 78ff, 83,
85n, 87ff, 128, 135ff, 199, 276; Kuan
Yin Kuo-t'ou, 88; *huan-shen*, 99;
tso-fu, 99; *hsia-yüan*, 112; *shang-yüan*,
112–13, 125; *chung-yüan*, 112–13
New Year, 112–16, 129, 133–34; for
T'u Ti Kung, 113; seventh-month
festival, Mountainstreet, 127; for
immigrants dead in battle, T'u-ch'eng,
199–200; Spring and Autumn

Festivals, Ping Shan, 217; *chao-fen*,
275f; Chung-yeung, 275f; Great
Sacrifice, A-lien, 313; Li Ch'un
Festival, 331. *See also chiao*; rituals
fen: defined, 77n
Feng-kui-tien, 72, 75, 78, 84, 88. *See
also* Shu-lin
feng-shui, see geomancy
fertility: gods of, 116, 214; ritual
symbols, 286–89 *passim*
Feuchtwang, Stephan: paper discussed,
8–9, 339; cited, 181
fictive relationships (bonding), 207,
222–24, 228, 242–50
fire-walking, 76, 133, 142
FitzGerald, C. P., 23
five elements (*wu-hsing*), 35, 39, 122
Five Thunder magic, 17, 327n, 328–36
flower trees, 213–14, 238ff
flowers: as ritual symbol, 286–87
folk medicine, 237f. *See also* curing
folk religion, 23, 32–33, 38n, 39–40, 43,
203–5
food: social significance of, 176; polarized types of, 236f. *See also*
propitiation
fortune-telling, *see* divination
Freedman, Maurice: paper discussed,
1–2, 340–41; cited: 1–3 *passim*, 14f,
164, 168n, 173–74, 279
fu (*hu*): charm, 49, 64, 331, 335;
Heavenly Court, 123; supernatural
sages, 140
Fu-an Miao, Fu-lai, 190
Fu Te Cheng Shen, *see* T'u Ti Kung
Fu-te Kung, T'an-ti, 77, 80, 86f
funerals and funerary rites, 28–29, 117–
22, 210n, 224–25, 273–74, 284–85,
294–99, 302, 333n. *See also* burial

generation names, 261n
geomancy, 2, 29, 35–40 *passim*, 83, 98,
122f, 186–87, 225, 273ff, 285. *See also*
divination
ghost marriages, 150–52, 188
ghosts: character, 7–8, 38n, 39, 123–28
passim, 169–81 *passim*, 194f, 209–13
passim, 220–23 *passim*, 229–30, 245–
46; and worship, 44, 107, 110, 114,
188f, 194, 195–96; offerings to, 110f,
170, 178–79, 180, 184, 194, 196, 208ff,
212–13, 223; control of, by gods, 115,
125–26, 134; of the neglected and unnaturally dead, 117, 123, 189–90, 193,
198f, 205, 208–9, 217, 229; place in